The Racketeer's Progress

The Racketeer's Progress explores the contested and contingent origins of the modern American economy by examining the violent resistance to its development. Historians often portray Chicago as an unregulated industrial metropolis, composed of factories and immigrant laborers. In fact, the city was home to thousands of craftsmen – carpenters, teamsters, barbers, butchers, etc. – who formed unions and associations that governed commerce through pickets, assaults, and bombings. Working together, these groups forcefully challenged the power of national corporations and physically managed the development of mass culture in the city.

Scholars often ignore this defiance, painting modernization as consensual and craftsmen as reactionary, corrupt, and criminal. Prompted by cinematic stereotypes and business rhetoric, many authors conflate organized crime and organized labor. This is ironic, for the tradesmen's reputation derives not only from their brutality, but also from their successful fight against modernization, the emergence of a consumer economy, and gangsters like Al Capone.

The struggle between tradesmen, corporations, and reformers redirected American law. Progressive-era courts rebuked the craftsmen for governing trade. In the 1920s, elite attorneys crusaded against unions and associations, inventing the term "racketeering" to sway criminal juries. But the Great Depression reversed harsh laws. Amidst falling prices and wages, urban craftsmen became a model for New Deal recovery statutes and a focus for constitutional debates in cases like *Schechter Poultry v. U.S.* (1935). Politicians redefined racketeering, enacting new provisions to protect unions against gunmen, strengthening connections between labor and the Democratic Party, and allowing craftsmen access to the growing power of the state.

Andrew Wender Cohen is an Assistant Professor of History at the Maxwell School of Citizenship and Public Affairs, Syracuse University.

CAMBRIDGE HISTORICAL STUDIES IN AMERICAN LAW AND SOCIETY

SERIES EDITOR
Christopher Tomlins, *American Bar Foundation*

The Racketeer's Progress

Chicago and the Struggle for the Modern American Economy, 1900–1940

Andrew Wender Cohen

Syracuse University

CAMBRIDGE
UNIVERSITY PRESS

PUBLISHED BY THE PRESS SYNDICATE OF THE UNIVERSITY OF CAMBRIDGE
The Pitt Building, Trumpington Street, Cambridge, United Kingdom

CAMBRIDGE UNIVERSITY PRESS
The Edinburgh Building, Cambridge CB2 2RU, UK
40 West 20th Street, New York, NY 10011-4211, USA
477 Williamstown Road, Port Melbourne, VIC 3207, Australia
Ruiz de Alarcón 13, 28014 Madrid, Spain
Dock House, The Waterfront, Cape Town 8001, South Africa

http://www.cambridge.org

First published 2004

Printed in the United States of America

Typeface ITC New Baskerville 10/12 pt.   *System* LATEX 2$_\varepsilon$ [TB]

A catalog record for this book is available from the British Library.

Library of Congress Cataloging in Publication Data
Cohen, Andrew Wender, 1968–
The racketeer's progress : Chicago and the struggle for the modern
American economy, 1900–1940 / Andrew Wender Cohen.
p.   cm. – (Cambridge historical studies in American law and society)
Includes bibliographical references and index.
ISBN 0-521-83466-x
1. Working class – United States – History – 20th century.
2. Skilled labor – Illinois – Chicago – History – 20th century.   3. Labor unions –
Illinois – Chicago – History.   4. Racketeering – Illinois – Chicago.
5. Crime – Illinois – Chicago – History.   6. Social conflict – United States – History.
7. Chicago (Ill.) – Economic conditions.   8. Labor laws and legislation –
United States. I. Title. II. Series.
HD8072.C69   2004
331.88'09773'1109041 – dc22   2004043554

ISBN 0 521 83466 x hardback

To Randy, in fond memory of M.W.C.

Contents

Illustrations

Acknowledgments

Like all works of scholarship, this book is less the product of individual inspiration than an outgrowth of my personal experience with a large number of colleagues, friends, and relatives. This acknowledgment is a necessary, but not in any way sufficient, reminder of their kind assistance.

The University of Chicago nurtured this project, shaping the ideas that fill its pages. In particular, I thank George Chauncey, my dissertation advisor, for his continual support. From the beginning, he emboldened me to follow my curiosity and encouraged me to challenge convention. Kathleen Conzen offered wise counsel and rigorous readings of the text. I also thank William Novak for his enthusiastic intellectualism and uplifting camaraderie. I owe a deep debt to my graduate cohort at Chicago, an unparalleled group of young scholars. Kathy Brosnan, Susan Radomsky, Mark Schmeller, David Tanenhaus, and Michael Willrich have had a formative impact on my approach to history.

Christopher Tomlins has been more than an editor. He has also been a good friend and mentor. Many others have offered me comments on the text or other forms of professional assistance: Burton Bledstein, Alan Brinkley, Richard Bulliet, Howard Erlanger, Daniel Ernst, Carol Faulkner, Tim Gilfoyle, Sally Gordon, Neil Harris, Roger Horowitz, Ronald Inden, Robert Johnston, Barry Karl, Norman Kutcher, Elisabeth Lasch-Quinn, Fred Marquardt, Arthur McEvoy, Peter Novick, William Sewell, Scott Strickland, Joel Tarr, and the anonymous reviewers for Cambridge University Press.

I thank a select group of wonderful archivists, without whom this book could not exist. Philip Costello, Jeannie Child, and Tom Sobun of the Cook County Circuit Court Archives found not only the cases I requested, but also many records I would never have discovered. The expertise of Martin Tuohy of the National Archives, Great Lakes

Division, proved invaluable during the second wave of research. I also thank the staffs of the University of Chicago's Joseph Regenstein Library and D'Angelo Law Library, the Chicago Historical Society, the Newberry Library, the Wisconsin Historical Society, Syracuse University's Bird Library, and the Kheel Center at Cornell University Library.

The insightful comments of the scholars at various research communities helped me refine my thinking. I found presentations at the Syracuse University History Department, the Syracuse University College of Law, the Hagley Library, the University of Chicago Social History Workshop, and the Comparative Legal History Workshop extremely useful.

A number of institutions generously funded the project. I thank the University of Chicago, the Andrew Mellon Foundation, the Harry Frank Guggenheim Foundation, the American Historical Association, the University of Wisconsin Law School, the Institute for Legal Studies, the Maxwell School's Appleby–Mosher Fund, the National Association of Scholars, and the John M. Olin Foundation. I would be remiss if I did not thank Deans John Palmer and Michael Wasylenko of Syracuse University's Maxwell School of Citizenship and Public Affairs for granting me time to complete the manuscript and the money to secure the images that appear within it.

Pieces of this manuscript have appeared previously in other forms. Parts of Chapters 1 and 2 appear as "Obstacles to History? Modernization and the Lower Middle Class in Chicago, 1900–1940," in *The Middling Sorts: Explorations in the History of the American Middle Class*, Burton Bledstein and Robert Johnston eds. (New York: Routledge, 2001). Specific sentences and paragraphs first appeared in "Business Myths, Lawyerly Strategies, and Social Context: Ernst on Labor Law History," *Law and Social Inquiry* 23:1 (1998): 165–84. Parts of Chapters 6 and 7 appear as "The Racketeer's Progress: Commerce, Crime, and Law in Chicago, 1919–1929," *Journal of Urban History* 29:5 (July 2003): 574–97. I thank the publishers of these essays for permitting me to reuse this material.

My friends deserve recognition for giving me good times and everyday encouragement: Pamela Buchbinder, Lisa Cohen, Rob Kaplan, Jeff Rake, Louise Redd, and Patrick Woodall.

I have benefited from the strong support of my family. My wife Carol Faulkner has brought me greater happiness than I imagined possible. My sister, Sheryl Cohen Fine, and my aunts, Elaine S. Wender and Lois Feldstein, have always encouraged me. From an early age, my father, Robert Baer Cohen, thrilled me with stories of his experiences in politics. These tales, sufficient to fill another book, have profoundly shaped my interpretation of the world.

Though my beloved mother, Marilyn Wender Cohen, tragically passed away before I could finish this work, I hope her spirit pervades it and everything else I do. But this history belongs to the living. For that reason, I dedicate it to my brother, Randolph Baer Cohen, whose contributions to my life are too numerous to relate here.

Common Abbreviations in Text and Notes

Organizations

CFL	Chicago Federation of Labor
ISFL	Illinois State Federation of Labor
BTC	Building Trades' Council of Chicago
IBT	International Brotherhood of Teamsters
CMB	Chicago Masons and Builders' Association
EA	Employers' Association of Chicago
BCC	Building Contractor's Council
BCEA	Building Construction Employers' Association
CCLA	Citizens' Committee to Enforce the Landis Award
IMA	Illinois Manufacturers' Association
NAM	National Association of Manufacturers
NMTA	National Metal Trades' Association
AABA	American Anti-Boycott Association

Courts

Sup.C.C.	Superior Court of Cook County
Circ.C.C.	Circuit Court of Cook County
Crim.C.C.	Criminal Court of Cook County
USCA	United States Court of Appeals
USDC, ND, E. IL	United States District Court, Northern District, Eastern Illinois

Archives

NARA-GL	National Archives and Research Administration, Great Lakes Division

CHS   Chicago Historical Society

Government Documents

IC, *Reports*, v. 7   U.S. Congress. *Report of the Industrial Commission on the Relations and Conditions of Capital and Labor Employed in Manufactures and General Business Including Testimony with Review*, v. 7 (Washington, DC: Government Printing Office, 1901).

IC, *Reports*, v. 8   U.S. Congress. *Report of the Industrial Commission on the Chicago Labor Disputes of 1900 with Especial reference to the Disputes in the Building and Machinery Trades*, v. 8 (Washington, DC: Government Printing Office, 1901).

Racket Hearings   U.S. Senate. *Hearings before a Subcommittee of the Committee on Commerce United States Senate Investigation of So-Called "Rackets,"* v. 1, Parts 1–6 (Washington, DC: Government Printing Office, 1934).

Newspapers

CDN   *Chicago Daily News*
CDT   *Chicago Daily Tribune*
CRH   *Chicago Record-Herald*
NYT   *New York Times*
WP   *Washington Post*

Introduction

Between the Progressive Era and the New Deal, small businessmen and craft workers in Chicago defied the corporate transformation of American capitalism, redirecting the course of American political and economic development. In trades such as trucking, construction, and shopkeeping, unions and associations enacted self-styled laws that favored small, local, and labor-intensive businesses at the expense of large national firms. They enforced their laws not through the legal system, but through fines, strikes, boycotts, pickets, assaults, bombings, and shootings. Unsurprisingly, the men who owned Chicago's department stores, warehouses, railroads, and factories condemned these forms of economic order, favoring a regime friendly to property rights. Their opposition provoked a series of violent confrontations between local craftsmen and corporate magnates that spilled into the city's streets, markets, and courts.

This struggle shaped American law. Case law felt its imprint, as judges defended private property rights by limiting practices such as picketing and the boycott. Indictments, injunctions, and contempt citations littered the dockets, as courts ruled Chicago's craft organizations to be criminal conspiracies, violating the rights of individuals and usurping the sovereignty of the elected government. With the support of reformers, tradespeople gradually undermined the idea of conspiracy and established a limited legitimate space for themselves in Chicago's economy. The conflict led to new areas of criminal law, including statutes barring "racketeering." In time, craft governance influenced powerful public officials like Raymond Moley, who wrote New Deal statutes mandating trade agreements. Thus, the forms of industrial order established in the United States between 1890 and 1940 resulted not from a progressive "search for order," but from the local struggle between reformers, elite businessmen, small proprietors, and craft workers.

Though largely absent from the literature, these clashes greatly affected American economic development. Most historians see corporatization as a consensual process. For example, Martin Sklar describes this transformation as "a relatively peaceful affair," requiring "neither civil war nor revolution, but rather political and economic reorganization and reform."[1] This book suggests the opposite: that modernization was violent, contingent, and contested. Routine protest, beatings, bombings, and shootings kept national corporations from dominating whole sectors of Chicago's economy. The book shows that the bloodiest strikes and lockouts of the early twentieth century pitted the power of a business elite against the authority of local tradesmen. It argues that these showdowns greatly affected the shape of the nation Americans live in today.

As such, it questions five powerful ideas that dominate early twentieth-century history: modernity, synthesis, voluntarism, corporatism, and legitimacy. The myth of *modernity* contends that the United States had achieved industrial maturity by the Progressive Era, laying the material groundwork for a modern American state and society. During the nineteenth century, historians claim, American businessmen had integrated the nation's commerce, mechanized its production, and incorporated its companies. With the new economy, distinct social classes had formed, one composed of managers, stockholders, and professionals, and another composed of ethnic industrial workers and their families. This modern economy, scholars argue, triggered an unprecedented set of social problems eventually addressed by a new political order.[2]

---

[1] Martin J. Sklar, *The Corporate Reconstruction of American Capitalism: The Market, the Law, and Politics* (New York: Cambridge University Press, 1993), 21; James Weinstein, *The Corporate Ideal in the Liberal State, 1900–1918* (Boston: Beacon Press, 1968), ix–xv, 3–6, 254; Robert Wiebe, *The Search for Order, 1877–1920* (New York: Hill and Wang, 1967); Ellis W. Hawley, *The Great War and the Search for a Modern Order: A History of the American People and Their Institutions, 1917–1933* (New York: St. Martin's Press, 1979); Olivier Zunz, *Making America Corporate, 1870–1920* (Chicago: University of Chicago, 1990).

[2] Alfred Chandler, *The Visible Hand: The Managerial Revolution in American Business* (Cambridge, MA: Harvard University Press, 1977). The business historians who reject notions of corporate dominance nevertheless emphasize manufacturing over other sectors. See Philip Scranton, *Proprietary Capitalism: Textile Manufacture at Philadelphia, 1800–1885* (New York: Cambridge University Press, 1983) and *Figured Tapestry: Production, Markets, and Power in Philadelphia Textiles, 1885–1941* (New York: Cambridge University Press, 1989). Labor historians tend to assume a Marxian model of class struggle, even when they study nonindustrial workers. See David Montgomery, *The Fall of the House of Labor: The Workplace, the State, and American Labor Activism, 1865–1925* (New York: Cambridge University Press, 1989); Dorothy Sue

Chicago's economy was far more diverse and "premodern" than such accounts indicate. Giant corporate steel mills, managed by Protestant gentlemen, employing thousands of immigrant laborers, selling to a national market, were less typical of urban commerce than the small shops and yards of the city's construction, trucking, retail, and service trades. These establishments provided Chicago's exploding population with food, shelter, transportation, infrastructure, and public culture. Hundreds of thousands of men and women labored in these sectors, aware of, but largely separate from, the city's dark factories. They often worked in public, even outdoors, and their jobs had changed little since the Industrial Revolution.[3]

Because craft production relied more upon the skill, strength, and intelligence of workers than upon capital investments, social classes remained relatively permeable. Local proprietors, partnerships, and family firms provided the city with most of its construction, teaming, retail, and service. Some workers started their own businesses, while many failed entrepreneurs returned to wage labor. For example, William H. "Red" Curran was an officer of the plumber's union, president of the Chicago Building Trades Council, and Illinois state factory inspector. He also worked as a bailiff, a deputy sheriff, a brewery agent, an aldermanic candidate, and a plumbing contractor. His immediate family included a Republican state representative, a county employee, a city bridge tender, a municipal court judge, a bailiff, and the superintendent of the Bridewell jail.[4]

Cobble, *Dishing it Out: Waitresses and Their Unions in the Twentieth Century* (Chicago: University of Illinois Press, 1991).

[3] Special Reports, *Occupations at the Twelfth Census* (Washington, DC: Government Printing Office, 1904), 516–23; Bureau of the Census, *Thirteenth Census of the United States Taken in the Year 1910, v.4, Population, 1910: Occupations* (Washington, DC: Government Printing Office, 1914), 544–47. A few recent scholars argue that the focus on industrialization hides those working outside factories as well as their distinct forms of protest. Dipesh Chakrabarty, *Rethinking Working-Class History: Bengal, 1890–1940* (Princeton: Princeton University Press, 1989), 226; Alice Kessler-Harris, "Treating the Male as 'Other': Redefining the Parameters of Labor History," *Labor History* 34 (1993): 192; Christopher Tomlins, "Why Wait for Industrialism?: Work, Legal Culture, and the Example of Early America – An Historiographical Argument," *Labor History* 40:1 (February 1999): 5–34; Andrew Wender Cohen, "Obstacles to History?: Modernization and the Lower Middle Class in Chicago, 1900–1940," in *The Middling Sorts: Explorations in the History of the American Middle Class*, Burton Bledstein and Robert Johnston, eds. (New York: Routledge, 2001), 189–200.

[4] "Thomas Curran Dies in Auto Crash," *CDT*, November 13, 1928, 1; "Tips On Aldermen by Voters' League," *CRH*, April 1, 1905, 3; *Lakeside Directory, 1902*, 519; *Lakeside Directory, 1910*, 335; *Lakeside Directory, 1917*, 420; Royal Ewart

Social divisions existed, of course, but the relationships between workers and employers were antagonistic rather than contradictory. Unions and employers' associations often bridged their differences, forming stable agreements that governed commerce in their crafts. Sometimes labor and capital fought violently, but in other instances workers and employers allied themselves against rival associations, factions, and business communities. The most heated episodes in Chicago labor history occurred when external agents challenged craft orders. The most blatant example is the Teamsters' Strike of 1905, in which the city's great merchants intervened to shatter agreements between local teamsters' unions and their respective employers' associations. The strike was indeed a class struggle, but only if we complicate our notions of class rather than shoehorn the conflict into conventional categories.[5]

Advocates of *synthesis* promote the production of a broad national and even international history. The case-study methodology, which proved so fruitful for a generation, has recently fallen into disfavor, and any book considering a single city may seem distinctly unfashionable. Scholars not only suggest the folly of constructing an objective history of the United States from an accretion of regional studies, they also refute the notion that any single locale can represent the experience of other cities or the nation as a whole. Some authors even blame this method for declining popular interest in history, noting the desire of the mainstream audience for interpretive works that unify the experiences of a range of Americans.[6]

But historians cannot understand the contingency of economic development and the modern nation unless they do local research. Nowhere is this fact more apparent than in political history, where the dominant scheme – the so-called "organizational synthesis" – is explicitly totalizing. Here, breadth leads some authors to portray transformation as inevitable, ignoring the individuals who resisted the rise of the national, corporate, and industrial economy, but never appeared on a larger stage. These Americans struggled, sometimes violently, against the developing social order, but they did not fight in halls of the

---

Montgomery, *Industrial Relations in the Chicago Building Trades* (Chicago: University of Chicago Press, 1927), 286–87.

[5] Ernesto Laclau, *New Reflections on the Revolution of Our Time* (New York: Verso, 1990), 7. For another view of the Teamsters' Strike of 1905, see David Witwer, "Corruption and Reform in the Teamsters Union, 1898 to 1991" (Ph.D. diss., Brown University, 1994).

[6] Thomas Bender, "Wholes and Parts: The Need for Synthesis in American History," *Journal of American History*, 73:1 (June 1986): 120–36, esp. 125.

Capitol. Indeed, they often predicated their defiance upon the value of self government.[7]

Because of its size, economic might, and political significance, Chicago is the ideal place to study the relationship between local resistance and the development of the nation state. A not inconsiderable number of Americans lived in the city. In 1920, Cook County, Illinois (3.05 million) had almost as many residents as California (3.43 million), and a larger population than Boston, Baltimore, Pittsburgh, and Los Angeles combined. As an emblem of modernity and a locus of corporate authority, Chicago's only rival was New York, making it the natural place to consider the rise of the new American economy. Initially the center of American Republicanism, later a pivot for Progressive-era reform, and eventually home to the nation's most powerful Democratic political machine, Chicago was a testing ground for social experimentation and a major source for national policy. In a very real sense, New Deal statutes, Supreme Court decisions, and racketeering law emerged from the shores of Lake Michigan.[8]

Third, this book questions the notion of *voluntarism.* Labor historians often describe early twentieth-century American craft unions and

---

[7] Eric H. Monkkonen, "The Dangers of Synthesis," *American Historical Review* 91:5 (December 1986): 1146–57; "Bias and Synthesis in History," *Journal of American History* 74:1 (June 1987): 109–12. For other reactions, see pieces by Richard Wightman Fox, Roy Rosenzweig, and Bender again in "A Round Table: Synthesis in American History," *Journal of American History* 74:1 (June 1987): 107–30. For the "organizational synthesis," see Louis Galambos, "The Emerging Organizational Synthesis in Modern American History," *Business History Review* 44 (1970): 279–90. Even those historians who see modernization as a conflicted political process seldom discuss physical conflict, perhaps because they focus on national policy rather than the history of a specific locality. Barry Karl, *The Uneasy State: The United States from 1915 to 1945* (Chicago: University of Chicago Press, 1983); Morton Keller, *Regulating a New Economy: Public Policy and Economic Change in America, 1900–1933* (Cambridge, MA: Harvard University Press, 1990); James Livingston, "The Social Analysis of Economic History and Theory: Conjectures on Late Nineteenth-Century American Development," *American Historical Review* 92:1 (1987): 72.

[8] Department of Commerce, Bureau of the Census, *Fourteenth Census of the United States Taken in the Year 1920*, v. *3, Population: Composition and Characteristics of the Population by State* (Washington, DC: U.S. Government Printing Office, 1923); Marco d'Eramo, *The Pig and the Skyscraper: A History of Our Future*, trans. Graeme Thomson (New York: Verso, 2001); Michael Willrich, *City of Courts: Socializing Justice in Progressive Era Chicago* (New York: Cambridge University Press, 2003), xxvi; Thomas Pegram, *Partisans and Progressives: Private Interest and Public Policy in Illinois, 1870–1922* (Chicago: University of Illinois Press, 1992), 3–6.

the American Federation of Labor (AFL) as conservative voluntary associations antagonistic to the state, opposed to legislative reforms, and unwilling to form a political party dedicated to broad social change. This voluntarism subsumed two related principles: business unionism and contractualism. Business unionism implied a narrow concern with bread-and-butter issues, such as wages and hours. Contractualism suggested reliance upon private, legally enforceable trade agreements rather than upon universal statutory protections.[9]

Historians base this interpretation upon statements conceived to gain access to and protection from the Progressive-era state. Union officers hoped to convince the voting public that American workers had no interest in radically undermining capitalism or the party system. Officials like AFL president Samuel Gompers also tried to deflect hostile formalist judges by portraying unions as expressing the combined wills of individual members. By presenting their organizations as wholly private bodies, labor leaders hoped to earn public sympathy and evade public regulation.[10]

Union behavior contradicted this rhetoric. Craftsmen in Chicago never accepted a strict divide between the public and private spheres essential to the idea of voluntarism. Local labor federations lobbied the Illinois legislature for protective legislation long after they purportedly became quiescent. Union officials took public jobs seeking to enroll thousands of government employees. In 1899, an investigation showed

[9] John Commons et al., *History of Labor in the United States*, v. 4 (New York: Macmillan, 1935); Ruth L. Horowitz, *Political Ideologies of Organized Labor: The New Deal Era* (New Brunswick, NJ: Transaction Books, 1978); Leon Fink, "Labor, Liberty, and the Law: Trade Unionism and the Problem of the American Constitutional Order," *Journal of American History* 74 (December 1987): 905–25; William Forbath, *Law and the Shaping of the American Labor Movement* (Cambridge, MA: Harvard University Press, 1991); Victoria C. Hattam, *Labor Visions and State Power: The Origins of Business Unionism* (Princeton: Princeton University Press, 1993); David Montgomery, *Workers' Control in America: Studies in the History of Work, Technology, and Labor Struggles* (New York: Cambridge University Press, 1979). A few recent scholars have complicated this picture of political quiescence and voluntarism. Julie Greene, *Pure and Simple Politics: The American Federation of Labor and Political Activism, 1881–1917* (New York Cambridge University Press, 1998); Michael Kazin, *Barons of Labor: The San Francisco Building Trades and Union Power in the Progressive Era* (Chicago: University of Illinois Press, 1989); Georg Leidenberger, "'The Public is the Labor Union': Working Class Progressivism in Turn-of-the-Century Chicago," *Labor History* 36:2 (Spring 1995): 187–210.
[10] See, for example, *American Federationist*, November 1907 reprinted in Samuel Gompers, *Labor and the Common Welfare* (New York: E. P. Dutton, 1919), 15–6.

that nearly two-thirds of the officials of the Building Trades Council and of the Chicago Federation of Labor held public offices such as brick inspector, examiner of engineers, and others. By 1929, economist Carroll Lawrence Christenson calculated that the city of Chicago, Cook county, and various public contractors employed 163,310 union teachers, janitors, teamsters, repairmen, inspectors, and building tradesmen – more than 70 percent of the workers in these occupations. These employees accounted for 10 percent of the city's total workforce, but more than half of its union membership.[11]

Craft organizations themselves acted as governments, enacting constitutions, passing bylaws, electing officers, and levying taxes. Though tradesmen signed contracts, the courts did not enforce them. This reflected not only the absence of any system of state-sponsored collective bargaining, but also the workers' suspicion of judges, whom they saw as irredeemably biased. Instead, craftsmen formed their own legal systems to administer rules stipulating wages, hours, prices, and materials. Beginning in the 1890s, building-trades unions and associations began hiring "walking delegates" to represent them at the worksites scattered around the city of Chicago. These men policed the city, checking for nonunion workers, banned machinery, and out-of-state materials. When the walking delegate found violations, he notified the offender and attempted to negotiate a resolution. Many unions and trade associations tried defendants in their own judicial proceedings, sentencing them to fines, suspensions, and boycotts.[12]

---

[11] Eugene Staley, *History of the Illinois State Federation of Labor* (Chicago: University of Chicago Press, 1930); Leidenburger, 187–210; Jane Addams, "The Present Crisis in Trades–Union Morals," *North American Review* 179 (August 1904): 188–90; Ernest Bogart, "Chicago Building Trades Dispute. II.," *Political Science Quarterly* 16:2 (June 1901): 227–28; Industrial Commission, *Report of the Industrial Commission on the Chicago Labor Disputes of 1900 with Especial Reference to the Disputes in the Building and Machinery Trades,* v. 8 (Washington, DC: Government Printing Office, 1901), 6, 276, 305, 353–54, 395, 435. Henceforth listed as IC, *Reports,* v. 8; Garth L. Mangum, *The Operating Engineers: The Economic History of a Trade Union* (Cambridge, MA: Harvard University Press, 1964), 6, 89; *Adams v. Brenan,* 177 Ill. 194, 197 (1898); James A. Miller, "Coercive Trade Unionism as Illustrated by the Chicago Building-Trades Conflict," *Journal of Political Economy* 9:3 (June 1901): 336; Carroll L. Christenson, *Collective Bargaining in Chicago: 1929–1930, A Study of the Economic Significance of the Industrial Location of Trade Unionism* (Chicago: University of Chicago Press, 1933), 2, 11, 13, 15, 17.

[12] IC, *Reports,* v. 8, 62, 118, 286–87, 471–72, 555–63; Bill of Complaint, June 30, 1899, in *Union Pressed Brick v. Chicago Hydraulic Press Brick,* case #196935 in the Circuit Court of Cook County (henceforth listed as Circ.C.C.); Robert A. Christie, *Empire in Wood: A History of the Carpenters Union* (Ithaca, NY:

Contrary to the literature, these organizations seriously threatened the city's corporations. Craftsmen denied the sovereignty of the state, provoking the continual reaction of legal institutions. In the craft mind, organizations had the primary right to rule their jurisdictions. The government could be a rival or an ally, but never the sole legitimate regulatory authority. Judging tradesmen by the standards of radical unions like the Industrial Workers of the World, which attacked capitalism itself and proposed the wholesale transformation of state and society, historians underestimate the militant implications of craft governance in its time. Alarmed by the immense power of craft unions, corporations spent the early part of the century trying to break their hold on industries like construction, trucking, retail, and service.

This book also considers the myth of *corporatism*. Advocates of corporatism argue that Progressive-era and New Deal reforms were merely aspects of an emerging national, corporate, industrial, bureaucratic society. In this history, reform-minded executives managed peacefully to deflect both socialism and laissez-faire capitalism by advocating a political and economic order composed not of individuals but of large interest groups such as corporations, labor unions, and political parties. Their ideals, which historians call "corporate liberalism," allowed for public regulatory bodies such as the Interstate Commerce Commission (ICC), statutory protections such as unemployment insurance, and the arbitration of labor disputes.[13]

Yet scholars massively overstate corporate authorship of these initiatives. Though some executives joined influential reform groups like

Cornell University, 1956), 63–6; Royal E. Montgomery, *Industrial Relations in the Chicago Building Trades* (Chicago: University of Chicago Press, 1927), 8–9; *Minutes Book of the Chicago Building Trades Council*, 1912–1914, Chicago Historical Society; Bill of Complaint, June 30, 1899, *Union Pressed Brick Co. v. Hydraulic Pressed Brick Co.*, case #196935, Circ.C.C. (1899); Bill, January 12, 1903, *Gavin v. Bricklayers and Masons International Union*, case #227562 in the Superior Court of Cook County (hereafter listed as Sup.C.C.).

[13] Ellis Hawley, "The Discovery and Study of a 'Corporate Liberalism,'" *Business History Review* 52 (1978): 309–20; Robert Wiebe, *The Search for Order, 1877–1920*; Weinstein, *The Corporate Ideal in the Liberal State*; Martin J. Sklar, *The Corporate Reconstruction of American Capitalism*; Daniel Ernst, "The Closed Shop, the Proprietary Capitalist, and the Law, 1897–1915," in *Masters to Managers*, Sanford Jacoby, ed. (New York: Columbia University Press, 1991), 132–48; Robert Himmelberg, *The Origins of the National Recovery Administration: Business, Government, and the Trade Association Issue, 1921–1933* (New York: Fordham University Press, 1993); Colin Gordon, *New Deals: Business, Labor, and Politics in America, 1920–1935* (New York: Cambridge University Press, 1994).

the National Civic Federation (NCF), most did not. Many more joined the Illinois Manufacturers Association (IMA), which opposed nearly every reform proposed in the legislature. Corporations were especially incensed by collective bargaining. At the turn of the century, one would be hard-pressed to name a single large firm in the city of Chicago that had signed a union contract. Thirty years later, the picture was little different, as unions had become concentrated in crafts controlled by small employers. These contractors and shopkeepers were, not coincidentally, strong supporters of Chicago's Kelly–Nash Democratic political machine and the Roosevelt administration during the 1930s.[14]

If we are to write a history of the New Deal "from the bottom up," we must look to the craft economy rather than to the corporate sector. Chicago's craft producers established a thriving associational culture by 1910, over a decade before the Hooverian corporate associationalism that many historians identify as a model for the New Deal. With urban craft governance specifically in mind, New Deal architects enacted policies like the National Industrial Recovery Act (NIRA) ratifying trade agreements. Finally, nearly all of the cases testing the "corporatist" arrangements of the first New Deal involved urban trades such as drycleaning, kosher foods, and milk delivery.

The reluctance of scholars to acknowledge the craft economy as the birthplace of many New Deal regulatory policies ironically flows from that economy's central role in legal controversies preceding the New Deal. Historians often fail to distinguish evidence showing graft, violence, and manipulation in trades like construction from the mere allegations of hostile businessmen. A professional strikebreaker invented the term "racketeering" in 1927 to condemn leaders of craft organizations in Chicago. The word's power grew in the 1930s as the federal government legitimized collective bargaining while maintaining strict legal limits on the use and abuse of organizations. In other words, the craft economy's reputation for "racketeering" reflects its influence on the evolving New Deal regime.[15]

---

[14] David Montgomery, *Fall of the House of Labor*, 272–75; Alfred H. Kelly, "A History of the Illinois Manufacturers' Association" (Ph.D. diss., University of Chicago, 1938), 21, 33–4; IC, *Reports*, v. 8, 4; Harold F. Gosnell, *Machine Politics: Chicago Model* (Chicago: University of Chicago Press, 1937), 47.

[15] Lizabeth Cohen, *Making a New Deal: Industrial Workers in Chicago, 1919–1939* (New York: Cambridge University Press, 1990), 251–89; Himmelberg, *The Origins of the National Recovery Administration*, passim; Peter H. Irons, *The New Deal Lawyers* (Princeton: Princeton University Press, 1982), 55; Raymond Moley, "Behind the Menacing Racket," *NYT Magazine* (June 23, 1930), 1–2, 19.

Finally, this work questions the progressive narrative of *legitimacy*, tracing the ascent of organized labor from "conspiracy to collective bargaining." Every year, early twentieth-century commentators heralded an end to the "outlaw" phase of industrial relations that found unionists and allied businessmen often in the criminal courts. In 1905, after the Chicago teamsters defrocked their president for alleged financial impropriety, economist John Commons announced that the industry had ceased to be "a criminal phenomenon." Within months, grand jury witnesses mocked the professor, charging teamsters and their employers with bribery, collusion, and violence. Even New Deal labor laws failed to stem such allegations, indicating that reforms forced the reconfiguration rather than the abatement of criminal prosecutions.[16]

In this light, it seems reasonable for historians to focus upon what behaviors became criminal as the state offered its blessing to new forms of economic governance. The long process of union legitimization, beginning in 1843 with Justice Lemuel Shaw's decision in *Commonwealth v. Hunt*, was accompanied by a concomitant recriminalization of many practices. Between 1843 and 1940, unions moved not between two unlike terms, conspiracy and collective bargaining, but between two competing conceptions of criminal law, conspiracy and "racketeering." This shift affected the character and reputation of American labor unions nearly as much as the better-studied positive law of the New Deal. And the contested origins of the word "racketeering" help explain the apparent contradictions in racketeering law today.

This history sees the origins of an integrated national economy and a pluralist polity as conflicted, violent, and perhaps even overdetermined. It suggests that the modern corporate order bears the deep impress of its opposite: the local craft economy. Chicago's craftsmen both countered the corporate faith in absolute property rights and provided the most vital example of commercial governance available to American policymakers from the Progressive Era to the depths of the Great Depression. After four decades of conflict, the modern legal order ironically legitimized the culture of the least industrial, least national, and least corporate sectors of the American economy. In doing so, the United States government validated the continuing defiance of craft producers and their struggle for order.

---

[16] John R. Commons, "Types of American Labor Organizations: The Teamsters of Chicago," *Quarterly Journal of Economics* 19 (1905): 407; U.S. Congress, *Investigation of So-Called "Rackets,"* v. 1, Parts 1–6 (Washington, DC: Government Printing Office, 1934).

In telling this story, this manuscript crosses certain field boundaries, jumping from labor to business, from city to nation, from law to politics. Indeed, I argue that no one class, region, or form of state power alone can provide full understanding of American history. This breadth has a cost. I assume my attempts at scope will aggravate those specialists who deem inadequate a history spread thin across subjects. Yet the benefits should be equally clear. Work, business, politics, and law are hardly autonomous realms in life, and no history, however deeply researched, can capture experience when so tightly constrained.

Chicago's corporations dreamed of rationalizing local commercial traffic by bringing it underground. The tunnel system, begun in 1899, eventually allowed the largest Loop firms to bypass the streets, and, more importantly, the craftsmen who controlled local transport. The top image shows a clogged street during a 1902 teamsters' strike. The bottom shows the completed subway in 1924. Courtesy of Chicago Historical Society (DN-003842, DN-077911).

1

Modernization and Its Discontents, 1900

At the turn of the twentieth century, in the city of Chicago, two business communities struggled for the right to determine the shape of the modern urban economy. Steel manufacturers, meatpackers, wholesalers, merchants, and bankers formed a business elite. Members of this elite advocated corporate forms of organization, mechanized production, streamlined distribution, and a private economy, legally protected from the entreaties of governments, labor unions, and even trade associations. In their ideal economic order, property and productivity were the sole determinants of commercial, social, and political power.

The self-made men, skilled workers, idealists, and scoundrels of the craft economy favored a distinct, if not always savory, alternative to the values of Chicago's corporate elite. Tradespeople in construction, transportation, retail, and service aimed at keeping their businesses nonindustrial and proprietary. Craftsmen created a public economy governed by unions, associations, and political parties rather than by the market. In their world, success depended less on capital than on connections, less on competitive advantage than on consensus. Through various forms of governance, these craftsmen resisted the modernization of the American economy and shaped the law, politics, and society of the twentieth-century United States.

In the public imagination, turn-of-the-century Chicago evokes an advanced industrial economy, composed of mechanized factories, owned by corporations, and operated by immigrant laborers. This imagined Chicago was home to the Union Stockyards, the steel mills, and the harvester plants. It was the terminus for the Illinois Central Railroad and the "Gateway to the West." This Chicago was also the center of class conflict, the city that hanged the Haymarket anarchists in 1887, and the city where the Industrial Workers of the World based their revolutionary labor organization in 1905. This Chicago, producing smoke, wealth, poverty, and strife, embodied capitalism in its most advanced stages.

These images reflect the myth of the modern economy. Following close behind the development of mechanized factory production were writers, artists, and scholars who depicted the imminent domination of industrial capitalism. In 1900, the dynamo at the Paris Exposition prompted Henry Adams to eulogize traditional life. A few years later, Upton Sinclair's novel *The Jungle* portrayed Chicago's meatpacking plants as representative of production in general. By the 1920s, economist Thorstein Veblen predicted a future economy so technologically sophisticated as to necessitate the political rule of engineers. Filmmaker Fritz Lang envisioned this idea most dramatically in *Metropolis*, the story of a city populated by elite planners and machine tenders, but without shopkeepers, skilled craftsmen, municipal employees, or servants.[1]

The themes explored in these fictional accounts hold surprising sway among scholars. Since progressive historians Charles and Mary Beard first analyzed the development of an urban, national, industrial, corporate America in 1927, modernism has set the terms for the study of late nineteenth and early twentieth-century United States history.[2] With a few notable exceptions, labor historians make the rise of an industrial working class the primary object of their inquiry.[3] In

[1] Henry Adams, "The Dynamo and the Virgin," in Ernst Samuels and Jayne Samuels, eds., *Novels, Mont Saint Michel, The Education* (New York: Library of America, 1983), 1066–76; Upton Sinclair, *The Jungle* (New York: Signet Classics, 1964); Thorstein Veblen, *The Engineers and the Price System* (New York: W. B. Huebsch, 1921); *Metropolis*, Fritz Lang, dir. (Germany: Universum Film A. G. Studios, 1926), feature film.

[2] Charles Beard and Mary Beard, *The Rise of American Civilization* (New York: Macmillian, 1927); Richard Hofstadter, *The Progressive Historians: Turner, Beard, Parrington* (New York: Alfred Knopf, 1968). See also John Patrick Diggins, "Power and Authority in American History: The Case of Charles A. Beard and His Critics," *American Historical Review* 86:4 (October 1981): 701–30.

[3] David Montgomery, *Workers' Control in America* (New York: Cambridge University Press, 1979); David Brody, *Workers in Industrial America*, 2nd ed. (New York: Oxford University Press, 1993). Recent scholars question the emphasis on industrialization. See Christopher L. Tomlins, *Waiting for Industrialism: Work, Law, Culture, and the Rediscovery of Early America*, working paper #9614 (Chicago: American Bar Foundation, 1996); Dorothy Sue Cobble, *Dishing it Out: Waitresses and Their Unions in the Twentieth Century* (Chicago: University of Illinois Press, 1991); Susan Porter Benson, *Counter Cultures: Saleswomen, Managers, and Customers in American Department Stores, 1890–1940* (Chicago: University of Illinois Press, 1986). Although some historians of nineteenth-century labor depart from the study of industrial workers, scholars of the twentieth century do so only when craft workers were radicalized or

business history, the corporation's once steely grip on the literature has weakened, but manufacturing remains the dominant area of investigation.[4] American political historians make the corporation and the large proprietary manufacturer the protagonists in the story of local and national government.[5] Taken together, scholars present early twentieth-century America as a land of industrial manufacturers and unskilled workers, without much in between.

This broad belief in a modern urban economy also undergirds much that historians write about Chicago. In Volume 3 of her famous *History of Chicago*, appropriately subtitled, *The Rise of a Modern City, 1871–1893*, Bessie Louise Pierce emphasizes agricultural products, manufacturing, merchandizing, and finance. More recently, William Cronon's *Nature's Metropolis* reaffirms Pierce's notion of the city as a manufacturing, processing, and distribution center for the region and the nation. Similarly, Lizabeth Cohen's *Making a New Deal* explicitly focuses on industrial workers, painting Chicago as the home of corporations, factories, and ethnic machine operatives fabricating goods for a national market. Cohen illuminates how workers patronized local shops, bars, and theaters, but not how people earned their living in these same spaces.[6]

---

politicized. Peter Way, *Common Labour: Workers and the Digging of North American Canals, 1780–1860* (New York: Cambridge University Press, 1993); Arnesen, *Waterfront Workers of New Orleans: Race, Class, and Politics, 1863–1923* (New York: Oxford University Press, 1991); Michael Kazin's *Barons of Labor: The San Francisco Building Trades and Union Power in the Progressive Era* (Chicago: University of Illinois Press, 1989).

[4] Alfred Chandler, *The Visible Hand: The Managerial Revolution in American Business* (Cambridge, MA: Harvard University Press, 1977). Mansell Blackford notes how large firms have held hegemony over business history, yet, as his literature review shows, even historians specializing in small business hardly examine retail, service, construction, and trucking. Mansell G. Blackford, "Small Business in America: A Historiographic Survey," *Business History Review* 65 (Spring 1991): 1–26, esp. 10–1; Mansell G. Blackford, *A History of Small Business in America* (New York: Twayne Publishers, 1991), 53–57. For small manufacturers, see Philip Scranton, *Proprietary Capitalism: Textile Manufacture at Philadelphia, 1800–1885* (New York: Cambridge University Press, 1983) and *Figured Tapestry: Production, Markets, and Power in Philadelphia Textiles, 1885–1941* (New York: Cambridge University Press, 1989).

[5] Robert Wiebe, *The Search for Order, 1877–1920* (New York: Hill and Wang, 1967); Martin Sklar, *The Corporate Reconstruction of American Capitalism: The Market, the Law, and Politics* (New York: Cambridge University Press, 1993).

[6] Bessie Louise Pierce, *A History of Chicago: Volume 3: The Rise of a Modern City, 1871–1893* (New York: Alfred A. Knopf, 1957); William Cronon, *Nature's Metropolis: Chicago and the Great West* (New York: W. W. Norton, 1991);

These important works tend to minimize the commercial diversity of urban life. Manufacturing, however striking its growth around the turn of the century, was only one sector of the city's economy. Crucial, if mundane, forms of commercial activity that one might call the "craft economy" surrounded industrial production. This "craft economy" included four groups of workers and proprietors. First, the category refers to skilled building tradesmen, such as bricklayers, carpenters, and plumbers. Second, the term includes flat janitors, stationary engineers, and realtors responsible for the management and maintenance of buildings. Third, it covers shopkeepers, some of them craft producers like butchers and bakers, others service providers such as barbers, tailors, or launderers, and still others who were retailers providing clothing, beer, coal, milk, and groceries. Finally, the craft economy refers to the Chicagoans who loaded and carried goods throughout the city and the region, such as teamsters, teaming contractors, longshoremen, and sailors.

The craft economy looked quite different from the modern economy imagined by Adams, Veblen, and Lang. Trades like construction, trucking, and shopkeeping were not industrial; factory production was uncommon. The craft economy was overwhelmingly proprietary, dominated by small, unincorporated firms with few employees. Although a gap existed between workers and bosses, this gap was not wide, class relations were fairly fluid, and many workers established themselves as businessmen. While an integral part of early twentieth-century commerce, the craft economy resembled nothing more than the urban economy of the previous century.

However antiquated their methods, thousands of Chicagoans worked in the craft economy, building the city's homes, cutting its hair, and delivering its coal. In 1900, more than 55,000 men, or 10 percent of all working males over ten years of age in the city, found their occupation in just eleven construction trades. Another 34,864 men (6.3 percent of working men) and 45,747 women (30.5 percent of working women) engaged in selected service fields including barbering, laundering, and building maintenance. Many men engaged in local transportation; teamsters, draymen, and hackmen alone accounted for 23,203 men, or 4.2 percent of all male workers.[7]

Lizabeth Cohen, *Making a New Deal: Industrial Workers in Chicago, 1919–1939* (New York: Cambridge University Press, 1990), 11–52, esp. 30–1.

[7] In the category "building trades," I count carpenters, electricians, masons, painters, plumbers, roofers, stonecutters, brickmakers, paperhangers, cabinetmakers, and plasterers. For male "service trades," I count barbers, bartenders, bootblacks, janitors, launderers, servants, waiters, watchmen,

A surprising number of men and women were shopkeepers and semi-independent producers working outside of factories. In 1905, the city sustained 852 bakeries, most of them small retail shops owned by individuals. In 1900, more than 23,000 men, or one out of every twenty-four, were "retail dealers," the third most common occupation among the 555,515 employed men in the city. Significant numbers of women operated small businesses. At the turn of the century, more than 1,500 women, or a little more than 1 percent, were retailers, with an additional 3,432 (2.3 percent) working as milliners and millinery dealers. In 1910, more than 15,000 women worked outside factories as dressmakers and nearly 5,000 more as tailoresses. Combined, these two jobs constituted 8.5 percent of the female workforce.[8]

These tradespeople had immigrated to the United States not only from Germany, Ireland, and Scandinavia, but also from southern and Eastern Europe. Contrary to common assumption, "old" immigrants did not monopolize craft employment. Rather, specific ethnic groups dominated tightly defined niches. German-Americans were building tradesmen and shopkeepers in disproportionate numbers. Irish-Americans were slightly overrepresented in construction and transportation, but greatly under represented in retail and service sectors. Newly arrived Polish-Americans worked in the craft economy as masons, as carpenters, and as bakers. Few Russians worked in construction, but nearly 12 percent of all Russian men were retail dealers, and significant numbers were bakers, barbers, and other tradesmen.[9]

police, and firemen. I count barbers, housekeepers, janitors, laundresses, servants, and waitresses as female service workers. Bureau of the Census, Special Reports, *Occupations at the Twelfth Census* (Washington, DC: Government Printing Office, 1904), 516–23.

[8] Because the census groups together retail and wholesale bakers, it is difficult to determine the extent of retail baking in the city. A quick inspection of the city directory shows that only thirty-two were wholesalers. *Census of Manufactures* (1905), 232; *Lakeside Directory, 1902*, 2235. The two most common occupations were "Laborers (not specified)" and "Clerks and copyists." Included in the category "retail dealer" are managers and superintendents of stores. I shift to 1910 because that census distinguished between dressmakers working inside and outside factories. Bureau of the Census, Special Reports, *Occupations at the Twelfth Census* (Washington, DC: Government Printing Office, 1904), 516–23; Bureau of the Census, *Thirteenth Census of the United States Taken in the Year 1910, v. 4, Population, 1910: Occupations* (Washington, DC: Government Printing Office, 1914), 544–7.

[9] Continuing immigration and industrialization altered the occupational distribution of each nationality. Because the census abstracts abandoned the ethnic breakdowns in 1910, it is difficult to estimate these changes. *Occupations at the Twelfth Census*, 516–23. In baking, painting, woodworking,

For centuries, these tradespeople had wielded significant economic and political power in American cities. In colonial New York, cartmen figured so prominently in local commerce and in public service that the city granted them the "freehold" – the right to vote and participate in urban government – usually reserved for property holders. In 1774, the decision of the First Continental Congress to meet in Philadelphia's Carpenters' Hall, home to a guild called the Carpenters' Company, was a response to the power of the city's artisans. Barbers, bakers, and butchers were a less potent but nevertheless significant presence in early American cities.[10]

With the growth of Chicago around the turn of the century, these trades became further entrenched in urban life. Between 1890 and 1904, the city gained more than 830,000 new residents, as well as thousands of new businesses. Immigrants to the city required food and shelter, services and government. Businesses required transportation and infrastructure. If steel and oil were the sinews of the new national economy, bread and meat, coal delivery and garbage removal, as well as housing and plant construction underpinned Chicago's commercial life. Stores, restaurants, bars, and barbershops did not provide essential goods, but they were the important neighborhood institutions and spaces that defined public life in the city.[11]

This prominence made the craft economy a public economy. Factory walls hid manufacturing from the outside world, making what transpired inside a private activity. Most of the city's population had no idea how workers assembled harvester machines, for example. By contrast, few barriers separated the people from the teamsters who carried

butchering, hod carrying, printing, and tailoring, Polish, Bohemian, Jewish, and Italian workers were populous enough to demand separate union locals. See *Lakeside Directory, 1906*, 72–3.

[10] Graham Hodges, *The New York City Cartmen, 1667–1850* (New York: NYU Press, 1986); John J. Zimmerman, "Charles Thomson, 'The Sam Adams of Philadelphia,'" *The Mississippi Valley Historical Review*, 45:3 (December 1958): 464; Sharon V. Salinger, "Artisans, Journeymen, and the Transformation of Labor in Late Eighteenth-Century Philadelphia," *William and Mary Quarterly*, Ser. 3, 40:1 (January 1983): 77.

[11] Hugo S. Grosser, *Chicago: A Review of its Governmental History from 1837 to 1906* (Chicago: Municipal Information Bureau, 1906), 74. For the effects of urbanization and technology on small-scale enterprise and the service sector, see Clay McShane and Joel Tarr, "The Centrality of the Horse in the Nineteenth-Century American City," in *The Making of Urban America*, Raymond Mohl ed. (Wilmington: Scholarly Resources, 1997), 107; Richard Hofstadter, *The Age of Reform: From Bryan to F.D.R.* (New York: Vintage, 1955), 220.

goods upon the streets. Building tradesmen worked on lots open to public inspection, while building maintenance personnel lived and worked in close proximity to tenants. Retail stores engaged in commerce directly with customers. Barbershops and saloons were public spaces open to consumers and nonconsumers. While steel mills were black boxes of production, mysterious physical manifestations of an increasingly abstract corporate economy, teaming, construction, and retail businesses were familiar local commercial institutions.

Visitors to Chicago marveled at the exploding city, and they commented on its bustling, public craft economy. In 1906, no less an observer than Max Weber noted the visibility of many different trades in Chicago:

> The Greek shining the Yankee's shoes for five cents, the German acting as his waiter, the Irishman managing his politics, and the Italian digging his dirty ditches. With the exception of some exclusive residential districts, the whole gigantic city, more extensive than London, is like a man whose skin has been peeled off and whose entrails one sees at work.

Scarcely noticing manufacturing, the great sociologist reported instead the readily visible trades, such as shoe shining, waiting, and ditch digging.[12]

Nor did Weber distinguish politics from the other crafts he listed. This is no surprise, for Chicago's local governments were deeply involved in the craft economy, ratifying the publicity of its trades. Teams, carts, and trucks were common carriers, subject to statute and common law. Building codes and license laws regulated construction. Fire codes, smoke ordinances, and license laws governed the stationary engineers who manned the boilers that kept the city's homes warm. Just as important, trades produced the staples of local government expenditure: construction and construction materials, hauling, printing, and coal. While negotiating regulations and scrambling to obtain lucrative government contracts, workers and proprietors in these fields took an active interest in government and in local politics and became the backbone of the local party factions.[13]

[12] Mariane Weber, *Max Weber: Ein Lebensbild* (Tubingen, 1926), 300 quoted in Hans Gerth and C. Wright Mills, *From Max Weber: Essays in Sociology* (New York: Oxford University Press, 1958), 15.
[13] Many crafts were subject to licensing laws. For steam engineers, see Garth L. Mangum, *The Operating Engineers: The Economic History of a Trade Union* (Cambridge, MA: Harvard University Press, 1964), 6, 89; Industrial Commission, *Report of the Industrial Commission on the Chicago Labor Disputes of 1900 with Especial Reference to the Disputes in the Building and Machinery Trades*, v.8

Despite their publicity, these crafts are virtually absent from "modernist" depictions of the twentieth-century city. Seeking to shock and warn, Sinclair, Veblen, and Lang omitted these public and familiar areas of the economy from their modernist dystopias. They put a funhouse mirror to commerce, exposing the most mysterious and private things, such as the factory, the machine, and the corporation, and obscuring the comforting, commonplace, and public commercial things, such as retail shops and delivery wagons. The effect of this on contemporaries was immense, for readers knew well what was absent from these imaginary worlds, and what remained startled them.

Present-day readers lack this first-hand knowledge, a fact that underlines the urgency of research on the craft economy. In recent years, awareness of these trades has grown, as historians of public space have studied the saloons, restaurants, stores, parks, and bathhouses where urban dwellers socialized, rebelled, and spent their hard-earned income. These historians have made an important contribution to our understanding of craft businesses as sites of consumption and culture.[14] But they suggest another history yet to be written – a history of craft businesses as areas of production. To see modernization as

(Washington: Government Printing Office, 1901), 303–5. Henceforth listed as IC, *Reports*, v.8. For barbers, see "The Barber Shop Law," *CRH*, October 14, 1909, 8; "Law Held Constitutional," *CRH*, April 29, 1910, 10; W. Scott Hall, *The Journeymen Barbers' International Union of America* (Baltimore: Johns Hopkins, 1936), 79–92. For the pipe trades, see Martin Segal, *The Rise of the United Association: National Unionism in the Pipe Trades, 1884–1924* (Cambridge, MA: Harvard University Press, 1970), 15–6, 108–33, 216–17; John Mangan, *History of the Steam-fitters Protective Association of Chicago* (Chicago: Steam-fitters Protective Association, 1930), 35–7. Such interventions have a long history. See William Novak, *The People's Welfare: Law and Regulation in Nineteenth-Century America* (Chapel Hill: University of North Carolina, 1996), 84–113, esp. 286; William Blackstone, *Commentaries on the Laws of England*, v. 4. adapted by Robert Malcolm Kerr (Boston: Beacon Press, l962); William W. Crosskey, *Politics and the Constitution in the History of the United States* (Chicago: University of Chicago Press, 1953), v. 2, 1286.

[14] George Chauncey, *Gay New York: Gender, Urban Culture, and the Making of a Gay Male World, 1890–1940* (New York: Basic Books, 1994), esp. 151–226; Roy Rosenzweig, *Eight Hours for What We Will: Workers and Leisure in the Industrial City* (New York: Cambridge University Press, 1983); Kathy Peiss, *Cheap Amusements: Working Women and Leisure in Turn-of-the-Century New York* (Philadelphia: Temple University Press, 1986); Gunther Barth, *City People: The Rise of Modern City Culture in Nineteenth-Century America* (New York: Oxford University Press, 1980); Cohen, *Making a New Deal*, 99–158. For a work that examines saloons as spaces of both consumption and production, see Perry Duis, *The Saloon: Public Drinking in Chicago and Boston, 1880–1920* (Chicago: University of Illinois Press, 1983).

the contested process it was, one must look at those trades that had not yet mechanized, in which small proprietors remained viable, and where the social order was considerably more fluid. The business elite loathed these trades for their unions, their politics, their provincialism, and their inefficiency. These crafts became the locus for clashes over the shape of the urban economy in the early twentieth century.

Corporate Industrialism in Chicago

Although the corporate industrial economy is well-trod historical ground, it is worthwhile to detail its contours to accurately assess its place in Chicago's history. At the turn of the century, Chicago's manufacturing, merchandizing, and railroad firms were both the products and the progenitors of the most extreme forms of capitalism. In these industries, William Blake's "Satanic mills" had indeed emerged as the dominant sites of production. In these firms, production was mechanized, ownership was corporate, and sales were national in scope. Operated by a fixed and subjected working population and managed by an increasingly powerful elite, these firms were the sites of particularly dramatic class warfare.

The managers of these firms conceived a powerful political economy, which asserted for corporations the primary, if not sole, power to govern the economy. In recent years, scholars have suggested that the sweeping effects of industrialization divided the business community, causing some corporate businessmen to advocate government regulation of the market. This may be so in other places, but not in Chicago. Background, education, and interest unified industrial manufacturers, railroad executives, bankers, and attorneys. Accentuating these commonalties were the shared belief in the private rule of corporations, acceptance of a distinctively hierarchical form of industrial relations, and contempt for any form of governance. Though some of these businessmen tolerated regulation, they seldom advocated any significant intrusion in their private affairs.[15]

Chicago's development as the productive center of the national economy began during the nineteenth century, partly in response to massive improvements in transportation. Good portage between

---

[15] For the idea that large corporations favored regulation and unionization, see Robert Wiebe, *Businessmen and Reform: A Study of the Progressive Movement* (Chicago: Ivan R. Dee, 1962), esp. 167. Martin Sklar's nuanced interpretation of corporate ideology overstates the extent to which corporations tolerated regulation and craft unionism. Sklar, *The Corporate Reconstruction of American Capitalism: The Market, the Law, and Politics*, 14–40, esp. 19.

Lake Michigan and the Mississippi River spurred the early growth of the city, and shipping remained an important industry into the twentieth century. The development of Chicago railroad facilities began in the 1830s and grew explosively in the 1850s; by 1932, more than forty trunk, belt, switching, and industrial railroads terminated in the city, the most prominent of which was the Illinois Central. Not coincidentally, during this same period, the city grew rapidly in size and economic prominence.[16]

Retail and wholesale merchants took advantage of Chicago's place in the transportation web to establish the city as the hub of national distribution. From the city, the mail-order houses such as Sears, Roebuck and Montgomery Ward sold goods advertised in their famous catalogs to the rest of the nation. The downtown shopping district grew with the city, anchored by immense department stores like Marshall Field's and Carson, Pirie, Scott, which offered products from all over the globe. Less famous were Steele–Wedeles and Hibbard, Spencer, Bartlett, wholesale houses distributing groceries and hardware, respectively, to retailers throughout the Midwest.[17]

Manufacturers just as successfully exploited the city's convenience. By 1890, Chicago had become the second largest manufacturing city in the United States, filled with large, well-equipped factories, each staffed with hundreds of workers. Best known were stockyards and packinghouses, where men and machines slaughtered and prepared the nation's meat. Companies like Armour, Swift, and Libby, McNeil and Libby operated the Union Stockyards, which employed thousands of workers and dominated a southwestern chunk of the city. Chicago's steel works were hardly less famous than its packinghouses. Located at the southern tip of Lake Michigan, stretching from Illinois into Indiana, were gigantic mills, each filled with fire, machines, and thousands of men, owned by famous firms such as Republic, Inland, Jones and Laughlin, and Carnegie. These factories produced the raw material of American industrialism, from which other factories in Chicago and around the world fabricated their goods.[18]

---

[16] Pierce, *A History of Chicago: Volume 3*, 64–5; Cronon, *Nature's Metropolis*, 63–74; Glenn A. Bishop, *Chicago's Accomplishments and Leaders* (Chicago: Bishop Publishing, 1932), 184–88.

[17] Pierce, *A History of Chicago: Volume 3*, 176–84; Cronon, *Nature's Metropolis*, 324–40.

[18] Pierce, *A History of Chicago: Volume 3*, 64, 108–44; 155–57. In 1904, the Chicago's five steel firms averaged over 1,000 workers each. The fifty-eight slaughterhouses in the city employed 22,767 workers, but the majority of these worked for a smaller set of corporate meatpackers. *Census of Manufactures*, 1914 (Washington, DC: Government Printing Office, 1918), 338–40.

Chicago's businesses manufactured more than meat and steel. The International Harvester Company, formed from the 1902 merger of the McCormick and Deering Companies, operated massive factories in the city. Down the coast of Lake Michigan, the Pullman Company was America's foremost manufacturer of railroad sleeper cars. Famous firms like Hart, Schaffner & Marx produced clothing. Plants owned by Western Electric, Stromberg–Carlson, and Kellogg Switchboard made the city strong in electrical equipment manufacture, a strength solidified in 1905 when Western Electric began shifting all its operations to the massive Hawthorne works in bordering Cicero. Other important products of the city were beer, pianos, musical instruments, printing, wagons, and metal goods.[19]

These firms were at the forefront of industrialization. They succeeded in a national market by using technology to reduce the costs of production and distribution. In the nineteenth century, meatpackers like Gustavius Swift and Philip Armour developed techniques of mass production that allowed them to sell their products cheaply. Using an automated line to slaughter and dissemble hogs and cattle, they were able to greatly speed the butchering process. By the early twentieth century, a newer set of highly automated industries had surpassed packing. In particular, the steel industry showed "unlimited opportunities for improvement," and, by 1900, engineers had invented machines capable of "handling of materials, integration of production stages, and continuous rolling of steel." Yet even in light industry, such as printing, technological innovations such as linotype had a dramatic effect on work and business. Moreover, the technology of the railroad itself enabled merchants to sell to a national market.[20]

Where machinery could not increase productivity, manufacturers sought to reduce costs by streamlining production. Managers often sought to "rationalize" their operations. For example, by using improved cost-accounting methods to closely supervise all aspects of production, steel executives like Andrew Carnegie whittled down their company's expenses. At the same time, steel manufacturers vertically

---

[19] Pierce, *A History of Chicago: Volume 3*, 145–91; Chandler, *The Visible Hand*, 503–12; Cohen, *Making a New Deal*, 33.

[20] Livingston, "The Social Analysis of Economic History," 83–5; James R. Barrett, *Work and Community in the Jungle: Chicago's Packinghouse Workers, 1894–1922* (Chicago: University of Illinois Press, 1990), 20–8; David Brody, *Steelworkers in America: The Nonunion Era* (New York: Harper & Row, 1960), 9; Emily Clark Brown, *Book and Job Printing in Chicago* (Chicago: University of Chicago Press, 1931), 56–69; Cronon, *Nature's Metropolis*, 324–25.

integrated their firms – purchasing mining, shipping, and coke-manufacturing companies, and then eliminating wasteful duplication by coordinating their interaction.[21]

Light manufacturers and merchants also used vertical integration and strict management to lower prices. Most piano manufacturers had begun as shopkeepers who, unable to purchase affordable pianos from wholesalers, decided to produce them themselves. Mail-order houses used hierarchical organization to enable the orderly and efficient operation of their firms. The famous cover drawing of the 1900 Montgomery Ward catalog portrays the "Busy Bee-Hive" that existed behind the walls of its Michigan Avenue establishment. The picture shows a many-floored warehouse divided into sections according to type of merchandise. From offices on the first and second floor, managers coordinated hundreds of workers working in unison to speed products to consumers.[22]

These firms also increased the productivity of human labor by reskilling work, breaking it into constituent parts. Between 1820 and 1900, many industries restructured their production. Meatpackers assigned each line worker a very specific part of the animal to cut and handle. "It would be difficult to imagine another industry," economist John Commons wrote, "where the division of labor had been so ingeniously and microscopically worked out . . . The animal has been surveyed and laid off like a map."[23]

These forms became more complex and intrusive around the turn of the century as a new breed of "scientific managers," led by Frederick Winslow Taylor, offered employers detailed analyses of the physical movements of workers. By studying the most productive employees, they determined the "one best way" to perform any task. They then proposed that employers implement "piece-work" pay scales for workers to increase their efficiency. With the exception of "incentive wages," few of these recommendations were fully integrated, but Taylor and

---

[21] Brody, *Steelworkers in America*, 18–22; Naomi Lamoreaux, *The Great Merger Movement in American Business, 1895–1904* (New York: Cambridge University Press, 1985), 27–37; Chandler, *The Visible Hand*, 249, 290–92, 300–1.

[22] George P. Bent, *A Pioneer's Historical Sketches: Four Score and More Years of American History in the Making* (Chicago: Geographical Publishing Co., 1928), 156–60; Cronon, *Nature's Metropolis*, center, 337–38.

[23] John Commons, "Labor Conditions in Slaughtering and Meat Packing," quoted in Barrett, *Work and Community*, 26. For an early history of reskilling see Sean Wilentz, *Chants Democratic: New York and the Rise of the American Working Class, 1788–1850* (New York: Oxford University Press, 1984), 107–45.

his acolytes deeply influenced manufacturers in the tool and dye, steel, and railroad-car industries.[24]

Mechanization and reskilling intensified the capital requirements of manufacturing. In 1905, the average manufacturing firm in Chicago owned $2,670 in capital goods per worker. Some firms carried lighter capital loads. The Kellogg Switchboard Company, the second largest Chicago-based manufacturer of electrical equipment, operated with an investment of $1,000 per worker. In "heavier" industries like agricultural implements, Illinois firms averaged $4,647.65 in assets for every worker. The most capital-intensive firm was probably the Pullman Company, with $9,000 invested per worker in 1897, rising to approximately $12,000 per worker in 1910.[25]

Companies multiplied such investments by thousands of workers, building giant industrial firms with millions in assets. In 1900, Chicago had three plants employing over 6,000 workers each: Armour Meat, Deering Harvester, and Illinois Steel. Pullman Sleeper Cars, Swift Meats, McCormick Harvester, and Western Electric each employed more than 4,000 workers. The five steel mills in the city in 1905 averaged nearly $3.4 million in assets. The twenty-four meatpackers in the city averaged more than $2.9 million in assets.[26]

Only a few manufacturers were so massive, but most were sizeable institutions. For example, in 1905, only two piano producers in the entire state held over $1 million in assets, but the average manufacturer of pianos in Chicago still held over $400,000 and employed 175 workers. Other industries populated by firms of this scale were malt liquors ($506,298 in assets and forty-nine employees per establishment) and foundry and machine tools ($131,534 in assets and fifty-one workers per establishment). In other words, by 1900, smaller manufacturers

---

[24] Daniel Nelson, *Managers and Workers: Origins of the Factory System in the United States, 1880–1920* (Madison: University of Wisconsin Press, 1975), 55–78; Frederick W. Taylor, *Scientific Management* (New York: Harper Brothers, 1947).

[25] *Census of Manufactures, 1905, Part II, States and Territories* (Washington, DC: GPO, 1907), 232–33. For Kellogg's assets, see *Dunbar v. American Telephone and Telegraph*, 238 Ill. 456 (1909). For the investments among heavy manufacturers, see *Census of Manufactures, 1905, Part II*, 209. In 1897, the Pullman Company employed 4,000 workers and held capital stock worth $36,000,000. By 1910, the firm had divested itself of its holdings in local real estate and trade, but held capital stock worth $120,000,000 and employed around 10,000 workers. Stanley Buder, *Pullman: An Experiment in Industrial Order and Community Planning, 1880–1930* (New York: Oxford University Press, 1967), 207–18.

[26] Nelson, *Managers and Workers*, 7–8; *Census of Manufactures, 1905, Part II*, 236.

were seldom "mom and pop" operations; they employed many work-ers and owned substantial capital.[27]

Businesses raised this capital by soliciting local, regional, and na-tional investors. Initially, firms borrowed from Eastern bankers. As commerce tied the city to its hinterland, a regional network of lenders emerged, and, with the success of merchants and manufacturers, a well of capital became available locally as well. Chicagoans formed promi-nent banks like the Northern Trust Company and the First National Bank of Chicago. But national investment in Chicago's businesses con-tinued into the twentieth century. During the merger movement of the period between 1895 and 1904, Wall Street financiers like J. P. Morgan obtained the massive capital needed to consolidate whole industries and create firms like U.S. Steel, International Harvester, National Lead, and so many others.[28]

To attract such investors, businessmen sought the legal protections of incorporation. Since the 1830s, the law had made corporations attractive investments by allowing stockholders to limit their liability to their initial investment. By the late nineteenth century, states had enacted general rules for incorporation, making the legal status more easily available to average businessmen. Beginning in 1888, states like New Jersey allowed corporations to purchase stock in other companies, an important precondition for widespread mergers.

By the early twentieth century, corporations were common and even dominant in banking, in rail transportation, in large-scale merchan-dizing, and in manufacturing. In 1905, 2,474 (30.3 percent) of the 8,159 manufacturing establishments in Chicago were incorporated. These firms held over 89 percent of Chicago's manufacturing capital, hired nearly 76 percent of its manufacturing workers, and fabricated 82 percent of its products. Moreover, the few industries where pro-prietorships and partnerships retained a majority share of the market skew these figures downward. In 1905, more than half of the propri-etary manufacturers in Illinois (53.52 percent) made baked goods, tobacco products, and clothing.

---

[27] *Census of Manufactures, 1905, Part II*, 210, 216, 232–39; *Bent v. Piano and Organ Worker Union*, case #204497 Sup.C.C. (1900). In 1903, the Piano and Organ Supply Company operated a plant worth $300,000, employing 260 workers. *Piano and Organ Supply Company v. Piano and Organ Worker Union*, case #232465 Sup.C.C. (1903); *Piano and Organ Workers Union v. P. & O. Supply Co.*, 124 Ill. App. 353 (1906).

[28] Pierce, *A History of Chicago: Volume 3*, 192–205, 231; Edward C. Kirkland, *A History of American Economic Life*, Third Edition (New York: Appleton-Century-Crofts, 1951), 416–19.

The industrialization, corporatization, and nationalization of manufacturing and merchandizing had mixed effects upon competition. On one hand, the market continued to be a battlefield for large, mechanized, managed, and corporate businesses. By removing geographic barriers to entry, improvements in transportation shattered local monopolies. Moreover, improvements in the efficiency of production encouraged price-cutting in many industries, including steel and metal manufacture. The gigantic scale of production, however, made entry almost impossible for new producers. With little competition from socially mobile tradespeople, corporate manufacturers needed only to consolidate their firms in order to obtain monopoly profits.[29]

In these industries, more than any others, labor and capital had developed into the distinct classes predicted by Karl Marx and other social critics. A gaping canyon separated manufacturers and merchants from the men and women who toiled in the city's factories, yards, and warehouses. Most obviously, employers and employees frequently quarreled over wages and work conditions. Almost as significant were their widely divergent origins, educational attainment, and level of social cohesion. This gap was cemented by the rise of the capital-intensive corporation, which eradicated social mobility and fixed these two classes at the opposite ends of production.

The characteristics of the industrial working class at the turn of the century are well known. Industrial workers were frequently immigrants and the children of newcomers to the United States. Many were "old" immigrants. For example, 6,642 (or 46 percent) of the 14,477 workers employed in Chicago's iron and steel industry in 1900 had German, Irish, or Scandinavian parents. Increasingly, however, manufacturing workers were "new immigrants," born in Eastern and southern Europe. By 1900, 32,360 Polish men worked in Chicago, more than 45 percent of them (14,466 men) in "manufacturing and mechanical pursuits," and 3,331 in the steel and iron mills alone. Other ethnic groups established niches in the different sectors of the city's corporate economy. Bohemians established an enclave in the bordering town of Cicero around General Electric's Hawthorne works. Russian Jews established

[29] Kirkland, *A History of American Economic Life*, 311, 401–2, 406–7, 414. Tobacco, garment, and baking – trades in the gray area between manufacturing and the craft economy – accounted for less than 6 percent of the corporations in the state. Others of this type were brickmaking, carriage making, sheet metal, lumber, and printing. *Census of Manufactures, 1905, Part II*, 212.

a presence in the garment industry; and, after 1900, Italians dominated various forms of common labor.[30]

A small but growing number of women carved their niches as industrial workers. In 1905, 46,987 women worked in manufacturing, about one-fifth of all manufacturing workers over the age of sixteen. In the production of various garments, candy, paper boxes, and furnishing goods, women comprised the bulk of the work force. In the department stores, women came to predominate as clerks and salespersons. In heavy manufacturing, women were a tiny minority, but 2,477 women worked in meatpacking, 2,802 in printing and publishing, and 1,131 in electrical machinery.[31]

These industrial workers had little formal education. In 1911, the U.S. Industrial Commission reported that three-fourths of all Slovak and Lithuanian immigrants had been farmers or farm laborers in Europe. Less than half spoke English. Although their children received free schooling in the United States, poverty minimized its duration. The family economy, which required that able-bodied children make money to support both close and distant relations, made high school a luxury and college a fantasy.

Workers had few marketable skills, and employers had scant need for those they possessed. As often as possible, through machines, management, and organization, employers eradicated positions requiring significant knowledge and training. The remaining jobs fell into two general categories: semiskilled machine operatives and laborers. Both types of industrial workers found themselves poorly paid and highly replaceable, their market position weakened by employers who needed brawn and dexterity more than intelligence or ability.[32]

Corporatization and industrialization impeded social mobility and hardened the distinctions between workers and employers. In most manufacturing trades, as corporations became bigger and more mechanized, start-up costs became massive, and entrepreneurship required strong connections to capital. The reskilling of work exacerbated this, because the techniques learned on the job hardly prepared workers for

[30] *Occupations at the Twelfth Census*, 516–23; Cohen, *Making a New Deal*, 30–1; Humbert Nelli, *Italians in Chicago, 1880–1930: A Study in Ethnic Mobility* (New York: Oxford University Press, 1970), 66, 74–5, 79–81.

[31] Only 23 women worked in steel mills. In the foundry and machine tool business, only 410 out of the 21,664 workers, or less than 2 percent, were women. *Census of Manufactures, 1905, Part II*, 232–39.

[32] Barrett, *Work and Community*, 45–6, 91–5; Montgomery, *Workers' Control in America*, 117–21. For a detailed discussion of these two industrial types, see David Montgomery, *The Fall of the House of Labor* (New York: Cambridge University Press, 1987), 58–170.

any independent form of business activity. For most industrial workers, the option of quitting their employment to compete with their employer did not exist.

Industrial workers responded to this subordinate condition in a number of ways. Most often, manufacturing workers simply quit their employment, skipping days or switching firms. With increasing vigor and violence, though, industrial workers proposed organizational solutions to their problems, ranging from anarchism and socialism to a more conservative combination of trade unionism and governmental regulation. The latter position proposed the determination of daily wages, establishment of an eight-hour day, prohibition of unsafe work conditions, and the protection of women and children. In general, workers demanded that industry accept some form of public regulation.[33]

But divisions within the industrial labor force weakened solidarity and stymied these efforts at resistance. Differences of ethnicity, gender, race, and party segmented the labor market. Workers developed their own forms of social life, but these modes did little in the short term to foster broad class unity. Saloons catered to different ethnicities, neighborhoods, and trades. Theaters performed in foreign languages. Protestant workers were divided among various denominations while Catholic parishes tended towards ethnic segregation. Thirty years later, unions affiliated with the Congress of Industrial Organizations (CIO) successfully appealed to these cultural affiliations, but in 1900, differences of faith and origin divided industrial workers.[34]

At the other end of Chicago's socioeconomic spectrum, a highly unified business elite fortified barriers to solidarity, preventing both the organization of working people and the operation of reform legislation. An employer class had coalesced, with its roots in manufacturing, but with branches in merchandizing, wholesaling, railways, finance, and

---

[33] Turnover became such a problem after 1914 that companies instituted widespread changes in labor policy. Nelson, *Managers and Workers*, 83–6, 148–56; Cohen, *Making a New Deal*, 162–72. For the varied political responses to industrialization, see Melvyn Dubofsky, *We Shall Be All: A History of the Industrial Workers of the World* (New York: Quadrangle Books, 1969); Paul Avrich, *The Haymarket Tragedy* (Princeton: Princeton University Press, 1984); James Weinstein, *The Decline of Socialism in America* (New York: Monthly Review, 1967); Leon Fink, *Workingmen's Democracy: The Knights of Labor and American Politics* (Chicago: University of Illinois Press, 1983); John Commons et al., *History of Labour in the United States*, v. 3 (New York: Macmillan, 1936).

[34] Cohen, *Making a New Deal*, 4, 11–52; Barrett, *Work and Community*, 36–58; Brody, *Steelworkers in America*, 96–111, 119–21.

the professions. Manufacturers like Gustavius Swift, Cyrus McCormick, and George Pullman made fortunes producing meat, agricultural implements, and sleeper cars, respectively. Marshall Field, Montgomery Ward, and Julius Rosenwald led the city's merchants. Marvin Hughitt, the president of five different lines, including the Chicago and Northwestern Railroad Company, was Chicago's foremost railroad executive. An aggressive set of bankers including Byron Smith of the Northern Trust Company and James B. Forgan of the First National Bank of Chicago built the nation's second most important financial center. And finally, a community of professionals, including attorneys like Levy Mayer and Horace Tenney, developed to assist businesses seeking to raise capital, to evade legal regulation, to restrain the workforce, and to organize production.[35]

This business elite had a number of distinguishing characteristics. Most of Chicago's wealthiest businessmen were born in the United States of English-speaking forebears. In 1900, more than 65 percent of the 3,540 males the census identifies as "bankers and company officials" had American, Anglo-Canadian, or British parents. The remaining 24 percent were Irish, German, and German-Jewish ethnics, each group sufficiently populous to justify its own exclusive club, yet small enough to make assimilation a common business stratagem. That so many German, Irish, and Jewish businessmen joined mainstream clubs like the Union League reflects their broader acceptance of an Anglo-American business culture and that culture's striking acceptance of them.[36]

---

[35] The other four railways were the Chicago, St. Paul, Minneapolis, and Omaha, the Fremont Elkhorn and Missouri, the St. Paul Eastern Grand Trunk, and the Sioux City and Pacific. *Directory of Directors, 1900–1901*, 94. For bankers, see *The Book of Chicagoans, 1905*, 302; Cronon, *Nature's Metropolis*, 305; Thomas Goebel, "The Uneven Rewards of Professional Labor: Wealth and Income in the Chicago Professions, 1870–1920," *Journal of Social History* 29:4 (1996): 749–77; Edgar Lee Masters, *Levy Mayer and the New Industrial Era: A Biography* (New Haven: Yale University Press, 1927), 40–68; Daniel Ernst, *Lawyers Against Labor: From Proprietary Capitalism to Corporate Liberalism* (Chicago: University of Illinois Press, 1996).

[36] The clubs, respectively, were the Sheridan, the Germania, and the Standard. *Chicago Blue Book of Selected Names of Chicago and Suburban Towns . . . for the Year Ending 1906* (Chicago: Chicago Directory Company, 1905), 385, 448, 452. Given that the Irish and Germans comprised nearly 40 percent of the city's working population, they were underrepresented in Chicago's business elite, though less so than the city's Scandinavians, Austrians, Russians, Italians, and Poles. *Occupations at the Twelfth Census*, 516–18.

Because most Chicago manufacturers, merchants, and executives had migrated from elsewhere in the United States, it is unsurprising that they embraced a national economy. Some, like Frederick Delano, an executive at the Wabash Railroad, were from prominent Eastern families. Many others, like department store magnate Marshall Field, were from the farms and towns of New England, northwestern New York, rural Ohio, and Illinois. Still others came to booming Chicago from more slowly growing cities. Jewish businessmen, such as Inland Steel vice-president Philip Block, Sears, Roebuck president Julius Rosenwald, and attorney Levy Mayer hailed, respectively, from Cincinnati, Ohio, Springfield, Illinois, and Richmond, Virginia.

These geographic ties frequently further encouraged the development of a national market. For example, Chicago's financial community grew on the strength of its exogamous connections to banks in its hinterland. These connections were personal as well as contractual, as many prominent bank executives had begun their careers as ambitious rural cashiers. George M. Reynolds, the president of the Bankers' Club and the vice-president of the Continental National Bank, started as a clerk in Panora, Iowa, while D. A. Moulton and W. D. C. Street, the vice-president and secretary, respectively, of the club, had similar origins as rural clerks and messengers.[37]

The business elite was comparatively well educated. In 1906, the membership of the Commercial Club of Chicago, a club with sixty prominent members, was split between men who attended university in their teens and those who directly entered the business world. Although twenty-seven finished no more than high school, twenty-one graduated from college or professional school. The scions of Chicago's best families, such as dry goods merchant John V. Farwell, Jr. and meatpacking heir J. Ogden Armour, obtained college degrees before entering the family business. Attorneys, whose number and prestige grew in the late nineteenth century, were particularly lettered. Finally, men like Enos Barton of Western Electric Co. used their education in engineering and science to run highly technical industries.[38]

[37] For the backgrounds of Delano, Field, Block, Rosenwald, and Mayer, see *The Book of Chicagoans, 1905*, 67, 159–60, 204, 498, 402. For the development of regional banking systems, see Cronon, *Nature's Metropolis*, 305; Pierce, *A History of Chicago: Volume 3*, 202–5; *Chicago Blue Book, 1906*, 331; *The Book of Chicagoans, 1905*, 483, 422, 555.

[38] The Commercial Club was the city's most elite businessmen's society. It served as a social club, reform group, and debating society. Pierce, *A History of Chicago: Volume 3*, 190; *Chicago Blue Book, 1906*, 370–1; *The Book of Chicagoans, 1905*, 199, 24, 46.

Yet solidarity was the most distinctive characteristic of Chicago corporate business elite. Mutual economic dependence forged bonds among manufacturers, merchandisers, and railroad executives. The railroad made the production and distribution of goods for and to a national market possible. Conversely, the wide range of products offered by department stores like Marshall Field's and Carson, Pirie, Scott depended upon their access to America's productivity. Banks derived their assets from the industrial wealth of the city, while offering to businessmen the credit they needed to purchase supplies and expand their operations. Businesses hired professionals for the expertise they offered, and paid them handsomely for their advice.

These connections were often genealogical. Children of tycoons frequently diversified their holdings by venturing into new areas of enterprise. John B. Drake, Sr. of the Grand Pacific Railway, had two sons, John B., Jr. and Tracy Drake, who built the Drake and the Blackstone Hotels. After Richard R. Donnelley became the city's foremost printer, his younger son, Thomas, took over the family business while his older son, Reuben, established Knight, Donnelley and Co., an investment bank and brokerage house. In innumerable other cases, marriage forged bonds between different lines of business. In 1908, Potter Palmer, Jr., the son of the drygoods merchant and real estate speculator, married Pauline Kohlsaat, the daughter of Herman H. Kohlsaat, the newspaper publisher, wholesale baker, and landowner.[39]

These relationships were inscribed in the structure of commerce. A network of corporate directorships linked these men to one another. The directors of the Northern Trust Company Bank were a diverse set of businessmen: two bankers, an investor, a plow manufacturer, a wholesale grocer, a hardware dealer, a railroad executive, and a retail merchant. Added together, these nine men dictated the affairs of twenty-nine other corporations. Individual men connected a wide range of businesses. Banker John J. Mitchell was a director for twelve corporations, while railroad speculator Norman B. Ream directed fourteen firms, including many railroads, two streetcar lines, banks, a steel firm, a cemetery, the National Biscuit Company, and the Pullman Company. Mitchell and Ream were exceptional but integral figures in the web that controlled the city's 2,474 corporations.[40]

[39] *Notable Men of Chicago, 1910*, 98; *Chicago's Accomplishments*, 177–79; *The Book of Chicagoans, 1905*, 169; "Love President's Topic; Congratulates Bride," *CRH*, July 25, 1908, 1.

[40] *Directory of Directors in the City of Chicago, 1900–1901* (Chicago: Audit Company of New York, 1900), 135; *The Book of Chicagoans, 1905*, 414; *Directory of Directors*, 160; Sklar, *The Corporate Reconstruction*, 29.

Common beliefs unified the business elite. Broadly speaking, manufacturers and merchants staunchly opposed any and all public governance, believing instead in a private, well-capitalized, and corporate economy. The physical manifestation of this private economy was the factory whose walls hid the workers and machines from public view; the legal embodiment of this principle was the corporation. By the turn of the century, manufacturers, merchants, bankers, and railway officials began seeing the corporation as the optimal institution for organizing business activity, proposing that it replace the individual as the constitutive unit of American economy and society, while retaining all the basic rights guaranteed to citizens. They imagined a private economic sphere, subject to the will of its owners and their representatives and exempt from all forms of regulation except the corporate law and the "natural law" of competition. As a corollary, they envisioned a minimal role for institutions, including trade associations, unions, political parties, and the state, in the economic life of the city.

The general consensus in support of a private corporate economy contrasts with scholarly representations of this group. In the past, historians such as James Weinstein, Martin Sklar, and most recently Daniel Ernst have argued that corporations advocated "corporate liberalism," a public economy regulated by unions, trade agreements, and government. Their rivals were small businessmen, or "proprietary capitalists," who continued to favor individualism and private property. These two interest groups, represented respectively by the National Civic Federation (NCF) and the National Association of Manufacturers (NAM), engaged in a dramatic struggle to determine the shape of industrial capitalism. In this portrayal, the executives of the NCF defeated the entrepreneurs of the NAM, establishing a pluralist order that abandoned older notions of individualism and deflected more radical alternatives such as socialism.[41]

Two facts suggest that this binary opposition is inapplicable to Chicago's business community. First, while local manufacturers, merchants, railroad executives, bankers, and professionals favored the

[41] Ellis Hawley, "The Discovery and Study of a 'Corporate Liberalism,'" *Business History Review* 52 (1978): 309–20; Scranton, *Proprietary Capitalism,* passim; James Weinstein, *The Corporate Ideal in the Liberal State, 1900–1918* (Boston: Beacon Press, 1968), esp. 5; Daniel Ernst, "The Closed Shop, the Proprietary Capitalist, and the Law, 1897–1915," in *Masters to Managers,* Sanford Jacoby, ed. (New York: Columbia University Press, 1991), 132–48. For a more complex version of this thesis, see Sklar, *Corporate Reconstruction,* 15–6.

corporation, they opposed "corporatist" schemes under which unions, trade associations, corporations, and the state governed the economy. At the very least, executives opposed the participation of labor organizations in any economic decisions. Though the NCF advocated labor arbitration, its Chicago branch notably did not; indeed, it avoided the "labor question" entirely. Second, the "small businessmen" who joined groups like the Illinois Manufacturers Association (the local branch of the NAM) were hardly contingent entrepreneurs yearning for a competitive past. By 1901, the IMA had enlisted "two hundred and fifty of the biggest manufacturers in Illinois, all but seventy-five of whom were located in the Chicago area." While claiming to be small businessmen, these men were managers of corporations like Armour Meat, selling to national and even international markets. They lobbied government in the name of proprietorship, yet their rhetoric merely served to mask the rapacity of ambitious corporations.[42]

The Chicago Association of Commerce (CAC) best represented the values of the business elite. Uniting the city's most prominent firms, the CAC pushed to create a climate favorable for continued economic growth. Beneath its umbrella was the Employers' Association of Chicago (EA), the city's most vocal opponent of labor unions and trade agreements. Founded in 1903 by local corporate executives including Charles Thorne of Montgomery Ward, Mark Morton of Morton Salt, Frederick Delano of the Wabash Railroad, and hardware merchant and NCF member Adolphus C. Bartlett, the EA became a major opponent of local craft producers, consistently favoring chains, large contractors, and ambitious businessmen who promised to break with agreements between employers and unions.[43]

---

[42] NCF members were often quite hostile to labor. NCF president August Belmont broke a streetcar strike in New York in 1905. The anti-union U.S. Steel corporation belonged to the NCF. And, in 1906, the manager of the bitterly anti-union Lyon & Healy Piano Company served as president of the Chicago Civic Federation. Weinstein, *The Corporate Ideal*, 12–3; Sidney Fine, *"Without Blare of Trumpets": Walter Drew, the National Erectors' Association, and the Open Shop Movement, 1903–1957* (Ann Arbor: University of Michigan Press, 1995), 10; Daniel Levine, *Varieties of Social Reform* (Madison, WI: University of Wisconsin Press, 1964), 57; Montgomery, *Fall of the House of Labor*, 272; *Lyon & Healy v. Piano and Organ Workers Union*, case #236230, Supp.C.C. (1904); Alfred Kelly "A History of the Illinois Manufacturers Association" (Ph.D. diss., University of Chicago, 1938), 21. For corporations using small business rhetoric, see C. Wright Mills *White Collar: The American Middle Classes* (New York: Oxford University Press, 1951), 34–59.

[43] The connection between the Chicago Association of Commerce and the Employers' Association of Chicago was a secret for many years, revealed

Chicago corporations founded few stable trade associations. When corporations did organize, they generally refused to grant their associations any real governing power. Beginning in the late nineteenth century, manufacturing groups like the National Founders Association (NFA) and the National Metal Trades Association (NMTA) emerged, but a more general associationalism did not catch fire, and new organizations emerged slowly. Until the 1920s, the striking refusal of corporations to abide by their own agreements hampered associational efforts to set prices or wages. For example, in April 1896, members of the Tin Plate Manufacturers' Association established standard prices through a "gentlemen's agreement." Within one month, the agreement had been widely violated and by August, its largest adherent had resigned from the association.

Manufacturers rejected organizational governance in favor of more private forms of industrial rule, a fact reflected in the rash of mergers during the years directly before and after 1900. As Naomi Lamoreaux has argued, the extraordinary consolidation of America's manufacturing and rail sectors during this period was a result of the failure of associational price controls between 1870 and 1895. Indeed, investors measured a consolidation's success not only by its effect on efficiency, but also by its effect on prices. Choosing the merger over the trade association, executives made the corporation the basic unit of an industrial order privately controlled by property holders.[44]

Employers supported trade associations that advocated the free market, an altogether common paradox of the time. The most successful groups were associations of corporate manufacturers like the NMTA that resisted the efforts of unions to regulate wages and hours. Contrary to the widespread belief that large corporations tolerated unionization, Chicago's corporations signed wage agreements only under extreme duress. In 1900, manufacturing unions were strongest in the industries where corporations were least common – printing, tobacco, garment, etc – and within these unionized trades, the most adamantly anti-union employers were usually large corporations, like R. R. Donnelley Sons, the largest nonunion printer in the Midwest. In

only during the 1930s. "Organized Labor's Protest Against the Abuse of the Legal Powers of the State's Attorney's Office by a Participant," *Federation News*, October 11, 1930, 14. All thirteen of the EA's original members were from major firms. Five managed department and dry goods stores, four were wholesalers, three were manufacturers, and one was a railroad executive. *Employers' News*, April 1928, 6; Louis Menand, *The Metaphysical Club: A Story of Ideas in America* (New York: Farrar, Straus & Giroux, 2001), 296.

[44] Lamoreaux, *The Great Merger Movement*, 1–13, 14; Livingston, "The Social Analysis of Economic History," 84–7.

unorganized trades, corporate employers, including the "Big Six" meatpacking houses, the railroads, the piano manufacturers, and the wholesale and retail merchants, fought the unions with the help of their associations.[45]

Corporate antipathy to state regulation mirrored its broad opposition to other forms of public governance. The Illinois Manufacturers Association, a branch of the NAM, consistently opposed any new factory safety regulation in the legislature and in court. Moreover, these businesses struggled to avoid age-old forms of economic policing. For example, in 1901, Sprague, Warner, and Company, the largest wholesale grocer in the United States, and Hibbard, Spencer, Bartlett and Company, a leading hardware wholesaler, decided to challenge laws requiring the licensing of carts. The city argued that the law of common carriers, the ancient principle allowing the state to make rules for transportation, gave it the power to license wagons. The wholesalers successfully argued that, since their teams were not available for hire by the public, they were not common carriers subject to regulation in the public interest.[46]

In the minds of Chicago's corporate managers, government existed to protect the private property of individual and corporate persons. When unions and associations organized workers and employers, corporations were the businesses most likely to go to court demanding the legal protection of their property. Corporations used injunctions and indictments to restrain pickets, boycotts, and price fixing. They demanded help from local police and asked the city to deputize armed guards and private detectives.[47]

[45] For NMTA success, see Lewis Lorwin, *The American Federation of Labor* (Washington, DC: Brookings Institution, 1933), 79. Looking at the rhetoric of open shop groups, many scholars conclude that small business opposed labor unions more assiduously than corporations. In fact, the strongest opponents of organized labor were corporations in largely proprietary industries such as printing. Daniel Ernst, *Lawyers Against Labor*, esp. 4–5, passim. See Wiebe, *Businessmen and Reform*, 167; Lamoreaux, *The Great Merger Movement*, 171. Barbara Warne Newall, *Chicago and the Labor Movement: Metropolitan Unionism in the Thirties* (Urbana: University of Illinois Press, 1961), 27; Harold Barton Myers, "The Policing of Labor Disputes in Chicago: A Case Study" (Ph.D. diss., University of Chicago, 1929).

[46] Earl R. Beckner, *A History of Illinois Labor Legislation* (Chicago: University of Chicago Press, 1929), 224–31; Kelly, "A History of the Illinois Manufacturers Association," 44–70; *Forbes Cartage Co. v. City of Chicago*, 1 Ill. C.C. 473 (1901); *The Book of Chicagoans, 1905*, 543, 45.

[47] Edwin Witte, *Government in Labor Disputes* (New York: McGraw-Hill Book Company, 1932); William Forbath, *Law and the Shaping of the American Labor Movement* (Cambridge, MA: Harvard University Press, 1991); Victoria

Manufacturers and merchants were, not coincidentally, ambivalent towards party politics. While currying the favor of public officials, they advocated the strict separation of business and politics. These businessmen seldom personally ran for government office, choosing instead to financially support candidates. Such political values produced wildly different types: both prominent reformers like Sears Roebuck president Julius Rosenwald, as well as the progenitors of graft on an unprecedented scale like streetcar tycoon Charles Tyson Yerkes. But few corporate executives held public office.[48]

Taken together, corporate businessmen advocated a private economy governed by corporations assisted by the courts. They insisted upon a system of industrial relations that placed workers in a subordinate relationship to the firm and a pattern of competition, which made prices subject to each corporation's ability to dominate the market. Although they accepted the state's authority, they believed in strictly limiting its jurisdiction to the protection of private property rights. However much they diverged from their own principles in practice, indulging in the monopolistic protections of pools, agreements, and laws, corporations did not tolerate those who diverged from these principles in theory. Over the next four decades, they battled unions, associations, political parties, and the state, while proselytizing to the workers and proprietors of the craft economy with the gospel of the private corporation.

The Craft Economy in the New Century

In many regards, the craft economy was everything the manufacturing economy was not. The differences were partly material. If industrial workers tended machines, the denizens of the craft economy used their hands. While manufacturers were often large corporations with many employees and national ambitions, firms in the craft economy were

---

Hattam, *Labor Visions and State Power: The Origins of Business Unionism in the United States* (Princeton: Princeton University Press, 1993).

[48] Outside of the building-materials industry, few manufacturers gained elected office. In 1904, the city elected thirty-five aldermen, only three of whom worked in manufacturing. Five were saloonkeepers or liquor dealers, five were contractors or material men, and two were team owners, while others worked in law, real estate, banking, wholesale, and brokerage. "Tips on Council Needs," *CRH,* April 2, 1904, 4; "Honest Council Given Big Vote; League Victory," *CRH,* April 6, 1904, 4; "Tips on Aldermen by Voters League," *CRH,* April 1, 1905, 3; "Council Chosen is Republican" *CDT,* April 5, 1905, 4; Harold Ickes, *Autobiography of a Curmudgeon* (New York: Reynal & Hitchcock, 1943); Sidney Roberts, "Portrait of a Robber Baron: Charles T. Yerkes," *Business History Review* 35 (Winter 1961): 344–71.

provincial proprietorships hiring few workers. Although employers and employees had emerged as sharply divided classes in the manufacturing sector, social relations were significantly more fluid in the craft economy. The modesty of craft enterprise, the mobility of workers, and a common business culture mitigated the significant differences between bosses and workers and encouraged peaceful bargaining between their representatives.

The craft economy and the industrial economy were also culturally distinct. Craft producers expressed an ideology hospitable to the regulation of public and semipublic institutions including business associations, unions, political parties, and government bodies. Tradespeople of the craft economy seldom questioned the need for some sort of organizational governance. They implemented rules that protected local workers and proprietors from the ravages of the market, allowing them to mitigate the transformative effects of capitalism. Although the craft economy was a site of routine and heated conflict, various groups of workers and employers fought to enforce industrial order, to define the rules, and to determine the beneficiaries. In sharp contrast to the elite, tradespeople questioned only who would govern and under what provisions, rather than whether they should be subject to some sort of regulation.

By 1900, industrial capitalism had touched the craft economy, but it had not radically remade its day-to-day operation. Factory production was largely unknown. For barbers and retail dealers, machines were of little use. In retail baking and butchering, mixing, kneading, chopping, and wrapping were done by hand. Into the 1920s, local commercial transportation continued to rely upon horse-drawn wagons loaded by powerfully built teamsters rather than by forklifts. In the building trades, manufacturers had begun producing materials in factories, but skilled journeymen still did most work with hand tools devised centuries before, while thousands of laborers lifted, carried, and hauled materials with little mechanical assistance at all.[49]

---

[49] Ursula B. Stone, "The Baking Industry with Special Reference to the Bread Baking Industry of Chicago" (Ph.D. diss., University of Chicago, 1929), 124; John Commons, "Types of American Labor Organization – The Teamsters of Chicago," *Quarterly Journal of Economics*, 19 (1905): 414–20; Robert A. Christie, *Empire in Wood: A History of the Carpenters Union* (Ithaca, NY: Cornell University, 1956), 19–28, 79–82; Joel Tarr, "Note on the Horse as an Urban Power Source," *Journal of Urban History* 25:3 (March 1999: 437). American contractors today use fewer machines than their counterparts in other countries. See Ronald E. Yates, "U.S. Builders Lose Ground," *CDT*, June 5, 1994, 7:1.

Only grazed by technology, work in the craft economy required somewhat different traits and abilities than did work in the manufacturing economy. Historians generally identify these trades as "skilled," and, indeed, certain occupations did demand more technical knowledge, learned either through a period of apprenticeship or through formal schooling. Bakers, butchers, and barbers began as apprentices. Building construction required men familiar with masonry, carpentry, electricity, plumbing, and many other fields of study.[50]

Skill, however, was hardly the sole distinguishing feature of craft work. Entrepreneurial abilities were critical in a milieu where employees and employers had to hustle to maintain steady trade and employment. The shopkeepers of the craft economy depended upon their relationships with local communities to establish a clientele. These trades also demanded substantial salesmanship from the clerks and teamsters they employed. Milk, bread, and laundry drivers who delivered goods directly to houses were expected to solicit business for their bosses, and they earned commissions on their sales. In an industry favoring short-term labor contracts and subject to boom-and-bust cycles, building tradesmen struggled to find continuous employment.[51]

Raw strength was another talent these jobs demanded. Craft work could be more physically taxing than manufacturing work. Drivers guided horsedrawn wagons through the city, but they also carried goods from their carts. As one teaming contractor reminisced:

> You had to like work to do the job. Five loads ... one hundred ... 135-pound coffee sacks to a load. You carried each sack from a tailboard ... 17 feet to the front of the wagon ... that's 67,000 lbs. on – 67,000 lbs. off – 134,000 lbs. per day with which to wrestle.

In building construction, a class of common laborers did this heavy lifting. In 1920, when the U.S. Census gave such workers their own categories, 18,259 laborers and 2,271 helpers worked in construction, three times the number employed in the famous packinghouses.

[50] Paul H. Douglas, *American Apprenticeship and Industrial Education* (New York: Columbia, 1921), 65, 74. As Bernard Elbaum has noted, apprenticeship continued much longer in unionized trades than other industries. "Why Apprenticeship Persisted in Britain but Not in the United States," *Journal of Economic History* 49:2 (June 1989): 348–49.

[51] Commons, "Types of Labor Organization," 414–20; Sterling Rigg, "The Chicago Teamsters Unions," *Journal of Political Economy* 34 (1926): 21; William Haber, *Industrial Relations in the Building Industry* (Cambridge, MA: Harvard University Press, 1930), 95–126; Richard R. Myers, "Interpersonal Relations in the Building Industry," *Applied Anthropology* 5:2 (Spring 1946): 3–4.

Although "skill" was a hallmark of the craft economy, strength was an equally distinctive feature.[52]

Having evaded the most radical effects of industrialization, the craft economy barely felt the corporate revolution. Corporations, though prominent in manufacturing, were not yet common in the craft economy. Bakers, barbers, teaming contractors, and building contractors operated small companies, partnerships, and proprietorships. For example, in 1902, most of the teaming firms in the city of Chicago were proprietorships. Out of the 284 listings in the *Lakeside Annual Directory*, 241 were for individuals, three for partnerships, and twelve were family firms. Only twenty-eight were large enough to call themselves "companies."[53]

The predominance of proprietorships and family firms reflects the minimal capital requirements of teaming enterprises. The Chicago Teamsters' Strike of 1905 revealed the ease with which one might start a teaming firm. During the dispute, the department stores, wholesale houses, and express companies decided to replace 5,000 striking teamsters. Finding that local teaming firms refused to hire nonunion drivers, the Employers' Association of Chicago raised $1 million in capital stock with which to purchase carts, lease wagons, and buy a few firms outright. Thus, teaming required $200 for every worker, less than one-thirteenth the capital investment per worker of the average Chicago manufacturing firm.[54]

Low entry costs narrowed the gap between employers and employees. For example, despite the emergence of large bread, cookie, and cracker factories, baking remained into the second decade of the century diffused among a large number of small establishments with few workers. In 1904, 852 bakeries served Chicago. Ten years later, 1,305 firms produced bread for the city. Over the same period, the number of workers per establishment actually declined, from 6.80 to 5.89. Among barbers, the distance between masters and journeymen was even smaller. According to the 1900 census, 4,628 men and 475 women in Chicago stated their occupation as "barber." The 1902 city directory listed 2,025 barbers operating shops. In other words,

---

[52] Typescripts, Howard Levansellaer Willett papers, CHS, 2; Department of Commerce, Bureau of the Census, *Fourteenth Census of the United States Taken in the Year 1920*, v. 4, *Population 1920: Occupations* (Washington, DC: Government Printing Office, 1923), 1076–77.

[53] *Lakeside Directory, 1902*, 2651–52.

[54] Luke Grant, "Rights and Wrongs of the Chicago Strike," *Public Opinion* 38:23 (June 10, 1905): 888–89; Commons, Types of American Labor Organization," 403–6; *Census of Manufactures, 1905, Part II*, 232–33.

roughly 40 percent of the city's barbers were proprietors rather than employees.[55]

Some businessman had few or any employees and earned little. Individuals bought coal, ice, and milk wholesale and retailed them to consumers out of homes, trucks, and storefronts rather than working directly for dealers or manufacturers. Such entrepreneurs eked out a living. Thomas Kidd, the president of the Amalgamated Wood Workers Union, admitted that: "Sometimes they don't even make money. I was a small employer once, and after every pay day, I discovered that my men had more than I. So I went back to work."[56]

In these trades, successful employers were seldom highly educated. One labor economist noted that "the rugged, 'self-made' businessman . . . for some reason, seems to be more common in the construction industry than in other lines of business." In 1899, F. B. Robinson, a twenty-three-year-old attorney who worked as the assistant secretary of the Chicago Masons and Builders Association, described the stone contractors who paid his salary as "ordinary common laboring men," not "college-bred men." Though Robinson exaggerated, few contractors had bachelor's degrees, and many had either ended their schooling in the sixth grade, or had attended technical schools such as Bryant & Stratton Business College to learn bookkeeping and basic math.[57]

The employers often came from backgrounds remarkably similar to their employees. They were often immigrants who had entered a trade apprenticeship in their youth. Instead of remaining journeymen, they had become foremen and then contractors. One example

---

[55] The *Census of Manufactures* omits contracting, service, and retail in its estimates of firm size, effectively cutting out the city's smallest employers and exaggerating the scale of business enterprise. *Census of Manufactures, 1914, Part 1* (Washington, DC: Government Printing Office, 1918), 338–40.

[56] The independent cartman has had a long and proud history of defying class boundaries in the urban United States. See Graham Russell Hodges, *The New York City Cartmen, 1667–1850* (New York: New York University Press, 1986). For Kidd's comments, see Hutchins Hapgood, *The Spirit of Labor* (New York: Duffield & Company, 1907), 361.

[57] Royal E. Montgomery, *Industrial Relations in the Chicago Building Trades* (Chicago: University of Chicago Press, 1927), 30. Robinson's comments came in response to a brick manufacturer's lawsuit. The attorney asked if the master masons were "college bred men," and Robinson answered "No, they are not." Testimony before Master of Chancery, July 6, 1899, *Union Pressed Brick v. Chicago Hydraulic Press Brick*, case #196935, Circ.C.C. (1899), 27–8; "An Attempt at Autobiography," v.1, 44–9 in Eugene Prussing Papers, Newberry Library; *Industrial Chicago: The Building Interests*, v.1 (Chicago: Goodspeed Publishing, 1891), 666–67; Edward C. Kirkland, *Dream and Thought in the Business Community, 1860–1900* (Chicago: Ivan R. Dee, 1956), 77.

was Joseph Downey. Downey's father had died in his youth, and his mother took his family from Ireland to Cincinnati to Chicago. A mason named James McGraw hired Downey as an apprentice, eventually making him a partner. As *Industrial Chicago*, a precis on local business published for the World's Fair described contractor Joseph Downey as "a self-made man in the truest and best sense of the phrase, and yet is absolutely devoid of the egotism which is so often apparent in those who have been the architects of their fortunes." As this suggests, the contracting class contained sufficient numbers of former journeymen like Downey both to justify the late nineteenth-century American myth of upward mobility and to rebuke those who had inherited their stations.[58]

Most craft workers either rejected such aspirations or found them impractical. But opportunity was more than a myth in the competitive craft economy. Thousands of small businesses scrambled for trade, many of them earning meager profits. But with opportunity came "cutthroat" competition, which clouded hope for the future. A magazine for teaming contractors noted in 1910:

> The larger teaming contractors when consulted as to the future of the teaming business in Chicago usually say 'Future? There is no future; look at it right now, a man can't figure on a thing; it's cut, cut, cut, the competition is so keen in the teaming business that there is not a cent in it . . .' Says another: 'What's the use of looking to the future? Everything is so expensive all the possible profits go into show bills, doctor bills, harness bills, feed bills, etc. If we have a good contract there are three or four other fellows after it. They will install new equipment, wagons, harness, to be new and painted, lettered to suit and at a price so low that it's folly to try to meet it.'[59]

The pool of able workers, some only a small capital investment away from independence, continually threatened to undercut existing firms. This threat encouraged employers to pay high wages, for well-paid workers were more likely to be satisfied with wage labor and less likely to become contractors.

The material closeness of workers and employers merely established the possibility of comity between the different groups. No vast educational, ethnic, and financial differences separated workers from

---

[58] *Industrial Chicago: The Building Interests*, v.1, 670. For attitudes toward the "self-made man," see Daniel T. Rogers, *The Work Ethic in Industrial America: 1850–1920* (Chicago: University of Chicago Press, 1978), 35–9.

[59] "The Teaming Contractor: A Glimpse into the Future," *Chicago Team Owners' Journal*, Special Edition, May 1910, 1.

proprietors, as they did in heavy manufacturing. In the small shops, yards, and stables of cities like Chicago, occupational mobility enabled workers to become employers. Workers and employers vehemently disagreed over wage and control, but their differences were hardly unresolvable.

The Looming Transformation

Though the proprietor and the skilled worker still dominated the craft economy, immigration, mobility, industrial production, and incorporation become serious concerns with the new century. Competition from below threatened these craft producers, undercutting their prosperity without fundamentally transforming their trade. Every day, men and women came to Chicago from Europe and from the American countryside, many hoping to become craftsmen and shopkeepers. Those who took manufacturing jobs bore children who might eventually enter these crafts. The low cost of entry allowed skilled workers to easily establish their own businesses. Indeed, in trades like construction, a master was little more than a journeyman with a set of tools, and many workers took small side contracts for extra money. Though established craft producers enjoyed the relative fluidity of social relations that allowed their ambitions free rein, such conditions threatened their livelihoods in the long term.[60]

More fearsome were the large corporations, ambitious local entrepreneurs, and out-of-town investors that generated new competition and threatened the fluid, labor-intensive, proprietary conditions in the craft economy. In transportation, construction, retail, and service, firms looked to establish dominance by lowering costs through improved administration, streamlined distribution, and reskilled work. Entire new industries, dominated by a few large firms using new technologies, offered cheaper alternatives to older trades of the craft economy. These industrial, corporate, and national firms threatened price and wage standards, encouraging the development of an organized opposition among craft producers.

Corporations slowly entered through many different doors. In some cases, local firms became national corporations through the processes of growth and merger. In 1885, E. A. Shedd, the city's foremost ice dealer, purchased twelve ice firms to form Knickerbocker Ice, Inc. In 1898, "eastern capitalists" bought the firm and thirty-five other ice

---

[60] Royal Montgomery estimated that more than half of the city's subcontractors were previously journeymen building tradesmen. *Industrial Relations*, 7.

companies, forming a new Knickerbocker Company, which not only monopolized local ice production and distribution, but also moved into selling building materials.[61]

In retail and service trades, the chain store, a group of shops owned and operated by the same corporation, represented the most significant threat. Some massive chains had grown from single storefronts. In the early twentieth century, two remarkably similar tycoons competed for the city's lunch trade. Herman Henry Kohlsaat, an emigrant from western Illinois, began his career in drygoods before turning a single lunch counter into a wholesale bakery and a chain of eateries. Born in eastern Illinois, John R. Thompson also worked in drygoods before moving to Chicago and establishing a chain of eleven restaurants and a commissary. Both men were reform Republicans and owned important Progressive publications, the former publishing a daily newspaper, the *Chicago Record-Herald*, and the latter publishing a muckraking journal, the *World To-Day*.

In other cases, predatory corporations formed chains by purchasing the most prominently located existing shops. In 1901, James Duke of the American Tobacco Company, secretly took over the United Cigar Stores Company, and began acquiring cigar shops in New York, Chicago, and other cities. The "tobacco trust" believed that control over distribution would allow it to maintain its dominance over production. By 1906, there were thousands of "United" shops in America.[62]

In construction, new architectural forms like the skyscraper encouraged the development of a national contracting elite. In 1889, Worcester, Massachusetts native George A. Fuller, completed the Tacoma, one of the Chicago's first skyscrapers. Colonel W. A. Starrett, an admirer and fellow contractor, called him:

> A new type of contractor, pioneering an administrative revolution in construction. Contractors until now usually had been boss carpenters or masons, men of little capital and foremanship, but generally of no technical education, who executed sub-contracts under the supervision of the architects. This was feasible in small enterprises, but as buildings grew in magnitude architects were overwhelmed with a multiplicity of burdens for which many of them had little training and no aptitude. Fuller raised contracting from a limited trade to

---

[61] *The Book of Chicagoans, 1905*, 203, 523; "Ice wagons," *Chicago History* 5:8 (Summer 1959): 245–51.

[62] *The Book of Chicagoans, 1905*, 341; *The Book of Chicagoans, 1905*, 568; Maurice Corina, *Trust in Tobacco* (New York: St. Martins Press, 1975), 67, 121, 128; Reavis Cox, "Competition in the American Tobacco Industry, 1911–1932" (Ph.D. diss., Columbia University, 1933), 325–60.

both an industry and a profession, visualizing the building problem
in its entirety – promotion, finance, engineering, labor and materials.

As demand grew for huge downtown buildings with steel superstructures, the need for contractors like Fuller expanded, and with it the
influence of a corporate elite of "general contractors." Lodged within
the most heavily proprietary part of the urban economy, these builders
were allied as closely with wealthy manufacturers as with other contractors. After Fuller's untimely death, his company became an arm
of John D. Rockefeller's real estate holding corporation, the United
States Realty Company.[63]
Employers like Starrett and Fuller pushed for increased efficiency in
contracting and purchasing, but other general contractors envisioned
improvements in construction itself. Bricklaying, a repetitive craft requiring tremendous precision, continually seduced dreamy eyed engineers who believed they could mechanize or systematize the trade.
In 1905, the magazine *Architecture* lamented:

> The coming of the brick-laying machine has been announced again
> and again, but the machine has never materialized. The last number
> of the "American Contractor" claims that an inventor in Williston,
> North Carolina, has perfected a machine which will do this seemingly
> impossible thing.

This new invention never took off. More influential were the efforts
of scientific managers like Frank B. Gilbreth. Gilbreth devoted an entire book to the subject of systematizing and improving bricklaying.
He also started his own contracting firm that successfully put these
improvements into practice.[64]

[63] W. A. Starrett, *Skyscrapers and the Men Who Build Them* (New York: Scribners, 1928), 32–4; Pierce, *A History of Chicago: Volume 3*, 499–500; *Industrial
Chicago*, v. 1, 690–91; Chad Wallin, *The Builders Story: An Interpretive Record of
the Builders Association of Chicago Inc.* (Chicago: Builders Association, 1966),
4–13; Ray Stannard Baker, "The Trust's New Tool – The Labor Boss," *Mc-
Clure's Magazine* 22 (1903–1904): 39.
[64] *Architecture* 12:2 (August 15, 1905): 119. Gilbreth's innovations served less
to deskill work than to eradicate what he saw as wasteful practices. For
example, he introduced adjustable scaffold that reduced stooping, saving a
bricklayer's spine without challenging craft mysteries. Gilbreth took great
pride in his own abilities as a bricklayer, using them to impress his future
wife during their courtship. The story of the Gilbreth family, captured in
the famous book, *Cheaper by the Dozen*, suggests the connections between
gender, class, and reform during the Progressive Era. Frank B. Gilbreth,
Bricklaying System (Chicago: M. C. Clark, 1909); Frank B. Gilbreth, Jr. and

Building-material manufacturers instigated the most aggressive efforts at the mechanization of construction, shifting production from building sites to factories. In the nineteenth century, skilled carpenters custom-made wood doors and window sashes. Journeymen masons sawed stone in pieces at the building site. After the Civil War, a new group of manufacturers began mass-producing wood-trim, and cut stone using machines tended by semiskilled operatives. Corporate manufacturers thus encroached on the craft economy, moving certain trades from the urban public economy to the private sphere of the factory and rural quarry.[65]

Investors proposed still bolder schemes to circumvent the craft economy. The most audacious was the network of catacombs built under the city's downtown in which ran small underground electric trains for carrying freight. In 1899, the Illinois Telephone and Telegraph Company began digging conduits for a new subterranean telephone network. In January 1904, the Illinois Tunnel Company, a national corporation with $30 million in capital stock, bought the operation intending to use it for local transport. Connecting the rail yard with the basements of the largest Loop concerns, these tunnels promised to replace the public streets, teaming contractors, and teamsters of the craft economy with a private, corporate, and "modern" form of transport.[66]

Massive corporations threatened to completely eradicate the fluid, labor-intensive, proprietary character of the craft economy. Chicago's heating industry provides the most drastic example. At the turn of the century, gas lit the city's streets and homes, but coal warmed its residences and businesses. Looking for new markets, People's Gas Light and Coke, commonly called "the gas trust," began convincing businesses to use gas for heat as well as light. These efforts established a rivalry, more between craftsmen and corporations than between coal and gas. Coal epitomized the craft economy. Sold by small neighborhood dealers, delivered by teamsters, burned in cast-iron stoves by residents, and shoveled into steam furnaces by stationary firemen and

Ernestine Gilbreth Carey, *Cheaper by the Dozen* (New York: Bantam, 1972), 24–6, 58; Taylor, *Scientific Management*, 77–85.
[65] Christie, *Empire in Wood*, 19–28; George E. Barnett, "The Stonecutters' Union and the Stone-Planer." *Journal of Political Economy* 25:5 (May 1916): 417–20.
[66] George W. Jackson, "Freight Tunnels in Chicago," *Independent* 57:3 (1904): 1018–22; William Hard, "Building the Chicago Subway," *Public Opinion* 38:20 (May 20, 1905): 769; Bishop, *Chicago's Accomplishments*, 482–88. These tunnels flooded in 1992 when a pylon broke through to the Chicago River. "Maze Down Under Opened in '04," *Chicago Sun-Times*, April 14, 1992, 18.

engineers, its distribution required thousands of tradesmen. Although the "gas trust" burned coal to produce methane, its distribution was deeply "modern": corporate, centralized, and mechanized.[67]

This transformation startled craft producers. Reflecting upon his highly successful career in the teaming business, Howard Levansellaer Willett noted the market's deadly power:

> Here in America, just one weapon . . . cut-throat competition. Respectable old businesses who clung to old ways . . . old methods . . . quietly passed away. Hundreds of thousands of them . . . millions of workers displaced. Most found new skills and a few 45 year old men threw in the sponge . . . refused to work. They puttered around the house . . . one suspender unbuttoned . . . "Everybody works at our house but my old man." Dead is dead! Firing squad or competition . . . But competition is an American word. It is a friendly everyday, "on our side" word, so we shrug it off, forget its deadly implications.[68]

Yet Willett's memory exaggerated the speed with which competition transformed his line of business. New firms armed with new technologies reshaped the teaming trade only slowly, in large part because craft producers organized against economic transformation.

Craft Governance and its Administrators

In response to this looming transformation, craft producers began to assert governmental authority over their trades. Beginning in 1890, a wide array of local labor unions and business associations inundated the city. Today, commentators blame the decline of organized labor on the rise of the "service economy," as if no precedent existed for unions in this sector. Yet service and retail workers aggressively organized at the beginning of the century. Until manufacturing workers unionized during the Great Depression, craft workers formed the backbone of the Chicago Federation of Labor. As late as 1929, the great majority of the city's 293,546 unionists worked in the building trades (98,369),

---

[67] For a discussion of technology and corporate consolidation in the gas trade, see Harold L. Platt, *The Electric City: Energy and the Growth of the Chicago Area, 1880–1930* (Chicago: University of Chicago Press, 1991), 42–52. In 1900, People's Gas produced methane by burning coal in a factory in a North-Side neighborhood then known as "Little Hell," now known as Cabrini Green. It was not until the 1920s that improvements in metallurgy allowed the piping of large amounts of natural gas from fields in the southwest U.S. to Chicago. "Old King Coal," *CDT*, May 18, 1994, Section C, 1–2.

[68] "SHARKEY," typescript in Howard Levansellaer Willett Papers, Chicago Historical Society, 3.

teaming (43,517), service (20,965), retail and wholesale trade (13,193), the public sector (21,424), and amusements (13,667). The craft economy was also home to most of the city's local trade associations. Proprietors created groups like the Chicago Masons and Builders, the Coal Team Owners, and the Chicago Master Bakers not only to negotiate with the unions, but also to regulate competition.[69]

For these groups, the ideal was not an integrated national corporation, but a well-governed agreement. For example, in 1910, the *Chicago Team Owners Journal* nonchalantly noted the arrangement in one area of the carting industry:

> Dwelling in our midst is a happy family of team owners. They rise early, work hard and are contented with their lot. They are known as the Chicago Commission Team Owners' Association . . . When they advocate a change in the prices of cartage they elect a committee. The South Water Street Commission Merchants' Association also appoint a like body. The two committees get together and adjust cartage rates to the satisfaction of all concerned and then peace and good will prevail. The two associations are governed by these rates and everybody is satisfied. We might state that their last agreement has been in force six years.

This preference for associations over private mergers or management perhaps reflected the guild history of these trades, a history acknowledged in the names of associations such as the "Master Plumbers Association" and "Journeymen Horseshoers Union."[70]

With these values in mind, producers began controlling the market through a patchwork of associational rules, agreements, ordinances, and alliances. Each union and association passed bylaws, which determined, for example, standard prices, locations, and legitimate workers,

---

[69] For the belief that a growing service economy accounts for the decline of unionization, see Richard Rorty, "The People's Flag in Deepest Red," in Steven Fraser and Joshua Freeman, eds., *Audacious Democracy: Labor, Intellectuals, and the Social Reconstruction of America* (New York: Houghton Mifflin, 1997), 62. Carroll Lawrence Christensen, *Collective Bargaining in Chicago: 1929–30: A Study of the Economic Significance of the Industrial Location of Trade-Unionism* (Chicago: University of Chicago Press, 1933), 8, 11, 13, 15, 17, 27; *Lakeside Directory*, 1904, 59–65.

[70] "The Happy Family," *Chicago Team Owners' Journal*, Special Edition, May 1910, 2; *Lakeside Directory*, 1906, 68, 76; Elbaum, "Why Apprenticeship Persisted," 345–49. For guilds in modern Europe, see William H. Sewell, Jr., *Work and Revolution in France: The Language of Labor from the Old Regime to 1848* (New York: Cambridge University Press, 1980); Antony Black, *Guilds and Civil Society in European Political Thought from the Twelfth Century to the Present* (Ithaca, NY: Cornell University Press, 1984).

products, and businesses. Collective bargaining was common in the craft economy, as different groups signed agreements setting wages and hours, restricting the use of machines, and limiting the entry of new firms and workers.

Rather than relying on the courts, each organization administered its own rules and agreements, hiring an ambitious new class of professional administrators rooted in labor, business, and politics. A diverse set of labor leaders exercised immense power over Chicago's craft economy. Many were upright, progressive, and militant. In 1905, the *Chicago Tribune* described Steve Sumner, an officer of the Milk Drivers Union from 1902 into the 1930s, as "a man of exemplary habits," a "zealot" who was also "a jovial sensible man" who "neither drinks nor smokes, and he never loses a chance to preach total abstinence." In 1906, Sumner declined to run for public office on a reform slate for fear that he might appear self-interested to his constituents. Nevertheless, Sumner's local was known for its rough rule. Though Sumner claimed his methods were peaceful, newspapers, grand juries, and businessmen repeatedly questioned his forceful control over the milk delivery trade.[71]

Some officers were effective organizers but questionable administrators. In 1894, William T. Stead, the famous British journalist, ranked William C. Pomeroy, an officer for the Waiters Union, the Chicago Trades and Labor Assembly, and the Illinois State Federation of Labor (ISFL), as one of the nation's four most important labor leaders. Pomeroy orated against "Mammon," and authored a utopian novel, titled the *Lords of Misrule*. In it, Pomeroy predicted the transition from capitalism to militaristic socialism to Christian democracy. Pomeroy's profligacy eventually overshadowed his abilities as a promoter. One unionist commented that Pomeroy "used to get $10 and go straight to the saloon and spend it all." The money he spent came from real estate ventures, advertising, bribes, and the waiters' union treasury. According to another peer, Pomeroy preferred to "make five dollars the crooked way than ten dollars honestly, because the one involved

---

[71] "Indict Leaders of the Strikers," *CDT*, April 30, 1905, 2. In 1907, a union member described Sumner as "a lily white reformer, on the water wagon and very religious." Hapgood, *The Spirit of Labor*, 314; "Labor's New Party Names Full Ticket," *CRH*, April 30, 1906, 6; "Probe Labor Assault," *CRH*, August 18, 1908, 3; John Landesco, *Organized Crime in Chicago*, Part III of the Illinois Crime Survey, 1929 (Chicago: University of Chicago Press, 1968), 140–41; True Bill, August 29, 1921, case #25695, Criminal Court of Cook County (henceforth "Crim.C.C."), IR 274, 41–3; U.S. Senate, Subcommittee of the Committee of Commerce, *Investigation of So-Called "Rackets,"* 1:3 (Washington, DC: Government Printing Office, 1934), 370–72.

scheming and the other didn't so much." In 1896, reformers challenged his leadership; by 1900, he was persona non grata in the labor
movement.[72]

Turn-of-the-century business associations also relied upon a new
class of secretaries, agents, and business managers to negotiate and
enforce their rules. The first professional associationalists were cler-
ical workers with strong backgrounds in the craft economy. Edward
Marshall Craig, the long-time secretary of the Building Construction
Employers' Association (BCEA), began as an office boy employed by an
attorney in Philadelphia. When he reached his majority, he learned the
trade of steamfitter, but he quickly returned to the white-collar world,
working as a boiler salesman, and later as a Republican Pennsylvania state legislator. After moving to Chicago, he started a steam-fitting
firm, but he almost immediately began a second career running local
and national associations. In 1897, he was elected general manager of
the Master Steam-fitters Association. By 1905, he had accepted positions in several associations including secretary of the Western League
of Steam-fitters, the Building Contractors Council (later called the
BCEA), and the National Building Trades Employers' Association.[73]

As with the unions, some of the most aggressive organizers
were suspect administrators. John C. Driscoll was the most potent
associationalist of the era. Like E. M. Craig, Driscoll came from a cleri-
cal background. Brought to Chicago as an infant in 1860, he received
a bachelor's degree from St. Ignatius College and became a clerk earning less than $700 a year. In 1902, Driscoll became the secretary of the
Coal Team Owners Association of Chicago. Success there led Driscoll

---

[72] The others were Samuel Gompers, Eugene Debs, and the Sovereign of
the Knights of Labor. William T. Stead, *Chicago To-Day, of the Labor War in
America* (London: Review of Reviews, 1894), 127–38. Pomeroy led Stead
on a tour of Chicago and may have gulled the reverend into inflating his
importance. William T. Stead, *If Christ Came to Chicago* (New York: Living
Books, 1964), 390–93; Staley, 92; William C. Pomeroy, *The Lords of Misrule:
A Tale of Gods and Men* (Chicago: Laird & Lee, 1894); "Chicago's Welcome to
Labor," *Lowell Daily Sun*, January 6, 1894, 2; "W. C. Pomeroy's Speech," *Fort
Wayne Gazette*, September 6, 1898, 1, 3. For Pomeroy's expulsion, see Staley,
History of the Illinois State Federation of Labor (Chicago: University of Chicago,
1930) 90, 89, 87–93, 136–39; Matthew Josephson, *Union House, Union Bar:
A History of the Hotel and Restaurant Workers International Union* (New York:
Random House, 1956), 19–30; Samuel Gompers, *Seventy Years of Life and Labor*
(New York: Dutton, 1923), 375–77; Jay Rubin and M. J. Obermeier, *Growth
of a Union: The Life and Times of Edward Flore* (New York: The Historical Union
Association, Inc., 1943), 50–1.

[73] *The Book of Chicagoans, 1905*, 142; "Autobiography of E. M. Craig," 72 in
Folder 7, Gerhard Meyne Papers, CHS.

to organize the rest of the industry, forming both narrow groups like the Truck Team Owners Association and broad umbrella groups, such as the Associated Teaming Interests and the Chicago Board of Arbitration. By 1903, Driscoll was earning $8,000 a year. By 1905, however, revelations of bribery and extortion forced him out of power.[74]

Given the fluid social structure of the craft economy, it is unsurprising that members of this leadership class were ambitious and mobile. Officers of local labor unions often became businessmen, professionals, and white-collar workers after leaving union office. In 1904, exhausted by his duties as the first business agent of the Flat Janitors Union, William Feather resigned, eventually becoming an attorney. Others remained in the same trades. In 1903, Clinton D. Hyre was the president of Local #73 of the Amalgamated Sheet Metal Workers International Association. By 1917, Hyre was a hardware dealer. As a young man, during the teamsters' strike of 1905, James B. Barry led the railway express drivers against the powerful express delivery companies. By 1917, Barry was the secretary of the Chicago Contracting Team Owners Association. Charles Dold was president of the new Piano and Organ Workers Union. After leaving the unions in the 1920s, he managed a piano store.[75]

Such life courses were most common among building trades unionists. William Schardt and John Brittain both left offices with the United Brotherhood of Carpenters to become contractors. In 1917, Schardt returned to the union as president.[76] William D. O'Brien ran the local bricklayers union in the 1870s, but he abandoned his fellow

---

[74] "John C. Driscoll, Central Figure Just Now in Labor "Graft" Rumors," *CRH*, June 14, 1905; Myers, "Policing of Labor Disputes," 373; Ernest Poole, "How a Labor Machine Held Up Chicago and How the Teamsters Smashed the Machine," *The World To-Day* (July 1904) 7:1. After 1905, the name "Driscoll" became synonymous with "manipulator." "End of an Industrial Brigand," *The Survey* 22 (June 12, 1909): 401–2.

[75] "William Feather, The First Business Agent of a Chicago Union Who Ever Resigned," *CRH*, January 30, 1904, 3; *Lakeside Directory, 1902*, 669; *Lakeside Directory, 1910*, 429; Bill of Complaint, April 25, 1903, *Holland Construction v. Amalgamated Sheet Metal Workers*, case #229657, Sup.C.C. (1903), 1; *Lakeside Directory, 1917*, 847, 157; "Indict Leaders of the Strikers," *CDT*, May 30, 1905, 2; *Lakeside Directory, 1917*, 157; *Platt v. Barry*, case #244201, Sup.C.C. (1905); "Charles Dold Elected As President of the Chicago Federation of Labor," *CRH*, January 16, 1905, 7; Eugene Staley, *History of the Illinois State Federation of Labor*, 186.

[76] Minutes, October 4, 1912, in *Minute Book of the Chicago Building Trades Council, 1912–1914*, Chicago Historical Society, 50; *Lakeside Directory, 1904*, 66; *Lakeside Directory, 1912*, 1235; *Lakeside Directory, 1917*, 1580; Christie, *Empire in Wood* 153; *Lakeside Directory, 1906*, 75; *Lakeside Directory, 1917*, 261.

journeymen to become a powerful mason contractor and building material manufacturer, as well as the president of both the Building Contractors Council and the National Building Trades Employers' Association. In this new role, "Billy O'Brien" was unpopular among union men. In 1900, the current president of the union, George P. Gubbins, called him, "a man who stands around with a fat roll of money in his pocket, and he calls men everything under the sun. It is fortunate for O'Brien that I never worked for him, or else there would be a case for the coroner." By 1912, however, Gubbins himself no longer held union office; he had also become a mason contractor.[77]

Of course, many union officers like Steve Sumner stayed in office for decades, remaining stalwart representatives of organized labor. Others returned to the rank and file after losing authority. Daniel J. Evans, the president of the Painters District Council in 1906, was an obscure union painter again by 1910. Yet the possibility and acceptability of such social mobility is telling, for it helps explain the collegial relations between organized craft employers and craft workers.[78]

For Chicago's labor leaders and businessmen, politics was another arena for mobility, association, and compromise. The craft economy and local politics overlapped substantially. Chicago's municipal governments inspected buildings, restaurants, and stores. Inspectors had discretion to enforce or ignore ordinances specifying the quality of brick, asphalt, coal, and lumber purchased by these governments. In the first decades of the century, licensing boards regulated the activities of engineers, plumbers, common carriers, barbers, mason contractors, moving picture operators, liquor dealers, and motor vehicle operators. For their success, building tradesmen, as well as dealers in materials, coal, and feed relied upon the purchasing power of the city, the county, the parks, the Board of Education, the Sanitary District, and the federal government.[79]

[77] IC, *Reports*, v.8, 479; *Industrial Chicago: The Building Interests*, v.1, 579, 673, 786; *Lakeside Directory, 1906*, 63; IC, *Reports*, v.8, 233; *Lakeside Directory, 1912*, 564.

[78] *Lakeside Directory, 1906*, 64–6; *Lakeside Directory, 1910*, 420; U.S. Senate, *Hearings before a Subcommittee of the Committee on Commerce United States Senate Investigation of So-Called "Rackets."* (hereafter *Racket Hearings*), v. 1, Parts 1–6 (Washington, DC: U.S. Government Printing Office, 1934), 416–19.

[79] *Lakeside Directory, 1917*, 5; J. C. Grant, "The Gild Returns to America, I," *Journal of Politics* 4 (1942): 313–14; William F. Brown & Ralph Cassidy, "Guild Pricing in the Service Trades," *Quarterly Journal of Economics* 61 (February 1947): 313; Richard Oestreicher, "Urban Working-Class Political Behavior and Theories of American Electoral Politics, 1870–1940," *Journal of*

With so much at stake, local government was dominated by, in the words of one writer, "business men, with politics for a specialty." The author referred not to merchants like Marshall Field, but to men like U.S. Senator William Lorimer, who owned a brick yard, or lesser lights like sheriff James Pease, who operated a painting concern, and appellate court clerk Thomas N. "Doc" Jamieson, who ran a drugstore. The connection between the construction industry and local politics was so enduring that it calls into question the very distinction between economy and polity. Among the thirty-five victors in the 1905 aldermanic elections were a city cement tester, a master plumber, a paint dealer, a general contractor, and a mason contractor. The city's leading producers of brick and stone, including Martin Barnaby Madden (no relation to union officer Martin B. "Skinny" Madden), Martin Emerich, Spencer Kimbell, Dillwyn Purington, William Schlake, Bernard Weber, and Thomas Carey, all held major public offices. Seeing parties and business as intersecting paths to success, these men took a proprietary interest in an ordered economy.[80]

Labor organizations and their officers were also deeply vested in local politics. Chicago's craft unions seldom affiliated publicly with either the Republican or the Democratic Party, but specific leaders developed close ties to specific parties and factions. George Gubbins, the president of the Bricklayers Union, called himself a "red hot Democrat."

American History 74:4 (March, 1988), 1273; Udo Sautter, "Government and Unemployment: The Use of Public Works before the New Deal," *Journal of American History* 73: 1 (June, 1986), 59–86.

[80] Hoyt King, *Citizen Cole of Chicago* (Chicago: Holders, 1931), 60; Samuel Hays, "The Politics of Reform in Municipal Government in the Progressive Era," *Pacific Northwest Quarterly* 55 (1964): 161–63; Irving Dillard, "William Lorimer," *Dictionary of American Biography*, v. 11 (New York: Scribners & Sons, 1931), 511–12; Joel Tarr "The Chicago Anti-Department Store Crusade of 1897: A Case Study in Urban Commercial Development," *Journal of the Illinois State Historical Society* 64 (Summer 1971): 166; Idem, *A Study in Boss Politics: William Lorimer of Chicago* (Urbana: University of Illinois Press, 1971); Idem, "The Urban Politician as Entrepreneur," *Mid-America* 49:1 (January 1967): 55–67. Between 1894 and 1915, Chicago's public-works budget rose from $2.25 to $15 million, prompting these men to seek public office. William A. Koelsch, "Modernizing Urban Government," Bessie Louise Pierce Papers, Box 23, Folder 2, University of Chicago Special Collections; "Tips on Aldermen by Voters' League," *CRH*, April 1, 1905, 3; "Council Chosen is Republican," *CDT*, April 5, 1905, 4; *Dictionary of American Biography*, v. 12 (New York: Scribner's, 1933), 180–81; Obituary, "Martin Emerich," *CDT*, September 28, 1922, 19; *Notable Men of Chicago and Their City* (Chicago: Chicago Daily Journal, 1910), 346; Harrison, *Growing Up With Chicago*, 233–34; *The Book of Chicagoans, 1905*, 189, 332, 388, 472, 599.

He was not alone. AFL organizer William C. Pomeroy supported Democratic Mayor Carter Harrison II. After Pomeroy's power declined, building trades leader Martin "Skinny" Madden helped elect Harrison, maintaining the alliance between Bricklayers' Hall and City Hall. In exchange for his support, Harrison gave "Skinny" a position as vehicle inspector with the rank and salary of a police sergeant. An 1899 investigation showed that between thirteen and twenty-two union officials held public offices such as brick inspector, examiner of engineers, and others.[81]

Reformers within the CFL believed that political ties corrupted local labor activism, and they condemned those officials linked to the parties. In 1904, Jane Addams reported that "certain 'old time' tradesunionists" charged that civil service reform had pushed "a number of adroit politicians" out of public jobs. "Finding 'nothing doing' in politics," she observed, these men "turned their attention to 'grafting' among trades-unions." But even scrupulous officials worked for the city. George Schilling of the Coopers' Union and John J. Sonsteby of the Garment Workers served as honest but stalwart Democratic bureaucrats. Likewise, the United Brotherhood of Carpenters chided officers holding government jobs, but Carpenters District Council president James Kirby ran for alderman, and his predecessor, Timothy Cruise, held a number of political posts including secretary of the West Park Board.[82]

These men were ethnic working class leaders with roots in neighborhood organizations, in politics, and in labor unions. In 1904, John Kikulski became a business agent for Local #44 of the Amalgamated Wood Workers' International Union. During his career, he was a real estate dealer, an active member of the Polish National Alliance, the president of the Polish Falcons, and the publisher of a newspaper, *Labor's Voice*. A decade later, the Amalgamated Meat Cutters and

---

[81] Ernest Bogart, "Chicago Building Trades Dispute. II," *Political Science Quarterly* 16:2, 227–28; IC, *Reports*, v. 8, 6, 395, 244; Luke Grant, "Rise and Fall of Skinny," *CRH*, May 30, 1909, 3; Staley, *History*, 185.

[82] Jane Addams, "The Present Crisis in Trades-Union Morals," *North American Review* 179 (August 1904): 188; "Labor's New Party Names Full Ticket," *CRH*, May 30, 1906, 6; Staley, *History*, 97, 216, 291; *Book of Chicagoans, 1905*, 509; *Who Was Who in America, v. 1, 1897–1942* (Chicago: A. N. Marquis, 1942), 1156–57; *Lakeside Directory, 1902*, 513, 1907; *Lakeside Directory, 1910*, 1244; *Lakeside Directory, 1917*, 21; Christie, *Empire in Wood*, 153; "Tips on Council Needs," *CRH*, April 2, 1904, 4; "Honest Council Given Big Vote; League Victory," *CRH*, April 6, 1904, 4; Bogart, "Chicago Building Trades Dispute. II.," 229; Carter H. Harrison, *Growing Up With Chicago* (Chicago: Bobbs Merrill, 1944), 368.

Butcher Workmen hired Kikulski to organize Polish and Lithuanian workers.[83]

The same families produced prominent politicians, union officers, and businessmen. Over the course of his career, William H. "Red" Curran worked as a bailiff, a deputy sheriff, a brewery agent, a Republican aldermanic candidate, a plumbing contractor, an officer of the plumber's union, the president of the Building Trades Council, and as Illinois state factory inspector. Curran's "long tailed tribe" included Thomas Curran, a Republican state representative and former saloon-keeper, as well as a county employee, a city bridgetender, a municipal court judge, a bailiff, and the superintendent of the Bridewell jail. Jimmy Carroll, brother of Plasterers' Union president Edward Carroll, was a saloonkeeper and alderman in Evanston. Siblings Anthony and Joseph D'Andrea controlled unions of hod carriers, tunnel, sewer, and water pipe laborers, and macaroni manufacturers. At different times, Anthony was a priest, linguist, pimp, alderman, and committeeman in Chicago's nineteenth ward.[84]

Consider Simon O'Donnell, Jr., the president of the Chicago Building Trades Council during the second decade of the century. In 1879, his father, Simon, Sr. served as chief of the highly partisan Chicago police department. Though demoted in 1881 for opposing the use of police in labor disputes, O'Donnell, Sr. used a whip and pistol to break an 1886 strike against the McCormick Reaper Works, an event leading directly to the famous Haymarket explosion. He eventually retired to start a plumbing business. In his youth, Simon, Jr. dealt coal, worked in the pipe trades, and eventually joined the police department. But he soon took a position as a business agent for the Journeymen Plumbers' Union, spending some brief time on both payrolls. In 1904 and 1905, O'Donnell ran as an independent candidate for nineteenth ward alderman, returning to the Democratic fold after his defeats. Meanwhile, his brothers Edward D. and Joseph worked over the years for the city clerk's office, the police force, the sheriff's department, and a plumbing supply business.[85]

---

[83] Barrett, *Work and Community*, 196; *Lakeside Directory, 1904*, 66; *Lakeside Directory, 1910*, 716; "Kikulski, Labor Leader Shot by Sluggers, Dies," *CDT*, May 22, 1920, 3.

[84] "Tips On Aldermen by Voters' League," *CRH*, April 1, 1905, 3; *Lakeside Directory, 1902*, 519; *Lakeside Directory, 1910*, 335; *Lakeside Directory, 1917*, 420; Montgomery, *Industrial Relations*, 286–87; "Thomas Curran Dies in Auto Crash," *CDT*, November 13, 1928, 1; Harrison, *Growing Up*, 225; "Bullies Aid his Plans," *Chicago Times-Herald*, August 19, 1900, 3; Landesco, 121–24.

[85] William Z. Foster, *Misleaders of Labor* (n.c.: Trade Union Educational League, 1927), 165–71; *Lakeside Directory, 1893*, 1236; *Lakeside Directory, 1894*, 1271;

These men negotiated their own world, slightly apart from the corporate economy and the business elite. This separation was evident on March 22, 1911, when a man walked into the saloon of the Briggs House, a hotel on Randolph Street that served as a headquarters for Mayor Carter Harrison's campaign and for various building-trades unions. The man pulled out a thirty-eight-caliber pistol, and shot Vincent Altman, a business agent for the International Association of Steam-fitters. As nearly sixty people scrambled for cover, Mossie Enright, a walking delegate for the rival United Association of Plumbers, fled the scene. John J. Brittain, a former officer of the carpenters' union, blocked his exit. Enright cried to his friend, "For Christ's sake, John, let me go!" Brittain released him, and Enright hustled away. Meanwhile, another union official, William "Dutch" Gentleman, dashed up the stairs, hands in his overcoat pockets, past the mayor. Witnesses to the crime included the vice-president of an electrical workers' local, an auto salesman, a steam-heat contractor, a cigar salesman, a master plumber, a doctor, a stenographer, an electrician, and a gambler.[86]

Lakeside Directory, 1895, 1311; *Lakeside Directory, 1896,* 1469; *Lakeside Directory, 1902,* 1531; *Lakeside Directory, 1910,* 995–96; *Lakeside Directory, 1917,* 1345; "'Jack' Shea, Great Thief Catcher; Twenty-Seven Years a Policeman," *CTH,* July 30, 1900, 9; *Report of the General Superintendent of Police of the City of Chicago* (Chicago: Department of Police, 1909), 10; Richard C. Lindberg, *To Serve and Collect: Chicago Politics and Police Corruption from the Lager Beer Riot to the Summerdale Scandal, 1855–1960* (Carbondale: Southern Illinois University Press, 1998), 61–5; "City Clerks Are Out," *CRH,* June 9, 1906, 5; "Tips on Council Needs," *CRH,* April 2, 1904, 4; "Honest Council Given Big Vote; League Victory," *CRH,* April 6, 1904, 4; Allen F. Davis, *Spearheads For Reform: The Social Settlements and the Progressive Movement* (New York: Oxford University Press, 1967), 151–62; Humbert Nelli, "John Powers and the Italians in a Chicago Ward, 1896–1921," *Journal of American History* 57:1 (June 1970): 67–84, esp. 74–5; "Tips on Aldermen by Voters League," *CRH,* April 1, 1905, 3; "Council Chosen is Republican," *CDT,* April 5, 1905, 4.

86 The gambler was also an epileptic, an alcoholic, and a pedophile, facts used to impugn his testimony. *People v. Enright,* 256 Ill. 221 (1912); "Enright's Trial Near; 'Men Higher Up' Safe," *CRH,* July 22, 1911, 3; "Special Grand Jury for Labor Sluggers," *CRH,* August 6, 1911, 1; "Life Sentence Given Enright; New Charge Up," *CRH,* October 29, 1911, 1; Nathaniel R. Whitney, *Jurisdiction in American Building-Trades Unions* (Baltimore: Johns Hopkins University Press, 1914), 135. Harrison suspected that the man on the staircase, William "Dutch" Gentleman, was the killer, but a jury convicted Enright. Governor Dunne pardoned Mossie in 1913. Harrison, *Growing Up with Chicago,* 174–76; Foster, *Misleaders,* 172–73.

Altman died in a room without corporate executives, bankers, or merchants. None of the elite businessmen who supported the Harrison campaign, such as Potter Palmer, Jr., were in the Briggs House that night. Of all those who admitted witnessing the murder, only one was a professional, and none worked in any capacity in the manufacturing sector. This was more than coincidence; it was a direct reflection of the broad space between Chicago's craft and corporate economies. Contractors, for example, were employers, but their status was as far from the city's business elite as that of their employees. Events like the assassination of Vincent Altman hardly made contact between the educated bourgeoisie and craft producers more likely. The social mixing, the dealmaking, and the violence found in the Briggs House stigmatized the craft economy in the minds of many bourgeois Chicagoans.

While the city's corporate elite relaxed in their well-appointed clubs, the denizens of the craft economy mingled along the brass rails of political clubs, saloons, hotels, and brothels. These haunts served as official and unofficial hubs of political, commercial, and even criminal activity in which people from different occupations negotiated differences of power, income, and status. Other such venues included The Kentucky Home, a saloon and brothel at 2317 Indiana Avenue favored by various union officials. Ten years later, the Chicago Board of Business Agents made Johnson's Saloon the nerve center of their efforts at organizing all construction workers in the Loop district. In these spaces, a new leadership class governed the craft economy.[87]

---

[87] "Labor Shooting is Traced to the 'Kentucky Home,'" *CDT*, August 25, 1905, 5; Witwer, "Corruption and Reform," 92; *People v. Curran*, 286 Ill. 302 (1919); "54 Indicted as Labor Graft Ring Leaders," *CDT*, December 4, 1915, 1–2. For a similar community, see Eliot Gorn, "'Good Bye Boys, I Die a True American': Homicide, Nativism, and Working-Class Culture in Antebellum New York City," *Journal of American History* 74:2 (September 1987): 388–410.

Turn-of-the-century workers used an array of charters, buttons, labels, directories, and banners to mark men, goods, shops, and unions as legitimate. These items were often the sole physical manifestation of associations that lacked any legal or material existence independent of the members themselves. For this reason, as this 1902 image shows, these items inspired immense pride and, in times of instability, possessiveness. Courtesy of Chicago Historical Society (DN-000082).

2

Ruling the Urban Economy

On May 27, 1903, more than one hundred master and journeymen barbers picketed outside John Kluck's Chicago shop after he refused to close at eight o'clock p.m. The police arrived at the corner of Madison and Wells Streets and arrested two sheet-metal workers for "trying to incite the crowd to violence." The crowd dispersed but re-formed around five other renegade businesses. Stephen McCauley, the vice-president of the barbers' union, told the newspapers, "Kluck is the man we are after. All the others have told us they would close if he shuts his doors." To this, Kluck defiantly responded, "I will never close my shop so long as I can get a barber to stand by me."[1]

The rally against Kluck was a distinctive form of protest, specific if not unique to Chicago's craft economy. In the past, historians have taken similar anecdotes as evidence of the conflict between capital and labor. In fact, the episode suggests a more subtle set of social relationships. The barbers picketed not to convince an employer class to accept the ten-hour day, but to force independent masters and journeymen to accept standard operating times. Rather than joining Kluck's struggle against the union, the master barbers aided their journeymen in pressuring him to close at eight o'clock.

The barbers' protest was an example of craft governance. During the early twentieth century, Chicago's craft workers and proprietors established a wide range of unions, associations, and agreements to regulate prices, wages, and production. In construction, teaming, retail, and service, producers enforced self-styled laws through fines,

---

[1] The same day, 500 north-side grocery clerks paraded down North Avenue, seeking to encourage shopkeepers to close at six o'clock on Wednesdays and Fridays. All but one complied with the request. "Disorder Marks Barbers Fight for Early Closing," *CDT*, May 28, 1903, 3. On May 29, Kluck called the police again. "Barbers Dispersed by Police," *CDT*, May 29, 1903, 3.

strikes, boycotts, pools, deals, and violence, if necessary. These practices allowed producers to control competition, to resist corporations
seeking to enter local markets, and to limit modern industrial modes
of production and distribution. These craft orders, although privately
controlled, asserted public power, claiming to be legitimate, authori-
tative, and exclusive governments.

This resistance rebuts those historians who portray American craft
workers and proprietors as compliant in the face of economic transformation. Many labor historians see the local branches of the American
Federation of Labor (AFL) as narrow organizations emphasizing the
improvement of basic material conditions such as wages and hours
for skilled tradesmen rather than any broad revolutionary program
for social change, government regulation of the wage bargain, or an
independent labor party.[2] Other scholars describe craft proprietors
as ardent individualists, hostile to unions, and susceptible to fascism.
The term *petit bourgeois* contains all of these ideas, and additionally
implies a certain narrow gaze, blind to any public interest beyond the
accumulated private desires of individuals.[3]

[2] John Commons et al., *History of Labour in the United States*, v. 3–4 (New York:
Macmillan, 1935); Ruth L. Horowitz, *Political Ideologies of Organized Labor:
The New Deal Era* (New Brunswick, NJ: Transaction Books, 1978). Recent
authors endorse the idea of "business unionism" while being sensitive to the
political context for the turn away from republicanism. William Forbath,
Law and the Shaping of the American Labor Movement (Cambridge, MA: Harvard
University Press, 1991); Victoria C. Hattam, *Labor Visions and State Power:
The Origins of Business Unionism* (Princeton: Princeton, 1993); Julie Greene,
*Pure and Simple Politics: The American Federation of Labor and Political Activism,
1881–1917* (New York: Cambridge University Press, 1998). Other authors
have either reclaimed the AFL's most radical elements, or rehabilitated
specific craft unions. Dana Frank, *Purchasing Power: Consumer Organizing,
Gender, and the Seattle Labor Movement, 1919–1929* (New York: Cambridge
University Press, 1994), 167, 200–4, 224–27; Dorothy Sue Cobble, *Dishing
it Out: Waitresses and the Unions in the Twentieth Century* (Urbana: University
of Illinois Press, 1991), 7; Michael Kazin, *Barons of Labor: The San Francisco
Building Trades and Union Power in the Progressive Era* (Chicago: University of
Illinois Press, 1989); Georg Leidenberger, "'The Public is the Labor Union':
Working-Class Progressivism in Turn-of-the-Century Chicago," *Labor History*
36:2 (Spring 1995): 187–210.
[3] Scholars generally favor corporate executives over other members of the
commercial classes, perhaps because of their education and philanthropic
endeavors. *Anti-intellectualism in American Life*, 233–34, 260; Alfred Chandler, *The Visible Hand: The Managerial Revolution in American Business* (Cambridge, MA: Harvard University Press, 1977); Robert Wiebe, *Businessmen
and Reform: A Study of the Progressive Movement* (Chicago: Ivan R. Dee, 1962);
Edward Kirkland, *Dream and Thought in the Business Community, 1860–1900*

Such portrayals do not account for the overwhelming surge in organization among craft workers and small businessmen between 1890 and 1910. A multi-million-dollar construction project, the World's Fair of 1893, allowed building trades workers to form stable local unions with property and national affiliations. By 1897, for example, the United Brotherhood of Carpenters needed nineteen local branches to serve their members.[4] The turn of the century saw broad efforts at organizing other workers into craft unions. Between May 1, 1902 and May 1, 1903, the number of "recognized" unions in the city jumped from 327 to 550. Meanwhile, the membership of local unions doubled, growing from 120,000 to twice that figure. Perhaps the most significant new unions were those affiliated with the Teamsters' Joint Council, which rose from nonexistence to the dizzy heights of power in a matter of years. In 1900, the teamsters were disorganized, but by 1902 they had formed nineteen locals. By 1904, the city was home to forty-eight local teamsters unions.[5]

In this same period, local business associations inundated the craft economy. In 1897, the *Lakeside Directory* of Chicago listed thirty-eight trade associations, twenty-seven of them local in orientation, including associations of bottle dealers, carpenters, cooks, drapers, jewelers, liquor dealers, masons, plumbers, tailors, retail druggists, theatrical mechanics, and undertakers. By 1902, thirty new associations had appeared on the rolls, including the Chicago Grocers and Butchers' Association, the Chicago Master Steam-fitters, the Master Horseshoers' Protective Association, the Northwest Side Grocers and Butchers'

(Chicago: Ivan R. Dee, 1990). For small business as antilabor, see Daniel Ernst, *Lawyers Against Labor: From Individual Rights to Corporate Liberalism* (Chicago: University of Illinois Press, 1995); Wiebe, *Businessmen and Reform,* 167; *Oxford English Dictionary* (Oxford: Clarendon Press, 1989), v. 11, 632. A number of scholars suggest that craftsmen were susceptible to right wing extremism, e.g., Arthur M. Schlesinger, Jr., *The Politics of Upheaval* (Boston: Houghton Mifflin, 1960), 69; Seymour Martin Lipset, *The Politics of Unreason: Right Wing Extremism in America, 1790–1970* (Evanston: Harper Torchbooks, 1970), 178. Alan Brinkley presents a more nuanced and humane picture of lower middle-class reaction in *Voices of Protest: Huey Long, Father Coughlin, and the Great Depression* (New York: Vintage, 1983), 194–215, esp. 198, 201. For a recent rebuttal, see Robert Johnston, *The Radical Middle Class: Populist Democracy and the Question of Capitalism in Progressive Era Portland, Oregon* (Princeton: Princeton University Press, 2003), 3–17.

[4] Royal E. Montgomery, *Industrial Relations in the Chicago Building Trades* (Chicago: University of Chicago Press, 1927), 13–6; *Lakeside Directory, 1897,* 50–1.

[5] "Prosperity of Labor," *CRH,* May 1, 1903, 9; John Commons, "The Teamsters of Chicago," 400; *Lakeside Directory, 1902,* 59; *Lakeside Directory, 1904,* 68.

Association, and the West Chicago Liverymen and Undertakers' Association. Over the next two years, the total number of groups jumped from sixty-seven to ninety. Of the twenty-three new organizations, twenty were local, and nearly all of them were craft-centered, including the Chicago Drug Trade Club, the Chicago Master Bakers' Association, the Chicago Master Painters' Association, and others.[6]

The intense violence and frequent protests in these trades seem also to rebut notions of the conservative craft producer. Tradespeople did not support an independent labor party, demand abolition of private property, or endorse any broad social movement, but they did actively oppose the transformation of the economy, often with a physical passion terrifying to commentators of the time. Workers in many different trades engaged in a heated strikes and boycotts, as they labored to organize new members and maintain union rules and standards. Beatings, bombings, and even shootings were not uncommon. For example, during an 1899 construction lockout, newspapers reported 250 separate assaults in a five-month period. Nor, as the story of John Kluck suggests, was direct action limited to workers. At the peak of its power, for example, the Chicago Masons and Builders' Association commanded attacks on workers and businesses alike. By physically asserting authority over their trades, they challenged a corporate political economy rooted in property and the legal authority of the state.[7]

Dream, Thought, and Action among Craft Workers

Even by the standards of turn-of-the-century craft workers, the 1904 annual convention of the American Federation of Labor (AFL) was a rough-and-tumble event. Earlier that year, the AFL had ordered the Chicago Federation of Labor (CFL) to expel members of the

---

[6] *Lakeside Directory, 1897,* 45–51; *Lakeside Directory, 1902,* 52–7; *Lakeside Directory, 1904,* 59–65. The literature on local business associations is scant. Louis Galambos, *Competition and Cooperation: The Emergence of a National Trade Association* (Baltimore: Johns Hopkins University Press, 1966) and Clarence E. Bonnett, *Employers' Associations in the United States: A Study of Typical Associations* (New York: The Macmillan Company, 1922). For an insightful essay on small business protest, see Joel Tarr, "The Chicago Anti-Department Store Crusade of 1897: A Case Study in Urban Commercial Development," *Journal of the Illinois State Historical Society* 64 (Summer 1971): 161–72.

[7] For a complete list of the most heated clashes, see Harold Barton Myers, "The Policing of Labor Disputes in Chicago: A Case Study," (Ph.D. diss., University of Chicago, 1929); Bogart, "Chicago Building Trades Dispute. II.," 226; Testimony before the Dailey Commission, March 25, 1921, in Montgomery, *Industrial Relations,* 189.

International Association of Steam-fitters (IA) after these workers refused to dissolve their organization and join the United Association of Plumbers. When the CFL refused to bar the steamfitters, the AFL revoked the powerful local federation's charter. The Chicago crowd attended the San Francisco convention anyway, bringing IA president John Mangan with them. When the AFL denied the CFL delegates their credentials, a floor fight ensued, splintering the meeting into factions. The debate ended only when the national federation finally seated the local officials.[8]

Near the end of the convention, three labor leaders from the British Commonwealth addressed the weary delegates, delivering a fraternal message in sharp contrast with the preceding fracas. But as Canadian John A. Fleet closed a heartfelt speech inviting the federation to hold its next convention in his homeland, warm feelings gave way to confusion. Policemen entered the hall and arrested the three dignitaries. The foreigners were terrified, but the laughter of the crowd broke the tension. Revealing themselves to be unionists in costume, the "police officers" awarded each Briton a gold watch and badge. "For a time the Englishmen were completely nonplused," wrote the *Chicago Tribune*, "but the joke took tremendously with the throng present."[9]

These events illustrate much about the distinctive craft worldview. Both the victory of the Chicago delegation and the "arrest" of the foreign delegates attest to the continuing power of localism in the AFL. The story also indicates the intense factionalism that, for decades into the century, made the federation little more than an umbrella for a wide array of different unions. The prank and the crowd's reaction to it suggest organized labor's opinion of the state, a product of frequent arrests, criminal indictments, contempt of court citations, and physical confrontations. By playfully impersonating the police, the unionists parodied the harsh realities of state discipline.

The story also suggests the fundamentally governmental character of craft unions affiliated with the AFL. On one hand, this governmentality was *formal.* Federation conventions resembled political conventions. Member unions quarreled over jurisdiction, like different courts, commissions, departments, and states. On the floor, delegates debated the rules defining legitimate representatives, an essentially legal issue.

---

[8] "Schardt May Give Up," *CRH,* November 16, 1904, 6; "Labor Body in Clash," *CRH,* November 17, 1904, 4; "Seat Mangen in Federation," *CDT,* November 17, 1904, 7.

[9] The other two delegates, James Wignall and William Abraham, hailed from England. Wignall was a union official, Abraham, a member of Parliament. "Chicagoans Win Again," *CDT,* November 18, 1904, 2.

Though the AFL existed to help workers protect themselves from the deprivations of wage labor, it resembled a government in both its institutional form and in the content of its debates. Yet unions were also governments in *substance*. The unionists who donned police livery in San Francisco did so with the knowledge that organized labor rivaled and even exceeded the state in the governance of the economies of cities like Chicago. "Walking delegates" policed the urban economy, strolling from worksite to worksite, enforcing rules through strikes, fines, and boycotts.

This policing was a component of a broader system of craft governance established by labor unions and business associations in Chicago during the early twentieth century. A varied set of organizations enacted rules, asserting the right to determine which goods might be sold and who might work in Chicago. Their plans, schemes, and deals were fragile, subject to frequent challenge and routine factionalism, yet they were also potent and adaptable. Craft workers and proprietors were practical only in that their values emanated from the concrete set of market *practices* adopted to stem the transformative effects of competition. Craft organizations forcefully, even violently, set the terms for commerce in the city, limiting the ability of ambitious small businesses, struggling outsiders, and national corporations to compete in the city.

Craft workers modeled their economic institutions upon political bodies, enacting constitutions, electing officers, obeying parliamentary procedures, passing laws, levying taxes, establishing courts, and exacting punishments. Though commentators make much of the dictatorial craft union, many such organizations were committed in principal to regular elections. In 1900, Herbert Lillien stated that the 5,000 members of his hod carriers' union voted on walking delegates every six months, while Structural Iron Workers' Union business agent (and later United States Congressman) Frank Buchanan testified that his organization used the Australian (or secret) ballot to elect its officials.[10]

---

[10] Industrial Commission, *Report of the Industrial Commission on the Chicago Labor Disputes of 1900 with Especial Reference to the Disputes in the Building and Machinery Trades*, v. 8 (Washington, DC: Government Printing Office, 1901), 62, 118, 471–72, 555–63. Henceforth listed as IC, *Reports*, v. 8; "Slug at Labor Elections," *CDT*, January 19, 1903, 1; Bill for Injunction, December 5, 1906 in *Schmidt v. United Order of American Bricklayers*, case #276661, Circ.C.C. (1906); John Mangan, *History of the Steam-fitters Protective Association of Chicago* (Chicago: Steam-fitters Protective Association, 1930), 60–1.

These unions were no more perfect than the governments they imitated; officers schemed to remain in power, using violence, thievery, and forgery to sway the rank and file. But struggles within the leadership only illustrated the immense power these organizations exerted. In the law, these unions found a powerful metaphor for their efforts. Designating workers, firms, and products "legitimate" and others "criminal," organizations attempted to assert their authority over the economy, an authority the state reserved to itself. Craft workers insisted that within their trades, they were the government, entitled to designate who might succeed or fail. They did so by marking workers, products, and shops as "legitimate" or "criminal" with buttons, uniforms, cards, labels, and banners.[11]

Unions similarly used the word "scab" to designate workers who defied organized labor's governing authority. A "scab" was an employee who broke union rules by crossing a picket line, accepting a wage below scale, or refusing to accept union discipline. From its origins in the eighteenth century, the word suggested betrayal and lawlessness. In 1792, a British worker answered the question, "What is a scab?" with the rejoinder, "He is to his trade what a traitor is to his country." In 1850, the London newspaper, the *Morning Chronicle* described the legal overtones to the word, noting:

> Having thus given the characteristics of the "legal" or honourable trade, I next turn my inquiry to the state of the labouring men, women, and children employed by the slop masters, who are distinguished from the "wages" (or legal) shops by the terms "illegal," "scab," or "slaughtershop" keepers.[12]

Unlike the expressions "wages" and "slaughtershop," the word "scab" survived into the twentieth century, as did its implication of treachery and criminality. In 1899, Jane Addams noted that unionists saw a worker who crossed a picket line as a "traitor" and "deserter." In 1903, John Stiles, one of the few nonunion painting contractors in the city, complained that members of the Brotherhood of Painters called his workers "scabs," "son[s] of bitches," and, most tellingly, "god damned

---

[11] As early the eighteenth century, journeymen's associations began claiming the right to designate legitimate goods and workers, assuming authority previously held by state-chartered guilds of master craftsmen. Christopher L. Tomlins, *Law, Labor, and Ideology in the Early American Republic* (New York: Cambridge University Press, 1993), 116–18.

[12] *Oxford English Dictionary*, 2nd ed., v. 14 (Oxford: Clarendon Press, 1989), 550.

anarchists." Craft unions saw workers who defied their rules as lawless (and perhaps godless) radicals.[13]

A "scab" was not merely a nonunion worker, but rather a person who defied union rules. In 1899, George P. Gubbins, the president of Local #21 of the Bricklayers and Masons International Union explicitly marked "scabs" as criminals and union rules as laws. He explained:

> A nonunion man is a man who never belonged to a labor organi-zation, but who would not take any other man's place when he is out on a strike. There are many of these men in town, and there is never any controversy between them and the union men. The man we consider a scab is a man who follows from place to place, who is not a mechanic, who is wrong somewhere – he is degenerated into something else – he is wrong because if he was not he would belong to a labor organization . . . But it is either a man who has designs to *break the laws* of some organization which he agreed to uphold, or he has done some *criminal act* and had to get out and travel under an assumed name. [italics added]

So-called "scabs" resented the epithet's implications for their sanity, morality, and skill. In 1900, for example, James Gavin claimed that his expulsion from the Bricklayers and Masons Union #21 for "an alleged 'crime,'" marked him an "unreliable, unskilled, incompetent and scab workman at the aforesaid craft." In 1903, the Brotherhood of Painters suspended John Burgher for cheating his business partner out of a fee. Shunned by his former comrades, unable to find work in Chicago's unionized construction industry for two years, Burgher lamented, "I was the same as a criminal."[14]

Each organization asserted the right to define a legitimate worker within its self-defined jurisdiction, and members of one union could be "scabs" in the view of another. In 1903, two groups of sheet-metal workers, Local #73 and Local #275, claimed authority over the same

---

[13] Jane Addams, "Trade Unions and Public Duty," *American Journal of Sociol-ogy* 4:4 (1899): 454; Amended Petition, February 27, 1903, *Builders Paint-ing and Decorating v. Advisory Board Building Trades*, case #227537, Sup.C.C. (1903), 23; *Builders' Painting and Decorating v. Advisory Board Building Trades of Chicago*, 116 Ill. App. 265 (1904); Affidavit of John G. Stiles, September 10, 1903, *Stiles v. Brotherhood of Painters*, case #232122 in Sup.C.C. (1903), 2.

[14] IC, *Reports*, v. 8, 235; Second Amended Bill, February 9, 1903, *Gavin v. Bricklayers and Masons International Union*, case #227562, Sup.C.C. (1903); Bill, January 12, 1903, *Gavin v. Bricklayers and Masons International Union*, case #227562, Sup.C.C. (1903); Bill of Exceptions, December 20, 1905, *Burgher v. Painters, Decorators and Paper Hangers of America*, case #234118, Sup.C.C. (1903) 26.

set of jobs. Local #73 was affiliated with the Amalgamated Sheet Metal Workers Union, an organization strong in New York, Chicago, and Pittsburgh. Local #275 was a weak subordinate of the Sheet Metal Workers International Association, a parent union operating all over the country. When two firms decided to hire members of Local #275, pickets from Local #73 hooted and hollered, threatened and cajoled the new workers, calling them "scabs" and other "vile names." When members of Local #275 produced a letter from Samuel Gompers naming them the legitimate union of sheet-metal workers in the city of Chicago, members of Local #73 called it a forgery and persisted in asserting their right to control the trade.[15]

Unions not only disparaged rivals, they also invented a wide range of markers to identify their own members. In 1891, the Retail Clerks International Protective Association became the first union to use a button to mark members. Renewed monthly, buttons allowed them to identify and solicit outsiders as well as to encourage members to pay their dues. In 1903, the *Chicago Record-Herald* described the button system as "universally in vogue." The badges told "their own story without question as to what union a man is a member of, and shows him to be in good standing." Workers felt peer pressure to obtain their new pins promptly at the start of each month, making the system "the best scheme for collecting dues yet proposed." The button was most popular with service and retail workers. Although laborers in other fields, such as coal mining, wore it at different points, teamsters, retail clerks, barbers, bartenders, waiters, actors, horseshoers, steam engineers, stationary firemen, musicians, and theatrical stage employees sported the badges most frequently.[16]

Some unions experimented with using uniforms to distinguish their members. In 1898, a group of musicians proposed that the American Federation of Musicians (AFM) adopt standard livery, but the union decided instead to use a button. In 1905, the Chicago Federation of Musicians, Local #10 AFM passed a resolution, with the support of its parent union and two-thirds of its membership, requiring its members

---

[15] Bill of Complaint, April 25, 1903, *Holland Construction v. Amalgamated Sheet Metal Workers*, case #229657, Sup.C.C. (1903), 5; Affidavit of O. C. Wiehle, April 29, 1903, *Holland Construction v. Amalgamated Sheet Metal Workers*, case #229657 (1903), 3; Affidavits from Thure Loeb and Anton Fuertch, March 30, 1903, *Sykes Steel Roofing v. Amalgamated Sheet Metal Workers*, case #228903, Sup.C.C. (1903); "Seeks to Enjoin War of Unions," *CDT*, March 19, 1903, 7.

[16] "Prosperity of Labor," *CRH*, May 1, 1903, 9; Ernest R. Spedden, *The Trade Union Label* (Baltimore: Johns Hopkins, 1910), 30; William O. Weyforth, *The Organizability of Labor* (Baltimore: Johns Hopkins, 1915), 115.

to wear a standard outfit with the word "Chicago" and a small lyre embroidered on the collar. In the end, a rebellious minority of the organization obtained an injunction from the Circuit Court of Cook County blocking this resolution.[17]

Unions also identified legitimate craftsmen with working cards and permits. International unions adopted these licensing systems to enable union shops around the country to identify members from other cities. The union issued a new card each month, or marked the card when the worker paid dues. For example, the working card of the International Brotherhood of Blacksmiths read: "The Brother named is in Good Standing for the months as punched with the Anvil Punch." Permits allowed craft unions in seasonal industries, such as brewing and building construction, to respond to fluctuations in the labor market. In flush times, employers demanded more craftsmen than the unions could provide. Rather than recruiting new members, the union sold temporary permits, giving businesses the help they needed without creating a future surplus of union workers or ceding authority over the labor market.[18]

Unions used labels to license products. In 1880, cigarmakers' unions began marking every box with the phrase, "made by a first class workman, a member of the Cigar Makers International Union, an organization opposed to inferior rat shop, Coolie, Prison, or Filthy Tenement House Workmanship." By 1900, thirty-seven international unions had distinct labels. Organizations, such as the Women's International Union Label League, promoted its use on all union-made

---

[17] The musicians exempted members in National Guard and regimental bands from wearing the union uniform. The CFM hoped to stop bandleaders from forcing their employees to rent costumes at rates exceeding $15 a year. Not wanting to lose their investment, bandleaders opposed the standard outfits, but the rank-and-file endorsed the rule, charging that their employers rented them suits that had become "unsanitary, ill-smelling, unwholesome, and unclean." Answer, July 7, 1905, *Weldon v. Chicago Federation of Musicians*, case #263907, Circ.C.C. (1905). See also Affidavit of William Meyer, July 19, 1905 and Affidavit of Benjamin C. Dillon, July 8, 1905, in *Weldon v. Chicago Federation of Musicians*, case #263907 Circ.C.C. (1905).

[18] Millis and Montgomery, *Organized Labor*, 260–61; Industrial Comission, *Report of the Industrial Commission on the Relations and Conditions of Capital and Labor Employed in Manufactures and General Business Including Testimony with Review*, v. 7 (Washington, DC: Government Printing Office, 1901), 632. Henceforth IC, *Reports*, v. 7. Montgomery, *Industrial Relations*, 88; William Haber, *Industrial Relations in the Building Industry* (Cambridge, MA: Harvard University Press, 1930), 202–04.

goods. Labels allowed union workers and their families to recognize union-made consumer goods, such as clothing, bread, and printing.[19]

The union label often figured prominently in transactions between different producers, rather than between producers and consumers. Unions like the United Brotherhood of Carpenters and Joiners and the Amalgamated Sheet Metal Workers Union, Local #73 refused to handle unlabeled material and marked their own finished work with the union signet. Even coffin-makers belonging to the Amalgamated Wood Workers Union used the label in solidarity with the nascent gravediggers union. A mock-scandalized *Chicago Times-Herald* commented that this burgeoning organization threatened to refuse burial to any body not buried in a union made coffin. The newspaper continued:

> No exception will be made in any case, whether poor or rich, infidel or believer, union or non-union sympathizer. The man who believes that death ends all will see the union label following his friends into the grave. The man who has made a Herculean struggle against labor unions in life will be triumphed over them by death.

Noting the union labels on cribs, the editors jokingly concluded that labor's object was to "unionize everything from the cradle to grave exclusive." The prediction proved sound; by 1908, a strong union agreement governed the undertaking trade.[20]

While local unions marked workers, employers, and products, larger labor bodies labeled the unions themselves. The AFL, the national and international unions, city federations, and craft councils all issued charters, the physical manifestation of the union's right to exist. When a national union sought to dissolve a local, it demanded that the local return the piece of paper itself to the parent body. If the union remained in existence, it was an "outlaw," and, until its members joined a sanctioned local, they were "scabs." In 1906, members of International Freight Handlers' Union Local #4 believed that their charter's

[19] In 1893, the CMIU ceased equating prisoners, immigrants, and Asians, substituting the phrase "devoted to the moral, material, and intellectual welfare of the craft." Spedden, *Trade Union Label,* 9–14, 15, f.1, 16–22, 25, f.1; *Lakeside Directory, 1902,* 60; IC, *Reports,* v. 7, 628–33; Frank, *Purchasing Power,* 212–46.

[20] Christie, *Empire in Wood,* 161–69, 188–97. At times, the United Brotherhood of Carpenters accepted the Amalgamated Wood Workers Union label. In 1898, a Chicago "woodworkers council," agreed to a common mark. IC, *Reports,* v. 8, 402; *Engel v. Walsh,* 258 Ill. 98 (1913); "Union Stamp on Coffins," *Chicago Times-Herald,* March 17, 1900, 1; *Allen v. Chicago Undertakers' Association,* 232 Ill. 458 (1908).

revocation branded them "scabs," unemployable at the nation's railroad terminals. A charter entitled a union to sit in AFL councils. The national federation defended its decision to refuse to seat the Chicago delegate at the 1904 convention by commenting "the Chicago Federation of Labor ceased to exist November 1 and had no *legal* existence in the labor movement of the country [italics added]."[21]

Umbrella organizations like the CFL and the Building Trades Council of Chicago (BTC), kept the public aware of their member organizations through directories. These directories were a lucrative source of revenue, as promoters solicited advertisements and subscriptions from employers, earning according to one estimate in the 1920s, between $20,000 and $50,000. More importantly, directories existed to differentiate "bona fide" labor unions from rival organizations. In 1914, over a half-million unionists existed outside of the AFL. Some unions, such as the bricklayers, had evolved independently of the federation. Competing organizations sprouted up like weeds, their roots strangling recognized unions. In 1903, AFL unions condemned an unrecognized group, the "Building Maintenance Council" for organizing stationary engineers, boiler firemen, and flat janitors in competition with established unions. Renegade labor leaders like P. F. Doyle, a former officer of the International Association of Steam Engineers and former president of the CFL, founded rival unions rather than returning to manual labor. Central organizations used directories to notify employers which organizations had their seal of approval and which were unauthorized usurpers.[22]

Yet these directories themselves were subject to fraud and abuse. In 1912, the BTC complained that John J. Brittain, a contractor and the former secretary of the carpenters, was selling labor directories marked "the Chicago Business Agents Association," a name suspiciously similar to that of the well-established Chicago Board of Business Agents. The BTC condemned Brittain's conduct as "misleading" and "reprehensible" and demanded he "confine himself to contracting and leave

[21] Bill of Complaint, June 7, 1906, *International Freight Handlers Union Local #4 v. International Freight Handlers Union*, case #254260, Sup.C.C. (1906). The CFL had refused to expel a steamfitters' local whose parent had lost its AFL charter. "Seat Mangen in the Federation," *CDT*, November 17, 1904, 7; "Chicagoans Win Again," *CDT*, November 18, 1904, 2.
[22] Foster, *Misleaders*, 264–65; Lorwin, 484; "Peace in Gas Strike," *CRH*, April 27, 1903, 3; "Labor Censures P. F. Doyle," *CDT*, May 24, 1901, 11; *Lakeside Directory*, 1906, 75.

the labor game alone as he is in no way connected with any central body."[23]

Enforcement of Craft Union Government

To appreciate the radicalism of this behavior, one must understand that unions and associations took it upon themselves to maintain agreements, arbitrate disputes, and discipline violators. Many scholars assert that early twentieth-century craft unions favored "contractualism," or the use of private agreements to establish economic conditions. But while unions signed contracts, they seldom enforced these agreements in court. Lawmakers often asked union officials why they called strikes against employers rather than suing them for damages. Sheet metal workers' delegate Fred "Frenchy" Pouchot responded that, "Labor people are not anxious to go into court; they never have been." Pouchot admitted the benefits of civil action, but confessed that courts were too "slow." Ironworker's officer Frank Ryan agreed; the legal system was too deliberate, too costly, and arguably too biased to be effective.[24]

Craft workers instead defined legitimacy and criminality for themselves. Though often willing to accept the assistance of local government, unions tried to control the workforce so fully that they became the state within their jurisdictions. Ruminating upon statutes regulating the plumbing trade, steamfitters' president John Mangan commented, "The best substitute for any "License Law" is for each trade organization to perfect themselves and their own members to such a state of perfection that they will be dependent on their own organization only, and thus retain self-government in their own household." By organizing all the workers in each craft, maintaining firm discipline, and directly enforcing its rules, a union "perfected" itself, gaining exclusive authority over its craft without the need for coercion.[25]

Enforcement depended upon an administrator known as the business agent (BA) or walking delegate. The real "men of power" at the

---

[23] Only weeks earlier, the BTC complained that, "irresponsible parties were misrepresenting themselves as organizers for the Building Trades." Minutes, August 2, 1912 and October 4, 1912, *Minute Book of the Chicago Building Trades Council*, 1912–1914, 40, 50 in CHS.

[24] IC, *Reports*, v. 8, 286–89, 440. For Gompers view, see IC, *Reports*, v. 7, 600–8.

[25] Forbath, *Law and the Shaping of the American Labor Movement*, 130; Mangan, *History of the Steam-fitters Protective Association*, 55; "'Recognition' as Explained and Defined by Chicago Trade Union Leaders," *CRH*, June 18, 1903, 2.

turn of the century, these local officials ran the unions, determining their strategy, safeguarding their treasuries, and, most importantly, maintaining their agreements. Beginning in the 1890s, members of unions and sometimes trade associations elected business agents to represent them at the workplaces scattered around Chicago. Traveling from site to site, walking delegates checked for violations of trade agreements and associational rules. Infractions might include the employment of a nonunion worker, or the payment of wages below scale, or the purchase of materials manufactured by an unrecognized firm. When a walking delegate found such violations, he notified the offending employer or worker and attempted to negotiate a resolution. Failing conciliation, he returned to his central office to confer with his organization and determine its course of action. The options included fines, strikes, and boycotts.[26]

Contemporary journalists and reformers described the walking delegate as a notorious character much like a ward boss or precinct captain. However apt this comparison, it reveals the extent to which both critics and advocates saw unions as institutions that ruled the economy, and business agents as officials with governmental powers. The walking delegate was, as one skilled worker aptly noted in 1906, "the policeman of the union," but his responsibilities often exceeded those of the ordinary patrolman. In 1903, the *Independent Magazine* delineated the different functions of the walking delegate:

He becomes the union's expert on all matters of wages, hours, and conditions of labor. He is their detective to discover the weak points of the employers and to advise them when and where to strike, when to acquiesce and what may be the tricks and traps contrived against them. He is their lieutenant in time of strike or lockout. He collects the evidence when a member has a grievance. He is their labor bureau for members out of work. He is their solicitor, to bring in the nonunionist, and their watcher to inspect members' "cards" and keep them in good standing. He is, in fact, their executive, their representative and the very type of unionism. As a piece of mechanism the

---

[26] C. Wright Mills, *The New Men of Power: America's Labor Leaders* (New York: Harcourt, Brace & Co, 1948), 10–1; Warren Van Tine, *The Making of the Labor Bureaucrat: Union Leadership in the United States, 1870–1920* (Amherst: University of Massachusetts, 1973), 161–81; Christie, *Empire in Wood*, 6, 9, 63–6; Kazin, *Barons of Labor*, 102–3; Fine, *Without Blare of Trumpets*, 15; Montgomery, *Industrial Relations*, 8–9.

union is no more than a device for joint action through a business agent.[27]

In short, business agents were the figures centrally responsible for maintaining private economic governance and market control. Successful rule of the urban economy demanded that persons patrol the city, ensuring that work proceeded according to the laws of the trade.

Business agents were most numerous and powerful in the construction industry, a domain ruled by the largest, wealthiest, and most aggressive unions. Production in the building trades was diffused among thousands of contractors, building on scattered sites, and the district councils relied upon walking delegates to maintain agreements. Since many jobs lasted only a few weeks, hustling contractors and chronically underemployed building tradesmen needed administrators to match workers with the work. But unions of manufacturing, service, and professional workers also employed business agents to negotiate disputes and enforce work rules. The Chicago Teachers Federation hired Margaret Haley as "business manager," making her one of the first female union representative in Chicago. Since unions paid business agents salaries, the number of delegates reflected the wealth of the union. In 1904, the Amalgamated Wood Workers Union had four agents, the International Association of Machinists #8 had three, while the Iron Molders Union, and the United Garment Workers District Council each hired only one walking delegate.[28]

[27] Luke Grant, "Industrial Democracy: The Walking Delegate," *Outlook* 84 (November 10, 1906): 615–21, esp. 617; "The Walking Delegate," *The Independent* 55:2846 (June 18, 1903): 1467; Franklin Clarkin, "The Daily Walk of the Walking Delegate," *Century Magazine* 67:2 (December 1903): 304; Baker, "The Trust's New Tool," 30–43, esp. 30–1; Jane Addams, "Trade Unions and Public Duty," *American Journal of Sociology* 4:4 (1899): 455; Kazin, *Barons of Labor*, 102–3; Richard R. Myers, "Inter-Personal Relations in the Building Industry," *Applied Anthropology* 5:2 (Spring 1946): 7.
[28] Montgomery, *Industrial Relations*, 8–9, 18–9, 35; Christie, *Empire in Wood*, 6, 9–10, 15, 153–57. The business agents listed in the 1904 *Lakeside Directory* were: Thomas Dawson, John Kikulski, George Lang, and Joseph Mech (Amalgamated Wood Workers), Lee Fisher, J. J. Keppler, and William Rossell (Machinists District Lodge #8), James Brown (Iron Molders), and S. H. Mowatt (United Garment Workers). *Lakeside Directory, 1904*, 66–71; Theodore W. Glocker, *The Government of American Trade Unions* (Baltimore: Johns Hopkins, 1913), 150; Katherine K. Sklar, *Florence Kelley and the Nation's Work: The Rise of Women's Political Culture, 1830–1900* (New Haven: Yale University Press, 1995), 214–15; Margaret Haley, *Battleground: The Autobiography*

Local unions defined the walking delegate's powers, but these officials often seemed unaccountable to either the union bylaws or the rank and file. According to the constitution of the Painters' District Council of Chicago, business agents could not order men off their jobs, but they often did so. The membership obeyed, fearing fines and suspensions. Although subject to yearly elections, delegates managed to convince the rank and file to reelect them through a mixture of generosity and coercion. Even charges of graft seldom resulted in expulsion. Though technically craftsmen controlled the business agents, workers seldom in fact defied his authority.[29]

Business agents were just one component of an expanding regulatory apparatus that disciplined and fined union members. The Chicago Federation of Musicians (CFM) established a fairly advanced court system to enforce its wage and price rules, which allowed appeals to local and national bodies. In September 1904, the CFM fined Henry Doehne, the musical director of the Garrick Theater and a member in good standing for thirty years, $260 for thirteen violations of the price list and threatened to expel him if he did not pay within twelve days. In 1906, the federation expelled Charles Quinn, the musical director of the Great Northern Theater, after discovering that he paid his musicians half of the union scale. His musicians quit and began picketing the theater.[30]

Workers and employers usually paid the fines, for suspension from the union often meant unemployment or bankruptcy. In 1903, Peter Anderson charged D. C. Hanson, the delegate of the Lake Seamen's Union, with neglecting his duties. A committee investigated Anderson's charges, found them baseless, and fined him ten dollars. Anderson claimed that he had tried to pay the fine, but that the leadership would not permit him. The union rebutted that Anderson had not sought redress in the proper manner. In the meantime, Anderson

of Margaret A. Haley, ed., Robert Reid (Chicago: University of Illinois Press, 1982).

[29] For the limits on the power of the business agent, see Christie, *Empire in Wood*, 6; Bill of Exceptions, December 20, 1905, *Burgher v. Painters Decorators and Paper Hangers of America*, case #234118, Sup.C.C. (1903), 34–43; IC, *Reports*, v. 8, 345, 118, 398, 432; Grant, "Industrial Democracy: The Walking Delegate," 616.

[30] Doehne declined to appeal the case within the CFM, choosing instead to obtain a court order restraining the union. Bill, September 12, 1904, *Doehne v. Chicago Federation of Musicians*, case #255329, Circ.C.C. (1904). In desperation, Quinn hired members of the rival American Musicians Union. "Orchestra on Strike for Dual Grievances," *CRH*, February 20, 1906, 9. See also *Bindley v. Chicago Federation of Musicians*, case #255626 Circ.C.C. (1904).

lost his membership. As a consequence, his former brethren "looked down upon and sneered at" him, causing him "great mental pain and worry and discomfort and inconvenience."[31]

In trades where unions had obtained the closed shop, suspension meant unemployment. In June 1897, the Bricklayers and Masons International Union Local #21 signed an exclusive contract with the Chicago Masons and Builders Association. That same year, the union suspended James Gavin for failing to pay a $100 fine. From then on, the union declared him "unfair" and a "scab," while the daily papers called him "the only nonunion bricklayer in Chicago." Gavin lied to get jobs, but his former union brethren refused to work with him, fearing a $50 fine. And since the Chicago Masons and Builders' Association had agreed to hire none but union men, contractors such as Angus and Son dismissed Gavin. Unable to make a living at his chosen profession, Gavin faced bankruptcy and threatened to become, in his own words, "dependent" and "a charge on the public."[32]

Unions also punished employers who violated the standards of each craft community. Building trades unions often fined contractors for straying from the terms of their agreements. In 1903, Turk Brothers, a clothing manufacturer, expelled a walking delegate named Minken of the International Ladies Garment Workers Union from their shop. Minken's superior Ben Schlesinger demanded the firm pay a $150 fine to avert a walkout. Unions demanded security from employers who refused to sign labor contracts. Contractor John Stiles claimed that in 1898 the painters' union agreed to cease picketing his establishment if he posted a $500 bond against his employment of nonunionists. In August 1908, Channing Ellery, "a musician of keen appreciation" and

---

[31] Narr., January 27, 1905, *Anderson v. Lake Seamen's Union*, case #241609, Sup.C.C. (1905); Demurrer, June 6, 1906, *Anderson v. Lake Seamen's Union*, case #241609 (1905).

[32] "Bar Sympathy Strike," *CDT*, January 13, 1903, 10; "Union Sued for Damages," *CDT*, October 24, 1903, 3; Bill, January 12, 1903, *Gavin v. Bricklayers and Masons International Union*, case #227562, Sup.C.C. (1903); Amended Bill, January 21, 1903, *Gavin v. Bricklayers*, case #227562, Sup.C.C. (1903); 2nd Amended Bill, February 9, 1903, *Gavin v. Bricklayers*, case #227562, Sup.C.C. (1903); Supplemental Bill to 2nd Bill, October 9, 1903, *Gavin v. Bricklayers*, case #227562, Sup.C.C. (1903); Answer to 2nd Amended Bill, November 11, 1903, *Gavin v. Bricklayers*, case #227562, Sup.C.C. (1903); Answer to 2nd Supplemental Bill, November 11, 1903, *Gavin v. Bricklayers*, case #227562, Sup.C.C. (1903). For another building tradesman unable to find employment after breaking with his union, see Bill of Exceptions, December 20, 1905, *Burgher v. Painters, Decorators, and Paper Hangers of America*, case #234118, Sup.C.C. (1903).

the owner and operator of a traveling military band with fifty musicians, came to Chicago to perform at Ravinia Park. According to Ellery, the union harassed and embarrassed him, finally demanding that he pay a $1000 cash bond to ensure that he would obey the union price list.[33]

Craft unions used walkouts to punish employers and maintain control over the labor market. The strike, or more appropriately, the threat of a strike, deterred employers from violating work rules, cutting wages below scale, or hiring nonunion craftsmen. In 1898, E. A. Davis, an officer of the Hoisting Engineers Union, demanded that the Thomas Elevator Company fire two nonunion workers named Charles and Dennis. The employer complied. Had he refused, Davis could have called the engineers off their jobs, citing union rules that prohibited members, upon threat of fines and suspension, from working with outsiders. Just as often, however, workers acted without the guidance of union officials and asked their agents to negotiate the dismissal of nonunionists.[34]

Unions worked together to enforce their rules. Construction workers, for example, honored the walkouts of other unions affiliated with various building trades councils. A sympathetic strike affected the many different contractors working on a given project, pitting all against the offending company and leading them to police one another. In particular, general contractors, responsible for the entire building, could not afford to hire companies that had experienced labor problems. Even one nonunion subcontractor might delay the project indefinitely. As a consequence, union employers avoided nonunion companies just as union workers avoided "scabs." For example, in 1902, Chicago's construction unions combined to stymie John Stiles. Because Stiles hired primarily nonunion painters, the Painters District Council could not call Stiles' employees out on strike. It could, however, ask other craft unions to refuse to work for general contractors who hired Stiles' firm. When Clark Construction, a general contractor, paid Stiles to paint the Magnus Foundry, unions affiliated with the Associated Building Trades League (ABTL) threatened to call

---

[33] IC, *Reports*, v. 8, 340, 437–38, 484; "Want to Strike; Fear Outcome," *CDT*, May 27, 1903, 3; Bill, August 14, 1908, *Ellery v. American Federation of Musicians*, case #286182 Circ.C.C. (1908); "The Passing Show," *WP*, February 27, 1910, n.p.

[34] *People v. Davis*, 3 Ill. C.C. 516 (1898). Labor officials often denied that they coerced members into quitting, arguing that workers simply refused to work with nonunionists. IC, *Reports*, v. 8, 438.

strikes against all Clark jobs. Seeking to avoid conflict, Clark broke its contract with Stiles.[35]

Such sympathetic strikes gave the ABTL the ultimate power to determine legitimate contractors and workers. Whole unions were shut out. In 1906, a group of ABTL affiliates, including the plumbers, steamfitters, ironworkers, boiler coverers, and electrical workers, boycotted any employer who hired members of the independent National Stonecutters' Society of the United States (NSS) instead of the ABTL-affiliated Journeymen Stonecutters' Association of North America (JSA). Pushed to the margins, the NSS eventually brokered a settlement in 1913. But even after, the JSA and their allies continued to exclude NSS members who refused to pay initiation fees.[36]

A second method of disciplining employers was the boycott. In the consumer-products, retail, and service trades, unions marked legitimate retail and service businesses with shop cards. In 1891, the Journeymen Barbers Union began allowing "fair" shopkeepers to solicit working-class consumers by displaying union cards in their windows. By 1914, the AFL reported ten organizations issuing such cards, including the grocers' and bartenders' unions. By contrast, unions publicized "unfair" workers and firms in weekly labor publications. Pickets distributed leaflets, held placards, and shouted "opprobrious names." In 1904, officers of the Bakery and Confectionary Workers Local #2 followed the delivery wagons of the Heusner Bakery on bicycles and distributed notices printed in English and German telling their patrons:

Union Bread. International Union Made B & C W I U of A (registered) An Appeal to Organized labor and its Friends. The Heusner Baking Co. 2616 S. Park Ave. and Coyne's on Lake and Madison St. still refuse to recognize the Bakers Union. WE appeal to Organized

---

[35] *Builders' Painting and Decorating Company v. Advisory Board Building Trades of Chicago*, 116 Ill. App. 264 (1904); *Stiles v. Brotherhood of Painters*, case #231675, Sup.C.C. (1903); *Stiles v. Brotherhood of Painters*, case #232122, Sup.C.C. (1903). Stiles' troubles began when he supported the lockout of 1899. See IC, *Reports*, v. 8, pp. 339–45, 452–54.

[36] *Chicago and Cook County Branch National Stonecutters Society of the United States v. Journeymen Stonecutters Association of North America*, 2 Ill. C.C. 118 (1906). This rivalry began with debates whether to tolerate the use of the mechanical stone planer. George E. Barnett, "The Stonecutters" Union and the Stone Planer," *Journal of Political Economy* 24:5 (May 1916): 439–40.

Labor and the public in general to refuse to trade in places where non-union goods are consumed. Ask for union made bread.[37]

Similarly, the barbers boycotted shops that did not abide by the eight o'clock closing time. In 1904, the Barbers Union issued a circular stating:

> Unionism! An appeal to the Public in the name of Organized Labor – Attention! Do not patronize a barber shop that does not close at 8 o'clock week days 10 o' clock Saturdays and 12 o'clock noon Sundays and Holidays. The Barbers of the City of Chicago do respectfully ask the Public and Union Men in particular 352 W. Division St. Proprietor of said shop refuses to be a Union Man and runs a non-union Barber Shop. All genuine barber shops have their signs in plain view of the public. Be sure that the shop you patronize has the Union Sign before you get shaved therein.

In the same year, Chicago's brewery workers union posted a more threatening notice. The figure of a skull and crossbones loomed ominously over text reading: "Boycott the Eagle Brewing Co . . . It is produced by scab labor."[38]

Unions restricted the materials members used in their work, labeling some goods legitimate and boycotting the rest. Members of the United Brotherhood of Carpenters often refused to use wood trim produced either by nonunion labor or by industrial workers belonging to the Amalgamated Wood Workers Union. Other unions supported material manufacturing workers. In 1899, the new Chicago Building Material Trades Council allied itself with the Building Trades Council. Metal polishers declined to handle nonunion brass. Bricklayers, teamsters, and hod carriers all refused to use brick without the brickmakers' union label, effectively making "unfair" brick "worthless."[39]

---

[37] Spedden, *The Trade Union Label*, 30; Weyforth, *The Organizability of Labor*, 70–1 esp. f.44, f.45; W. Scott Hall, *The Journeymen Barbers' International Union of America* (Baltimore: Johns Hopkins, 1934), 115–18; Bill and Affidavits, June 29, 1906, *Heusner Baking Co. v. Bakers and Confectioners #2*, case #272931 Circ.C.C. (1906); True Bill, November 30, 1904, *People v. Spiess*, case #75430, Crim.C.C., IR 134, 179–82.

[38] True Bill, September 30, 1904, *People v. Bausk*, case #74791, Crim.C.C., IR 134, 169; True Bill, January 26,1904, *People v. Obermeyer*, case #72033, Crim.C.C., IR 134, 137.

[39] Christie, *Empire in Wood*, 112–13; Leo Wolman, *The Boycott in American Trade Unions* (Baltimore: Johns Hopkins, 1916), 43–72, esp. 62, 69; IC, *Reports*, v. 8, 431.

Trade Association Governance and its Expansion

Like their employees, Chicago's master craftsmen, contractors, and shopkeepers presumed that business was a public pursuit, subject to rules and contingent upon peer approval. Businessmen formed trade associations that adopted constitutions that established administrations and enumerated the requirements of membership. Though their language was comparatively mild, they nevertheless distinguished between the legitimate economic activity of their members and the "disreputable," "criminal," and "unfair" activities of their rivals. Like craft unions, proprietors' associations continually struggled to contain their swelling ranks and to assert an exclusive authority over specific areas of commerce. The most prominent example was the Chicago Masons and Builders Association (CMB). In 1897, two-thirds of all mason contractors belonged to the CMB, and the organization controlled 95 percent of all brick construction in the city.[40]

Whereas unions used the term "scab," associations employed the word "unfair." In 1905, the Jobbing Confectioners' Association published a history of their trade in Chicago, featuring biographies of prominent members, proclaiming their belief in quality merchandise, "fair" profits, and opposition to "unfair measures." Agreements setting prices were the material manifestation of these attitudes. In 1901, Jewish bakers met in the Great Northern Hotel to discuss, matter-of-factly, how to limit competition and raise profits. They decided to form an association that would establish a standard price for bread in the city. Groups devised price schedules, often working in tandem with larger bodies. For example, Chicago launderers submitted price lists to the National Laundrymen's Association for approval.[41]

Some associations adopted buttons and labels for their salesmen and products. In January 1903, for example, Chicago tobacco sellers formed the National Cigar Dealers Association (NCDA) to oppose the "tobacco trust" and to stem "ruinous and unfair competition."

[40] For examples of association constitutions, see pamphlets attached to Bill of Complaint, June 30, 1899, in *Union Pressed Brick v. Chicago Hydraulic Press Brick*, case #196935, Circ.C.C. (1899); *People ex rel Emerich v. Chicago Masons and Builders Association*, case #219410, Circ.C.C. (1901), 9.

[41] Henry G. Abbott, *Historical Sketch of the Confectionary Trade of Chicago* (Chicago: Jobbing Confectioners' Association, 1905); "Jewish Bakers May Combine," *CDT*, June 24,1901, 11; "Coal Jury Grist is Forty-Four," *CRH*, January 20, 1903, 2; *Sanford v. People*, 121 Ill. App. 619 (1905). "Laundry Bills to Soar; Soaps Price the Cause," *CRH*, June 26, 1907, 5; IC, *Reports*, v. 8, 204–5.

To mark its salesmen, the association adopted a button. More often, trade groups relied upon lists of "fair" and "unfair" proprietors. Because each firm had its own label, and because the number of businessmen in Chicago was comparatively small, purchasers could easily check a product's trademark against the list of "legitimate" firms. For example, in the late 1890s, groups such as the Pressed Brick Association supplied lists of acceptable vendors to contractors to be checked against trademarks stamped in the clay itself. In some sectors, associations put disobedient firms on "unfair lists." The Retail Coal Dealers Association of Illinois and Wisconsin and the National Association of Retail Druggists both kept lists of retailers that undercut standard prices.[42]

Like craft unions and Chicago government generally, trade associations occasionally deviated from the high principles of their constitutions. Members often charged officials with malfeasance. In June 1903, the Chicago Restaurant Keepers accused their president, George Walton, of offering a bribe to leaders of the striking waiters union. Walton's attorney responded that businessmen "forcibly ejected him from the room, thereby committing an assault on his person" and "denied him the opportunity to explain and wrongfully deposed him," violating the bylaws the association. Other officers attempted to hold power despite the will of their members. In 1903, the recently formed National Cigar Dealers Association declined to reelect its president, Thad H. Howe. After losing the election, Howe refused to relinquish the records of the organization he had founded.[43]

Associations, like unions, also battled against factionalism, rivalry, and fraud. In 1901, Frank C. Koebel and Martin Campe founded the Landlord's Protective Department, an organization charging city's

---

[42] "Convene to Fight Trust," *CDT*, January 14, 1903, 3; "Cigar Men Ask for Laws," January 15, 1903, 3. Labeling eventually gained adherents among manufacturers' associations. Emmett Hay Naylor, *Trade Associations: Their Organizations and Management* (New York: The Ronald Press Company, 1921), 126. "Coal Jury Grist is Forty-Four," *CRH*, January 20, 1903, 2; *Platt v. National Association of Retail Druggists et al.*, 1 Ill. C.C. 1 (1905). Trademarks on brick were common even in Ancient Mesopotamia in the Third Millennium B.C. Indeed this practice became so accepted that U.S. government required brand names on brick it purchased in 1925. Karl Gurcke, *Bricks and Brickmaking: A Handbook for Historical Archeology* (Moscow, ID: University of Idaho, 1987), 120–25; Bill of Complaint, June 30, 1899, *Union Pressed Brick v. Chicago Hydraulic Press Brick*, case #196935 Circ.C.C. (1899).

[43] "To Sue Cafe Owners," *CRH*, June 13, 1903, 2; "Convene to Fight Trust," *CDT*, January 14, 1903, 3; "Cigar Men Ask for Laws," January 15, 1903, 3; "Thad Howe, Leader in the Cigar Dealers' War," *CRH*, June 18, 1903, 2.

landlords a $1 membership fee in exchange for a membership certificate and free legal services. The Chicago Landlords' Protective Bureau, incorporated in 1886, charged $10 for admission, provided more extensive services, and claimed over 7,000 past and present members. Discovering that agents of the new association were taking advantage of the similarity of the names, the Bureau asked Koebel and Campe to change the name of their organization. When these men refused, the older organization took them to court.[44]

To govern commerce in their trades, local associations relied heavily upon contractual and commercial forms of pressure. Although their surveillance paled beside that of the unions, trade associations hired representatives to police the economy. In 1899, the Chicago Masons and Builders allegedly hired "business agents" to travel about the city looking for building sites using pressed brick and "to spy out and ascertain from whom the pressed brick required for said building had been purchased or contracted to be purchased and to report such facts to the said Chicago Masons & Builders Association." In 1903, the Central Supply Association (CSA), administered by blue-blooded manufacturer Paul Blatchford, regulated prices of brass and lead fixtures in the plumbing trade. The association periodically issued a schedule called the "Price Current." The CSA hired detectives, stenographers, and a bookkeeper, Emil Larson, who checked the ledgers of member firms to determine which firms had obeyed the schedule. Offenses were punishable by fines and boycotts.[45]

Like unions, trade associations frequently used boycotts to isolate and impoverish proprietors who violated their rules or refused to join their organizations. In the late nineteenth century, the Chicago Laundrymen's Association began asserting its right to govern the businesses that washed clothes in the city. In 1890, the association punished a woman named Mary Hennessey for refusing to increase her prices. Because Hennessey operated a storefront laundry that sent

---

[44] The bureau sued and eventually obtained an injunction upon appeal. *Koebel v. Chicago Landlords' Protective Bureau*, 210 Ill. 176 (1904).

[45] Affidavit of Martin Emerich, July 11, 1901, *People ex rel Emerich v. Chicago Masons and Builders Assn.*, case #219410, Circ.C.C., 9. Paul Blatchford initially supported unions and craft governance, but he and his fellow plumbing manufacturers eventually rejected craft practices, supported the anti-union National Metal Trades Association, and accepted a more corporate form of industrial relations. "Pool Secrets Bared," *CRH*, October 3, 1903, 9; "Expose Pools to Grand Jury," *CDT*, October 3, 1903, 7; "Pool on Rack To-Day," *CRH*, December 3, 1903, 9; "Writs are Voted in Plumbing Pool case," *CRH*, December 4, 1903, 7; True Bill, November 1, 1903, *People v. Sanitary Specialty Manufacturing Company*, case #71392, Crim.C.C., IR 134, 131.

clothes to an outside factory, she was vulnerable to boycotting. The agents of the association instructed the laundry plants not to serve Hennessey and threatened to ruin those who continued to take her business.[46]

Business associations joined together to enforce standard prices and maintain exclusive control over markets. The first such agreement arose in common brick. In December 1897, negotiations began between the Chicago Masons and Builders Association (CMB) and a new organization called the Brick Manufacturers Association (BMA). The BMA united nearly 95 percent of all the manufacturers selling common brick in Cook County, including leading dealers such as Dillwyn Purington, Adam Weckler, Frederick LaBahn, Louis Reimer, Edward Harland, and William Schlake. On April 1, 1898, the CMB agreed to buy brick only from the manufacturers in exchange for a discount of $1 per thousand. The BMA paid the masons' association an additional bounty of $1 per thousand if any member sold brick to an outside contractor. This handsome rebate encouraged contractors to join the CMB and enforce the brick rules.

The CMB then created disciplinary structures to regulate the purchase and use of brick in the city. First, the masons promised the material dealers that their association would use its power to push prompt payment of debts. For years, the material men had struggled to collect money for the goods they provided. Fly-by-night contractors would receive payment for constructing a building and then refuse to pay their bills. Under the new rules, contractors had thirty days to reimburse their creditors before the CMB suspended their membership. After another fifteen days, the association expelled the contractor pending payment of the debt, miscellaneous fines, and a readmission fee.[47]

Building-material manufacturers also regulated the local market by pooling receipts. Pools were central funds, maintained by groups of producers, who agreed to collect a percentage of their gross

---

[46] *Doremus v. Hennessey*, 176 Ill. 608, 613 (1898). By 1910, drycleaners had formed the Master Cleaners and established a "closed solicitation" agreement that prohibited members from "stealing stops" by lowering prices. Unified, the plant owners could pressure the retailers, and, in turn, this control allowed them to enforce boycotts upon their own members. Morrison Handsaker, "The Chicago Cleaning and Dyeing Industry: A Study in Controlled Competition" (Ph.D. diss, University of Chicago, 1939), 106–12.

[47] *Purington v. Hinchliff*, 219 Ill. 159, 164 (1905); Information in Nature of Quo Warranto, July 11, 1901, *People ex rel Martin Emerich v. Chicago Masons and Builders*, case #219410, Circ.C.C. (1901).

earnings for later distribution. In industries where bidding was common, pools effectively discouraged low bidding by ensuring that all producers would gain when a contract was awarded. But more importantly, with a large chunk of their profits going to the community of producers, pools induced firms to charge higher prices. Pools were not unique to the craft economy; railroads had made similar arrangements to stem competition in the late nineteenth century. What made these pools unprecedented was their integration with a broader system of craft governance.

A complex pooling arrangement produced a deep reservoir of cash that unified the brick business for a time. In 1897, the owners of two of the largest brickyards in the city, Leonard H. Harland and Dillwyn V. Purington, founded a dummy corporation, the Cook County Brick Company (CCB). In exchange for a mere $13 per year, Harland and Purington obtained leases from thirty-seven other local brickyards. CCB then subleased the yards back to the manufacturers at a rate of $1.50 per thousand bricks sold. In a city where a large brickyard would sell over 20 million bricks per annum and over 3 million bricks per month during the summer building season, this variable rent induced the city's brick firms to raise prices and limit production.[48]

The Cook County Brick Company collected this revenue and then distributed the income among its stockholders. In exchange for signing a lease and sublease with CCB, proprietors and managers of brick firms obtained the right to purchase a limited number of shares of CCB at a price of $25 apiece. The brickmakers fixed the percentage of CCB each manager could own according to each firm's share of the brick business in 1897. The effect of this policy was to stabilize the hierarchy of brick firms. It discouraged small brickmakers from cutting prices to increase their business, but it guaranteed them profits from the aggregate earnings of the industry.

The shares paid massive dividends, which compensated for a firm's losses due to rent. For example, in November 1897, Peter F. Kaehler, the operator of Mayer & Towle Brick was given the opportunity to buy nine shares of CCB for $225 in exchange for signing the proper leases.

[48] The $1.50 rent represented nearly half of the total cost of brick during this period, a percentage brickmakers might reduce by increasing prices. One account claims that thirty-seven firms signed leases with Cook County Brick while another claims forty-four firms joined the pool. *The Book of Chicagoans*, 263; *Cook County Brick Co. v. Lebahn Brick Co.* 92 Ill. App. 526, 529 (1900).

After he signed the rental agreements, Mayer & Towle began losing money. With the company's output restricted and its profits diverted to pay rent on its own property, Mayer & Towle lost at least $1,850 during Kaehler's tenure. But Kaehler personally earned $1012.50 in dividends from his CCB stock. And when CCB decided to buy him out, the courts forced the firm to pay him $6,000 for his stock. Thus, on a $225 investment, he made over $7,000 dollars.[49]

The combination of pools and agreements spread rapidly from the common brick market to other sectors of the building-material business. In late 1898 and early 1899, Martin Barnaby Madden, the president of the Western Cut Stone Company, and Spencer Smalley Kimbell, the president of the Chicago Hydraulic Press Brick Company, invited the largest pressed brick manufacturers to the Chamber of Commerce Building for a series of meetings. Kimbell informed the seven of his peers, representing the Chicago Hydraulic Press, Cayuga, Thomas Moulding, Charles Bonner, Union Pressed, Jenkins & Reynolds, and Kulage, that the Chicago Masons and Builders' Association had offered to help regulate the pressed brick market in exchange for between $2 and $6 per thousand bricks sold.

Some brickmakers opposed the scheme. Though the association offered Martin Emerich's Union Pressed Brick Company 12 percent of the pool, Emerich refused to sign the agreement. He claimed that he favored competition and doubted the prospects for solidarity, commenting:

> The entire talk at this meeting, both on the part of Mr. Kimbell and the others present, was on the assumption that all the pressed brick dealers in Chicago were to be treated alike, and were to act harmoniously; but it seemed very doubtful from the talk of those present, whether Mr. Kimbell's suggestions would ever be approved by all the pressed brick dealers in Chicago.[50]

In April that year, four of the seven firms – Chicago Hydraulic Press, Cayuga, Thomas Moulding, and Charles Bonner – agreed to establish a "Pressed Brick Association." On May 9th, they enacted "Pressed Brick

---

[49] *Jarrett, Admr. for Peter Kaehler v. Johnson*, 216 Ill. 212 (1905).

[50] Affidavit of Martin Emerich, July 15, 1899, *Union Pressed Brick v. Chicago Hydraulic Pressed Brick*, case #196935, Circ.C.C. (1899), 4. Politics affected Emerich's defection. In 1902, Emerich, a Democrat, later defeated Madden in his bid for the U.S. House of Representatives. "Col. Martin Emerich, Newly Elected Congressman from First Illinois District," *CRH*, November 6, 1902, 2; L. Ethan Ellis, "Martin Barnaby Madden," *Dictionary of American Biography*, v. 12 (Scribners, 1933), 180–81.

Rules," raising the price of brick $3 per thousand and defining "acceptable" manufacturers. Finally, they adopted a simplified pool that divvied up the accumulated funds according to a fixed percentage and disbursed one third of the money to the CMB.[51]

Emerich's Union Pressed Brick Co. experienced an immediate and massive decline in sales after the establishment of the agreement.[52] Contractors made deals with Union only to renege when they realized the situation. Charles Schleyer, a member of the CMB, paid $140 to Emerich for 10,000 bricks. Thirty minutes later, Schleyer returned and informed Emerich the CMB had forbidden his material. Schleyer then purchased "legitimate" brick from the Thomas Moulding Company for $20 more. The material Moulding sold Schleyer was identical to the banned brick, for Moulding had bought it from Emerich only a short time before the rules went into effect. Success depended upon membership alone, not upon the quality or the origin of the merchandise.[53]

[51] As with the Cook County Brick Company, the pressed brick pool discouraged low bids and firmly established the hierarchy of firms. Affidavit of Martin Emerich, July 15, 1899, *Union Pressed Brick v. Chicago Hydraulic Pressed Brick*, case #196935, Circ.C.C. (1899); Bill of Complaint, June 30, 1899, *Union Pressed Brick v. Chicago Hydraulic Pressed Brick*, case #196935, Circ.C.C. (1899); Information in Nature of Quo Warranto, July 11, 1901, *People ex rel Emerich v. Chicago Masons*, case #219410, Circ.C.C. (1901); IC, *Reports*, v. 8, 91, 168, 220, 229, 236, 277.

[52] In April and early May, Union Pressed Brick sold 1,150,000 bricks. After May 9, the pressed brick rules took effect. In the next three weeks, UPB sold only 17,200 bricks. In June, their sales dropped below 9,000 units. Other firms suffered similar downfalls. W. G. Beyerly, the General manager of the Jenkins and Reynolds Brick Company, refused to join PBA. In the following two months, Jenkins and Reynolds sales dropped more than 90 percent. Affidavit of W. G. Beyerly, July 15, 1899, *Union Pressed Brick v. Chicago Hydraulic Pressed Brick*, case #196935, Circ.C.C. (1899); Bill of Complaint, June 30, 1899, *Union Pressed Brick v. Chicago Hydraulic Pressed Brick*, case #196935, Circ.C.C. (1899); Affidavit of Martin Emerich, July 15, 1899, *Union Pressed Brick v. Chicago Hydraulic Pressed Brick*, case #196935, Circ.C.C. (1899).

[53] On May 9, 1899, CMB member E. W. Sproul entered Emerich's office seeking to purchase brick. When the manufacturer admitted he did not belong to the PBA, Sproul declined to purchase any material, fearing a $500 fine. Affidavit of Martin Emerich, *Union Pressed Brick v. Chicago Hydraulic Pressed Brick*, July 15, 1899, case #196935, Circ.C.C. (1899); Information in Nature of Quo Warranto, November 7, 1901, *People ex rel Emerich v. Chicago Masons*, case #219410, Circ.C.C. (1901).

Working Together

Though their interests diverged with regard to wages, unions and associations often operated in tandem. They shared a common faith in their own right to determine legitimate firms, enforce prices favorable to their members, and freeze social hierarchies. Collective bargaining became a tool for the joint control of competition, all the more powerful for harnessing the growing strength and legitimacy of labor unions in the city. When major work stoppages did cripple construction, teaming, and other trades, the instigators of these disputes were often ambitious corporations within these trades and elite merchants and manufacturers in other industries, seeking to promote a hierarchical corporate form of commerce in the city.[54]

Trade agreements often lay upon a foundation of friendship and familiarity. John Mangan, the president of the International Association of Steam-fitters, commented on the debt he felt toward his employers and their association:

> After our first agreement of October 1892, we met at regular intervals with our employers and as time wore on wages and working conditions were improving and our relations with our employers getting better, and even though slight differences appeared on the surface at times, still to the credit of both sides be it said those outside the conference never heard of any disputes or differences and I feel that the harmonious feeling prevailing can be attributed largely to the fairness of our contractors, and I may further say that while we were making steady and reliable progress and proud of it we were equally proud of the advancement of the Master Steam-fitters, and I may express the hope that the present pleasant relations may long continue as I feel they will.[55]

In toasting his rivals, Mangan exaggerated the tenderness of their relationship. Journeymen and masters quarreled – sometimes violently – at the end of every contract. Yet his statement suggests that they hardly saw their interests as contradictory or necessarily antagonistic.

[54] For the possibility of comity between small employers and workers, see Johnston, *The Radical Middle Class*, 76–8; Herbert Gutman, "Class, Status, and Community Power in Nineteenth-Century American Industrial Cities," *Work, Culture, and Society in Industrializing America: Essays in American Working-Class and Social History* (New York: Random House, 1977), 234–60.

[55] Mangan also noted that: "after a lapse of forty years[,] friendly relations are still in existence between our fair minded employers and our Association." Mangan, *History of the Steam Fitters*, 24, 38.

Craft employers also asserted the need for harmonious relations. In 1910, the *Chicago Team Owners Journal* remembered "the old time teamster" and waxed nostalgic about the period before a heated 1905 strike had soured relations between drivers and the larger employers such as the department stores:

> Why they thought as much of the stock they drove as if they were members of their own family, and the team owner felt the same towards the teamster. If he were sick or laid up he got his envelope paid the same, by jove! as if he worked, and the relations of the employer and employee were ideal. It was a happy family, and the horses were included.

Comparing workers to livestock, employers hardly proposed social levelling. Nor were their emotions necessarily honest; they invoked their kinship to dissuade workers from demanding higher wages. But the patriarchal model was evocative in the craft economy where the family firm remained a fixture, where workers routinely became bosses and hired their own relatives. Craft unionists did not ridicule the domestic analogy. Bartenders' Union official William C. Pomeroy saw the family was the natural model for social relations, and his expression of this notion made him an effective organizer into the 1890s. In his dystopian novel, *The Lords of Misrule*, Pomeroy portrayed a world passing through capitalism into socialist tyranny and finally into a society based upon brotherhood and Christian charity. But while employers emphasized their own parental generosity, Pomeroy accused bosses of failing to live up to their filial obligations.[56]

The institutional manifestation of these aspirations was the "exclusive agreement." The brick trade again furnishes a case in point. The United Order of American Bricklayers Local #2, also known as the Bricklayers and Masons International Union Local #21 (BMIU), enforced rules regarding the "legitimacy" of prices, contractors, and material. Union bricklayers would not work for contractors outside of the Chicago Masons and Builders Association (CMB). Those who violated the "brick rules" not only lost their lucrative rebates from the pool, but also suffered work stoppages on unfinished projects and a radical labor shortage on any new contracts. On March 27, 1900, George P. Gubbins, the president of BMIU Local #21 testified before

[56] "The Object of the Parade for Owners and Drivers," *Chicago Team Owners' Journal*, Special Edition, May 1910, 2; William C. Pomeroy, *The Lords of Misrule: A Tale of Gods and Men* (Chicago: Laird & Lee, 1894), 17–9; William T. Stead, *Chicago To-Day, of the Labor War in America* (London: Review of Reviews, 1894), 127–38.

the Industrial Commission of the United States that his union had pressured ninety contractors into joining the CMB.

The CMB looked to the BMIU for rough enforcement of their rule. In his testimony, Gubbins noted that builders "even went so far as to try to hire laboring men to put some of these independent contractors in the hospital." When pressed by a commissioner as to what he meant, Gubbins replied "Breaking their legs and arms, something of that kind . . . assaulting them – putting them out of business when they could not put them out through the material men." Gubbins claimed that he had refused this request, but, in 1921, a business agent remembered the ways of his youth:

> If there was a building to be put up, if it was not put up, and the man did not belong to the bosses' association, that building did not go up. If it did go up, it cost the contractor from one to two dollars more a thousand for brick . . . there was a delegate for the bricklayers' union and the stonecutters and the carpenters and the plumbers and we met at the bosses association. Twenty to fifty dollars apiece was handed out and divided four ways . . . and we went out to the building and pulled off the labor and if necessary put someone out the second story window into a sand pile. The bosses financed that and organized it with the unions.[57]

In a real sense, then, the bricklayers enforced the rule of the master masons. In return, they received money and help governing their own jurisdiction.

The compliance of the bricklayers and hod carriers also strengthened the rules governing building material. George Hinchliff, for example, was a mason contractor and a member of the CMB. Around 1892, he decided to move into the brick manufacturing business, building a plant in Hobart, Indiana. In 1898, the exclusive agreements went into effect, and Hinchliff asked a committee of manufacturers and contractors if he might join the BMA. Rather than welcoming Hinchliff, they asked him "to sell no more brick in the city of Chicago or Evanston." In disbelief, Hinchliff asked if there had been an error. But the chair answered, "there is no mistake on my part." Hinchliff demanded the brickmaker "Go right back in there and tell them they are a bigger lot of fools than I thought they were, and I make a

---

[57] IC, *Reports*, v. 8, 220; Montgomery, *Industrial Relations*, 189. For a similar agreement in other trades, see *Allen v. Chicago Undertakers' Association*, 232 Ill. 458 (1908); "The Happy Family," *Chicago Team Owners' Journal*, Special Edition, May 1910, 2.

similar request of them." Hinchliff's bravado, however, was misplaced. He found that his brick had become "absolutely worthless.... The workmen all belonged to the union, practically, and the hod carriers would not handle them or the bricklayers wouldn't lay them."[58]

The bricklayers' local president, George Gubbins, confirmed these practices before the U.S. Industrial Commission of 1900. He described an incident where contractors named Burns and Thorheimer ordered 4.5 million bricks from the Davis, Snyder, Whittaker Company. When the union bricklayers refused to handle the material, the contractors reneged on the deal costing the manufacturer thousands of dollars. Gubbins later summarized the union's role in governing the market: "They [the CMB] used us as a whip."

Building tradesmen also used their power to further their own agenda, demanding union-made building material. In 1897, as agreements restricting the use of brick and stone fell into place, a new Building Materials Trades Council began organizing material-manufacturing workers. Assisting this new organization, the bricklayers' union and the Building Trades Council also demanded material manufactured along certain specifications and from defined locations. Since Chicago was a "union town," while nearby towns remained unorganized, provincialism and unionism worked in tandem.[59]

As agreements tightened, unionism, associationalism, and localism became as one. In March 1899, when E. W. Sproul bought common brick from Evanston Brick Company, an association member. "When the brick came on the ground I was informed by the laborers that they wouldn't touch them," Sproul noted, "they were from outside the union, and the union label was not on them." Unhappily, Sproul canceled his order and bought brick from Purington Brick Co., one of the organizers of the exclusive agreement. Angry at having to purchase smaller and more expensive brick, Sproul protested to the president of the bricklayers, who responded, "It's an outrage, but my hands are tied in the matter." Despite appearances, the union likely enforced the prohibition against Evanston Brick on behalf of the manufacturers' association. The owners of Evanston Brick, the Lebahn family, had

---

[58] *Purington v. Hinchliff*, 120 Ill. App. 523, 528–29 (1905); *Purington v. Hinchliff*, 219 Ill. 159, 166 (1905).

[59] Though admitting the bricklayers' union had an agreement with the builders, Gubbins denied the direct role in enforcing the brick rules. Like virtually all of the witnesses, Gubbins contradicted himself to avoid the appearance of illegality. IC, *Reports*, v. 8, 235, 236, 515–6; Wolman, *The Boycott*, 69.

Charles Gilhooley was one of Chicago's first "professional sluggers." The Amalgamated Woodworkers' Union and the Carriage and Wagon Workers' Union allegedly paid him and his colleagues a fee for every replacement worker they assaulted. Gilhooley's career ended when one of his victims, nonunionist Christ Carlstrom, died of pneumonia following a beating. Courtesy of Chicago Historical Society (DN-003036).

refused to contract with Cook County Brick, thus alienating themselves from the association and the union.[60]

Collective bargaining itself became a method of exercising market control. Unions and associations allied themselves on boards of arbitration, new organizations empowered to enforce price and wage standards through fines. In 1903, Eli Rysdon decided to buck the Sheet Metal Contractors Association. When Rysdon underbid the favored firm to obtain the Rock Island Depot contract, the arbitration committee fined him $3,000. When Rysdon refused to pay, the association suspended him, his union employees stopped working, and the Building Trades Council placed him on their "unfair list." This boycott

---

[60] The bricklayers' union president eventually settled the matter, allowing Sproul to complete the job. By contrast, the Lebahns needed go to court for satisfaction. IC, *Reports*, v. 8, 480–82, 226; "Brick Deal Is Illegal," *CDT*, December 21, 1900, 13; Affidavit of Martin Emerich, July 11, 1901, *People ex rel Emerich v. Chicago Masons and Builders Association*, case #219410, Circ.C.C. (1901), 6.

reduced Rysdon's business to one contract and "a little repair work," forcing him to approach the State's Attorney for help.[61]

Violence and State Power

Violence sustained craft governance and permeated the overlapping realms of politics, business, labor, and the underworld. Labor assaults were often indistinguishable from other forms of coercion. In 1906, three men attacked urban reformer Raymond Robins. Newspapers attributed the crime to Edward Carroll, a candidate for alderman of the thirty-second ward and a former president of the Building Trades Council. The grand jury rapidly indicted unionists William Flannery and John Kane, as well as James Carroll, Edward's saloonkeeper brother. The interaction of politics, economic interest, and an intensely physical associational culture led to Robins' slugging.[62]

The Ragen brothers were the ultimate products of this environment. Raised in the "Back of the Yards" district south of the city's meatpacking

---

[61] The sheet-metal contractors also controlled bidding. When a builder announced a job, sheet-metal contractors first gave their estimates to the association, which decided which firm would receive the contract. The businessmen than reframed the bids so that a favored contractor entered the lowest bid at 15 to 100 percent above the actual cost and then paid half his profits back to the association for distribution among its members. "Indictments for Nineteen Contractors," *CDT*, October 4, 1903, 4; "Pool Secrets Bared," *CRH*, October 3, 1903, 9; "Expose Pools to Grand Jury," *CDT*, October 3, 1903, 7; "Unions With Slocum," *CRH*, May 5, 1903, 3; True Bill, October 3, 1903, *People v. Miller*, case #70799, Crim.C.C., IR 134, 104–9. A similar arbitration agreement existed in iron construction. See "Metz Loses Election," *CRH*, July 30, 1910, 2.

[62] "Claims to Have Clew to Robins' Thugs," *CRH*, February 19, 1906, 4; "Robins' Assault Bills In," *CRH*, March 29, 1906, 9. Assigning perpetrator and motive to violent acts was an explicitly political act. In 1910, the state tried union representative Vincent Altman for bombing a telephone exchange. Altman successfully argued that a clique of politically connected gamblers had committed the crime. "Bomb Case Brings Defense's Promise of Police Upheaval," *CRH*, January 17, 1910, 1; "Jury Has Bomb case," *CRH*, January 22, 1910, 16; "Jury Acquits Altman," *CRH*, January 23, 1910, 2. In 1912, a bomb exploded in the store of Antone Morici, an importer of Italian products. Morici blamed the bakers union, but police charged a "Black Hand" gang of extortionists. "Lays Blast to Labor War," *CRH*, May 16, 1912, 3. Both Altman and the Moricis died violently, and their deaths inspired similar debates. "Special Grand Jury for Labor Sluggers," *CRH*, August 6, 1911, 1; Harrison, *Growing Up With Chicago*, 174–76; "Two Millionaires Shot in Murder Fund War," *CDT*, January 28, 1926, 1.

facilities, James Ragen hired out his fists and guns to unions and anyone else who would pay him. Violent incidents punctuated his life. In
1906, James and four other men allegedly assaulted Dominick Monack,
Jacob Greenbaum, and Harry Wheeler. In 1908, the state indicted him
for murdering a "pugilist" named Richard Thors. In 1911, allegedly,
the United Association of Plumbers hired Ragen to shoot John Ramier,
a member of the rival International Association of Steam-fitters. In
1946, James was himself murdered by gamblers seeking control over
his lucrative horseracing wire service business.[63]

For brother Frank Ragen, fighting was both the logical conclusion
to any argument and a valuable source of political power. In 1912,
Ragen served on the Cook County Board of Commissioners, the body
charged with spending millions in public revenue. In a budget dispute,
Frank physically attacked fellow commissioner Joseph Mendel. Frank
also drew his political strength from a South Side athletic and political club called "Ragen's Colts." Taking the motto, "Hit me and you
hit two thousand," the Colts intimidated voters annually on Election
Day, African Americans during the Race Riot of 1919, and even British
Prime Minister David Lloyd George upon his 1923 visit to Chicago.
In that same year, 100 Colts allegedly travelled to Oklahoma to assist the Governor in his war on the Ku Klux Klan. Long after the decline of his political club, Ragen's supporters celebrated their leader's
athletic prowess, physical fitness, cruel sense of humor, and fighting
ability.[64]

Men like these came to power repeatedly in unions, associations,
and parties. Though some held power through brute force, craft attitudes towards violence, strength, and virility also gave these men a base
of support. Luke Grant, a journalist and former carpenter close to the

[63] True Bills, March 29, 1906, *People v. Eisenlord,* cases #80445, 80446, 80447,
Crim.C.C., IR 149, 47–9; "Shooting Case to Jury," *CRH,* July 10, 1908, 11;
"Special Grand Jury for Labor Sluggers," *CRH,* August 6, 1911, 1; "Ragen
Case Dismissed," *CRH,* June 29, 1912, 9; Death Notice, "James M. Ragen,"
CDT, August 17, 1946, 18; "Ragen Inquest Continued; Set Funeral Rights,"
CDT, August 16, 1946, 14.

[64] William M. Tuttle, Jr., *Race Riot: Chicago in the Red Summer of 1919* (New
York: Atheneum, 1970), 32–3, 54–5, 199; John Landesco, *Organized Crime
in Chicago: Part III of the Chicago Crime Survey, 1929* (Chicago: University
of Chicago Press, 1968), 99, 169–75, 240; "Join in Fist Fight Over Budget,"
CRH, January 27, 1912, 1; "Lloyd George Ill, but Rallies in Time for Chicago
Speech," *NYT,* October 18, 1923, 1; "100 'Ragen's Colts' to Aid of Gov.
Watton," *Port Arthur News,* October 3, 1923, 10; John Landesco, "Interview
with John Shields, August 23, 1927," 1, 8 in Burgess Papers, Box 34, Folder
9.

labor movement, told Hutchins Hapgood that he preferred the leadership of "Skinny" Madden, a brutal building tradesman, to that of Charles Dold, a mild-mannered socialist cigarmaker. Grant thought Dold a coward but credited Madden with physical courage, thus qualifying him for union office. When Madden's allies slugged Grant for writing unflattering columns about them, he replied not by condemning violence, but by sarcastically vowing to "uplift" the perpetrators.[65]

These attitudes toward violence extended to craft employers, who also used force to establish their rule. In drycleaning, plant owners enforced price agreements through assault and property destruction. In one case, the trade association hired men to attack the drivers of a plant owner who had left the organization. To repel such interference, he hired "sluggers" of his own. In another case, the association disciplined a member who switched to a renegade plant owner by throwing a brick through his shop window. For this rough work, employers often hired unionists who had a stake in the results.[66]

The craftsmen's brutality expressed a particular conception of political economy rooted in Chicago's violent culture. The city's wealthy businessmen also exalted pugnacity as manly, and the bourgeoisie generally supported anyone who bullied union workers. But unlike corporate executives, who fought in defense of private property, craft producers asserted their physical authority to determine who might buy, sell, and work in the city. Within certain spheres, craftsmen saw their organizations as governments, entitled to all the state's prerogatives, including the legitimate use of force. Chicagoans brawled and bombed during the early twentieth century, not because their lives were wild and chaotic, but because they struggled to rule the economy and to shape its future. Contrary to common assumption, violence derived from order rather than disorder.[67]

[65] Hutchins Hapgood, *The Spirit of Labor* (New York: Duffield, 1907), 296–97; Ernest Poole, "The Widening Sense of Honor," *Outlook* 84 (December 1, 1906): 820.

[66] Morrison Handsaker, "The Chicago Cleaning and Dyeing Industry: A Study in Controlled Competition" (Ph.D. diss., University of Chicago, 1939), 106–12; Testimony before the Dailey Commission, March 25, 1921 in Montgomery, *Industrial Relations*, 189.

[67] Philip Taft and Philip Ross, "American Labor Violence: Its Causes, Character, and Outcome," in Hugh Davis Graham and Ted Robert Gurr, eds., *Violence in America: Historical and Comparative Perspectives*, v. 1 (1969), 221–301; Louis Adamic's *Dynamite: The Story of Class Violence in America* (Gloucester, MA: Peter Smith, 1963); H. M. Gitelman, "Perspectives on American Industrial Violence," *Business History Review* 47:1 (Spring 1973): 1; Stephen

The professionalization of the "slugger" – a man hired to assault strikebreakers – illustrates the role of violence in ordering the craft economy. At first, many sluggers were amateurs from the rank and file. In 1903, Albert Fridley testified that he joined the Brass Molders Union and picketed the Western Electric and Stromberg–Carlson plants. The business agent, Jacob Johnson, offered Fridley $25 for each replacement worker he incapacitated; he accepted. Fridley's crew assaulted three men with billy club and revolver, although not forcefully enough to prevent them from working, and Johnson paid them only $25.

Unions quickly began hiring powerfully built specialists, expert in physical conflict, who knew how to fight, shoot, and burn. In 1905, Charles Gilhooley, Marcus Looney, and Edward Feeley declared themselves a "professional slugging committee" available for hire. Until the state imprisoned them for killing a nonunion worker, they plied their trade for both the Amalgamated Woodworkers and the Carriage & Wagon Workers Local #4. Other men dedicated themselves to the protection of particular unions and officials. In August 1905, Martin Murphy, the bartender for "the Kentucky Home," a brothel catering to labor leaders, criticized building trades' official "Skinny" Madden within earshot of James "Heine" Christiansen, Madden's bodyguard. Christiansen attacked Murphy, only to be shot by the bartender's brother Michael. "Heine" survived and remained Madden's close lieutenant.[68]

Unions hired men like Christiansen, Fridley, and Gilhooley both to obtain agreements and to enforce those contracts. Manufacturing lockouts inspired the most serious violence, as union pickets waited for replacement workers to pass the factory gates, while police, detectives, and strikebreakers stood ready to break up picket lines. To avoid this, union members followed replacements home, assaulting them where the employer could not protect them. In 1904, Percy Ford decided to defy a strike against Richman Brothers Cigars. One day, two cigar makers followed Ford and threatened to "disable him." Another Richman employee, Charles Tyler, charged that union men had offered him $25 to quit. When he refused, they promised to "hurt him at their hands," and to brand him "a scab all over the United States . . . .

Norwood, *Strikebreakers and Intimidation: Mercenaries and Masculinity in Twentieth Century America* (Chapel Hill, University of North Carolina Press, 2002).
[68] "Beat Workman for $25," *CDT*, January 14, 1903, 1; *Shields v. People*, 132 Ill. App. 109, 119 (1907); True Bill, *People v. Gilhooley* case #77030 Crim.C.C., IR 134, 217–18 (1905); "Labor Shooting is Traced to the 'Kentucky Home,'" *CDT*, August 25, 1905, 5.

so that he would be unable to obtain employment from any other manufacturer."[69]

More commonly, business agents used the threat of violence to maintain trade standards among craftsmen. John Has, a nonunion painter working for contractor John Stiles, testified that a union man had approached him on December 17, 1902 and told him: "If you keep your mouth shut, I'll give you a pointer. You fellows better get out of here, there is a lot of sluggars[*sic*] coming in to the building today to do you up. If you don't get away you will be killed." Has neither quit, nor was beaten. Instead, the business agent, Joseph Roach, told two policemen that Has had threatened him with a pistol. The officers then arrested Has and two other nonunion employees.[70]

Craft unions systematically attacked the property of disobedient businessmen. In 1902, Electrical Workers Local #134 allegedly hired John Gallagher to destroy "800 feet of electric wire, 100 insulators, bells, speaking tubes, and fixtures" belonging to Lakeside Electrical Construction Co. In 1903, striking employees of the Chicago City Railway Company threw clubs, stones, and bricks at the windows passing streetcars. And nonunion painting contractor John Stiles repeatedly charged that unionists destroyed his materials. Such harassment pressured employers to accept the union's terms while also eliminating their ability to continue operations on a nonunion basis.[71]

Perhaps nothing better illustrates the instrumental quality of craft violence than the internal efforts at controlling it. In 1904, the members of Carriage and Wagon Workers Local #2 walked out on their employer,

---

[69] Affidavits from Percy Ford and Charles Taylor, July 15, 1904, *Chicago Cigar Manufacturers Association v. Cigar Makers International Union*, case #238016, Sup.C.C. (1904). "Nonunion Man Beaten By Hired Sluggers," *CRH*, November 17, 1904, 4; "Nonunion Worker Slugged," *CDT*, November 17, 1904, 7; Bill, February 10, 1900, *Bent v. Piano and Organ Workers*, case #204497, Sup.C.C. (1900), 4, 6, 7, 9; True Bill, June 29, 1900, *People v. Dold*, case #59120, Crim.C.C., IR 133, 6–11; Bill of Complaint, September 25, 1903, *Piano and Organ Supply Company v. Piano and Organ Workers*, case #232465, Sup.C.C. (1903), 13, 16, 18; *Piano and Organ Supply Company v. Piano and Organ Workers*, 124 Ill. App. 353 (1904). Picket-line violence crossed the gender divide. See "Shake Off Union Nemesis," *CDT*, September 10, 1903, 4.

[70] Affidavit of John Has, *Stiles v. Brotherhood of Painters*, case #232122, Sup.C.C. (1903), 2.

[71] "Court Clerk Bribed," *CRH*, April 22, 1903, 2; True Bill, December 24, 1904, *People v. Conn*, Case #71812, Crim.C.C., IR 135, 135; True Bill, January 20, 1904, *People v. Foster*, case #71884, Crim.C.C., IR 135, 142; Amended Petition, February 27, 1903, *Builders Painting & Decorating Co. v. Advisory Board Building Trades*, Supp.C.C., case #227537 (1903).

the H. McFarlane Company. Caught up in the situation, David Bergquist, a unionist, assaulted Harry Stevens, a replacement hired by McFarlane. The police could not find him, but the union could. Local #2 disciplined Bergquist, fining him twenty dollars and remanding him to the police court, which released him on bond. The next year, the union reversed course. In January 1905, the 106 manufacturers locked out 1,400 unionists after they demanded a closed shop. The leadership decided to impede nonunion workers as they entered the factories. But when officials saw court costs bankrupt the union, they made contact with Gilhooley, Looney, and Feeley, "sluggers" who had assisted the woodworkers in a previous dispute. These professionals promised to "lick" eight men for $50. The executive board paid the three men a $2 retainer, and agreed to give them the remainder after completing the job.[72]

Such tactics were often quite effective. In September 1903, as janitor Marinius Hagen cleaned the first floor of the Home Insurance Building, five men came in the door. One asked him, "Where is your union card?" Hagen answered that he did not belong to the union. The man replied, "Why don't you?" and the five unionists attacked Hagen, knocking out two teeth and bruising his head. Only two weeks before, Hagen's coworker, Charles Johnson, had suffered a similar beating. Though nonunion janitor Martin Thorsen defiantly proclaimed that, "that sort of thing will not induce us to join the organization," other workers did submit. By the next year, the flat janitors' union had five locals, 3,000 members, and agreements with the rental agents and the real estate board.[73]

Just as importantly, through violence, craft producers asserted their governmental authority. Market pressures themselves did not require brutal responses; craft organizations had many alternatives. Through beatings and bombings, however, craft producers placed their associations on a par with the state itself, challenging its presumed monopoly on violence. In October 1904, W. J. Newman, an excavating contractor, angered the teamsters by hiring members of another union to haul material. In apparent reprisal, an unknown assailant attacked Newman with a wagon spoke, giving him a fractured skull. Newman called the

[72] "Union Fines Slugger," *CRH*, April 22, 1904, 4; "Lockout Hurts 1,400," *CRH*, January 25, 1905, 10; *Shields v. People*, 132 Ill. App. 109 (1907).
[73] "Janitor Badly Beaten for Not Joining Union," *CDT*, September 9, 1903, 7; *Lakeside Directory*, 1902, 841; "William Feather, the First Business Agent of a Chicago Union Who Ever Resigned," *CRH*, January 30, 1904, 3; True Bills, December 3, 1904, *People v. Olson*, case #s 75529–75530, Crim.C.C., IR 134, 176 (1904).

police, who brought suspects in for identification. Angered by the contractor's appeal to the law, a teamster named Larson proclaimed: "I'll show you the police force is no stronger than the union."[74]

Such episodes illustrate the craftsmen's challenge to the corporate transformation of American capitalism. Hardly a tame petit bourgeoisie, these skilled workers, shopkeepers, and contractors organized, enacted rules, and enforced them as laws, they asserted the publicity of economic activity, made themselves arbiters of legitimate commerce, and even threatened to exercise power over manufacturing. Their efforts signified not contractualism or business unionism but rather a broad claim to authority. Their governance created a city within the city, immodern and illiberal, existing in defiance of the Midwest's wealthiest businessmen. During the coming decades, Chicago's business elite dedicated substantial energy to breaking up craft governance and reestablishing an economic order governed by private property and the market. For this reason, the primary context for Progressive-era political economy was not the protest of industrial workers, but rather the conflict over craft rule.

[74] "Man Slugged; Police Defied," *CDT*, October 24, 1903, 3.

The battles over Chicago's economic future were among the most brutal in the history of the United States. Teamsters, for example, often denied the policemen's authority over the streets, leading to violent clashes and hundreds of casualties like the one shown above (from a 1902 strike). These confrontations attracted crowds of onlookers, many of them supporting the craftsmen. Courtesy of Chicago Historical Society (DN-000515).

3

The Struggle for Order

As economic development knitted the diverse regions of the United States into a new American nation, the consequences of modernization divided Chicago. Intense protests and counterprotests pummeled the city, costing residents millions of dollars, filling jails, leaving hundreds injured, and killing at least twenty-five. Between 1902 and 1904, a series of successful walkouts more than doubled the number of union members. Over 77,000 workers participated in ninety-two strikes in the first nine months of the year 1904. Waiters, chefs, launderers, and janitors, as well as employees of not-yet-public utilities like the streetcars and the gas works, dropped their tools. Workers producing meat, bicycles, apparel, printing, switchboards, carriages, pianos, bread, candy, and furniture fought for union recognition, shorter hours, and higher wages. Businesses continued operation, engaging hundreds of private detectives and more than 1,000 policemen to stop pickets from damaging property, threatening replacement workers, and impeding the flow of commerce.[1]

This wave of unrest captured the public imagination, providing the impetus for popular realist novels like Upton Sinclair's *The Jungle* (1906) and Arthur Jerome Eddy's *Ganton & Co.* (1908). This burst still intrigues historians, whose interpretations loosely parallel

[1] "Prosperity of Labor," *CRH*, May 1, 1903, 9; Montgomery, *Fall of the House of Labor*, 269–75; "Close Shops to Tailors," *CDT*, January 17, 1903, 1; "Car Men Have Voted," *CDN*, February 17, 1903, 2; "Avoid Bread Famine," *CRH*, May 2, 1903, 9; "Chinese Flocking In," *CRH*, May 6, 1903, 3; "Peace in Gas Strike," *CRH*, May 27, 1903, 3; "Almost Strike in Freight Sheds," *CDT*, May 28, 1903, 3; "Strike in Hotels and Restaurants," *CRH*, June 5, 1903, 1; "Shake off Union Nemesis," *CDT*, September 10, 1903, 4; "Hit Foes of Union," *CRH*, October 3, 1903, 9; Harold Barton Myers, "The Policing of Labor Disputes in Chicago: A Case Study" (Ph.D. diss., University of Chicago, 1929); Barrett, *Work and Community in the Jungle*, 176–77.

these two contemporary fictional descriptions. Some scholars, following Sinclair, portray industrial labor as struggling with corporate capital for survival, dignity, and control over production. Others, mirroring Eddy, describe educated liberal executives battling twin enemies: insurgent unionism and Gilded-age individualism. Though scholars disagree about the character and values of the business community, they concur that factory workers and employers fought over issues such as union representation, higher wages, shorter hours, and improved work conditions.[2]

In fact, the fiercest bouts pitted craftsmen against corporations with control over the city as the prize. In confrontations like the Building Trades Lockout of 1900 and the Teamsters' Strike of 1905, merchants, financiers, and manufacturers challenged the tradesmen's self-proclaimed jurisdictions. Chicago's wealthiest citizens staged "open shop drives" to dislodge the institutions blocking the city's future as a modern hub of a national corporate economy. Hoping to regain their authority over the market, reforge bourgeois solidarity, and replace disgruntled workers with loyal subordinates, corporations pushed fellow employers to shun unionists, and to abandon trade agreements. For sure, industrial workers engaged in traditional class warfare in the packinghouses and elsewhere. But even in these strikes, skilled craft workers, teamsters, and small employers played an instrumental role.

Though corporations won most of the major disputes, the tradesmen proved extraordinarily determined. Corporations neither broke the craftsmen's belief in their own authority, nor significantly eroded public acceptance of labor unions. The battles themselves produced an uneasy alliance of corporations, disgruntled entrepreneurs, and nonunion workers, crucial to the campaigns of the following decades. Elite victories halted the expansion of craft governance into meatpacking, metal work, pianomaking, carriage production, and other forms of manufacturing. But the craftsmen's defeat encouraged their insularity and hardened their resistance to an untamed market.

[2] Upton Sinclair, *The Jungle* (New York: The New American Library, 1906); Arthur J. Eddy, *Ganton & Co.: A Story of Chicago Commercial and Social Life* (Chicago: McClurg, 1908). For two of the best examples, see David Montgomery, *The Fall of the House of Labor: The Workplace, the State, and American Labor Activism, 1865–1925* (New York: Cambridge University Press, 1989), 272–73; Daniel Ernst, *Lawyers Against Labor: From Individual Rights to Corporate Liberalism* (Chicago: University of Illinois Press, 1995), 11–2.

The Opposition

The city's elite profoundly resented the set of powerful exclusive organizations that regulated the craft economy, raising wages, eliminating competition, and inhibiting the use of machinery and unskilled labor. Trade agreements offended their faith in property rights and impeded their unfettered dominance. Manufacturers and merchants were often boosters who worried that construction rates, for example, chased capital from the city, discouraged growth, and depressed property values. In 1900, for instance, George Harding, Sr., a South Side landlord, nonunion developer, and Republican politician, told the United States Industrial Commission that trade agreements had raised building prices 100 percent. He charged that unions and association had "ruined" many real estate investors and done "a great injury to the city."[3]

Larger builders, often masons, carpenters, or iron contractors who hired smaller businesses to paint, roof, electrify, and plumb a building, suffered under the rules governing construction. If a single master broke faith with his workers, the BTC called everyone off the structure, sometimes suspending production for weeks. This forced general contractors, who were responsible to their financial backers, to police the agreements of their subcontractors. For example, Clark Construction fired John Stiles in 1903 not to stop the painters from picketing, but to prevent the BTC from halting all work on the Magnus Foundry.[4]

When trade agreements did not restrict corporations per se, they protected local companies against the development of a national market. For example, the organizers of the Pressed Brick Association (PBA) were all successful manufacturers with ties to the city's elite. But the PBA's chief opponent was Martin Emerich, the owner of the Union Pressed Brick Company and an outsider in many respects. A native of Baltimore, Emerich had moved to Chicago only in 1887, starting his brick business in 1896. He was a Jewish reformer among machine politicians. But most significantly, his Union Pressed Brick merely sold material produced by a foreign corporation, the Fultonham Brick Company of Ohio. The PBA offered Emerich membership,

---

[3] IC, *Reports*, v. 8, 164.

[4] *Builders' Painting and Decorating Company v. Advisory Board Building Trades of Chicago*, 116 Ill. App. 264 (1904); *Stiles v. Brotherhood of Painters*, case #231675, Sup.C.C. (1903); *Stiles v. Brotherhood of Painters*, case #232122, Sup.C.C. (1903).

but passed rules preventing him from capturing more than 12 percent of the market. And when he declined this share on principle,
they pushed contractors to boycott his business.[5]

As in construction, local teaming interests passed rules restricting
corporate control that engendered resentment among Chicago's commercial elite. On May 21, 1902, the Coal Teamsters' Union #4 and the
Coal Team Owners' Association signed an agreement stating that contractors would hire only union drivers, and that teamsters would work
only for association members. When journalist Ray Stannard Baker
asked union secretary Milton Booth whether any nonunion teamsters
worked in the city, Booth answered: "No, unless they are in the hospital." When Baker asked the equivalent question of John C. Driscoll,
the representative of the team owners, Driscoll responded "You'll have
to look for them [independents] with a spy glass."[6]

To the horror of the city's elite, these teaming organizations began
asserting authority over the broader economy, acting as evangelists
for craft culture. After his success in coal, Driscoll organized other
team owners and established an umbrella group, the Associated Board
of Teaming Interests, to deal with the unions. In 1902, the drivers
asked the department stores for a closed shop contract. The employers
refused, but eventually granted the workers an increase in wages. But
by 1903, even the city's wealthiest merchants obeyed the teamsters' will.
This fact was evident when famed department store, Marshall Field &
Co., began using natural gas, sold by People's Gas, Light and Coke, for
heat and power during the summer. In response, the teaming interests
demanded the retailer remove its gas fixtures. When the firm ignored
these demands, the coal interests denied them fuel during the cold
winter months. Not wanting to freeze his customers, Field grudgingly
ordered workmen to remove the gas heaters.

This alliance intervened in a wide range of outside labor disputes,
using their control over the streets to assist the union employees of a
number of powerful corporate concerns, including the gas trust, the

[5] Affidavit of Martin Emerich, July 15, 1899, *Union Pressed Brick v. Chicago
Hydraulic Pressed Brick*, case #196935, Circ.C.C. (1899), 4; "Col. Martin
Emerich, Newly Elected Congressman from First Illinois District," *CRH*,
November 6, 1902, 2.

[6] David Witwer, "Corruption and Reform in the Teamsters' Union, 1898 to
1991" (Ph.D. diss., Brown University, 1994), 21–7. See also Ernest Poole,
"How a Labor Machine Held Up Chicago, and How the Teamsters' Union
Smashed the Machine," *The World To-Day* 7:1 (July 1904): 900–1; Baker,
"Capital and Labor Hunt Together," 451–57; John Commons, "Types of
American Labor Organization – The Teamsters of Chicago," *Quarterly Jour-
nal of Economics* 19 (1905): 406–7.

meatpackers, the railroads, the streetcar companies, garment manufacturers, and telephone equipment firms. For example, H. Kohlsaat & Co. was an ambitious corporation in baking, a trade dominated by organized small proprietors. Founded by wealthy Republican reformer and newspaper publisher, Herman Kohlsaat, the firm operated a wholesale house, a chain of lunch counters, and number of restaurants. In May 1903, bakers, teamsters, and waiters boycotted Kohlsaat for replacing "colored" union waiters with white union waitresses. According to rumors, the dismissal of the black waiters was merely a pretext; the unions were actually punishing Kohlsaat for refusing to join the Master Bakers' Association of Chicago. Five weeks later, the teamsters returned to work, having failed to push the firm into the association or to obtain reinstatement for the black waiters. Kohlsaat's sweet victory had cost him $80,000 in lost revenue.[7]

Despite such defeats, the drivers and their employers consolidated their power, founding the Chicago Board of Arbitration (CBA) in 1903. Though a private organization, the CBA assumed jurisdiction over all local labor disputes, offering its mediation services to workers and employers in every industry. Lacking any legal authority to enforce its rulings, the CBA compelled obedience by denying transportation services to recalcitrant firms. For this reason, executives, many of them ardent believers in the unfettered market, viewed the CBA as the very epitome of illegitimate regulation.

The CBA targeted corporations hiring nonunion workers and employing new technologies, forcing them to conform to rules set within each trade. The S. J. McLeod Company was a nonunion steam fitting manufacturer and contractor, producing a line of special fittings needed for the power piping in public utilities. Working ten hours a day, earning less than the union wage of $4 per shift, McLeod's employees decided to join the Steam-fitters' Protective Association (SFPA). But when the union approached McLeod, he flew "off into a rage declaring them traitors and ordering our Business Manager to get out of the office." The SFPA called its members on strike, suspending contract work for the Commonwealth Edison Company and the Elevated Power Houses. The SFPA asked the CBA to mediate, but

---

[7] Commons, "Types of American Labor Organization," 406; Baker, "Capital and Labor Hunt Together," 455, 462; Poole, "How a Labor Machine Held Up Chicago," 898; George C. Sikes, "The Chicago Labor Troubles and their Settlement," *Outlook* 71 (June 14, 1902): 449–50; Luke Grant, "Rights and Wrongs of the Chicago Strike," *Public Opinion* 38:23 (June 10, 1905): 888; "Avoid Bread Famine," *CRH*, May 2, 1903, 9; "Chinese Flocking In," *CRH*, May 6, 1903, 3; "Strike at Postoffice," *CRH*, June 19, 1903, 5.

McLeod refused their interference. The utility was more flexible. De-nied labor, coal, material, and drinking water, Commonwealth Edison, one of the city's largest corporations, bowed to the will of organized craft producers and replaced McLeod with a "fair" contractor.[8]

Some corporations found a novel means of accommodating craft governance: bribery. Many contractors alleged that walking delegates demanded cash payments to settle strikes, while union officials claimed that prominent employers offered bribes to prevent enforcement of union rules. Fuller Construction, a $20 million firm owned by the Rockefellers and responsible for Chicago's largest skyscrapers, appar-ently adopted a policy of appeasing unions through wholesale payoffs. Allegations of graft swirled in various disputes between 1902 and 1905, with some accusing unionists of creating unrest for financial gain, and others contending that corporations paid officials like teamsters' pres-ident Al Young to sabotage their rivals.[9]

But while some executives suborned craft officials, most raged at the developing limits on their managerial prerogatives. At his death in 1906, department store magnate Marshall Field left an estate valued at approximately $140 million. Possessing vast tracts of land – Field al-legedly paid more in taxes than any other American – he could claim a legitimate proprietary interest in the city. He was accustomed to total dominance. It was thus with most of Chicago's elite, who had fore-stalled unions in the warehouses, department stores, packinghouses, and mills only to find the leniency of shopkeeps and contractors had given mere craftsmen the keys to the city.

Trade agreements bound the weak, as well as the strong, pushing many ordinary Chicagoans to identify with the corporate elite. Frus-trated by the limits on their enterprise, some independent trades-men formed a discontented rump within the larger craft commu-nity. Painter John Burgher, bricklayer James Gavin, bandleader Henry Doehne, and sheet metal manufacturer Eli Rysdon freely joined unions and associations, rebelling only when disciplined for violat-ing the rules. Contractor George Hinchliff rejected the protections of

---

[8] John Commons, "Types of American Labor Organization," 400–33 esp. 406–7; Ernest Poole, "How a Labor Machine Held Up Chicago," 898–901; Mangan, *History of the Steam-fitters Protective Association,* 56–8.

[9] IC, *Reports,* v. 8, 325–26, 218–19, 430, 462; Baker, "The Trust's New Tool – The Labor Boss," 38–40; Ernest Poole, "How a Labor Machine Held Up Chicago, and How the Teamsters Union Smashed the Machine," *The World To-Day* 7:1 (July 1904): 896–905; "Grand Jury Stirs Volcano of Graft; Both Sides are Hit," *CRH,* June 16, 1905, 1–2; *Thorne v. Young,* case #244976, Sup.C.C. (1905).

his trade association only after it blocked his ambition to move into manufacturing. Only a few businesspersons like painter John Stiles and brick manufacturer Martin Emerich objected to the idea of governance itself. And this principled dissent was also mildly hypocritical, for governance was the context that made hiring nonunion workers, lowering prices, and using out-of-state material profitable. Despite pressure from their peers, many of these individuals remained in business, earning reasonable returns. In 1930, Stiles still owned a painting business and lived in a modest $7,500 home (about $80,600, adjusted for inflation) in Chicago. Rysdon was even better off, operating a sheet metal firm and owning in a $40,000 house (about $430,000 today).[10]

Of course, craftsmen denied many workers the opportunity to decide for themselves, impeding African-Americans and women from competing in the Chicago market. Though the AFL expressedly forbade its constituent internationals from formally restricting the race of their members, many craft unions managed to retain an entirely white membership. Some overtly barred female members, alleging they possessed insufficient skill to warrant membership. For example, W. E. Klapetzky, the secretary-treasurer of the Journeymen Barbers' International Union, excluded the many female barbers who annually petitioned him for membership, joking that they ought to join the "Butchers' Union" or the "Shaving Teamsters' Union." Similarly, many white men identified women, immigrants, and black workers with the introduction of machinery and elimination of skilled labor.[11]

Contractors, shopkeepers, and master craftsmen often shared this hostility to black and female workers. American tile floor

[10] John Stiles household, 1930 U.S. census, Cook County, Illinois, population schedule, city of Chicago, enumeration district 353, supervisor's district 29, sheet 6B, dwelling 90, family 102, National Archives micropublication T626, roll 428; Eli Rydon household, 1930 U.S. census, Cook County, Illinois, population schedule, city of Chicago, enumeration district 641, supervisor's district 7, sheet 1A, dwelling 2, family 2, National Archives micropublication T626, roll 443.

[11] Oscar D. Hutton, Jr., "The Negro Worker and the Labor Unions in Chicago," M.A. thesis, University of Chicago, 1939, 25–37; Clyde W. Summers, "Admissions Policies of Labor Unions," *Quarterly Journal of Economics*, 61:1 (1946), 66–107 esp. 72, 77; Bureau of the Census, Special Reports, *Occupations at the Twelfth Census* (Washington, DC: Government Printing Office, 1904), 516–23; "Notes and Comments," *The Journeyman Barber* 1:2 (March 1905): 44; John Commons, "Restrictions by Trade Unions," *The Outlook* 84 (October 27, 1906): 472–73; Ava Baron, "An 'Other' Side to Gender Antagonism at Work: Men, Boys, and the Remasculinization of Printers' Work, 1830–1920," in *Work Engendered: Towards a New History of American Labor*, Ava Baron, ed. (Ithaca: Cornell University Press, 1991), 47–69.

manufacturers were reluctant to hire women, as European employers did. Frank L. Davis, a mosaic contractor, told the United States Industrial Commission of 1900 that he refused to employ women, even though he could pay them half as much. His employees had not forced this decision. Davis, a national contractor hostile to unions, publicized his discrimination to defend himself against those who questioned his fairness or proclaimed his factory a sweatshop. Similarly, a New York builder defended his reluctance to hire African-American workers on grounds of "plain efficiency" rather than "sentiment." Though the contractor did employ a few black craftsmen, he shared the white workers' assumptions about the skill and discipline of African-Americans. Race was hardly his only filter; he also preferred Italians to Russian Jews, calling them "stronger workers."[12]

Moreover, sexual and racial restrictions were neither universal nor unchanging. In 1908 journalist Ray Stannard Baker found African-Americans, "mostly mulattos," employed as carpenters, masons, and ironworkers. The flat janitors', hod carriers', and teamsters' unions admitted all types, and, as the Kohlsaat strike shows, sometimes defended black workers' employment. Demography and culture help explain this openness. Because African-Americans comprised only 2 percent of Chicago's population in 1900 and because women seldom sought access to male-dominated trades such as construction, walking delegates focused primarily on preventing employers from hiring white, male nonunionists. This emphasis continued until World War I, when blacks and women entered the local workforce in greater numbers.[13]

But the craftsmen's broader obsession with self-government encouraged them to institionalize their prejudices, resulting in rules restricting membership. For instance, steamfitters' official John Mangan argued that an open-admissions policy destroyed "the validity, tenacity and family of the trade union, and the unity and discipline therein." Mangan certainly rationalized his own biases, but he also enunciated the governmental basis for exclusivity. Unions like the steamfitters maintained their wage standards primarily through internal discipline,

[12] IC, *Reports*, v.8, 423–24; Ray Stannard Baker, *Following the Color Line: American Negro Citizenship in the Progressive Era* (New York: Harper Torchbook, 1964), 133–34. For a similar consensus in the Philadelphia metal industry, see Howell John Harris, *Bloodless Victories*, 19.

[13] Hutton, "The Negro Worker," 37–60; Otis Dudley Duncan and Beverley Duncan, *The Negro Population of Chicago: A Study of Residential Succession* (Chicago: University of Chicago Press, 1957), 21–2; W. E. B. DuBois, *The Philadelphia Negro: A Social Study* (New York: Schocken Books, 1969), 128–29, 332–33; Baker, *Following the Color Line*, 133–36, 143–44.

not in court. Leaders prized consensus, abhorred factionalism, and dismissed the idea of equal opportunity as an individualist conceit inimical to stable governance. Towards this end, his union allowed few apprentices, charged high admissions fees, and violently opposed the employment of members of the equally lily-white Association of Plumbers. Mangan advocated barring blacks and women not only because of bigotry, but also because he believed that his organization's survival depended upon its exclusivity.[14]

Some officials rejected Mangan's narrowness, only to stumble over white rank-and-file distrust of black workers. In 1903, CFL organizers Charles Fieldstack and Sophie Becker met with thirteen washerwomen, many of them wives of union janitors, to form a laundresses' organization. The meeting ended when ten whites, hailing largely from the South Side, protested that three of the black women present had stolen their customers. Fieldstack complained, "I cannot understand these women. Their husbands visit resorts with colored men. Many of them live next door to colored families, but they object to having negroes in the union." Fieldstack did not, in fact, comprehend the white launderers, who expressed less personal revulsion than resentment of black competition and skepticism about the fidelity of African-American workers. A black washerwoman acknowledged this perception while denying its validity: "We ain't never done them no dirt. I never took any one's job, and I won't. I'se a union woman. My husband's in a union, and I intends to be, or there's goin' to be trouble." Nevertheless, the new local faltered due to white doubts about black obedience to the larger group.[15]

Union officials addressed these assumptions by creating racially, sexually, and occupationally homogeneous locals. Ethnic butchers, bakers, and painters' unions served as a precedent. Beginning as immigrant burial societies, this model accommodated the belief that diversity threatened the health of a union. On some occasions, segregated unionism was the voluntary result of involuntary workplace segregation. For example, "colored waiters" never worked with white servers, so they had their own union, Local #509. More often, African-American workers organized exclusive locals in reaction to the admissions policies of white unions. In 1906, African-American musicians formed Local #208 of the American Federation of Musicians, when Local #10 refused to accept them. Similarly, women founded their own

---

[14] Mangan, *History of the Steam-fitters Protective Association*, 13; Nathaniel Ruggles Whitney, *Jurisdiction in American Building-Trades Unions* (Baltimore: Johns Hopkins University Press, 1914), 135.
[15] "Color Line Kills Union," *CDT*, January 16, 1903, 3.

unions in response to a segmented job market and restrictive unions. Bindery women, janitresses, and waitresses had their own locals, as did "Lady Soap Workers" and seamstresses.[16]

The segregation and outright exclusion of some workers not only institutionalized the society's racial and sexual assumptions, but also encouraged an alliance of corporate employers, aggrieved entrepreneurs, and unorganized workers. In other words, prejudice proved to be self-fulfilling. Exclusionary policies effectively discouraged some young women and Southern blacks from supporting craftsmen on the picket lines. The decision to accept work during lockouts prompted white hostility and hardened union segregation. Craftsmen came to see women as unorganizable, while whites increasingly viewed African Americans as a "scab race." In the next decade, with the growing confidence of American women and the wholesale migration of black workers to the city, this rivalry grew both bitter and catastrophic.[17]

The Building Trades Lockout

Chicago's building trades lockout of 1899–1900 illustrates how corporate power clashed with the craftsmen's prerogatives during the Progressive Era, forcing both workers and employers to choose sides. The city's elite initiated this expensive conflict to eradicate craft governance, or at least those rules that inhibited improvements to productivity. At the expiration of labor agreements in 1899, the builders founded a new organization, the Building Contractors' Council (BCC). The BCC asked smaller associations not to renew agreements with the city's 30,000 union building tradesmen until they abandoned limits on efficiency, restrictions on the use of machinery, the right to interfere with the workmen during the day, the sympathetic strike, prohibitions on the employment of apprentices, and, most importantly, membership in the Building Trades Council. The employers looked not backward, but towards a future workplace, where technology, piecework, and semiskilled labor increased output.[18]

[16] *Lakeside Directory*, 1904, 66–71; Per Nordahl, "Swedish American Labor in Chicago," in Philip J. Anderson and Dag Blanck, eds., *Swedish American Life in Chicago* (Chicago: University of Illinois Press, 1992); Hutton, "The Negro Worker and the Labor Unions in Chicago," 61–9.

[17] William Tuttle, *Race Riot: Chicago in the Red Summer of 1919* (New York: Atheneum, 1970), 120–23; Emily Brown, *Book and Job Printing in Chicago* (Chicago: University of Chicago Press, 1931), 83–7.

[18] Ernest Bogart, "Chicago Building Trades Dispute. I.," *Political Science Quarterly* 16:1 (1901): 114–41, esp. 130; Ernest Bogart, "Chicago Building

Though the BCC appealed to entrepreneurs like painter John Stiles, most contractors were conscripts, not volunteers, in an army commanded by the city fathers. Financiers, manufacturers, and engineers organized the lockout to reconstruct the construction industry in the corporate image. Over two decades after the conflict, economist Royal Montgomery observed that the BCC "was not representative of nearly all the general contractors and subcontractors at that time," a fact leading to "more dissension within the ranks of the organization than was generally realized for a long time after the struggle." The BCC's power stemmed from "the support of the materials men, the architects, and most of the Chicago bankers." Writing many years later, BCC secretary E. M. Craig recalled that many companies defied the council after they saw independent firms violating the lockout and hiring union labor. And in some trades, such as painting, the majority of the master craftsmen never endorsed the BCC at all. The lockout expressed the desire of the largest contractors to join the corporate elite, and abandon their once fruitful alliances with their workers.[19]

The dispute dragged on for nearly two years, spreading throughout Chicago and to other cities. When the contractors began employing nonunion workers in February 1900, the manufacturers of lumber, brick, stone, and sheet metal decided to support the contractors, knowing that the BCC members could lock them out as well. This action caused the 20,000 members of Building Material Trades Council and the Wood Workers Council to strike in support of the BTC. The conflict escalated further, when the BTC asked its members to boycott all businessmen who "owned or rented buildings erected with nonunion labor," eventually calling for bars on any merchant expressing sympathy with the BCC. Finally, the BTC convinced the National Building

Trades Dispute. II.," *Political Science Quarterly* 16:2 (1901): 222–47; Royal E. Montgomery, *Industrial Relations in the Chicago Building Trades* (Chicago: University of Chicago Press, 1927), 28–32; S. V. Lindholm, "Analysis of the Building Trades Conflict in Chicago, from the Trades Union Stand Point," *Journal of Political Economy* 8:3 (1900): 327–46; J. E. George, "The Chicago Building Trades Conflict of 1900," *Quarterly Journal of Economics* 15:3 (May 1901): 348–70; James Miller, "Coercive Trade-Unionism as Illustrated by the Chicago Building-Trades Conflict," *Journal of Political Economy* 9:3 (June 1901): 321–50, 331; Industrial Commission, *Report of the Industrial Commission on the Chicago Labor Disputes of 1900 with Special Reference to the Disputes in the Building and Machinery Trades*, v. 8 (Washington, DC: Government Printing Office, 1901). Henceforth listed as IC, *Reports*, v. 8.

[19] Montgomery, *Industrial Relations*, 28–9; "Autobiography of E. M. Craig," 72 in Folder 7, Gerhard Meyne Papers, CHS; IC, Reports, v. 8, 452–54.

Trades Council to order locals in other regions to shun builders participating in the lockout.[20]

Efforts at resolving the dispute failed, and the state proved reluctant to intrude in the matter. Martin Barnaby Madden, a Republican alderman and a major stone contractor, and Graham Taylor, a professor at the Chicago Theological Seminary and president of the Chicago Commons, offered to arbitrate. But neither side was willing to compromise on the existence of the BTC. Meanwhile public officials feared the political consequences of decisive intervention. Mayor Carter Harrison II had appointed so many construction union officials to positions in city government that newspapers called the BTC the "City Hall Faction" of the Chicago Federation of Labor. Harrison also offered to mediate the dispute, but he hesitated to alienate his constituents by ordering police to protect replacement workers. And though the courts issued injunctions, grand jury investigations resulted in no major indictments.[21]

Tensions soon turned violent. To perform emergency work, the employers hired 1,000 men, including farmers, sailors, and local African-American tradesmen belonging to the independent Colored Federation of Labor. The BCC employed 500 detectives and a smaller number of black bodyguards to guard their worksites, employees, and themselves. The bricklayers responded by purchasing "twenty-five kodaks" and hiring "an official photographer" to take pictures of nonunion bricklayers. Publishing these photos in their national journal, the masons tried to ensure the replacements never worked in another union town. Bricklayers scoured the city for nonunion construction sites to disrupt. For example, on April 24, 1900, union president George P. Gubbins allegedly led over 100 men to 383 West Randolph Street where they threw bricks at contractor Dietrich C. Laue and his nonunion masons. During the first five months of the lockout, the newspapers reported 250 such cases of assault. Over the course of the

---

[20] Bogart, "Chicago Building Trades Dispute. I.," 132–33; Bogart, "Chicago Building Trades Dispute. II.," 223; George, "The Chicago Building Trades Conflict of 1900," 365.

[21] Montgomery, *Industrial Relations*, 30–1; Bogart, "Chicago Building Trades Dispute. I.," 127–28; Bogart, "Chicago Building Trades Dispute. II.," 227–28, 232; Miller, "Coercive Trade Unionism," 336; Lindholm, "Analysis of the Building Trades Conflict," 346; IC, *Reports*, v. 8., 108–13, 276, 305, 353–54, 435, 516, 528–53; Letter, E. M. Craig to Graham Taylor, May 18, 1900, Graham Taylor Papers, Newberry Library; "Fraud Charge by Labor," *CDT*, January 18, 1903, 7; *Winslow Brothers v. Building Trades Council*, case #198400, Sup.C.C. (1899); *Glay v. People*, 94 Ill. App. 598, 602 (1900); "To Investigate Labor War," *NYT*, April 29, 1900, 11.

dispute, participants suffered at least thirty serious injuries and four deaths.[22]

The lockout ended only when Chicago's financial community forced the mayor to protect BCC worksites and nonunion workers. The banks refused to loan the city any funds until Harrison removed BTC president Edward Carroll from the Civil Service Board and ordered the police to stop union assaults. Faced with fiscal collapse, the mayor shifted his support to the builders. Fearing a battle with armed policemen, a parade of unions walked out of the BTC, led by the carpenters.

The opponents of craft governance had won their first victory, but their gains were only temporary, and the conditions leading to the lockout quickly returned. Though the BTC was gone, nearly all its original leaders retained power over their specific unions. Eager to start building again, contractors shortly granted workers the closed shop in fact if not in name. By the end of April 1901, workers formed a new council, the Associated Building Trades League. Within a year, walking delegates were using strikes to enforce agreements. Unions like the stonecutters reinstated restrictions on machinery and material. BCC secretary E. M. Craig commented: "The recuperative powers of defeated unions is certainly marvelous, they simply won't stay licked and become convalescent quickly after a most serious shock." Over the next three decades, the building trades remained one of the city's bloodiest industrial battlegrounds.[23]

The Teamsters' Strike of 1905

The Chicago Teamsters' Strike of 1905 similarly pitted elite businessmen against insurgent craftsmen, with small employers and African-American workers playing significant roles in the outcome. One of the bitterest industrial disputes in American history, lasting 105 days, belligerents and bystanders suffered 415 serious injuries and twenty-one deaths. The use of black replacements inspired racial hostility in the city for decades to come. Moreover, with the teamsters' defeat, corporations stemmed the growth of unions and associations in the city.

---

[22] Bogart, "Chicago Building Trades Dispute. II.," 222, 226–27; "Autobiography of E. M. Craig," 71 in Folder 7, Gerhard Meyne Papers, CHS; "A Detective Kidnapped," *NYT*, May 30, 1900, 2; "Help for Local Unions," *Chicago Times-Herald*, March 14, 1900, 7; Amended declaration, March 29, 1902, *Fendl v. Gubbins*, case #207473, Circ.C.C. (1900); *People v. Gubbins*, case #58583, Crim.C.C., Box 9.
[23] IC, *Reports*, v.8, 6, 395; "Autobiography of E. M. Craig," 79 in Folder 7, Gerhard Meyne Papers, CHS; Bogart, "Chicago Building Trades Dispute. II.," 247. Montgomery, *Industrial Relations*, 33–5.

Nevertheless, local tradesmen retained almost total control over the teaming industry, not only after the strike, but also throughout the early twentieth century.[24]

The Kellogg Switchboard Strike of 1903 served as a proxy war for the showdown of 1905. Not content interfering in industries where craftsmen ruled, such as baking and construction, the Chicago Board of Arbitration began aiding craft workers employed by the corporations engaged in meatpacking, transit, and manufacturing. The best example was in the high-technology telephone industry. Before 1902, three firms controlled the nation's supply of telephone equipment: Western Electric, Stromberg–Carlson, and Kellogg Switchboard. Western Electric was the largest, but the latter two were significant. Kellogg Switchboard held $500,000 in capital stock and 500 employees. Its founder, Milo Kellogg, was the prototypical corporate elite often associated with progressive labor relations. He had been an executive with Western Electric and the Southern Telephone and Telegraph Company. The owner of over 150 patents, Kellogg came from a British-stock, ninth-generation, New England family, attended prep school, and earned two degrees from the University of Rochester. He was an avid clubman who married into one of Chicago's oldest families.[25]

Industrial consolidation had enhanced the corporate character of the business. For years, Stromberg–Carlson and Kellogg Switchboard had enabled competition in the telephone industry. While the giant American Telephone and Telegraph Company (ATT) bought equipment from its subsidiary, Western Electric, the independent telephone exchanges purchased goods from Kellogg Switchboard and Stromberg–Carlson. Western Electric allegedly planned to buy its competitors, shut them down, deny the independents access to equipment, and force them into the trust. When Kellogg fell deathly ill in 1901, he let his brother-in-law, Wallace De Wolf, run the company. After seeing the company's books, De Wolf panicked and sold a majority of Kellogg's stock to Western Electric. Soon afterward, with De Wolf's help, Western Electric attempted to purchase its remaining rival, the Stromberg–Carlson Company. Its stockholders refused, and in April 1902, they chose instead to reorganize as a New York corporation with a factory in Rochester.[26]

---

[24] Tuttle, *Race Riot*, 120–23; Montgomery, *Fall of the House of Labor*, 270, 312–13.

[25] *Chicago: Pictoral and Biographical*, v. 2, Deluxe Supplement (Chicago: S. J. Clarke, 1912), 127–8.

[26] Kellogg recovered and sued to stop the sale. After years of litigation, the courts eventually voided the deal. *Dunbar v. American Telephone and Telegraph*, 238 Ill. 456 (1909); *Brown v. Cragg*, 230 Ill. 299 (1907).

Some administrators of the teaming industry, circa 1905: (back, from right) Unknown, IBT president Cornelius Shea, CFL president Charles Dold, (front, from right) truck drivers' business agent Jerry McCarthy, truck drivers' president Hugh McGee, express drivers' business agent James Barry, and former team owners' secretary John Driscoll. Courtesy of Chicago Historical Society (DN-003577).

In 1902, metal workers' unions began organizing the workers in the city's switchboard firms. Disputes initially took a classic Marxian form, as capital battled labor. In January 1902, the Brass Molders' Union Local #83 demanded a closed shop contract from the Stromberg–Carlson and Western Electric companies. The firms refused, locked the unionists out, and brought in nonunion replacements, the union commenced picketing, spying, and threatening the strikebreakers. This violence escalated into beatings and shootings. On May 7, 1903, the dispute spread to the Kellogg Switchboard & Supply Company, by that time owned by Western Electric. Ninety percent of its employees, approximately 450 members of fourteen unions, refused to work until they received a closed shop contract. After three weeks, the firm hired replacement workers and resumed operation.

With the use of strikebreakers, the struggle spiraled into a confrontation between the craft and corporate economies. Local #83 invited the CBA to arbitrate, but the manufacturer declined their services. On June 24, 1903, local teamsters' unions instituted a boycott against Kellogg, members refusing to cart goods to or from the firm. The CBA's intervention angered Chicago's elite businessmen, who responded by forming the Employers' Association of Chicago (EA). Though some business groups like the National Business League (NBL) still favored conciliation, the Bell Telephone Trust (which owned over half of Kellogg's stock,) the EA, the Illinois Manufacturers' Association, and the American Anti-Boycott Association fell behind Kellogg, making this strike the first battle in a new campaign against craft governance.[27]

The craftsmen and the elite competed for public authority. The CBA positioned itself as a conciliator offering unbiased mediation. Even after Judge Jesse Holdom enjoined the drivers from interfering in the metal workers' strike, teamsters' president Al Young worked with the NBL to push both sides to the bargaining table. L. D. Kellogg refused to negotiate, positioning himself as his employees' protector. He commented, "The company will not discharge a single man now in its employ to make room for union men. Our employees have stood by us in time of trial, and we will not remove them." Evincing tolerance for unions, he continued, "We are not endeavoring to disrupt any organization. We simply demand the right to conduct an open shop and employ whom we please." The courts accepted this moderated defense of individual liberty, issuing contempt citations and criminal indictments. Protected by the law, Kellogg successfully resisted the agreement desired by 90 percent of his original employees.[28]

With this victory in hand, in October 1903, EA members like Marshall Field decided to wrest control of the Associated Teaming Interests – an umbrella group for team owners' associations – from

[27] Ernst, *Lawyers Against Labor*, 95–9; *Johnson v. People of Illinois*, 124 Ill. App 213 (1906); IC, *Reports*, v. 8, 295–301; *Dunbar v. American Telephone and Telegraph*, 238 Ill. 456 (1909); Poole, "How a Labor Machine," 901; *Kellogg Switchboard and Supply v. Brass Workers Union Local #127*, case #230199, Sup.C.C. (1903); *Christensen v. Kellogg Switchboard*, 110 Ill. App. 61 (1903); *O'Brien v. People ex rel Kellogg Switchboard and Supply Co.*, 216 Ill. 354 (1905); Kelly, "A History of the Illinois Manufacturers' Association," 33–4, 21; "Blow to the Unions," *CRH*, July 21, 1903, 1, 7. The National Business League should not be confused with Booker T. Washington's National Negro Business League. Wiebe, *Businessmen and Reform*, 20–1, 31; "National Business League," *NYT*, January 31, 1897, 5; "Ferdinand W. Peck," *NYT*, November 5, 1924, 19; "Volney W. Foster Dead," *NYT*, August 16, 1904, 7; "Urge Negroes to Migrate," *NYT*, August 25, 1900, 7.
[28] "Blow to the Unions," *CRH*, July 21, 1903, 1, 7; *Christensen v. Kellogg Switchboard*, 110 Illinois App. 61 (1903). The machinists avoided most criminal sanctions. True Bill, December 24, 1903, *People v. J. E. Johnson et al.*, Crim.C.C., case #71818, IR 134, 136; Entry, June 10, 1907, *People v. Johnson*, Crim.C.C., case #71818, Docket 36A, 16; *Johnson v. People* 124 Ill. App 213 (1906).

its petite bourgeois founders. They demanded the teamsters' unions quit the Chicago Federation of Labor and agree to stop striking in sympathy with other craft unions. Such action would prevent them from obstructing corporate decision making and keep them from assisting manufacturing, wholesaling, and merchandizing workers.[29]

When the teamsters endorsed the streetcar workers' strike against the City Railway Company, the EA determined to crush the drivers for good. Their chance came on December 15, 1904, when nineteen clothing cutters quit their work at Montgomery Ward and Company, protesting the firm's use of nonunion subcontractors. The garment workers and the CFL urged the Teamsters' Joint Council to show solidarity, and, on April 6, 1905, the teamsters stopped carting goods to and from the mail-order house pending settlement of the dispute. The EA made this their Waterloo, collecting $100,000 from its members and incorporating a new firm, the Employers' Teaming Company (ETC), in the state of West Virginia. The ETC purchased the horses and wagons of the Hough Teaming Company, Montgomery Ward's main contractor, and hired private detectives and African-American strikebreakers from St. Louis to man the carts.[30]

The team owners initially remained neutral, refusing the EA's requests that they lock out union teamsters. Dependent on unions for market regulation and accustomed to the sympathetic strike, the contractors expressed little compassion for the elite. The president of the Coal Team Owners' Association commented, "we will do our best to make deliveries," but "we do not care, of course, to force a lockout of our drivers nor to spread the strike in any way." Salt manufacturer Mark Morton persuaded the railroads to pressure team owners to join the lockout, but the contractors refused, risking millions in business with the railways. This resistance convinced some EA lawyers that the team owners had actually planned the strike.[31]

Sensing their growing vulnerability, the teamsters attempted to resolve the dispute, but the merchants smelled victory and stood firm. The drivers offered to end the strike if the mail-order house rehired them, but General Manager Robert Thorne refused on "principle." Faced with potential humiliation, and perhaps remembering their recent dominance, the teamsters decided to fight the EA itself. On

[29] "Long Peace for Team Interests," *CDT*, October 9, 1903, 4.
[30] "Plan War on Union," *CRH*, November 20, 1903, 2; Grant, "Rights and Wrongs," 887–89; "Editorial," *The Public* 8:373 (May 27, 1905): 113; Witwer, "Corruption and Reform," 65–7.
[31] Witwer, "Corruption and Reform," 68–71, esp. 68; Grant, "Rights and Wrongs," 888.

April 25, drivers for the railway express companies, the department stores, and the wholesale houses left their posts, leaving the city itself at a standstill. To pay replacements for the over 5,000 strikers and 2,000 carts, the ETC raised another $1,000,000 from local business elites, including $50,000 from the Chicago Bankers' Association alone.[32]

With 35,000 members, the teamsters themselves were a force, but they drew further support from the city's white tradespeople. When the nonunion Peabody Coal Co. delivered fuel to the schoolhouses, children went on "strike," refusing to attend their classes. The decision to hire Southern black replacements caused many to back the teamsters. Ordinary citizens blocked the streets, impeded the corporate wagons, and stoned the African-American drivers. Daniel Garrigan, a fireman unconnected with the teamsters, allegedly lobbed rocks at the replacements, crying, "hang the damned niggers." Armed with pistols, rifles, and shotguns, strikebreakers and police fired back, resulting in the staggering number of casualties. This violence subsided only when employers replaced the black drivers with whites.[33]

The courts offered the employers considerable assistance. Local judges issued injunctions not only restraining the teamsters, but also requiring express companies to serve Montgomery Ward and allied businesses. After extended hearings, United States District Court Judge Christian Cecil Kohlsaat (the brother of newspaper publisher, baker, and restauranteur Herman Kohlsaat) ordered the teamsters to cease their interference with the ETC and even held sympathizers like Daniel Garrigan in contempt. The Cook County Criminal Court convened a special grand jury to investigate the teaming industry. On April 29, a grand jury led by foreman A. A. McCormick, the reactionary publisher of the *Chicago Evening Post*, issued true bills of indictment accused the teamsters of conspiring to boycott Montgomery Ward, to interfere with its employees, and to deny supplies to businesses serving the mail order house.[34]

---

[32] Grant, "Rights and Wrongs," 889; Witwer, "Corruption and Reform," 74–7, 85.

[33] "Shot by Special Policeman," *CRH*, June 15, 1905, 2; "Shot in a Strike Riot," *CRH*, June 14, 1905, 2; *Employers' Teaming Co. v. Teamsters' Joint Council*, 141 F. 679 (1905); *Garrigan v. U.S.*, 163 F. 16 (1908); "Strike of Teamsters in Chicago," *CDN Almanac* 22 (1906): 351; Grant, "Rights and Wrongs," 889–90; Witwer, "Corruption and Reform," 83–4; Tuttle, *Race Riot*, 120–23.

[34] *Montgomery Ward v. International Brotherhood of Teamsters*, case #243939, Sup.C.C. (1905); *Marshall Field & Co. v. Becklenberg*, 1 Ill. C.C. 59 (1905); *Platt v. Barry*, case #244201, Sup.C.C. (1905); *Employers' Teaming Co. v. Teamsters'*

But allegations of corruption proved the most damaging to the strikers. As early as 1904, a CFL committee had accused team owners' secretary John C. Driscoll of bribing union officials. The June grand jury heard witnesses testify that the teamsters had instigated strikes solely to demand cash for their resolution. Ben F. Straus claimed that he overheard a labor official state that the drivers had assisted the garment workers only to obtain $10,000 from Montgomery Ward general manager Robert J. Thorne.[35]

Driscoll himself was the grand jury's star witness. During one week in June, the former "labor commissioner" testified to widespread graft, displaying cancelled checks proving that he funneled over $50,000 from employers to unionists. Driscoll denied that he had profited from these transactions, lamenting:

> What a fool I was. Thought to be on easy street. Look at the money I spent on getting the Associated Teaming Interests on its feet. The thousands of dollars that passed through my hands went to others, and then when I got things going right the whole thing blew up. I might just as well have kept my mitts on the whole pile.

Driscoll impugned everyone else, from Robert Thorne to international financier and arbitration advocate August Belmont. He also accused labor leaders of taking money, including his former ally, teamsters' union president Cornelius Shea, and his rival, labor reformer Michael Donnelly of the butcher's union.[36]

The charges of graft led to the defection of supporters and the defeat of the teamsters. Though aimed at corporations, contractors, and unionists alike, Driscoll's shotgun blast undermined the teamsters' stated justifications, providing in the words of one teamster the "greatest blow" to the workers' cause. Making a brothel called the Kentucky Home his unofficial headquarters, Cornelius Shea hardly pandered to the popular desire for respectable labor leaders. One reformer called

Joint Council, 141 F. 679 (1905); *Daily Labor Bulletin,* May 23–31, 1905; *Garrigan v. United States,* 163 F. 16 (1908); Witwer, "Corruption and Reform," 88; True Bill, April 29, 1904, *People v. Shea,* case #76994, Crim.C.C., IR 134, 206–12; "Indict Leaders of the Strikers," *CDT,* April 30, 1905, 1, 3.

35 Poole, "How a Labor Machine," 902–3; "Driscoll is Center of 'Graft' Inquiry," *CRH,* June 14, 1905, 2.

36 "Firm in Union Plot May Face True Bill," *CRH,* June 17, 1905, 1–2; "Driscoll Hides Facts," *CRH,* June 15, 1905, 2; "Grand Jury Stirs Volcano of Graft; Both Sides are Hit," *CRH,* June 16, 1905, 1–2; "To Renew Plot Grill," *CRH,* June 19, 1905, 3; "Graft Probe Held Up," *CRH,* June 20, 1905, 3; "Get New Graft Tales," *CRH,* June 21, 1905, 3.

him a "poisonous toad" and even teamsters referred to his behavior as "disreputable." Only the intervention of CFL president John Fitzpatrick convinced other craft unions to continue public affiliation with the strike committee. Privately, though, the teamsters were now alone. Drivers' locals gradually defected from the strike, their members agreeing to return to work shorn of their union buttons. On August 1, the employers victoriously called off the lockout.[37]

The city fathers had won, but, once again, their gains were oddly limited. The EA stopped only the expansion of craft governance, not its operation within the craft economy. After the strike, three quarters of the drivers returned wearing union buttons in defiance of their settlement. With the help of the contractors, who had never wanted the dispute, the unions reestablished the closed shop in each jurisdiction except those controlled by large corporations: the department store drivers and the express teamsters. A number of local drivers' unions defected from the Teamsters Joint Council, forming the independent Chicago Teamsters' Union, but these locals continued to be bastions of craft governance, hostile to the city's corporate interests.[38]

The Visible Fist

Though corporations promised Chicagoans lower prices, new technologies, and greater selection, their success depended upon their ability to overcome powerful associations that controlled important sectors of the economy such as construction and teaming. While supported by independent craftsmen seeking to operate unmolested by their peers, the lockouts of the Progressive Era reflected the elite's drive to create a climate favorable to their commerce. The struggle between labor and capital was in a very real sense a conflict over the extent of modernization and the power of craftsmen in the city. And the violence of this confrontation suggests both the difficulty of establishing a corporate order and the intense hostility this regime inspired.

With the backing of the state, the elite won these fights. But their modest returns blunted their aggressiveness, lowering expectations for a transformation of local conditions. The participants were exhausted.

---

[37] "The Chicago Strike, By a Teamster," *The Independent* 59:2953 (July 6, 1905): 18; Witwer, "Corruption and Reform," 34, 97–8, 105–6; Hapgood, *The Spirit of Labor*, 346; "Cornelius P. Shea, Labor Leader, Dead," *NYT*, January 13, 1929, 31.

[38] Myers, "Policing of Labor Disputes," 581, 636–37; Sterling Rigg, "The Chicago Teamsters Unions," M.A. thesis, Northwestern University, 1925, 23–7.

After the lockout, the BCC became the Building Construction Employers' Association, and in this new guise favored a cautiously conciliatory role towards unions. After defeating the teamsters, the EA remained labor's scold, but ceased taking direct action against craft governance. Unions consolidated their holdings and ceased risking core positions to aid manufacturing workers. Strikes and lockouts punctuated the succeeding decades, but years passed before anyone initiated another cataclysmic showdown.

Though inconclusive, the battles between craftsmen and corporations generated both debate and demands for new law. The conflicts themselves appealed to the concerns of Progressive-era public: the poverty of workers and the decline of small business, the wastefulness of work stoppages and the horrors of violence, the power of monopolies and the scourge of dishonesty. At the same time, events like the Teamsters' Strike posed a significant challenge for the courts, politicians, and police, inspiring them not only to intervene in that crisis, but also to establish new rules for industrial relations. The turmoil in the city's streets spilled into other realms, redirecting the political economy of the nation at large.

LIBERTY?

This cartoon from a 1903 issue of *Puck* shows a typical progressive view of the walking delegate. Many reformers saw union officers as tyrannical and corrupt politicians, exploiting the immigrant masses they purported to help. Courtesy Olin Library, Cornell University.

4

The Progressive Reaction

Craftsmen and corporations sought public approval by framing their arguments in the era's dominant rhetoric: Progressivism. Chicagoans of this time were fairly united in expressing dissatisfaction with existing institutions, such as political parties, unions, and corporations. But, rather than calling for the eradication of these institutions and a return to the individualism of the Gilded Age, citizens proposed to build new bodies consonant with ideals such as the public interest and the rule of law. This common purpose created the conditions for an extended discussion. Priorities like efficiency, justice, and democracy were not only subjective; they also often contradicted each other. Thus, while executives, reformers, and some craftsmen shared a language, their words served no single obvious vision. Rather, participants competed to define the meaning of reform values for economic development, with the citizenry serving as umpire.[1]

The elite's entry in this rhetorical sweepstakes was the idea of the "open shop" – a firm that employed union members but refused to offer them exclusive contracts. Affluent executives, often from philanthropic backgrounds, conceived of the open shop to justify their campaigns against craft governance to an audience frustrated with

---

[1] By investigating how different populations claimed the title of reformer and appealed to the public's desire for new governing institutions, scholars can move beyond debates over the definition of progressivism and the character of its adherents. Hofstadter, *The Age of Reform: From Bryan to FDR* (New York: Vintage, 1955), 215–71; Wiebe, *Businessmen and Reform: A Study of the Progressive Movement* (Chicago: Ivan R. Dee, 1962), 207–12; Idem, *The Search for Order, 1877–1920* (New York: Hill and Wang, 1967), 164–95; Daniel T. Rogers, "In Search of Progressivism," *Reviews in American History* 10 (December 1982): 113–82; David Green, *The Language of Politics in America: Shaping Political Consciousness from McKinley to Reagan* (Ithaca, NY: Cornell University Press, 1987), 54–85.

strikes, lockouts, and industrial violence. By granting unions a right to exist, then using themes such as antimonopoly, efficiency, and the rule of law to condemn agreements setting prices, wages, and work conditions, open shoppers portrayed themselves as moderate defenders of the public interest.[2]

Open shop arguments appealed to many "professional reformers": journalists like Ray Stannard Baker, activists like Jane Addams, and attorneys like Louis Brandeis. Yet these archetypal progressives refused to dismiss craft governance, for they believed workers needed protection against unfettered capitalism. They criticized craftsmen for violence, corruption, selfishness, and other allegedly irresponsible behavior, yet they also defended unions, arguing that labor's tenuous legal position allowed dishonest leaders to dominate industrial relations, resulting in bloodshed and graft. As a solution, these critics proposed the incorporation of worker organizations, the formalization of trade agreements, the use of arbitration, and, most importantly, the purification of union leadership. Once redeemed, reformers hoped that labor would take its place in a powerful new political alliance, dedicated to legislative goals such as social insurance, municipal ownership of the traction, and the regulation of business.[3]

The target of these criticisms, urban tradesmen, found it extremely difficult to defend themselves in the reformers' terms. If their attitudes towards trusts, workers' rights, and the market appealed to many Chicagoans, the mode and content of their activism remained highly controversial. Craftsmen believed in their own authority, and they rejected the formalization of trade agreements, the sovereignty of the law, and arbitration in most instances. Their organizations were explicitly exclusive and monopolistic, and they favored restrictions on

---

[2] Aside from Daniel Ernst, few historians discuss the history of open shop rhetoric in its progressive context. Ernst, *Lawyers Against Labor: From Individual Rights to Corporate Liberalism* (Chicago: University of Illinois Press, 1995); Howell John Harris, *Bloodless Victories: The Rise and Fall of the Open Shop in the Philadelphia Metal Trades* (New York: Cambridge University Press, 2000), 85–6; Sidney Fine, *"Without Blare of Trumpets": Walter Drew, the National Erectors' Association, and the Open Shop Movement, 1903–1957* (Ann Arbor: University of Michigan Press, 1995), 2, 5–7, 36.

[3] The literature on progressive labor policies focuses on the fight for arbitration and regulation, but often ignores the reformers views on legitimacy, governance, and corruption. Melvyn Dubofsky, *The State and Labor in Modern America* (Chapel Hill: University of North Carolina Press, 1994), 37–60; Weinstein, *The Corporate Ideal*, 3–39; Bruno Ramirez, *When Workers Fight: The Politics of Industrial Relations in the Progressive Era, 1898–1916* (Westport, CT; Greenwood Press, 1978), 65–85.

technology and the labor market that decreased productivity. Finally, many craft administrators were seduced by power, falling far short of the ideals they set for themselves. Unable to adopt the reformers' suggestions without shedding their core beliefs and allegiances, tradesmen often remained aloof.[4]

An uneasy consensus emerged from these clashes, one that seemed to favor Chicago's elite. The corporations won both the Building Trades Lockout and the Teamsters' Strike, in part because of their wealth and power, but also because they more successfully courted public opinion. But the reformers' charges of corruption had proved more damaging to labor's cause than elite attacks on the craftsmen's authority. And the popular concern about corrupt officials and the administration of trade agreements illustrated the growing perception of unions as potentially legitimate governors of the commercial realm, a perception inimical to the corporate ideal.

Rhetoric and the Building Trades Lockout

The Building Trades Lockout of 1899–1900 provides a good example of how different groups constructed ideologies consistent with the reform sentiments wafting through the city's public sphere. The length and scale of the dispute attracted national attention, prompting hearings before the United States Industrial Commission, which became a platform for contractors, workers, union officials, and executives. The combatants lobbied for the support of government, each claiming to represent the public, with varying degrees of success. While the Building Contractors Council (BCC) and its backers easily adapted classical liberalism to reform sensibilities, the Building Trades

---

[4] Many scholars paint craft unions as embracing contractualism, liberalism, and reform between 1880 and 1910. Others like David Montgomery and Christopher Tomlins assign labor's acceptance of liberal capitalism to later dates. William Forbath, *Law and the Shaping of the American Labor Movement* (Cambridge, MA: Harvard University Press, 1991); Richard Schneirov, *Labor and Urban Politics: Class Conflict and the Origins of Modern Liberalism in Chicago, 1864–1897* (Chicago: University of Illinois Press, 1998); Georg Leidenberger, "'The Public is the Labor Union': Working Class Progressivism in Turn of the Century Chicago," *Labor History* 36:2 (Spring 1995): 187–210; Karen Orren, *Belated Feudalism: Labor, the Law, and Liberal Development in the United States* (New York: Cambridge University Press, 1991); Montgomery, *The Fall of the House of Labor*, 411–64; Tomlins, *The State and the Unions: Labor Relations, Law, and the Organized Labor Movement in America, 1880–1960* (New York: Cambridge University Press, 1985).

Council (BTC) struggled to bend its principles to the assumptions of the new era.

The BCC advanced arguments that combined a traditional faith in individual rights with a utilitarian concern for the public interest. Though an organization dominated by the largest contractors, the BCC used popular antimonopoly sentiments against the workers. Successful attorney Samuel Henry Wright's 1899 address before the elite Chicago Literary Society, *A Local Phase of Labor Combination*, posited the existence of a "labor trust." Later published as a book, Wright's essay charged the BTC with seeking "special privileges" from the state and a "monopoly of the labor market, to be achieved by violent suppression of the nonunion laborer, destruction of free contract, the boycott, and the sympathetic strike." Similarly, Michael Havey, a former union steamfitter, described organized labor as "the father of all trusts." Unions protected their members at the expense of others. Drawing upon an old American fear of economic concentration, opponents used antimonopoly language to condemn the BTC as a threat to the public interest.[5]

Attacks on exclusive agreements expressed the BCC's faith in individual rights. When Wright called the BTC a "conspiracy against unorganized labor," he defended the freedom of nonunionists to accept employment on their own terms. The witnesses before the Industrial Commission saw this liberty as flowing from citizenship, the Constitution, and manhood. Mrs. J. S. Robb complained that the painters had denied her husband, a veteran of "George Washington's own" First Infantry Division, his rights to "life, liberty, and the pursuit

---

[5] Wright's career illustrates how corporate law, anti-unionism, and progressive reform overlapped. His partner, E. Burritt Smith, was a professor at Northwestern Law School, a director of numerous corporations, and an active participant in many philanthropic activities. In February 1900, the duo obtained an injunction against the Piano and Organ Workers Union for manufacturer George Bent. Wright died later that year from drinking contaminated water at the elite Midlothian Golf Club in Blue Island, Illinois. Samuel Henry Wright, *A Local Phase of Labor Combination* (Chicago: Chicago Literary Club, 1900), 27, 29; Bill, February 10, 1900, *George P. Bent v. Piano & Organ Workers*, Sup.C.C., case #204497; "Typhoid Ravages Golf Club," *NYT*, July 19, 1900, 1. In 1893, Havey started his own business but neglected to obtain a withdrawal card from the union. When his shop failed, he petitioned for reinstatement. The union demanded a $100 payment for readmission. He refused, choosing instead to move to the suburbs. IC, *Reports*, v. 8, 172, 173. For more on the "labor trust," see Ernst, *Lawyers Against Labor*, 90–109; Fine, *Without Blare of Trumpets*, 6.

of happiness." By limiting his ability to work, the union deprived Robb of the honor and self-respect that derived from his "individuality" as a "free agent." By reducing Robb's family to poverty, the painters' union feminized him and denied him the masculine rights of citizenship.[6]

Through their attacks on construction unions BCC members painted themselves as forward-looking businessmen, not antiquarians seeking a return to the unfettered capitalism of the Gilded Age. For example, prominent general contractor and BCC officer Victor Falkenau charged unions with promoting inefficiency. He attacked rules restricting the use of apprentices, which made it impossible to expand the city's labor pool. He further lamented that, "Thousands of dollars spent by contractors and manufacturers for special machinery with which to cheapen the cost of production of their various materials has been forced to lie idle in their shops and yards." Worst of all were strictures limiting workers' productivity. Falkenau estimated that employers paid a day's wage for no more than three hours work, citing a rule permitting plumbers to set only one washbasin, one toilet, and one bathtub and allowing steamfitters to lay only ninety feet of pipe per day. Noting the public costs of this waste, Falkenau condemned the BTC for ignoring "the harm they were doing to... the general prosperity and welfare of the community."[7]

The builders stressed that craftsmen threatened the rule of law, popular government, and the nation. Drawing upon Republican rhetoric dating back before the Revolutionary War, Samuel Wright described the BTC as a "conspiracy," a subversive "scheme of government," shaped in "secret sessions," which gave its leaders "absolute dominion." Authors like Wright argued that the BTC was criminal because it asserted ruling authority over the market, not only challenging the sovereignty of the state, but also interfering in a private realm to which the Constitution barred even elected officials. Wright claimed the BTC possessed:

Not a whisper of philanthropy, not a sentiment for the brotherhood of man, not one rallying-point for the great mass of citizens, not one sincere attempt to declare the rights of workingmen within the law, not one truly constructive principle of democratic self-government, but throughout inversion of the democratic idea, subversion of the citizen, the dogmatism of force and lawlessness, and lure to all those is in the promise of monopoly and gratification of greed.

[6] IC, *Reports*, v. 8, 81–2.
[7] IC, *Reports*, v. 8, 313–14, 341, 355–57, 391, 447–48.

Opponents described the BTC as treacherous and unpatriotic. John Stiles, the leader of the city's nonunion painting contractors, accused the painters' union of "espionage." He attacked the painters' loyalty, charging that the union demanded his son pay dues while serving in the Spanish-American War. Stiles even accused the BTC of anarchism, claiming a delegate told him that "the Government of the United States is rotten, and it will only be a short time till the labor unions take up arms and wipe it out of existence."[8]

Witnesses also emphasized the building tradesmen's lawlessness. Stiles charged the painters' union with "continual intimidation and crime." Mrs. Robb was more specific, alleging the painters' union hired an "entertainment committee" to give her husband "compulsory education" when he continued to defy the rules. Wilbur F. Behel, a carpenter contractor and the chair of the BCC executive committee, cited a workman chased "by a howling mob," who fled into a "residence in one of the most respectable neighborhoods," where "the lady of the house . . . presented him with a revolver to protect his life." True or not, Behel's picture of a lone worker hounded by "the Molly Maguires of Chicago" and aided in his self-defense by the flower of the city's upper classes illustrated how some businessmen demonized the BTC and idealized the elite during the lockout.[9]

Some witnesses charged union officials with personal corruption, applying the rhetoric of political reform to the local economy. Businessmen decried Mayor Harrison's appointment of Edward Carroll, the BTC president, to the civil service commission. James Miller, a leading sheet metal contractor, described Carroll as "a very poor man" for the job, who used the law to benefit his union constituents rather than the city at large. Even more damaging were allegations that union officials had accepted bribes for settling strikes. Victor Falkenau charged that a walking delegate ended a nine-week strike over the installation of nonunion window frames after receiving "consideration." Frederick P. Bagley, a wholesale marble dealer, charged business agents levied "tribute," using their power to extort cash from builders. Taken together,

---

[8] Wright, *A Local Phase*, 20, 31, 15. This Republican language found consistent expression in 18th and 19th century law. Christopher L. Tomlins, *Law, Labor, and Ideology in the Early American Republic* (New York: Cambridge University Press, 1993), 114–27; Hattam, 30–69; Francis Sayre, "Criminal Conspiracy," *Harvard Law Review* 35 (1922): 393–409; William J. Novak, *The People's Welfare: Law and Regulation in Nineteenth-Century America* (Chapel Hill: UNC Press, 1996), 12, 22, 246–48; IC, *Reports*, v. 8, 40, 341.

[9] IC, *Reports*, v. 8, 80, 340, 395, 396–97; "A Detective Kidnapped," *NYT*, May 30, 1900, 2.

the witnesses drew a picture of a labor movement both in cahoots with boss politics and advancing the machine's reputedly dishonest logic.[10]

Finally, the builders also maintained their reform credentials by downplaying the racial politics of the lockout. Though the contractors hired African-Americans as workers and bodyguards, none mentioned these men in Congressional hearings, fearing public disapproval. In an era when reformers condemned the use of black strikebreakers, seeing separation as a precondition for peace, it hardly behooved employers to mention their African-American employees.[11]

Building trades' unions framed their position for a progressive audience, with middling success. Labor's task was difficult because craft governance, even honestly enforced, ran counter to the values of many middle-class American reformers. For example, union officers chose to question the virtue of productivity rather than denying charges of inefficiency, a position not likely to appeal to the growing number of professionals favoring mechanization and management. M. H. Murphy, the vice-president of the Painters' District Council, responded to the employers' charge with a riddle: "The only man who ever limited a day's work . . . was the master painter, and the limit they put on it is the man's endurance." Though the first half of Murphy's retort seemed to blame employers for inefficiency, the second half justified the union's role in limiting production by focusing on the beleaguered craftsmen. Employers fired workers "when the gray hairs begin to show in a man's head," privileging speed over ability. Murphy attacked attempts to increase production as unfair to employees and deleterious to quality, positioning himself as the defender of skill, experience, and craft pride.[12]

Union officers derided notions of individual liberty espoused by employers, describing such freedom as a threat to the rights of the larger community of workers. M. H. Murphy commented:

> Mr. Stiles in our trade does not go for anything. He banks on what he calls American citizenship. He probably has $500 invested in tools, etc., out where he does business. His American citizenship is the amount he has invested; he thinks that ought to be protected. He

[10] IC, *Reports*, v. 8, 325–26, 353, 392.
[11] Tuttle, *Race Riot*, 112–20; Elisabeth Lasch-Quinn, *Black Neighbors: Race and the Limits of Reform in the American Settlement House Movement, 1890–1945* (Chapel Hill: University of North Carolina Press, 1993), 11–23. For the reformers' rejection of conflict, see Louis Menand, *The Metaphysical Club: A Story of Ideas in America* (New York: Farrar, Straus, Giroux, 2001), 313.
[12] IC, *Reports*, v. 8, 453–54.

does not consider that a man who works for a living – has served his time – is a citizen at all: has any rights of citizenship.

Murphy contended that one minor contractor from the outskirts of the city ought not to be allowed either to undermine the standards of the craft community or to dictate the rules governing painting by allying with wealthy contractors of the BCC.[13]

If such arguments appealed to the reformers' desire for communal order, then the craftsmen's contempt for the rule of law did not. Building tradesmen declined to accept the sole authority of the state, rationalizing violence as a legitimate response to the employer's instigations. John A. Long, president of the Board of Business Agents, stated: "when the contractors are solely responsible for the trouble that exists, they should not be given police protection to try to cause more trouble." Long suggested that the purpose of the law was the preservation of the status quo, claiming a right to punish employers for upsetting that order and denying the state's obligation to protect the property of those who undermined industrial peace.[14]

Union officials focused on personal responsibility rather than individual rights, reviling those critics who blamed organized labor for their misfortune. M. H. Murphy stated that he had forgotten about J. S. Robb's existence until his wife told her story to the committee. Murphy admitted that the painters had expelled Robb in 1888, but the business agent denied knowledge of any assault and claimed to have ignored the former unionist since that time. To check Robb's tale, Murphy went to their Maplewood home, asked their neighbors about the couple, and discovered that they were "inveterate pikers and betters on long shots." Murphy alleged that, "whenever he [Robb] got $5 or $6, he went to play the bangtails, the short horses . . . If they won they were all right, but if they lost I suppose they had to starve." By demanding that Robb take responsibility for his family, rather than making "the union . . . the hunchback to hang this poverty on," Murphy inverted Mrs. Robb's charge that unions destroyed her husband's individuality.[15]

Professional reformers generally found these arguments unconvincing. Industrial Commission chairman, Civil War veteran, and avid protectionist Col. Albert Clarke commented, "The labor men seem to enforce their own laws without respect to the laws by which we are

---

[13] IC, *Reports*, v. 8, 453.
[14] IC, *Reports*, v. 8, 206; Bogart, "Chicago Building Trades Dispute. II.," 227, ft. 2.
[15] IC, *Reports*, v. 8, 454, 455.

all bound." Theology professor and settlement house administrator Graham Taylor condemned labor's use of violence as "not only indefensible but suicidal," prompting, "not only the deeper alienation of nonunion labor, which is its only source of growth and power," but costing, "also the support and even the fair hearing of the public, which is the only hope of the ascendancy of its principles." Taylor charged the BTC's political affiliations had "very seriously impeded the growth of the legitimate influence of labor unions in the city." Though he believed that workers deserved representation on the civil service board, the professor concluded that "the appointment [of Carroll] was not such as would have been expected by friends of the civil service law, to say the least." And while Taylor doubted most of the graft charges, he urged the unions to "purge itself from any just suspicion of being bought and sold for blackmailing."[16]

But reformers like Taylor did not wholly embrace the employers. Viewing industrial peace as the ultimate priority, they blamed both sides for their selfish indifference to the broad effects of the lockout and their refusal to submit their grievances to an "impartial" representative of the people. Taylor commented:

> The cause of human brotherhood, for which organized labor in the main has stood through the past 600 years of English history, is more sacred than any labor organizations. That sacred cause is at stake in Chicago to-day. Its right to be heard transcends every other issue of mere policy or personal interest at stake. Its appeal must at last be made to the public. For it is the jury of public opinion which always returns the final verdict in this and every other issue. As the third and greatest party to this controversy, the public has the right to be heard. Whatever the cost of these struggles to either side, the public always pays the heaviest bills.

Taylor chastised businessmen like Victor Falkenau who favored arbitration only when it accomplished a permanent revision in the terms of employment. He granted labor's nobility, but denied its right to violate the law. Progressives demanded that both sides submit to public authority and work towards the public good. During the lockout, this principle favored the BCC, but this would not invariably be the case in future.[17]

---

[16] "Chicago's Labor Contest," *NYT*, April 1, 1900, 9; "Col. Albert Clarke Dead," *NYT*, July 17, 1911, 9; IC, *Reports*, v. 8, 535, 538, 541.
[17] IC, *Reports*, v. 8, 534–35.

Elite Reform and the Open Shop

During the succeeding years, a broader "open-shop" movement emerged in Chicago, utilizing many of the arguments developed in the Building Trades Lockout of 1899–1900. The authors of this crusade were not small businessmen or relics of the nineteenth century, but rather sophisticated corporate executives and elite attorneys who saw themselves as open-minded and public-spirited citizens of a modern American nation. As in the lockout, these men tried to present their own interests in a reform language that referenced both the public interest and private rights. The term "open shop" itself was a philosophical compromise between the staunch individualism of the Gilded Age and the institutionalism of the Progressive Era. By granting the workers' right to organize, but denying their authority over the workplace, businessmen tried to disable the unions' claims to sovereignty while courting both craft businessmen and a public sympathetic to labor.[18]

Executives with reform pedigrees conceived the idea of the open shop in response to the craftsmen's claims to authority over the market. Paul Blatchford was very nearly the stereotypical progressive businessman. Born in 1859, Paul personally connected a Protestant philanthropic tradition, emerging industrial trusts, laissez-faire jurisprudence, and new corporate associations. His father, an early Chicago settler and lead manufacturer named Eliphalet W. Blatchford, participated in innumerable charitable and religious organizations, serving as treasurer of the Northwestern branch of the Sanitary Commission and vice-president of the American Board of Foreign Missions. Paul's brother Edward spent his life helping Armenian Christians in Palestine. Yet Paul was also heir to a strain of classical liberalism that linked the family's political beliefs to its material interests. His uncle

---

[18] Daniel Ernst, *Lawyers Against Labor: From Individual Rights to Corporate Liberalism* (Chicago: University of Illinois Press, 1995); James Weinstein, *The Corporate Ideal in the Liberal State, 1900–1918* (Boston: Beacon Press, 1968), 5; Martin J. Sklar, *The Corporate Reconstruction of American Capitalism: The Market, the Law, and Politics* (New York: Cambridge University Press, 1993), 15–6; Andrew Wender Cohen, "Business Myths, Lawyerly Strategies, and Social Context: Ernst on Labor Law History," *Law and Social Inquiry* 23:1 (1998): 165–84. A few recent books discuss the connections between corporations and the open shop movement. Howell John Harris, *Bloodless Victories: The Rise and Fall of the Open Shop in the Philadelphia Metal Trades* (New York: Cambridge University Press, 2000), 4, 162–82; Sidney Fine, *"Without Blare of Trumpets": Walter Drew, the National Erectors' Association, and the Open Shop Movement, 1903–1957* (Ann Arbor: University of Michigan Press, 1995), 11, 214.

was U.S. Supreme Court Justice Samuel Blatchford, a New York Republican whose most famous decision, *Chicago, Milwaukee & St. Paul Railway v. Minnesota* (1890), established the principle of substantive due process, often used by judges to invalidate protective legislation during the following four decades.[19]

Blatchford's professional life grew from these diverse roots. After graduating from Amherst College, Paul helped manage his father's lead manufacturing business until 1902, when they sold the firm to the newly formed National Lead Company, a $60 million "trust" owned in part by Standard Oil. Rather than devoting his life to charitable endeavors, Paul embarked upon a new occupation: trade association executive. For the remainder of his life, he worked as an administrator, serving as president of the Central Supply Association (CSA), a group of plumbing equipment manufacturers, and secretary of both the Chicago Hotel Employers' Association (CHEA) and the Chicago Metal Trades Association (CMTA).[20]

In his capacity as representative of plumbing manufacturers and hoteliers, Blatchford proclaimed tolerance and even enthusiasm for organization, conciliation, and administration if these favored the employer's prerogatives. When a series of strikes among launderers, black and white waiters, cooks, and steam engineers paralyzed the city's hotel and restaurant industry in the spring of 1903, Blatchford agreed to negotiate with workers, but he made such meetings contingent upon the employees resuming work. When the unionists both refused to return and rebuffed offers of mediation from the teamsters and the National Civic Federation, Blatchford brought thousands of "colored" waiters from Missouri to replace the strikers, forcing the unions eventually to agree to arbitration. Similarly, as secretary of the Central

---

[19] Mary E. and Eliphalet W. Blatchford, *Memories of the Chicago Fire* (Chicago: Privately Printed, 1921); Charles Hammond Blatchford, Jr., *The Story of Two Chicagoans* (Chicago: Privately Printed, 1962), 35–6, 46; "American Board Debts," *NYT*, October 18, 1895, 3; Sarah E. T. Henshaw, Eliphalet W. Blatchford, Mark Skinner, *Our Branch and Its Tributaries; Being A History of the Work of the Northwestern Sanitary Commission and Its Auxiliaries, During the War of the Rebellion* (Chicago, A. L. Sewell, 1868). For the conjunction of Protestant philanthropy, paternalism, and the open shop, see Harris, *Bloodless Victories*, 178, 287–93.

[20] *Amherst College Biographical Record of the Graduates and Non-Graduates: Centennial Edition, 1821–1921*, ed. Robert S. Fletcher and Malcolm O. Young (Amherst, MA: Amherst College, 1927), 2654; "Lead Trust Organizing," *NYT*, September 30, 1902, 10; "'Lead Trust' Activity," *NYT*, August 22, 1903, 10.

Supply Association, Blatchford managed competition among plumbing manufacturers through price agreements, showing his willingness to experiment with governing schemes, as long as his constituents stood to benefit and the law proved no obstacle.[21]

At the same time, Blatchford and John D. Hibbard, the president of the CMTA, innovated the open shop approach to labor, arguing that employers could maintain normal dealings with unions without accepting their governing authority. Representing 100 firms with 15,000 employees, the CMTA officials argued that businessmen could eliminate dangerous and wasteful labor wars by maintaining friendly, but not exclusive, agreements with unions. To anyone who witnessed the building trades lockout of 1899–1900, the CMTA's principles were familiar; the association prohibited any limitations on output, all work stoppages, and the closed shop. The CMTA proposed that unions should raise wages not by obtaining exclusive agreements, but by assisting employers at increasing production. Blatchford saw this as a compromise position between the extremes of absolute individualism and craft governance.

Blatchford continued to present himself as a forward-thinking proponent of industrial peace even after the CMTA adopted a more militant posture late in 1903, ending its dalliance with the reformist National Civic Federation (NCF), affiliating with the staunch National Association of Manufacturers (NAM), and beginning a nationwide drive against the International Association of Machinists. In some sense, Blatchford's position had not changed. Though he publicly favored arbitration, his actions in the hotel dispute showed his commitment to conciliation was always contingent upon the maintenance of employer prerogatives. The CMTA's defection from the NCF merely revealed that Blatchford's passion for industrial peace was secondary to his faith in the manager's rights.[22]

---

[21] "Chinese Flocking In," May 6, 1903, 3; "Cafe Employes Lay Down Law," *CDT*, May 28, 1903, 3; "Strike in Hotels and Restaurants," *CRH*, June 5, 1903, 1, 3; "Laundries Open; Peace in Hotels," *CRH*, June 6, 1903; "To Sue Cafe Owners," *CRH*, June 13, 1903, 2; "Hotel Strike Fizzling," *NYT*, June 14, 1903, 1; "Strikers to Yield," *CRH*, June 17, 1903, 2; "Waiters' War Ends," *CRH*, June 18, 1903, 2; "Strike on Postoffice," *CRH*, June 19, 1903; "Pool on Rack To-Day," *CRH*, December 3, 1903, 9; "Writs are Voted in Plumbing Pool case," *CRH*, December 4, 1903, 7; True Bill, November 1, 1903, *People v. Sanitary Specialty Manufacturing Company*, case #71392, Crim.C.C., IR 134, 131.

[22] Baker, "Organized Capital Challenges Organized Labor: The New Employers' Association Movement," *McClure's* 23 (1904): 288–91; Montgomery, *Fall of the House of Labor*, 269–75.

The open shop campaign of the period 1903–1905 depended upon this combination of anti-union militancy and Progressive-era rhetoric, developed in the Building Trades Lockout of 1899 and refined by trade association officers like Blatchford. Anger over teamster intervention on behalf of brass workers in the Kellogg Switchboard strike of 1903 led not only to the revivification of the dormant Illinois Manufacturers' Association, but also to the founding of the Employers' Association of Chicago (EA), labor's nemesis for the next forty years. Its members included some of the city's wealthiest men, including department store executive John Shedd, railroad executive Frederic Delano, and mail order house executive Robert Thorne. Wholesale hardware merchant and philanthropist Adolphus C. Bartlett was also a founding member. Its counsel was the formidable Levy Mayer, the elite attorney responsible for the formation of trusts in sugar, meat, liquor, and other industries.[23]

These organizations hired men with reform professionals to promote the CMTA's combination of the open shop and mediation. The EA's first secretary was Frederick W. Job, a lawyer who, as chair of the Illinois State Board of Arbitration, had resolved the dispute between the teamsters and the department stores without giving in to the drivers' demand for an exclusive contract. When Job quit the state board after twenty months, he still expressed some sympathy for labor and high hopes for arbitration, blaming strikes on the rising cost of living and calling the state board of arbitration "one of the most important" branches of the government. He complained only that most such bodies lacked any means of enforcing their judgments and that "the salary paid boards of arbitration is so small that good citizens cannot be induced to accept the position," perhaps as a way of justifying his departure.[24]

Job's initial statements as EA secretary in April 1903 further delineated the open shop businessmen's appeal to the progressive public. The new secretary denied the antiunionism of the association,

[23] Alfred H. Kelly, "A History of the Illinois Manufacturers' Association," unpublished Ph.D. Diss., University of Chicago, 1938, 33–4, 21; "Not to Fight Labor," *CRH*, April 14, 1903, 2; *Employers' News*, April 1928, 6; *Book of Chicagoans*, 1905, 45–6; Edgar Lee Masters, *Levy Mayer and the New Industrial Era: A Biography* (New Haven: Yale University Press, 1927), 41–68, esp. 65–6.

[24] Job's credentials included his support for the open shop, his experience, his political connections, and his common attendance at the University of Michigan with CMTA president, John D. Hibbard. *The Book of Chicagoans* (Chicago: A. N. Marquis, 1905), 314; "John D. Hibbard," *NYT*, November 18, 1937, 3; "Why There Are So Many Strikes," *NYT*, March 30, 1903, 6.

announcing that, "our organization is in no way opposed to organized labor . . . the purpose of the Employers' Association of Chicago is to foster more amicable relations, and thereby reduce labor strife to a minimum." Its first press release expressed a desire to to secure freedom of contract "irrespective of whether or not an employer or employe[*sic*] is a member of any organization" and to oppose "restriction of output, sympathetic strikes and boycotts." Yet like BCC and CMTA, the EA combined this opposition to craft governance with a paper commitment, "to harmonize differences between employers and employees so that justice may be done to both sides, and to favor arbitration of serious differences." Thus, the city's most vocal advocate of the open shop positioned itself as the vessel of reform values and the best defender of the "welfare of Chicago."[25]

Open shoppers highlighted the plight of workers and businessmen crushed by corrupt and tyrannical union officials, but painted enlightened corporate paternalism as individualism's best defense. In 1908, Arthur Jerome Eddy, a corporate attorney and art collector, published a popular novel called *Ganton & Co.*, which later became a Broadway play, *The Great John Ganton*. This parable – based loosely upon the stockyards strike of 1904 – portrayed an alliance between selfish union officers and scheming trusts. The book's villain was John Ganton, Sr., a ruthless but successful meatpacker who pays teamsters to ruin his competitors and increase the price of beef. Eddy's heroes were Ganton's sons, John, Jr., an educated young elite whose enthusiasm for cooperation disappoints his father, and William, a muscular type uncomfortable with the managerial role he is expected to inherit. When Will takes a job on the plant floor, he discovers his true nature. With his bare hands, he disperses the picketers and protects the cowering African-American replacement workers. When the father dies, John, Jr. (brain) and Will (body) agree to run the family business together, establishing a new era of modern and ethical business operations.[26]

By defending black workers against corrupt craft unions, Eddy allowed his protagonists to regain the patriarchal masculinity robbed of them by their affluence, their education, their distance from production, and the workers' increasing independence. Eddy's portrayal of the strikebreakers was actually somewhat radical at a time when

[25] "Not to Fight Labor," *CRH*, April 14, 1903, 2; *Employers' News*, April 1928, 6.
[26] Arthur Jerome Eddy, *Ganton & Co.: A Story of Chicago Commercial and Social Life* (Chicago: McClurg, 1908), esp. 216–17; "Few Novelties in the Waning Theatrical Season," *NYT*, April 2, 1909, X8; "Arthur Jerome Eddy Dies After Operation," *NYT*, July 22, 1920, 10; *Book of Chicagoans* (Chicago: A. N. Marquis, 1917), 207.

most readers still hated African-American workers who crossed picket lines. Open shop executives like Blatchford, personally rooted in the antebellum antislavery movement, were indeed more sympathetic to African-Americans than were white craftsmen. But this profoundly condescending egalitarianism also served the employers' interests, helping to justify a mixture of corporate cooperation, employer paternalism, and staunch anti-unionism. In the succeeding decade, Eddy would call this idea "the New Competition," and it would secure his small but significant place in history.[27]

Progressive Reform and the Open Shop Critique

Professional reformers shared the elite's concerns, yet their sympathy for workers and their desire to channel labor's political strength prompted them to support the purification, rather than the eradication, of craft governance. Chicago's craft economy aggravated the contradictions in the progressive view of institutions. These men and women founded settlement houses, courts, and schools while condemning existing associations, agencies, and corporations as undemocratic, corrupt, and monopolistic. In sum, they favored organization and planning, but not the forms they found in Chicago; they desired a cooperative order, but they still trumpeted individual rights. The progressive community saw unions as tools for protecting citizens against the extremes of capitalism. But as strikes unfolded in the city, many concluded that irresponsible leaders turned unions into threats to the public good. The contrast between ideals and reality led activists, attorneys, journalists, and social workers to crusade for the sanitation of industrial relations.[28]

[27] For Eddy's less charitable view of Asian-Americans, see Carter H. Harrison, *Growing Up With Chicago* (Chicago: Ralph Fletcher Seymour, 1944), 188–90, 194, 196, 197; Arthur Jerome Eddy, *An Examination of the Conditions Underlying the Radical Change That Is Taking Place in the Commercial and Industrial World, the Change from A Competitive to A Cooperative Basis* (New York: Appleton, 1912).

[28] This ambivalence is reflected in the literature on progressivism itself. Richard Hofstadter, *The Age of Reform*, 215–71; Wiebe, *The Search for Order*, 164–95. If, as James Kloppenberg suggests, pragmatist philosophers created the intellectual conditions for the Progressive Era by finding a moral, democratic politics between socialism and free market capitalism, then this idealism had profoundly conservative implications, at least when applied to industrial conditions in Chicago. Kloppenberg, *Uncertain Victory: Social Democracy and Progressivism in European and American Social Thought, 1870–1920* (New York: Oxford University Press, 1986).

Among the groups clamoring for reform, the press most strongly supported the open shop, attacking unions for threatening the rule of law, the peace of the community, and the natural order. Their daily coverage of strikes, lockouts, injunctions, and settlements was hardly evenhanded, appealing to a middle-class public troubled by the so-called "labor problem" but suspicious of working-class leaders and frightened by protest. The papers emphasized the selfishness of union officers and the brutality of their members. One headline sarcastically described a retiring janitors' delegate as, "The First Business Agent of a Chicago Union Who Ever Resigned." Another proclaimed "Acts of Violence on Labor Day," emphasizing union lawlessness. Articles sensationalized physical conflict. For instance, the *Tribune* described a 1903 fight between striking female candy workers and their replacements in titillating detail, noting that, "Hair was pulled, faces were scratched, and clothes were torn." The stereotyped picture of female combat invited readers to envision scantily clad women engaged in a catfight. But the story also highlighted the rough speech and manner of the picketers indicating the unnatural effect of unions on femininity.[29]

In the pages of new popular magazines, muckraking journalists worried that the craftsmen conspired to usurp the sovereignty of the elected government. In a 1903 article in *The Century*, Franklin Clarkin lashed the craftsmen for presuming to establish their own private courts. John Keith's 1903 article in *Harper's Weekly* compared a streetcar strike to the "Terror of Revolutionary France," painting unions as mobs that denied freedom and unlawfully assumed public authority. Keith contended that organized labor had acquired "enormous power" over "unorganized labor, over capital, over the populace in general, over police and municipal authorities, and over the whole status of individual liberty." In 1904, Wendell Philips Garrison's *The Nation* argued that unions had become a despotic and irresponsible "*imperium in imperio*," exempt from punishment by "the sympathy of the mob," "the amiability of the Legislature," and their lack of corporate legal status. Capital's only hope, according to Garrison, was "to find refuge in some other quarter of the globe where there was till equality before the law."[30]

---

[29] "William Feather, The First Business Agent of a Chicago Union Who Ever Resigned," *CRH,* January 30, 1904, 3; "Acts of Violence on Labor Day," *CDT,* September 8, 1903, 3; "Shake Off Union Nemesis," *CDT,* September 10, 1903, 4; Stephen Norwood, *Strikebreakers and Intimidation: Mercenaries and Masculinity in Twentieth-Century America* (Chapel Hill, University of North Carolina Press, 2002), 49.

[30] Franklin Clarkin, "The Daily Walk of the Walking Delegate," *Century Magazine* 67:2 (December 1903): 301, 303; John Keith, "The Strangle-Hold of

The reformer's doubts about the craftsmen are unsurprising; few had any direct personal experience with manual labor. The leading figures came from both the new and old middle classes. Author Ernest Poole was raised in an affluent home in Chicago, the son of early settlers to the city, and attended Princeton before committing to life as a reformer. The son of a wealthy merchant, attorney Louis Brandeis was schooled in Germany and at Harvard Law School. Settlement house administrator and activist, Jane Addams, was the educated daughter of a prominent rural banker. Carroll Wright had been a colonel in the union army and a prosperous lawyer before becoming United States Labor Commissioner. Even those of modest rural backgrounds like economist John Commons, journalist Ray Stannard Baker, and writer Franklin Clarkin were nevertheless educated men from old American stock who had little in common with the workers they wrote about. Of the best-known commentators on the "labor question," only reporter Luke Grant had begun his career as a tradesman.[31]

But if middle-class reformers had difficulty shedding their revulsion towards the craftsmen's rough style, their broad sympathy for workers tempered their support for open shop arguments. Though author John Keith called for the suppression of strikers, comparing them to insurrectionists, he also lamented the hideous fate of "unprotected . . . little children working in the mines, and flogged when they fell, or shocked with buckets of cold water when they grow drowsy after fourteen hours of toil." Like all reform movements, Progressivism fed upon dramatic exposes and sentimental appeals that expressed heartfelt feelings for the workers themselves if not for their organizations.

These emotions led some progressives to see unions as obstacles to their goals. Observers like John Keith favored statutes protecting women and children and thus making the state the guarantor of the public good. Though the Illinois State Federation of Labor backed most such legislation, its member unions often refused to endorse any law that allowed the state to subsume their authority over work

Labor," *Harper's Weekly* 47 (December 5, 1903): 1940–41; "Remedies against Unions," *The Nation* 78:2023 (1904): 265–66.
[31] "Jane Addams A Foe of War and Need," *NYT*, May 22, 1935, 16; "Franklin Clarkin is Dead at 91," *NYT*, June 13, 1960, 27; "Carroll D. Wright Dies in Worcester," *NYT*, February 21, 1909, 7; "Ernest Poole, 69, Novelist is Dead," *NYT*, January 11, 1950, 20; Truman F. Keefer, *Ernest Poole* (New York: Twayne Publishers, 1966); Ernest Poole, "The Widening Sense of Honor," *Outlook* 84 (December 1, 1906): 820; Hofstadter, *Age of Reform*, 131–72; Wiebe, *The Search for Order*, 111–32. For a contrasting view, see Robert Johnston, "Re-Democratizing the Progressive Era: The Politics of the Progressive Era Political Historiography," *Journal of the Gilded Age and Progressive Era* 1:1 (January 2002): 68–92.

conditions. Locals often preferred laws that ratified their power over trade, making the state serve civil society rather than the reverse. To reformers tortured by nightmares of shoeless children slaving in fetid conditions for sadistic masters, the craftsmen's demands for barbers' licensing laws seemed less than humanitarian.[32]

Ray Stannard Baker exemplified the ambivalent muckraker, who endorsed the assumptions if not the conclusions of the corporate elite. If open shop businessmen were cynics posing as idealists, Baker was a staunch idealist posing as a worldly realist. In 1903, prompted by Lincoln Steffens' casual suggestion, Baker wrote a series of articles on labor relations for *McClure's*. Visiting Chicago, he marveled in horror at the collusion, violence, and corruption of the building and teaming trades. Baker contended that the craftsmen had attained industrial peace on their own terms, without consideration of the public or the rights of the individual. In his first article, "Capital and Labor Hunt Together: Chicago the Victim of the New Industrial Conspiracy," Baker lamented, "We have been sighing for labor and capital to get together; we have been telling them that they are brothers, that the interest of the one is the interest of the other. Here they are together; are we any better off?"[33]

Writers like Baker affirmed charges of a "labor trust," made previously by opponents of craft governance like attorney Samuel Wright. Baker portrayed unions and associations as stifling trade, creating "a close monopoly in which all health giving competition is completely shut out." He explained how sheet metal and brick "rings" ruined

---

[32] John Keith, "Cures for the Labor Problem," *WSJ*, February 29, 1904, 6; "Form Big Cigar Company," *CDT*, January 16, 1903, 3; "The Barber Shop Law," *CRH*, October 14, 1909, 8; Earl Beckner, *A History of Illinois Labor Legislation* (Chicago: University of Chicago Press, 1929), 382–84; Eugene Staley, *A History of Illinois State Federation of Labor* (Chicago: University of Chicago Press, 1930), 281–83; Daniel Rodgers, *Atlantic Crossings: Social Politics in a Progressive Age* (Cambridge, MA: Belknap, 1998), 19, 257–58; Forbath, *Law and the Shaping*, 17.

[33] Ray Stannard Baker, "Capital and Labor Hunt Together," *McClure's Magazine* 21 (1903): 451, 463; Lincoln Steffens, *The Autobiography of Lincoln Steffens* (New York: Literary Guild, 1937), 521–22. The articles flowed in close succession. Baker, "The Trust's New Tool – The Labor Boss," *McClure's Magazine* 22 (1903–1904): 39; Baker, "A Corner in Labor: What is Happening in San Francisco where Unionism Holds Undisputed Sway," *McClure's Magazine* 22 (1903–1904): 366–78; Baker, "The Lone Fighter," *McClure's Magazine* 22 (1903–1904): 194–97; Baker, "Organized Capital Challenges Organized Labor," *McClure's Magazine* 23 (1904): 279–92; Baker, "The Rise of the Tailors," *McClure's Magazine* 24 (1904–1905): 126–39.

independent businessmen like Eli Rysdon and George Hinchliff. In a 1904 article, "The Trust's New Tool – the Labor Boss," Baker accused union officials of aiding industrial giants. Baker described how iron-workers' official Sam Parks conspired with the George Fuller Co., a contracting firm owned by the Rockefeller family, to dominate construction in New York City. Rather than opposing one another, capital and labor formed a frightening conjunction of organized private interests.[34]

By attacking walking delegates, commentators reconciled their faith in collective bargaining with their anxieties about union behavior. In 1903, Baker described Sam Parks as a:

> Rough, tough nut of a man who loves to fight, he says, better than to eat. Ignorant, a bully, a swaggerer, a criminal in his instincts, inarticulate except in abuse and blasphemy, with no argument but his proficient and rocky fists, he yet possesses those curious Irish faculties of leadership, that strange force of personality, that certain loyalty to his immediate henchmen familiar among ward politicians, – so that he could hold his union with a hand of iron.

Baker adapted the rhetoric (and stereotypes) of political reform to industrial relations. He saw unions and associations as confronting the same problems as government itself, noting, "The honest, conservative, selfish, 'good' citizen remains at home and plays with his babies, while the able scalawag runs his organization." As graft tainted City Hall, the personal corruption of officials undercut the craftsmen's accomplishments.[35]

The ubiquity of this political metaphor, however critical its intent, actually illustrated the growing legitimacy of craft governance during this period. Humor magazines like *Puck* caricatured the walking delegate as a mustachioed dude sartorially resplendent in checked suit, derby hat, waistcoat, and tiepin, resembling Thomas Nast's iconic drawing of Boss Tweed. The most striking of these prints showed immigrants landing in the United States only to find the Statue of Liberty replaced by the towering figure of a walking delegate in bowler and ascot, a cigar between his lips. In one hand, he held a plaque reading "tyranny," in the other, a torch labeled "lawlessness." A caption underneath read "Liberty?" Bristling at such jibes, some unions renamed their walking delegates "business agents," but the political analogy actually created

[34] Baker, "Capital and Labor Hunt Together," 462, 463; Baker, "The Trust's New Tool – The Labor Boss," 40–3.

[35] Baker, "The Trust's New Tool," 30–43, esp. 30–1; Baker, "Capital and Labor Hunt Together," 451–52, 462; Poole, "The Widening Sense of Honor," 820.

a legitimate space for collective action. Representations of union officers as ward heelers, machine bosses, and corrupt cops shifted the focus from unions themselves to their leaders, comparing them to the sovereign state and presenting honestly administered organizations as valid. For this reason, labor's strongest supporters, Jane Addams and Luke Grant, defended the walking delegate by calling him the policemen for the union.[36]

Moreover, critics questioned the businessmen's claims to source of moral authority. Union critic John Keith commented, "almost any industrial war is better than the absolute power of the employer." Others questioned the authenticity of open shop businessmen, viewing their supposed tolerance for unions as mere public relations, hiding their fundamental intransigence. In his 1904 piece, "Organized Capital Challenges Organized Labor," Ray Stannard Baker canonized Paul Blatchford of the CMTA for establishing friendly, but not exclusive, relations with his unions. But within the same piece, Baker condemned EA members as phony reformers, summarizing their beliefs as "yes, we believe in unionism, but *damn the unions.*" Later that year, Baker disavowed the open shop entirely after investigating New York's garment industry. Famed attorney Clarence Darrow similarly commented, "The open shop furnishes, and always has furnished, the best possible means of destroying the organization of the union," noting the ease with which such employers found nonunion men to undermine the union's internal discipline. And writers increasingly blamed corporate employers for industrial violence. Labor journalist Luke Grant argued that the open shop groups pressured businessmen to fight workers,

---

[36] Luke Grant, "Industrial Democracy: The Walking Delegate, *Outlook* 84 (November 10, 1906): 615–21; Jane Addams, "Trade Unions and Public Duty," *American Journal of Sociology* 4:4 (1899): 454–55, 458; *Puck* 53:1365 (April 29, 1903): center; *Puck* 53:1374 (July 1, 1903): cover; *Puck* 53:1377 (July 22, 1903): cover; *Puck* 53:1372 (June 17, 1903): cover; Leroy Scott's Broadway play, *The Walking Delegate* (New York: Doubleday, 1905); Clarkin, "The Daily Walk of the Walking Delegate," 299–301, 304; John Mangan, *History of the Steam-fitters Protective Association of Chicago* (Chicago: Steamfitters Protective Association, 1930), 65. For other examples of the political metaphor, see "The Walking Delegate," *The Independent* 55:2846 (June 18, 1903) 1467; "A Walking Delegate Convicted," *The Outlook* 74 (August 29, 1903): 1010–11; Michael Kazin, *Barons of Labor: The San Francisco Building Trades and Union Power in the Progressive Era* (Chicago: University of Illinois Press, 1989), 102–3; Richard R. Myers, "Inter-Personal Relations in the Building Industry," *Applied Anthropology* 5:2 (Spring 1946): 7.

shunning the Illinois State Board of Arbitration, and rejecting peaceful solutions.[37]

No issue better exposes the reformers' doubts regarding both corporations and craftsmen than the employment African-American strikebreakers. Activists were divided in regard to the replacements themselves. Authors like Upton Sinclair vilified the strikebreakers, painting them in the most lurid racial terms as brutes, prone to gambling, fighting, and vice. But other reformers blamed white craftsmen for shunning black workers. In 1899, African-American sociologist W. E. B. DuBois described the plight of "negro artisans," denied a living by the closed shop. In 1903, *The Nation* argued that unions left blacks with few choices but to take replacement work. Amidst the racial violence of the teamsters' strike of 1905, leaders of Chicago's African-American community, including anti-lynching crusader Ida Wells-Barnett, organized a rally of 1,000 people to support equal opportunity generally and black replacements specifically. In 1908, Ray Stannard Baker chided craftsmen for using race to strengthen their "labor monopoly," blaming exclusive agreements for the isolation, unemployment, and poverty of many black workers.[38]

But, almost universally, reformers reprimanded the *employers* for hiring the Southern replacements. Observers charged that businesses scoured the slums and levees of St. Louis, bringing dissolute and desperate men to Chicago. More importantly, reporters like Luke Grant saw black strikebreakers as inflaming the passions of white workers, worsening the violence. Even W. E. B. DuBois, perhaps the first

[37] John Keith, "Cures for the Labor Problem," *WSJ*, February 29, 1904, 6; Baker, "Organized Capital Challenges Organized Labor," 283, 289–91; Baker, "The Rise of the Tailors," 137–9; Darrow quoted in Howard T. Lewis, "The Economic Basis of the Fight for the Closed Shop," *Journal of Political Economy* 20:9 (November 1912): 932; "Arbitration Discouraged," *NYT*, October 14, 1903, 5.

[38] Tuttle, *Race Riot*, 117–19; Upton Sinclair, *The Jungle* (New York: The New American Library, 1906), 265–67, 270–71; W. E. B. DuBois, *The Negro Artisan*, Atlanta University Publication, No. 7 (1902); W. E. B. DuBois, *The Philadelphia Negro: A Social Study* (New York: Schocken Books, 1969), 128–29, 332–33; "The Negro and the Trade Unions," *The Nation* 76:1966 (1903): 186–87; Norwood, *Strikebreaking and Intimidation*, 103; Ray Stannard Baker, *Following the Color Line: American Negro Citizenship in the Progressive Era* (New York: Harper Torchbook, 1964), 133–36, 143–44; Idem, "The Negro's Struggle for Survival in The North," *The American Magazine* 65 (March 1908): 473–85; "Conference to Aid Negroes," *NYT*, May 31, 1909, 3; "The Negro and the Unions," *The Nation* 91:2370 (1909): 515–16.

prominent critic of union discrimination, rejected the paternalistic egalitarianism of the city's corporations. In July 1905, DuBois led a secret meeting at Fort Erie, Ontario, from which came the Niagara Movement, a forerunner of the National Association for the Advancement of Colored People. In the aftermath of the Chicago Teamsters' Strike, the attendees issued a declaration of principles that decried not only white workers for, "boycotting and oppressing thousands of their fellow-toilers, simply because they are black," but also employers for, "importing ignorant Negro-Americans laborers in emergencies," "affording them neither protection nor permanent employment," and exacerbating "the war of labor and capital." Though appalled by union racism, DuBois refused to embrace opportunistically color-blind employers.[39]

Reformers resolved their uncertainty by promoting a vision of "responsible unionism." Activists desiring to help workers could not dismiss the unions. And to achieve their other goals, progressives needed a working-class constituency that could carry elections, justify their claims to the public interest, and rebut critics who accused them of being effete or sterile puritans. In the 1890s, Mary Kenney, a labor organizer affiliated with Jane Addams' Hull House, sided with notorious bartender's union official William C. Pomeroy in his dispute with Socialist union officials Thomas and Elizabeth Morgan. Similarly, in 1904, Addams endorsed plumbers' union official Simon O'Donnell in an unsuccessful aldermanic campaign against infamous "boodler" John Powers. In 1905, reformers joined with the teamsters, the teachers, and various honest unions to elect Democratic Judge Edward Dunne mayor, a major victory for advocates of municipal ownership of the streetcar lines.[40]

[39] Grant, "Rights and Wrongs," 890; "Declaration of Principles of the Niagara Movement," in *The Seventh Son: The Thought and Writings of W. E. B. DuBois*, v. 1, ed., Julius Lester (New York: Random House, 1971), 430; James McPherson, *The Abolitionist Legacy: From Reconstruction to the NAACP* (Princeton, NJ: Princeton University Press, 1975), 380; Elliot Rudwick, "The Niagara Movement," *Journal of Negro History*, 42:3 (July 1957): 179; August Meier and John H. Bracey, Jr., "The NAACP as a Reform Movement, 1909–1965: 'To Reach the Conscience of America,'" *Journal of Southern History* 59:1 (1993): 6.

[40] Ruth O'Brien, "'Business Unionism' v. 'Responsible Unionism': Common Law Confusion, the American State, and the Formation of Pre-New Deal Labor Policy," *Law and Social Inquiry* 18:2 (Spring 1993): 255–96; Katherine K. Sklar, *Florence Kelley and the Nation's Work: The Rise of Women's Political Culture, 1830–1900* (New Haven: Yale University Press, 1995), 214–15; "Tips on Council Needs," *CRH*, April 2, 1904, 4; "Honest Council Given Big Vote; League Victory," *CRH*, April 6, 1904, 4; Allen F. Davis, *Spearheads For Reform:*

The desire for these fruitful alliances forced reformers either to downplay their criticisms of the tradesmen, or to participate in violent inter-union disputes. Seeing unions as crucial to their political and humanitarian goals, progressives began rationalizing exclusivity, graft, and violence. In his 1905 study of the Chicago teamsters, institutional economist John Commons dispassionately described conditions in the industry. He noted the corruption of some officials, but then explained that the workers had learned "self-government," their union becoming an "economic" rather than "criminal" institution. Though favoring a rather different approach to labor policy than Commons, Jane Addams similarly defended walking delegates, sympathetic strikes, and boycotts, describing unions as democratic organizations engaged in a bitter but just war with employers. Addams blamed the youthful exuberance of newly formed unions for violence and the unscrupulousness of the business community for corruption.[41]

Others like journalist Ernest Poole and Luke Grant favored direct action, helping upright union officials like Charles Dold break Martin "Skinny" Madden's control of the CFL in 1903. During the packinghouse strike of 1904, Poole became the spokesman for Michael Donnelly's Amalgamated Meat Cutters' Union. When that walkout failed, Poole publicly charged teamsters' officials with betraying the butchers, leading to president Al Young's dismissal. After the 1905 strike, Grant described this common struggle:

> I'm not an uplifter of the ignorant poor; I'm only a democrat who believes people can uplift themselves. I believe in uplifting grafters, especially that man with the brick in his fist. And don't make any mistake. Most of the union boys think the same way. And we've been getting busy, and in Chicago, half the labor grafters have already been uplifted.

The Social Settlements and the Progressive Movement (New York: Oxford University Press, 1967), 151–62; Leidenberger, "'The Public is the Labor Union,'" 187–210; Ickes, *Autobiography of a Curmudgeon,* 101–3; Grant, "Rights and Wrongs," 888.

[41] John Commons, "Types of American Labor Organizations: The Teamsters of Chicago," *Quarterly Journal of Economics,* 19 (1905): 407, 430; Jane Addams, "Trade Unions and Public Duty," 453–59; Jane Addams, "The Present Crisis in Trades-Union Morals," *North American Review* 179 (August 1904): 181–83, 187; Katherine Kish Sklar, "Differences in the Political Cultures of Men and Women Reformers During the Progressive Era," in *Major Problems in American Women's History: Documents and Essays,* Norton and Alexander, eds., (New York: Houghton Mifflin, 2003), 263–71.

Grant saw the employers' portrayals of scheming union officials as caricatures, arguing that most walking delegates were honest public servants. But he nevertheless shared Arthur Eddy's belief that graft was an evil that tested his manly honor. Reform could neither be achieved by crusading to improve the morality of workers, nor by waiting for unions to develop, but by fighting with corrupt officials for supremacy.[42]

By contrast, attorneys like Louis Brandeis and Carroll Wright saw the legitimization of collective bargaining as the basis for "responsible" unionism. As the editor of *The Nation* commented in 1904, most unions were unincorporated associations, loose groups of individuals lacking "standing" or "capacity," that is, the ability to sue and be sued in court. Brandeis concluded that this status encouraged unlawful behavior. Workers resorted to strikes, boycotts, picketing, and violence only because they could neither sign contracts for their members, nor enlist the state in commanding obedience to agreements. At the same time, immunity from a range of tort actions allowed unincorporated unions to inflict damages without liability. An employer might sue the individual unionists, but he had no recourse against the union. Brandeis felt that this caused employers to respond with punitive legal remedies such as injunctions and criminal convictions that failed to discriminate between positive and negative forms of collective activity, punishing peaceful picketing as harshly as bloodshed.[43]

Incorporation promised simultaneously to solve the problems of liability and legitimacy. State-chartered unions were corporate persons

[42] Ernest Poole, "How a Labor Machine Held Up Chicago, and How the Teamsters Union Smashed the Machine," *The World To-Day* 7:1 (July 1904): 896–905; "Ernest Poole, 69, Novelist, Is Dead," *NYT*, January 1, 1950, 20; Grant quoted in Poole, "The Widening Sense of Honor," 819–23, esp. 820; Grant, "Rights and Wrongs," 890; Hutchins Hapgood, *The Spirit of Labor* (New York: Duffield & Company, 1907), 294–300, esp. 296, 297; Luke Grant, "Industrial Democracy: The Walking Delegate," *Outlook* 84 (November 10, 1906): 615; Graham Taylor, "End of an Industrial Brigand," *Survey* 22 (June 12, 1909): 401–3; Tuttle, *Race Riot*, 114–19.

[43] "Remedies against Unions," *The Nation* 78:2023 (1904): 265–66; Louis Brandeis, "The Incorporation of Trade Unions," *Green Bag* 15 (1903): 11–4; Carroll Wright, "Consolidated Labor," *North American Review* 174 (1902): 30–44 esp. 44. For labor's struggle to establish its legitimacy, see Christopher L. Tomlins, *The State and the Unions: Labor Relations, Law, and the Organized Labor Movement in America, 1880–1960* (New York: Cambridge University Press, 1985); Ernst, *Lawyers Against Labor*, esp. 147–64; William Forbath, *Law and the Shaping of the American Labor Movement* (Cambridge, MA: Harvard University Press, 1991); Ruth O'Brien, "'Business Unionism' versus 'Responsible Unionism': Common Law Confusion, the American State, and the Formation of Pre-New Deal Labor Policy," *Law and Social Inquiry* 18:2 (Spring 1993): 264–65.

legally responsible for damages they caused. Legal accountability would discourage unions from breaking contracts and engaging in violence. At the same time, incorporation gave unions the right to sign enforceable contracts for their members, thus eliminating the need for direct action. Finally, incorporation promised to deliver unions from punitive law. Like the stockholders of a corporation, members of a union chartered by the state could act collectively without fear of criminal conspiracy indictments. Brandeis finally argued that incorporation undermined the equity jurisdiction of courts issuing restraining orders, claiming that judges could not enjoin financially responsible labor unions. This belief was based upon a longstanding principle of equity law, stating that plaintiffs seeking injunctions must prove that no common law remedies exist. Historically, employers petitioned for equity jurisdiction by charging unions with incapacity and the individual defendants with financial irresponsibility. When unions gained financial and legal standing, Brandeis argued, employers lost their ability to enjoin them.[44]

Brandeis wanted to formalize craft governance, creating a framework allowing workers to set wages without costly strikes while protecting employers from arbitrary stoppages, property damage, and violence. In a 1903 speech harkening back to John Adams, he exhorted unions to show "that they are amenable to law," willing to accept the "consequences if they transgress," and "in full sympathy with the spirit of the people, whose political system rests upon the proposition that this is a government of law, and not of men." Having established stable contractual relationships, incorporated unions could engage in industrial arbitration, a much-heralded reform. An avid follower of efficiency expert Frederick Winslow Taylor, Brandeis undoubtedly believed such agreements could permit workers to trade increased productivity for higher wages and shorter hours. Hardly a partisan advocate of organized labor, Brandeis proposed a legal compromise and model for industrial relations that he believed offered significant benefits to all sides. But, like all progressive reforms, his attempt to adjust the interests of labor, capital, and society was itself speculative and dependant on the full faith of the participants, many of whom saw no need for any change at all.[45]

[44] Brandeis, "The Incorporation of Trade Unions," 13; Herbert Hovenkamp, "Labor Conspiracies in American Law, 1880–1930," *Texas Law Review* 66:5 (April 1988): 919–65, esp. 958–62.
[45] Brandeis, "The Incorporation of Trade Unions," 14; Beckner, *A History of Illinois Labor Legislation*, 21; Industrial Commission, *Report of the Industrial Commission on the Relations and Conditions of Capital and Labor Employed in Manufactures and General Business*, v. 7 (Washington, DC: Government Printing

Craftsmen Respond

Craft workers and employers experimented with the reforms that suited their interests, but viewed most such proposals with a mixture of alarm and skepticism. The lack of any intellectuals in the local labor movement complicated engagement between reformers and the craftsmen. While open shop attorneys like Fred Job easily adjusted their version of classical liberalism to the society's new utilitarianism, the craftsmen confronted a far more challenging theoretical task – finding justification for their authority in a progressive rhetoric preoccupied with the public interest and the rule of law. The job fell to union and association officials, who, like local party politicians, spent their energy building organizations, maintaining alliances, and enforcing agreements. Rather than writing treatises developing a coherent justification for their behavior, craftsmen cultivated public opinion by presenting themselves as voluntary associations committed to individual rights and self-improvement.[46]

Some tradesmen embraced calls for purification, overcoming gender, class, political, and geographic divisions. In the 1890s, unions began indemnifying themselves against losses due to fraud. A coalition of Socialists, women's trade unionists, and delegates from Southern Illinois purged profligate bartenders' organizer William C. Pomeroy from the Illinois State Federation of Labor. Expelling the stalwart Democrat turned McKinley Republican in 1896 for unpaid debts, the ISFL eventually passed a constitutional amendment to prevent him from returning to power. In 1903, an unlikely coalition of teamsters, largely female teachers, and manufacturing workers, led by Socialist cigarmaker Charles Dold, took control of the CFL from "Skinny" Madden's Harrisonite Democratic building trades' faction. In each case, elements severed labor's ties to party machines and marshalled the union vote behind candidates supporting municipal ownership of the streetcars and other progressive policies.[47]

Office, 1901), 803. Henceforth listed as IC, *Reports*, v. 7. Louis D. Brandeis, *Scientific Management and the Railroads: Being Part of a Brief Submitted to the Interstate Commerce Commission* (New York: Engineering Magazine, 1912).

[46] See, for example, IC, *Reports*, v. 8, 429–40.

[47] *Butchers and Grocery Clerks Association v. U.S. Fidelity & Guaranty*, case #205590, Sup.C.C. (1900); Sklar, *Florence Kelley*, 214–15; Eugene Staley, *History of the Illinois State Federation of Labor* (Chicago: University of Chicago Press, 1930), 100–40; Schneirov, *Labor and Urban Politics*, 320–21; "Federation of Labor," *Stevens Point Daily Journal*, December 16, 1896, n.p.; "Fraud Charge by Labor," *CDT*, January 18, 1903, 1; "Slug at Labor Elections," *CDT*, January 19, 1903, 1; "Booming Darrow; Mayor Worries," *CDT*, January 20,

Once in power, these reform unionists refined craft governance. They turned inward, investigating charges that team owners' official John Driscoll had paid bribes to union officers to end strikes. In May 1903, Michael Donnelly of the butchers' union alleged that Driscoll had offered John Floerch of the Packing Trades Council $75 every month for inside information regarding strikes. Donnelly's revelations led to a reform wave that felled the old regime without cutting its cultural roots. The teamsters' national body removed its president, Al Young, replacing him with Cornelius Shea, an official from Boston. In April 1904, the teamsters' unions broke with their own Chicago Board of Arbitration and pressured all but one trade association to dismiss Driscoll, whom they charged had placed "his personal advantage above all other considerations." Ernest Poole commented: "Here the men found that the exclusive union-shop agreement that Driscoll had given them could now be worked as well without him."[48]

But officials like Pomeroy, Madden, and Driscoll refused to retreat in the face of accusations. Madden tried everything to retain power in the 1903 CFL election, firing guns, initiating seven fights, hiring pickpockets, and distributing phony ballots. Seeking to regain office during the following years, Madden hired men to disrupt the CFL balloting and assault the judge of election, Amalgamated Meat Cutters' president Michael Donnelly. By contrast, John Driscoll inverted the allegations against him. Describing Donnelly as an "evil spirit," the team owners' official commented:

I don't care anything about the charges, for they were made by a man who has no business in the labor movement and belongs to an organization that has been outlawed by the American Federation of Labor as a grafting institution . . . The curse of the labor movement is their walking delegates. They are being paid in Chicago about $500,000 a year in wages and in spite of this they are holding up employers in every line of business. Let them get gay with me and I'll

1903, 3; "Labor Menaced by Disruption," *CDT*, September 8, 1903, 2; "For Smaller Central Body," *CDT*, September 9, 1903, 7; "Rise and Fall of Skinny," *CRH*, May 30, 1909, 3.
[48] "Evidence submitted by M. Donnelly and colleagues of the stock yard unions and J. C. Driscoll, secretary of the Team owners' association – Chicago, Illinois, July 9, 1903," John Fitzpatrick Papers, Box 1, Folder 1, CHS; Minutes, August 2, 1903, Chicago Federation of Labor Papers, Reel 1: 8 in CHS; Minutes, September 6, 1903, Chicago Federation of Labor Papers, Reel 1: 17–8 in CHS; Poole, "How a Labor Machine," 900–4; Witwer, "Corruption and Reform," 27–8, 33; Commons, "Types of American Labor Organizations," 407.

show them who has paid them money, when, and why. I have done it myself rather than submit to a strike, and I know what I'm talking about when I say they are a lot of grafters and cheap skates.

When such retorts failed to quell dissent, officials physically threatened their rivals. The teamsters' union punished Luke Grant for writing disparaging articles by hiring men to slug the reporter with a brick, push him against a wall, and threaten him with a revolver. Reformer Raymond Robins suffered a similar beating in 1906 after he criticized plasterers' official and machine politician Edward Carroll.[49]

Moreover, implicated officials still commanded the respect of hundreds of supporters, who rejected the reformers as weak and effete. Many workers actually appreciated the blandishments of bon vivants like Madden, who freely spent money, buying drinks for crowds of supporters. Even reformers often declined to initiate full-scale investigations of labor organizations, fearing their effects on solidarity and public perception. Others defended leaders who secured for the rank-and-file improved wages and working conditions, regardless of their personal excesses. In a sense, some workers viewed corruption as the price they paid for strong leadership. Anarchist woodworker Anton Johannsen opposed "Skinny" Madden but also questioned the leadership of upright officials like Charles Dold. Describing Dold as a coward, who quivered when threatened, Johannsen preferred the fearless Madden. Workers who saw their manly skill as the source of their authority responded to doubts about the reformers' masculinity.[50]

Unions were suspicious of the reformers' pet project: civil service reform. Craftsmen initially manipulated licensing and inspection bodies for their own purposes. P. F. Doyle, the president of both the Engineers Progressive Union sat on the City Board of Examining Engineers. Nonunion engineers protested that they could get no job working for the city, while property owners complained that they could not discharge a union man without receiving a notice for excessive smoke. After BTC

[49] "Fraud Charge by Labor," *CDT*, January 18, 1903, 1; "Slug at Labor Elections," *CDT*, January 19, 1903, 1; "Labor Menaced by Disruption," *CDT*, September 8, 1903, 2; Poole, "The Widening Sense of Honor," 820; Hapgood, *The Spirit of Labor*, 296–98; "Rise and Fall of Skinny," *CRH*, May 30, 1899, 3; "Claims to Have Clew to the Robins Thugs," *CRH*, February 19, 1906, 4. Forging corruption occasioned financial risks as well. In 1915, the Brotherhood of Painters published a report accusing a business agent of accepting bribes. He sued for libel and won a $10,000 judgment. *Kretchmar v. Brotherhood of Painters*, case #315610, Sup.C.C. (1915); *Kretchmar v. Brotherhood of Painters*, case #333282, Sup.C.C. (1917).
[50] "Rise and Fall of Skinny," *CRH*, May 30, 2009, 3; "For Smaller Central Body," *CDT*, September 9, 1903, 7; Baker, "The Trust's New Tool," 30–1; Hapgood, *The Spirit of Labor*, 298–300; Baron, *Work Engendered*, 49, 63–4.

president Edward Carroll lost his seat on the Civil Service Commission in 1900, unions found themselves in an adversarial relationship with the board. For instance, in 1906, the commission fired William Maynard, a fire fighter, on charges of drunkenness. The Fireman's Association pressured Maynard's colleague William G. Ball to lie on the unemployed man's behalf. When commissioner Frank Wenter learned of Ball's deceit, he fired him for obeying persons intent on "intimidating the commission."[51]

Craftsmen opposed the public mediation of strikes and lockouts, preferring private arbitration agreements. They expressed little enthusiasm for the intervention of reformers into their affairs, however well meaning. In 1903, one labor newspaper flayed the NCF and Illinois State Board of Arbitration, denying the need for "middle-men to settle labor disputes." He asked "Why is it that a college professor who never worked a day at manual labor . . . is so anxious to tell the world how to settle a strike between employer and employe [*sic*]?" He mockingly challenged condescending academicians, attorneys, and ministers to live as workers before involving themselves in adjusting labor disputes. Craftsmen tried to adapt the idea of mediation to their own notions of authority. Numerous trades, such as sheet metal, signed contracts empowering boards to adjudicate grievances and enforce standards through fines and boycotts. Some craftsmen like the bookbinders forged agreements that required adherents to negotiate new terms at the time of the bargain's expiration. And some groups usurped progressive language, using the idea of conciliation to justify their power. By calling their deliberative body the Chicago Board of Arbitration, teamsters and team owners claimed to represent the broader public interest in industrial peace.[52]

Such arbitration schemes created common ground for progressive businessmen and local craftsmen. George Prussing, the president of the Illinois Brick Company, was both the child and brother of well-known reformers. His father Ernst was a German Republican who

---

[51] IC, *Reports*, v. 8, 303–5; Garth Mangum, *The Operating Engineers: The Economic History of a Trade Union* (Cambridge, MA: Harvard, 1964,) 6, 89; "Painters Ask for an Accounting," CDT, August 18, 1900, 1; "Union Sued for Damages," *CT*, October 24, 1903; "To Fight Civic Unions," *CRH*, December 11, 1906, 6; "City Firemen on Rack," December 12, 1906, 9; "Fire Fighter is Out; Blow to Federation," *CRH*, December 13, 1906, 1–2; "Union Costs Fire Job," *CRH*, December 14, 1906, 1.

[52] "Is Fighting Both Union and Employers," *CDT*, October 4, 1903, 4; "Notes from the Labor World," *CRH*, June 5, 1903, 3; "Long Peace for Team Interests," *CDT*, October 9, 1903, 4; "Great People," *Union Labor Advocate*, June 1903, 15.

had fled his homeland's 1848 revolution. In Chicago, Ernst worked as the German language editor of the city's reform newspaper, the *Inter-Ocean*, helped found the Illinois Republican Party, and aided antislavery settlers in Kansas. In 1888, the Prussings became Mugwumps, leaving the G.O.P. and endorsing Democrat Grover Cleveland and his program for tariff revision. George's half-brother Eugene was a prominent railroad attorney, a committed agnostic, an advisor to Theodore Roosevelt, and the president of the Citizens' Association of Chicago, a good government group.[53]

George Prussing's picaresque business career bridged the gap between the craft economy and the emerging world of corporate commerce. Despite his relatively affluent origins, George left school in 1861 at the age of sixteen, when he grew too large for his teachers to handle. His father was displeased, but he arranged for the teenager to become an apprentice mason. By 1866, with Ernst's assistance, George had become a contractor. He spent some time in the 1870s as a brick inspector, a city job that led to his indictment on charges of corruption. After his acquittal, George moved into mason contracting, then brick manufacturing. In 1900, he became president of the new Illinois Brick Company (IBC), a corporation created by the merger of thirty smaller firms, controlling 85 percent of the local market.[54]

Unlike his contemporary, Paul Blatchford, Prussing worked to reconcile craft governance, corporate power, and the principles of progressive reform. In 1887, Prussing led the Chicago Master Masons' Association in an aggressive but ill-fated lockout that aimed at establishing the employers' right to hire without regard to union membership. The lockout continued for over a month before both sides began to question the wisdom of a long work stoppage. Under the supervision of Judge Murray Tuley, Prussing and the bricklayers negotiated a groundbreaking system of arbitration that served as a model

---

53 *Industrial Chicago: The Building Interests*, v. 1, 668–69; Hildegard Johnson, "Adjustment to the United States," in *The Forty Eighters: Political Refugees of the German Revolution of 1848*, ed., A. E. Zucher (New York: Columbia University Press, 1950), 61–3; "Great Kansas Meeting in Chicago," *NYT*, June 5, 1856, 2; "Democrats Claim Illinois," *NYT*, October 17, 1888, 5; "An Attempt at Autobiography," v. 1, 13 in Eugene Prussing Papers, Newberry Library; Citizens' Association of Chicago, *Bulletin* 17 (September 27, 1906); "The Agnostic Testified," *NYT*, December 23, 1885, 4; "Roosevelt Gets Ideas He Likes," *NYT*, November 11, 1907, 1; *The Book of Chicagoans*, 1905, (Chicago: A. N. Marquis, 1905), 471–72.

54 "An Attempt at Autobiography," v. 1, 44–9, 49–50, 77–83 in Eugene Prussing Papers, Newberry Library; "Chicago Customs House," *CDT*, May 23, 1878, 1; "The Chicago Customs House Cases," *NYT*, May 7, 1879, 4; *The Book of Chicagoans*, 1905, 263.

for other trades in the United States, Australia, and Germany. Henceforth, the principles of union recognition and arbitration guided Prussing's dealings with unions. Between 1900 and 1905, the IBC obtained exclusive agreements with masons, brickmakers, and the teamsters' union that exchanged high wages for help in limiting competition.[55]

The brickmakers' experiment ran headlong into the law. In January 1905, IBC executive Bernard F. Weber ran for the presidency of the corporation, which had strong ties to local unions. When Weber lost to fellow stockholder George C. Prussing, he left the firm, raised $500,000 in capital, and founded the National Brick Company. Weber immediately declared his corporation an open shop, shunning union teamsters, bricklayers, and brickmakers. When the industry responded with a boycott, Weber went to the state's attorney, who initiated an investigation. A subsequent grand jury, amidst the widening teamsters' strike, indicted Prussing, his sales agent, and multiple union officials, a charge eventually resulting in a guilty plea and fine. Weber eventually capitulated to the unions, and the masons, brickmakers, teamsters, manufacturers, and contractors remained close. But the legal system made it impossible for them to trumpet their agreements as solutions to the "labor problem."[56]

Tradesmen were divided in their reaction to union incorporation and other proposals to give labor organizations a formal legal status. Contrary to most scholarship, a significant number of unions tried incorporation. The BTC was incorporated under Illinois law. John S. Kelley, president of the United Association of Journeymen Plumbers,

[55] "Builders in Council," *NYT*, March 31, 1887, 2; "Chicago's Big Lock-Out," *NYT*, May 15, 1887, 2; "Too Strong a Platform," *NYT*, May 24, 1887, 1; James C. Beeks, *30,000 Locked Out: The Great Strike of the Building Trades in Chicago* (Chicago: Franz Gindele, 1887); *Industrial Chicago: The Building Interests*, v. 1 (Chicago: Goodspeed Publishing, 1891), 666–68; Schneirov, *Labor and Urban Politics*, 249–51; "True Bills Likely for Brick Officers," *CRH*, June 27, 1905, 2; IC, *Reports*, v. 8, 88–9, 366, 476–67, 533.

[56] "Quits Brick Company," *CRH*, January 24, 1905, 10; *The Book of Chicagoans*, 1905, 599; "May Indict Brick Men," *CRH*, June 24, 1905, 9; "See Plot in Cohen Charges," *CRH*, June 24, 1905, 9; "True Bills Likely for Brick Officers," *CRH*, July 27, 1905, 2; "Brick Men are in Net," *CRH*, June 29, 1905; "Jury Begins New 'Trust' Inquiry," *CDT*, December 2, 1905, 3; "Brick Men Are Indicted," *CDT*, December 3, 1905, 3; "'Brick Trust' Hit By Heavy Fines," *CDT*, December 19, 1905, 7; "Wage Gain is Million," *CRH*, February 10, 1906, 9; True Bill, July 1, 1905, *People v. Prussing*, case #s 77368–77572, Crim.C.C., IR 134, 264–78; True Bill, December 2, 1905, *People v. Illinois Brick Co.*, case #s 79340–79341, Crim.C.C., IR 134, 290–308; "To Prevent Strikes," *CRH*, June 12, 1911; "Indicted Brickmakers Would Quash True Bill," *CRH*, June 21, 1911, 3.

supported the idea before the Industrial Commission, noting that plumbers unions were incorporated in New York, New Jersey, and Illinois. G. W. Perkins, the president of the Cigar Makers International Union (CMIU), testified that, "They [unions] are not violators of the law. I favor being incorporated, first, because it would legalize us; second give us more standing before courts. We are willing to be brought into court any minute." For this reason, the CMIU – AFL president Samuel Gompers' own international – had five incorporated locals in Illinois alone.[57]

The unions that incorporated did so less to embrace Brandeis' vision of responsible labor unionism than to attain specific concrete benefits. Though Illinois law did not provide specifically for the incorporation of labor unions, it did provide for mutual benefit societies, and many unions obtained charters under these provisions so that they could offer death benefits to members. Others such as the United Order of American Bricklayers and the BTC incorporated so they

[57] Herbert Hovenkamp, "Labor Conspiracies in American Law, 1880–1930," 919–65, esp. 958–62; Victoria Hattam, *Labor Visions and State Power* (Princeton: Princeton University Press, 1993), 130 f.49; O'Brien, "'Business Unionism,'" 261–64; Ernst, *Lawyers Against Labor*, 147–64; IC, *Reports*, v. 7, 974, 171–72. In 1903, the *List of Illinois Corporations* included these Chicago groups: Architectural Iron Workers, Associated Union of Steam Shovel and Dredgemen, Brotherhood of Engravers #1, Chicago Federation of Musicians, Chicago German Hod-carriers' Union, Chicago Jewelers' Protective Union, Chicago Journeymen Horseshoers' Local #4, Chicago Journeymen Plumbers, Chicago Junior Union of Musicians, Chicago Printed Book Binders and Paper Cutters' Union #8, Cigar Makers' Progressive International Union #15, Cigar Makers' Union #47, Cigar Makers' Union #14, Franklin Union #4, Hod-carriers and Building Laborers' Union #4, Independent Hod-carriers and Building Laborers' Union of Chicago Heights, Independent Union of Musicians, International Brotherhood of Dinkey Locomotive Engineers, International Brotherhood of Steam Shovel, Dredge, Firemen, Dock Hands and Scowmen, Iron Moulders' Union #239, Local Union #147 of the Brotherhood of Painters, Decorators and Paperhangers of America, Packing House, Stock Yards and Manufacturers Carpenters' Union of North America, Polish Hod-carriers' Union #3 of Chicago, South Chicago and Calumet River Vessel Unloaders' Union #1, Subordinate Union of #30 of the Illinois Bricklayers and Masons' International Union, Supreme Union United States Midwives' Protective Union, United Order of Bricklayers and Stone Masons. *List of Illinois Corporations* (Springfield: Phillips Bros. State Printers, 1903). Nor was Illinois unique. New York's Commissioner of Labor Statistics John McMacklin and Secretary of State John T. McDonough told the Industrial Commission that 289 incorporated unions existed in that state. IC, *Reports*, v. 7, 803–4, 820–27; Bogart, "The Chicago Building Trades Dispute. I.," 115.

might own property, solicit funds, hold parties, and issue labor directories. Far from promoting responsibility, incorporation actually enabled business dealings that became a major source of graft and fraud.[58]

Incorporation became common among unions seeking to secure independent legal existence. For example, firms engaged in rivalries, such as the Chicago Federation of Musicians and the American Musicians Union, incorporated as they struggled for AFL sanction. The Indianapolis-based Brotherhood of Painters, Decorators, and Paper Hangers obtained a charter from Indiana during a showdown with a rival painters union based in Baltimore. After 1898, a number of locals affiliated with the largely defunct Knights of Labor (KOL) incorporated, as did many independent unions such as the Independent Hod-carriers of Chicago Heights. Finally, so-called "company unions," created by nonunion firms like McCormick Reaper, West End Mine, W. W. Kimball, and the Lyon and Healy Piano Company to give their workers token organization, also obtained corporate charters. In other words, some unions embraced incorporation, but seldom for the reasons envisioned by Brandeis.[59]

Despite these experiments, most AFL officials staunchly opposed obtaining state charters. Adolph Strasser, the former president of the cigar makers' union, noted that laws requiring incorporation and compulsory arbitration would combine to enslave workers by making

[58] *Law Relating to the Incorporation of Companies for All Purposes Except Banking Insurance, Building and Loan Associations Also for the Incorporation and Consolidation of Railroads, Illinois* (Springfield: Phillips Bros, State Printers, 1900), 8–10; James B. Kennedy, *Beneficiary Features of American Trade Unions* (Baltimore, Johns Hopkins, 1908); *List of Illinois Corporations* (1903); *Building Trades Council of Chicago v. State Bank of Chicago*, case #217048, Sup.C.C. (1901); *Gray v. United Order American Bricklayers*, case #212310, Sup.C.C. (1901); "Charge Fraud at Picnic," *CDT*, September 9, 1903, 7; "Labor Vows Bryan Aid," *CRH*, August 17, 1908, 3.

[59] *American Musicians Union v. Chicago Federation of Musicians*, case #271650, Circ.C.C. (1906); *Chicago Federation of Musicians v. American Musicians Union*, 234 Ill. 504 (1908); Elizabeth Fones-Wolf and Ken Fones-Wolf, "Rank-and-file Rebellions and AFL Interference in the Affairs of National Unions: The Gompers Era," *Labor History* 35:2 (Spring 1994): 243–44; Baker, "The Trust's New Tool – The Labor Boss," 37; *Burgher v. Painters, Decorators and Paper Hangers of America*, case #234118, Sup.C.C. (1903). IC, *Reports*, v. 7, 827. Affirming state power, the Knights accepted incorporation, at least as a temporary measure. But their locals may have also sought corporate charters to gain a legal existence independent of their extremely tenuous federation. Victoria Hattam, *Labor Visions and State Power*, 130 f.49; "Powderly in Error Say Labor Leaders," *CRH*, April 27, 1904, 3; IC, *Reports*, v. 7, 430.

unions liable for strikes. Having consulted "the best lawyers," Strasser predicted that judges would drain the treasuries of state-chartered unions. "I used to believe in incorporation, but I have changed my mind," he commented, "they [incorporated unions] cannot expect justice at the hands of the courts." Other leaders such as Mahlon Garland, the former president of the Architectural Iron Workers' Union, and Samuel Donnelly, president of the International Typographical Union, agreed it was foolish to expect a piece of paper to override judicial bias.[60]

AFL president Samuel Gompers contended that courts were unlikely to punish employers who abrogated contracts – one of the proposed benefits of incorporation – but were liable to award employers damages for harms inflicted by pickets. He worried that judges might tamper with the internal government of incorporated unions – not an idle fear. When *The Nation* demanded incorporation as a remedy for labor's "absolute despotism over their members," the journal explicitly envisioned the courts overseeing union discipline, enjoining officers from fining the rank and file. Finally, union incorporation undermined the power of AFL internationals to designate unions as legitimate. By issuing charters, the state granted unions existing outside of the "House of Labor" an alternate source of authority, usurping a function jealously guarded, not by the mass of workers, but by the AFL and its affiliates.

These arguments filtered down to the local level, and most Chicago union officials opposed incorporation. At the 1901 Illinois State Federation of Labor convention, an East St. Louis carpenters' local proposed a bill banning the incorporation of labor organizations as nonprofit corporations, noting that employers used such laws to legitimize "scab" (i.e., non-AFL) unions. The federation proposed a more moderate law, indicating that some officials supported incorporation. The revised legislation prohibited the secretary of state from issuing any charter to labor organizations in the same class of labor as an existing union affiliated with the AFL or one of its subsets. In other words, craft workers accepted progressive reforms if and only if those laws recognized each union's exclusive ruling authority over its trades.[61]

[60] IC, *Reports*, v. 7, 85, 261–62, 279.
[61] IC, *Reports*, v. 7, 600–5; Samuel Gompers, "Address before the National Civic Federation, New York City, published in the American Federationist, February 1903," in *Labor and the Employer*, Hayes Robbins, ed. (New York: E. P. Dutton, 1920), 276–77; *The Nation*, 78:2023 (1904): 265–66; Herbert Hovenkamp, "Labor Conspiracies," 961; O'Brien, "Business Unionism vs. Responsible Unionism," 262; Ernst, *Lawyers Against Labor*, 155–56; Fones-Wolf, "Rank-and-file Rebellions," 237–59. Eugene Staley, *History of the Illinois*

Ambivalence Unresolved

Struggling to purify their leadership and reluctant to accept the supremacy of the courts, craftsmen retained some hope of winning the battle for public opinion. Unions argued that their beneficial effects on workers outweighed the costs of monopoly, corruption, and violence. Reformers slowly warmed to this view. Hutchins Hapgood, the Harvard-educated son of a wealthy plow manufacturer, was the very prototype of the progressive journalist. In *The Spirit of Labor* (1907), a study of union politics in Chicago, Hapgood lambasted effete Puritanism and urged his readers to shift their gaze from "the eddies on the surface – 'graft' and violence" to "the big, underlying and significant facts of the human situation." Hapgood hoped to bridge the gap between middle-class morality and working-class ethics, forging an alliance between feminine reformers and masculine workers. The enlightened middle class, he claimed, needed to be less squeamish about fighting alongside powerful rogues and more manly in their advocacy of workers' rights. But until the 1920s and 1930s, bourgeois Chicago remained hesitant – intrigued by the promise of industrial order, but frustrated with labor's excesses.[62]

For the time being, this ambivalent consensus shaped the law. The business elite largely controlled the legal institutions of the city, and they used open shop rhetoric to push prosecutors and judges to attack craft governance. Through injunctions, contempt citations, and indictments, the state directly influenced the outcome of the era's major disputes. But public sympathy gave craftsmen a shield against the most extreme punishments. And while the corruption scandals undermined the tradesmen's popular support, the focus on official malfeasance actually affirmed the potential legitimacy of collective bargaining and undermined laws asserting a narrow faith in property and contract rights.

State Federation of Labor (Chicago: University of Chicago Press, 1930), 285–86; "Powderly in Error Say Labor Leaders," *CRH*, April 27, 1904, 3.

[62] Hapgood, *The Spirit of Labor*, 298–300; *Book of Chicagoans*, 1905, 261; "Hutchins Hapgood, Author, 75, Is Dead," *NYT*, November 19, 1944, 50. The Hapgood family was not coincidentally instrumental in the establishment of Al Smith's reform coalition, which managed to bridge the gender and class divides that hobbled Progressivism. "Norman Hapgood, Editor, Dies at 69," *NYT*, April 30, 1937, 22; Norman Hapgood and Henry Moskowitz, *Up from the City Streets: A Life of Alfred E. Smith* (New York: Grosset & Dunlap, 1928); "Powers Hapgood, CIO Leader, Dead," *NYT*, February 5, 1949, 15; Richard Hofstadter, *Anti-Intellectualism in American Life* (New York: Knopf, 1963), 172–96, esp. 193–96; Hofstadter, *The Age of Reform*, 272–316; Elisabeth I. Perry, *Belle Moskowitz: Feminine Politics and the Exercise of Power in the Age of Alfred E. Smith* (Boston: Northeastern University Press, 1992).

Painting contractor John M. Stiles fought the Brotherhood of Painters for decades. The very image of middle-class respectability, this small businessman eagerly supported the corporate crusade for the open shop, joining the Building Contractors' Council in 1899 and fronting the American Anti-Boycott Association's challenge to the legality of closed-shop agreements. Courtesy of Chicago Historical Society (DN-001229).

5

Rhetoric into Law

The courts actively participated in the dramatic clashes of this period, creating a law that seems simultaneously modern and reactionary, utilitarian and liberal, pluralist and individualist. The state was the single greatest factor determining the outcome of the era's sharpest confrontations. The Teamsters' Strike of 1905 alone prompted hundreds of arrests, multiple murder indictments, a grand jury investigation, two massive criminal conspiracy trials, a $25,000 tort action against union officials Cornelius Shea and James Barry, a $25,000 libel suit against former Teamsters' president Al Young, multiple state and federal injunctions, as well as numerous contempt citations. This onslaught enabled the executives of Employers' Association of Chicago (EA) to defeat the drivers and temporarily reestablish their hegemony in the city.

As corporations asked judges to contain tradesmen, they wrote their ambiguous reform values into the law. Perceiving the open shop as enlightened, not backward-looking, courts rendered decisions appealing not only to Gilded-age notions of property, but also to progressive ideas of the public interest and the rule of law. Seeing the craftsmen as conspirators challenging the sovereignty of the state, the bench granted unions an ostensible right to exist but raged at their attempts to govern the market. Judges chose to deflect the appeals of reformers like Louis Brandeis, who called for the legitimization and purification of collective bargaining. Only at the decade's end did the courts begin policing the administration of unions and their agreements.

The legal results satisfied no one. The state obstructed the craftsmen's ability to enforce their rules, imposed significant financial burdens on unions and associations, and turned officials into outlaws. Judges ignored the reformers' dream of stable, legally enforceable, and honest collective bargaining. But corporations were also frustrated. While the courts halted the spread of craft governance to manufacturing, they proved reluctant to interfere in union disciplinary

157

proceedings and incapable of freeing trades like construction from private regulation. Tradesmen proved surprisingly resolute, and their organizations, durable. Again and again, they survived punishments to maintain control over prices, wages, and conditions in Chicago's craft economy.

Open Shop Crusade and Progressive Law

American courts fixated on urban craftsmen, their restrictive rules, and their direct, physical modes of enforcement. Historians often see turn-of the-century law as the employer's blunt instrument, used to cudgel industrial workers or – depending on one's politics – to protect property rights and liberty of contract. If scholars disagree whether judges were Gilded-age individualists or modernizing progressives, then they concur that class warfare inspired the era's flood of injunctions, indictments, and citations. Neither interpretation explains why even the most conservative judges spoke so little about labor per se, and so much about lawlessness, monopoly, conspiracy, and sovereignty. Judges invited debate and even confusion by defending the workers' right to organize while simultaneously restraining union protest.[1]

To understand the contradiction between the courts' seeming tolerance for unions and their harsh decisions, one must see the emerging labor jurisprudence as a component of the open shop campaign

[1] William E. Forbath, *Law and the Shaping of the American Labor Movement* (Cambridge, MA: Harvard University Press, 1991); Victoria C. Hattam, *Labor Visions and State Power: The Origins of Business Unionism in the United States* (Princeton, NJ: Princeton University Press, 1993); Sylvester Petro, "Injunctions and Labor Disputes: 1880–1932. Part 1: What the Courts Actually Did – and Why," *Wake Forest Law Review* 14 (June 1978): 341–576; B.W. Poulson, "Criminal Conspiracy, Injunctions, and Damage Suits in Labor Law," *Journal of Legal History* 7 (September 1986): 212–27; Richard Epstein, "A Common Law for Labor Relations: A Critique of the New Deal," *Yale Law Journal* 92 (July 1983): 1357–1408; Howard Dickman, *Industrial Relations in America: Ideological Origins of a National Labor Relations Policy* (LaSalle, IL: Open Court Press,) 1987; Herbert Hovenkamp, *Enterprise and American Law, 1836–1937* (Cambridge, MA: Harvard University Press, 1991); Morton Keller, *Regulating a New Economy: Public Policy and Economic Change in America, 1900–1933* (Cambridge, MA: Harvard, 1990); Christopher Tomlins, *The State and the Unions: Labor Relations, Law, and the Organized Labor Movement in America, 1880–1960* (New York: Cambridge University Press, 1985); Daniel Ernst, *Lawyers Against Labor: From Individual Rights to Corporate Liberalism* (Chicago: University of Illinois Press, 1995); Andrew Wender Cohen, "Business Myths, Lawyerly Strategies, and Social Context: Ernst on Labor Law History," *Law and Social Inquiry* 23:1 (1998): 165–84.

against craft governance. Cases are the raw material for law, and a striking number hinged on the state's willingness to protect former unionists, nonunion workers, and ambitious entrepreneurs against organized craftsmen. In 1898, two nonunion elevator operators, Charles and Dennis, complained that the Building Trades Council (BTC) had forced their dismissal. Unionists suspended for violating rules, like bandleader Bohumir Kryl, bemoaned that their former brethren now refused to work with them, causing employers to shun them as well. Independent unions went to court to protest exclusionary policies of competing organizations. The American Musicians Union complained that their members could not obtain gigs in a market controlled by the more powerful Chicago Federation of Musicians (CFM).[2]

Businesses similarly appealed to judges and juries to stop unions and associations from enforcing rules regarding hiring, wages, and prices. In 1904, nonunion bakers, barbers, and brewers, all dependent upon worker patronage, complained when unions publicized their hiring policies. After the Lockout of 1899, painting contractor John Stiles repeatedly testified that general contractors refused to hire his firm, fearing that union tradesmen might walk off the job rather than work alongside his nonunion employees. Brick dealers like Martin Emerich, sheet-metal contractors like Eli Rysdon, and retail laundresses like Mary Hennessey asked the state to punish their competitors for

[2] *People v. Davis*, 3 Ill.C.C. 516 (1898); *Burgher v. Painters, Decorators, and Paper Hangers of America*, case #234118, Sup.C.C (1903); *Gavin v. United Order of American Bricklayers*, case #218594, Circ.C.C. (1901); *Gavin v. Bricklayers*, case #227562, Sup.C.C. (1903); *Gavin v. Bricklayers*, case #243717, Sup.C.C. (1905); *Gavin v. Bricklayers*, case #266991, Sup.C.C. (1908); *Anderson v. Lake Seamen's Union*, case #241609, Sup.C.C. (1905); *Kryl v. Chicago Federation of Musicians*, case #256083, Sup.C.C. (1906); *Allen v. Chicago Federation of Musicians*, case #234926, Sup.C.C. (1904) *Chimera v. Chicago Federation of Musicians*, case #256082, Sup.C.C. (1906); *Vessella v. Chicago Federation of Musicians*, case #254135, Sup.C.C. (1906); *Bindley v. Chicago Federation of Musicians*, case #255626, Circ.C.C. (1904); *Doehne v. Chicago Federation of Musicians*, case #255329, Circ.C.C. (1904); *Ellery v. Chicago Federation of Musicians*, case #286182, Circ.C.C. (1908). For the closed shop and rival unions, see *American Musicians Union v. Chicago Federation of Musicians*, case #271650, Circ.C.C. (1906); "Orchestra on Strike for Dual Grievances," *CRH*, February 20, 1906, 9; *Chicago and Cook County Branch National Stonecutters Society of the United States v. Journeymen Stonecutters Association of North America*, 2 Ill. C.C. 118, 120 (1906); "Seeks to Enjoin War of Unions," *CDT*, March 19, 1903, 7; *Holland Construction v. Amalgamated Sheet Metal Workers*, case #229657, Sup.C.C. (1903); *Sykes Steel Roofing Co. v. Amalgamated Sheet Metal Workers*, case #228903, Sup.C.C. (1903).

enacting boycotts to force them to join associations, hire union workers, and adopt standard rates.[3]

Mid-sized manufacturers of consumer goods such as musical instruments, carriages, printing, and electrical equipment went to court to stop their skilled workers from gaining closed shop agreements. When ambitious piano maker George Bent replaced the daily wage with piece rates, his carpenters and metalworkers responded by demanding an exclusive agreement guaranteeing a return to the old pay structure. Bent locked out his union workers, hired nonmembers to run his plant, and arrayed armed guards around his property. When union pickets blocked his factory, Bent asked the Superior Court protect his property and replacement workers.[4]

[3] True Bill, November 30, 1904, *People v. Spiess,* case #75430, Crim.C.C., Indictment Record Volume (henceforth "IR") 134, 179–82; *Heusner Baking Co. v. Bakers and Confectioners,* case #272931, Circ.C.C. (1906); True Bill, September 30, 1904, *People v. Bausk,* case #74791, Crim.C.C., IR 134, 169; True Bill, January 26, 1904, *People v. Obermeyer,* case #72033, Crim.C.C., IR 134, 137; *Builders Painting and Decorating Company v. Advisory Board Building Trades,* case #227537, Sup.C.C. (1903); *Builders' Painting and Decorating v. Advisory Board Building Trades,* 116 Ill. App. 265 (1904); *Stiles v. Brotherhood of Painters,* case #232122, Sup.C.C. (1903); *Union Pressed Brick Co. v. Chicago Hydraulic Pressed Brick.,* 3 Ill.C.C. 290 (1899); *Purington v. Hinchliff,* 219 Ill. 159 (1905); Baker "Capital and Labor Hunt Together," 460–62; True Bill, July 1, 1905, *People v. Prussing,* case #s 77368–77372, Crim.C.C., IR 134, 264–78; True Bill, December 12, 1905, *People v. Illinois Brick Co.,* case #s 79340–79341, Crim.C.C., IR 134, 290–308; True Bill, October 3, 1903, *People v. Miller,* case #70799, Crim.C.C., IR 134, 104–9; "Unions with Slocum," *CRH,* June 5, 1903, 3; "Expose Pools to Grand Jury," *CDT,* October 3, 1903, 7; "Pool Secrets Bared," October 3, 1903, 9; "Indictments for 19 Contractors," *CDT,* October 4, 1903, 4; *Doremus v. Hennessey,* 176 Ill. 608 (1898).
[4] George P. Bent, *A Pioneer's Historical Sketches: Four Score and More Years of American History in the Making* (Chicago: Geographical Publishing Co., 1928), 156–60; Bill, February 10, 1900 in *Bent v. Piano and Organ Worker Union,* case #204497, Sup.C.C. (1900); *Piano and Organ Supply Company v. Piano and Organ Worker Union,* case #232465, Sup.C.C. (1903); *Piano and Organ Workers Union v. P. & O. Supply Co.,* 124 Ill. App. 353 (1906); *Shields v. People,* 132 Ill. App. 109 (1907); "Danger in Union Idea," *CRH,* February 1, 1904, 7; Emily Clark Brown, *Book and Job Printing in Chicago* (Chicago: University of Chicago Press, 1931); Harold Barton Myers, "Policing of Labor Disputes in Chicago," 464–67; *Typothetae v. Franklin Union Number Four,* case #232708, Sup.C.C. (1903); True Bill, January 28, 1904, *People v. Lindemann,* case #72078, Crim.C.C., IR 134, 133–34; True Bill, October 16, 1903, *People v. Woerner,* case #71762, Crim.C.C., IR 134, 133–34; *Franklin Union #4 v. People,* 121 Ill. App. 647 (1905); *Franklin Union #4 v. People,* 220 Ill. 355 (1906); *Flannery v. People,* 127 Ill. App. 526 (1906); *Flannery v. People,* 225 Ill. 62 (1907); *Donnelley v. Franklin Union*

Powerful corporate interests often backed these complainants. Beginning with the Building Trades Lockout of 1899, the elite made new law a primary objective. High-powered attorney Levy Mayer complained of "a hungry, rapacious rebellion against property rights." Similarly, James Miller, chair of the legal committee of the Building Contractors' Council, detailed his program for dealing with "coercive trade-unionism," including laws barring unions from interfering with employers' rights, ordering strikes, and enforcing their rules. In the following years, the organizations that conceived the open shop – groups like the Employers' Association (EA), the Illinois Manufacturers' Association (IMA), the American Anti-Boycott Association (AABA), and the Chicago Metal Trades Association – provided the financial and legal backing for these disgruntled tradesmen to seek satisfaction in court.[5]

Two minor lawyers affiliated with the AABA, Alexander C. Allen and Adolph Wesemann, initiated many such suits, but elite attorneys with progressive credentials handled a high percentage of these cases. Frederick Job, the secretary of the EA and former chair of the Illinois State Board of Arbitration, founded a partnership that handled many cases. Nathan William MacChesney, a corporate director, YMCA counsel, and later a law professor and reformer, represented sailor Peter Anderson against the Lake Seamen's Union. Levy Mayer, the architect of the meat, sugar, and liquor trusts, helped the IMA contest antitrust laws and the Employers' Teaming Co. obtain a federal injunction against the teamsters. The firm of Tenney, Coffeen, Harding, and Wilkerson petitioned the appellate court in three of the period's most important cases: *Kellogg Switchboard* (1905), *Franklin Union #4* (1906), and *Barnes v. Chicago Typographical Union #16* (1908). Its lead partner, Horace Kent Tenney, was the president of the Chicago Bar Association and a professor at the University of Chicago Law School.

#4, case #234015, Sup.C.C. (1903); *Rand McNally v. Franklin Union #4*, case #233046, Sup.C.C. (1903); *Childs v. Franklin Union #4*, case #234227, Sup.C.C. (1903); *Ouclay v. Franklin Union #4*, case #232812, Sup.C.C. (1903); *Kellogg Switchboard and Supply v. Brass Workers Union Local #127*, case #230199, Sup.C.C. (1903); *Christensen v. Kellogg Switchboard* 110 Ill. App. 61 (1903); *O'Brien v. People ex rel Kellogg Switchboard and Supply Co.*, 216 Ill. 354 (1905); Myers, "Policing of Labor Disputes," 433–59; Ernst, *Lawyers Against Labor*, 95–100; *Dunbar v. American Telephone and Telegraph*, 238 Ill. 456 (1909).

5 IC, *Reports*, v.8, 73, 77; James Miller, "Coercive Trade-Unionism as Illustrated by the Chicago Building-Trades Conflict," *Journal of Political Economy* 9:3 (June 1901): 348–50; "Witnesses Dare Not Testify," *NYT*, September 12, 1903, 5.

His colleague, Milo Coffeen, was a director of the Kellogg Switchboard corporation.[6]

These attorneys had three legal instruments at their disposal: injunctions, judgments for damages, and criminal indictments. As historians often note, employers used injunctions to stem picketing during strikes and lockouts. But businessmen also asked judges to enjoin craftsmen from enforcing their rules. For example, brick manufacturer Martin Emerich requested the court protect his right to buck price agreements. Others like John Stiles, the Heusner Bakery Co., and the Sykes Steel Roofing Co. petitioned the courts to restrain unions from pressuring them to sign exclusive agreements or to shun a competing local. Suspended members of the CFM and the Bricklayers and Masons' International Union asked the courts to guard them from their own unions, while members of the National Stonecutters' Society asked the court to protect them from a rival organization.[7]

[6] Ernst, *Lawyers Against Labor,* 58, 96–9; *Chicago Cigar Manufacturers Association v. Cigar Makers International Union,* case #238016, Sup.C.C. (1904); *Anderson v. Lake Seamen's Union,* case #241609, Sup.C.C. (1905); John Leonard, ed., *Book of Chicagoans* (Chicago: A.N. Marquis, 1905), 314, 524; Edgar Lee Masters, *Levy Mayer and the New Industrial Era: A Biography* (New Haven: Yale University Press, 1927), 41–68, esp. 65–6; *Employers' Teaming Co. v. Teamsters Joint Council,* 141 F. 679 (1905); *Garrigan v. United States,* 163 F. 16 (1908); Edward M. Martin, *The Role of the Bar in Electing the Bench in Chicago* (Chicago: University of Chicago Press, 1936), 106; "Horace K. Tenney, Noted Lawyer, Dies," *NYT,* October 30, 1932, 36; *O'Brien v. People ex rel Kellogg Switchboard,* 216 Ill. 354 (1905); *Franklin Union #4 v. People,* 220 Ill. 355 (1906); *Barnes v. Typographical Union,* 232 Ill. 424 (1908).

[7] *Kellogg Switchboard and Supply v. Brass Workers Union Local #127,* case #230199, Sup.C.C. (1903); *Builders Painting and Decorating Co. v. Advisory Board Building Trades,* case #227537, Sup.C.C. (1903); *Builders Painting and Decorating Company v. Advisory Board Building Trades,* 116 Ill. App. 265 (1904); *Union Pressed Brick Co. v. Chicago Hydraulic Pressed Brick Co.,* 3 Ill.C.C. 290 (1899); *People ex rel Emerich v. Chicago Masons and Builders,* case #219401, Circ.C.C. (1901); *Stiles v. Brotherhood of Painters,* case #232122, Sup.C.C. (1903); *Heusner Baking Co. v. Bakers and Confectioners Union #2,* case #272931, Circ.C.C. (1906); "Seeks to Enjoin War of Unions," *CDT,* March 19, 1903, 7; *Holland Construction v. Amalgamated Sheet Metal Workers,* case #229657, Sup.C.C. (1903); *Sykes Steel Roofing Co. v. Amalgamated Sheet Metal Workers,* case #228903, Sup.C.C. (1903); *Vessella v. Chicago Federation of Musicians,* case #254135, Sup.C.C. (1906); *Doehne v. Chicago Federation of Musicians,* case #255329, Circ.C.C. (1904); *Ellery v. Chicago Federation of Musicians,* case #286182, Circ.C.C. (1908); *Gavin v. Bricklayers and Masons' International Union,* case #227562, Sup.C.C. (1903); *Chicago and Cook County Branch National Stonecutters Society of the United States v. Journeymen Stonecutters Association of North America,* 2 Ill. C.C. 118, 120 (1906).

Plaintiffs also demanded the court award them damages for harms caused by craft governance. Between 1904 and 1906, three bandleaders sued the CFM, demanding as much as $10,000 for interfering with their employment. In 1903, painter John P. Burgher sought $35,000 in damages from his former union, Local #147, while James Gavin, "the only nonunion bricklayer in Chicago," asked for $75,000. In 1904, Indiana brick dealer George Hinchliff asked a jury to award him $100,000 after being denied permission to sell material in the city. Painting contractor John Stiles sued 42,000 workers affiliated with eight unions for $50,000. Others demanding compensation included laundress Mary Hennessey and brick manufacturer Martin Emerich.[8]

Complainants pushed state's attorneys to expand the use of criminal law against tradesmen. Dismissed elevator operators Charles and Dennis asked the grand jury to indict union officers for blacklisting them. Bakers, brewers, and barbers all complained that unionists had conspired to discourage the public from buying their goods. Sheet metal contractor Eli Rysdon and brick manufacturer Bernard Weber pressed for charges against their peers for restraining trade through pools and exclusive agreements.[9] Employers used the criminal law to

[8] *Kryl v. Chicago Federation of Musicians*, case #256083, Sup.C.C. (1906); *Allen v. Chicago Federation of Musicians*, case #234926, Sup.C.C. (1904); *Chimera v. Chicago Federation of Musicians*, case #256082, Sup.C.C. (1906); *Burgher v. Painters, Decorators and Paper Hangers of America*, case #234118, Sup.C.C. (1903); *Gavin v. Bricklayers*, case #243717, Sup.C.C. (1905). Gavin also sued for $25,000 and $30,000. *Gavin v. United Order of American Bricklayers*, case #218594, Circ.C.C. (1901); *Gavin v. Bricklayers*, case #266991, Sup.C.C. (1908); *Purington v. Hinchliff*, 219 Ill. 159 (1905); Baker, "Capital and Labor Hunt Together," *McClure's Magazine* 21 (1903): 451–63; *Doremus v. Hennessey*, 176 Ill. 608 (1898); *Stiles v. Brotherhood of Painters*, case #231675, Sup.C.C. (1903); "Forty-Two Thousand are Made Defendants," *Marion Daily Star*, September 10, 1903, 1; *Union Pressed Brick Co. v. Chicago Hydraulic Pressed Brick Co.*, case #216762, Circ.C.C. (1901). See also *Anderson v. Lake Seamen's Union*, case #241609, Sup.C.C. (1905).

[9] *People v. Davis*, 3 Ill.C.C. 516 (1898); True Bill, September 30, 1904, *People v. Bausk*, case #74791, IR 134, 169; True Bill, November 30, 1904, *People v. Spiess*, case #75430, IR 134, 179–82; True Bill, January 26, 1904, *People v. Obermeyer*, case #72033, Crim.C.C., IR 134, 137; True Bill, October 3, 1903, *People v. Miller*, case #70799, Crim.C.C., IR 134, 104–9; "Unions With Slocum," *CRH*, June 5, 1903, 3; "Expose Pools to Grand Jury," *CDT*, October 3, 1903, 7; "Pool Secrets Bared," October 3, 1903, 9; "Indictments for 19 Contractors," *CDT*, October 4, 1903, 4; True Bill, July 1, 1905, *People v. Prussing*, case #s 77368–77372, Crim.C.C., IR 134, 264–78; True Bill, December 2, 1905, *People v. Illinois Brick Co.*, case #s 79340–79341, Crim.C.C., IR 134, 290–308; "May Indict Brick Men," June 24, 1905, *CRH*, 9; "Brick Men are in Net," June 29, 1905, *CRH*, 4.

implicate union officials in picket-line violence, testifying that unions hired men to harass replacement workers. Manufacturer Fred Meckel pressed the grand jury to indict Carriage Workers Union officers along with three members of a "professional slugging committee" for killing Christ Carlstrom, a replacement worker who died of pneumonia while recovering from a beating. And similar cases arose in other disputes, such as the piano workers' strike of 1900 and the metal workers' strikes of 1903, and the print feeders' strike of 1904.[10]

Though open shop plaintiffs were committed to Gilded Age notions of property and contract, their legal arguments also stressed carefully conceived reform values. Witnesses told grand juries how unions and associations conspired to hurt them physically or financially, interfering with their business or their right to sell their labor. But just as intensely, they focused on the craftsmen's claims to authority. Suspended union bricklayer James Gavin claimed his former brethren had "entered into a conspiracy," established "certain rules, regulations, laws, and by-laws," and "coerced all persons other than complainant living in Cook County and following the aforesaid trade . . . to become members." Attorneys asked the courts to restore the rule of law and the sovereignty of the elected government. Alexander Allen's briefs for painter John Stiles charged the Associated Board of Building Trades with conspiring to "hold meetings, elect officers, and enact pretended 'laws.'" The construction workers' unions "combined for the unlawful purpose of usurping the legislative, executive, and judicial powers belonging to the people of the State of Illinois." Lawyers gave the supremacy of the state priority over Stiles' property rights.[11]

[10] *Shields v. People,* 132 Ill. App. 109 (1907); True Bill, May 23, 1905, *People v. Miller,* case #77028, Crim.C.C., IR 134, 213–14; True Bill, June 29, 1900, *People v. Dold,* case #59120, Crim.C.C., IR 133, 6–11; True Bill, August 7, 1902, *People v. Johnson,* case #66201, Crim.C.C., IR 134, 1–4; *Johnson v. People,* 124 Ill. App. 213 (1906); True Bill, December 24, 1903, *People v. Johnson,* case #71818, Crim.C.C., IR 134, 136; True Bill, October 16, 1903, *People v. Woerner,* case #71762, Crim.C.C., IR 134, 133–34; True Bill, January 28, 1904, *People v. Lindemann,* case #72078, Crim.C.C., IR 134, 138.

[11] Bill, February 10, 1900, *Bent v. Piano and Organ Workers,* case #204497, Sup.C.C. (1900), 7; Bill of Complaint, April 25, 1903, *Holland Construction v. Amalgamated Sheet Metal Workers,* case #229657, Sup.C.C. (1903), 2; Bill, January 12, 1903, *Gavin v. Bricklayers and Masons' International Union,* case #227562, Sup.C.C. (1903); Amended Petition, February 27, 1903, *Builders Painting & Decorating Co. v. Advisory Board Building Trades,* case #227537, Sup.C.C. (1903), 23. All Allen's briefs made the same charge. See Bill, March 18, 1903, *Sykes Steel Roofing v. Amalgamated Sheet Metal Workers,* case #228903, Sup.C.C. (1903).

Similarly, by emphasizing the monopolistic aspects of craft governance, the plaintiffs moved beyond Gilded Age notions of individual rights to a broader emphasis on the public good. They accused craftsmen of establishing a "labor trust," which injured the society as a whole. Those protesting trade agreements in construction and laundry like Stiles, Martin Emerich, Eli Rysdon, and Mary Hennessey alleged conspiracies to "eliminate all competition" and monopolize "by secret agreement." Open shop attorneys thus appealed to a public concerned with high prices and justified the application of state antitrust laws.[12]

Lacking any real alternative, the craftsmen hired criminal lawyers, personal injury attorneys, and aspiring politicians to defend them. The most eminent litigator was Clarence Darrow, the famed writer, orator, and personality. Darrow did not practice labor law until 1894 when, at the relatively ripe age of thirty-seven, he decided to represent Eugene Debs, the president of the American Railway Union, against charges of conspiracy to obstruct the mails and contempt of court during the Pullman strike. Though he continued afterward to take both personal injury and corporate cases, he paused periodically to defend union officers in transportation, woodworking, electrical equipment manufacture, and mining.[13]

Darrow's high fees and erratic behavior forced local craftsmen to depend primarily upon the developing, but still not entirely reputable, plaintiffs' bar. John Bloomingston, George Dickson, and John Geeting had built their practices by representing injured workers in damage suits against employers, private insurance companies, and the developing public workers' compensation system. Seeking to cut costs during the strikes of 1903, the CFL hired Bloomingston and Dickson's firm, the Workmen's Legal Security Co. At other times, unions hired ambitious and idealistic ethnic attorneys like William Cunnea and Jacob LeBosky, who used labor cases to develop constituencies and build political careers.[14]

[12] Amended Petition, February 27, 1903, *Builders Painting & Decorating Co. v. Advisory Board Building Trades*, case #227537, Sup.C.C. (1903), 21; Bill, March 18, 1903, *Sykes Steel Roofing v. Amalgamated Sheet Metal Workers*, case #228903, Sup.C.C. (1903), 12; *Union Pressed Brick Co. v. Chicago Hydraulic Pressed Brick Co.*, 3 Ill.C.C. 290 (1899); *Doremus v. Hennessey* 176 Ill. 613 (1898); Ernst, *Lawyers against Labor*, 90–109.
[13] Irving Stone, *Clarence Darrow for the Defense* (Garden City, NY: Doubleday, Doran, & Co., 1941), 35–66; J. Anthony Lukas, *Big Trouble* (New York: Simon & Shuster, 1997), 288–328, esp. 310, 316, 324.
[14] Staley, 248–60; Lukas, *Big Trouble*, 324, 554; Minutes, August 16, 1903, Chicago Federation of Labor Papers, Reel 1: 11, 13–5, CHS; Weston Goodspeed and Daniel D. Healy, eds., *History of Cook County* (Chicago: Goodspeed

These lawyers appealed to the classical liberalism of the courts by denying the authority craft unions so forcefully asserted on the streets. In *Burgher v. Painters* (1903), John Burgher sued his union for suspending him, then boycotting his business. The union officers granted that they had disciplined him, but denied any power over the rank and file, who shunned Burgher of their own accord. Union attorney John Bloomingston argued that his clients merely exercised their freedom of contract by defining the terms for their continued employment. Just as open shoppers endorsed the idea of organization in order to appeal to the public's sympathy for workers, unions asserted their consensual character so as to deflect the discipline of the courts.[15]

Lawyers pushed judges to grant protestors greater latitude, arguing that workers deserved the right to picket peacefully. Clarence Darrow contended that unions intended to raise wages and educate the public, not to threaten replacement workers or obstruct trade. Appealing to American values such as the right of free political expression and voluntary association, he insisted that pickets were no more a conspiracy than a religious congregation or charitable society. Lawyers pushed the boundaries of liberal thought by asking the courts to permit union workers to strike in sympathy with other tradesmen and even to boycott nonunion workplaces in the absence of a labor dispute. In both cases, counsel contended that the unions were not third parties, interfering with the private contractual relations of others; rather, all workers possessed a natural connection that gave them the right to protest adverse conditions wherever they were found. Appealing to an emerging legal utilitarianism, lawyers suggested that the demands of the new industrial society necessitated the modification of formalist interpretations of contract law.[16]

Darrow finally attacked the machinery of justice, rejecting procedures that gave free rein to judicial bias by denying unionists a hearing. He questioned the fairness of ex parte injunctions, that is, court orders issued on the statements of plaintiffs alone. Just as significantly, Darrow questioned whether Illinois law and the Fifth Amendment of the U.S. Constitution permitted judges to sentence individuals to jail

Historical Association, 1909), 730–31; *Debs v. U.S.*, 249 U.S. 211 (1919); *People v. Lloyd*, 304 Ill. 23 (1922); *Who's Who in Chicago*, v.6 (Chicago: A.N. Marquis, 1936), 235; "Municipal Voters' League Reports on Aldemanic Candidates," *CRH*, April 1, 1914, 4.

[15] See the testimony of George Henshaw in Bill of Exceptions, December 20, 1905 in *Burgher v. Painters*, case #234118, Sup.C.C. (1903), 34–43.

[16] Ernst, *Lawyers Against Labor*, 96–7, 191–210.

for violating court orders, since these punishments seemed to deny defendants their right to a jury trial.[17]

The crude realities of craft governance undermined these doctrinal arguments. The craftsmen not only used violence, they also proclaimed the supremacy of their laws and organizations. In a period where judges prohibited *legislatures* from interfering in labor contracts, voiding reform statutes guaranteeing workers a minimum wage and maximum hours, it seemed highly unlikely they would permit private organizations such as unions to pressure individuals into obeying their rules. As the craftsmen would discover, few judges believed that unions expressed the collective free will of their members. And still fewer jurists wished to deny their own authority to make and enforce injunctions.

The Institutions of Law

The legal system hearing these arguments was largely antipathetic to craftsmen and their organizations, only slowly shedding the oppressive doctrines of the previous centuries. Beginning in the 1300s, British courts had prosecuted unrecognized economic associations as conspiracies. The United States inherited this legal tradition, repeatedly trying journeymen for organizing to improve wages in the nineteenth century. But with the growth of the free labor ideology during the antebellum market revolution, American law slowly but indisputably reversed course, legalizing some forms of collective action. In *Commonwealth v. Hunt* (1842), Massachusetts Justice Lemuel Shaw invalidated the conspiracy conviction of union bootmakers accused of blacklisting a former associate. Shaw held that the concerted actions of workers became conspiratorial only when their means or ends were unlawful.[18]

The ruling in *Hunt* signaled a very long-term trend away from the stringent limitations on collective action. In the decades after the Civil War, both judicial and statutory restrictions on unions tightened, but,

---

[17] "Strikers in Court," *CRH*, April 21, 1903, 2; *O'Brien v. People*, 216 Ill. 368–70; Edwin Witte, "Value of Injunctions in Labor Disputes," *Journal of Political Economy* 32:3 (1924): 335; IC, *Reports*, v.8, 69.

[18] *Commonwealth v. Hunt*, 45 Mass. 111 (1842); Christopher Tomlins, *Law, Labor, and Ideology in the Early American Republic* (New York: Cambridge University Press, 1993), 128–219, esp., 128–29, 212; Francis Sayre, "Criminal Conspiracy," *Harvard Law Review* 35 (1922): 393–427; Richard B. Morris, *Government and Labor in Early America* (New York: Columbia University Press, 1946).

by 1900, organized labor had secured the passage of new legislation defending the right to union membership and protecting the union label. At the same time, judges like William Howard Taft and Oliver Wendell Holmes, Jr. began building a new employment law. Seeing higher wages as a public good, these judges increasingly granted workers the right to associate (i.e., to join a labor organization) and the right to quit work collectively (i.e., to strike), and the right to peacefully protest work conditions, as long as they did not intend to injure. Though many jurists remained hostile to unions and trade agreements, these progressive judges reaffirmed Shaw's ends-means test while legalizing picketing if the harmful effects of that collective protest merely coincided with workers' efforts at self-improvement.[19]

At the same time, courts also endeavored, with very limited success, to subject labor to the rule of law by making unincorporated unions civilly liable. Lacking any legal standing, unions were largely immune to lawsuit, a fact noted by Louis Brandeis and others. Persons might sue individual members, but not their association. In 1901, the British House of Lords handed down the *Taff–Vale* decision, which held a railroad workers' union financially responsible for harm done to employers. Although *Taff–Vale* caused much discussion in the United States, American employers waited nearly twenty years for a similar precedent, during which time, the difficulties of the law left them with no civil redress besides injunction. When a plaintiff sued individual unionists for damages and won, as in the famous case *Loewe v. Lawlor* (1907), the plaintiff had a difficult time collecting the award.[20]

---

[19] Ernst, *Lawyers Against Labor*, 1–9; Daniel Ernst, "Free Labor, the Consumer Interest, and the Law of Industrial Disputes, 1885–1900," *American Journal of Legal History* 36 (1992): 19–37; *Moores v. Bricklayers' Union*, 23 Wkly. Cin. Law Bull. 48; Victoria Hattam, *Labor Visions and State Power* (Princeton, NJ: Princeton University Press, 1993), 69–73; Earl Beckner, *A History of Illinois Labor Legislation* (Chicago: University of Chicago Press, 1929), 13–20, 34–9. The Illinois Supreme Court ruled the law protecting the right to union membership unconstitutional in 1900. *Gillespie v. People*, 188 Ill. 176 (1900).

[20] *Taff–Vale Railway Co. v. Amalgamated Society of Railway Servants*, A.C. 426 (1901). Only one American case affirmed this precedent, *Hillenbrand v. Builders Trade Council*, 14 Ohio Decisions, N.P. 628 (1904). The courts established the liability of unincorporated labor unions in *United Mine Workers v. Coronado Coal*, 259 U.S. 344 (1922). See also James B. McDonough, "Liability of an Unincorporated Labor Union the Sherman Law," *Virginia Law Review*, 10 (1924): 304–11. In *Loewe v. Lawlor* (1903–1917), an employer won massive damages from members of the United Hatters Union with the help of the AABA. Unable to attach the union treasury, the plaintiff attached the houses of the defendants. In the end the AFL paid most of the debt.

These new doctrines appear moderate by the standards of Gilded Age, leading some historians to see them as expressions of a new pluralist utilitarianism friendly to unions. But these decisions were ideologically consistent with arguments made by open shop advocates like Paul Blatchford. Indeed, federal court judge William Howard Taft attended Yale during the 1870s, just like the lions of the open shop movement: Daniel Davenport, the chief executive officer of the AABA, and Levy Mayer, counsel to the IMA. Yale professor and Social Darwinist William Graham Sumner clearly influenced all three men. Sumner's 1883 lament for the "Forgotten Man," the public, trapped between the millstones of organized capital and organized labor, inspired not only Taft's assumptions, but also the rhetoric of the open shop movement.[21]

Though provocative during the Grant administration, Sumner's vision had become conservative by the time of Theodore Roosevelt. The intent-ends-means test for conspiracy directly challenged the ability of tradesmen to protest conditions and enforce associational rules. Illinois statutes forbade interference, boycotting, threats, and even a whiff of violence, making these tactics illegal means. If union pickets threatened passing replacement workers, a prosecutor could indict individual workers for assault and the union officers for conspiracy. Though the new doctrine liberated workers to quit work en masse, they could not use strikes to punish employers for violating an established agreement, for this could be construed as a malicious goal. Though Illinois antitrust statutes briefly exempted workers and small businessmen, the Illinois Supreme Court decisively struck down this exception in 1903 after pressure from Levy Mayer and the IMA. Thus, workers who demanded the termination of nonunion employees risked criminal conspiracy prosecutions, as exclusive agreements were an unlawful end.[22]

Ernst, *Lawyers Against Labor*, 152–55. For a full list of successful damage suits against unions, see Witte, *The Government in Labor Disputes*, 345–48.

[21] *In re Phelan* 62 F. 803 (S.D. Ohio 1894); William Graham Sumner: *The Forgotten Man and Other Essays*, ed., Albert G. Keller (New Haven: Yale University Press, 1918), 465–98; Ernst, *Lawyers Against Labor*, 30–7, 82–3; Gordon L. Hostetter and Thomas Q. Beesley, *It's a Racket!* (Chicago: Les Quin Books, 1929), vii; "Levy Mayer, Noted Lawyer, Found Dead," *NYT*, August 15, 1922, 11.

[22] The law exempted businesses whose costs were "mainly made up of wages" and organizations whose purpose was "to maintain or increase wages." *All the Laws of the State of Illinois Passed by the Fortieth General Assembly* (Chicago: Chicago Legal News, 1897), 153. The invalidation of this law was a victory for corporations, not only because it made unions more vulnerable to

If doctrine favored the open shop attorneys, so did the biases of the legal system. Cook County judges favored stern limits on unions, trade associations, and exclusive agreements. Judge Jesse Holdom authored more writs that any other magistrate in early twentieth-century Chicago, and perhaps in America as a whole. Born in England in 1851, Holdom arrived in the city at the age of seventeen and began practicing law at twenty-one. He entered the office of Joshua C. Knickerbocker, where he established a relationship with Victor Lawson, the conservative Republican publisher of the *Chicago Daily News*. With Lawson as his sponsor, Holdom was elected to the Superior Court of Cook County in 1898 and remained in various judicial positions until 1930.[23]

Holdom staunchly defended property, law, and order against insurgent workers. In 1905, he commented that Chicago was the "very storm center of industrial strife in this country," the home to a "deadly struggle between the armies of capital and labor." Labor's distinguishing characteristics were its "reckless disregard of life, law, and morality," the "cruelty and inhumanity" of its "barbarous" physical attacks, and its "grafting" leaders. He defended his use of injunction as a remedy to the indifference of local government to the rights of employers, arguing:

> Failing protection to property and liberty under the law at the hands of the municipal authorities and in a final effort to procure relief from an intolerable situation, a court of chancery has been asked to stretch out its strong arm and protect the property of the employer from destruction . . . to ameliorate past conditions and teach organized labor their duties as well as their rights under the law.

Only by protecting the sanctity of individual (and corporate) rights and the absolute rule of law, Holdom argued, could the city free itself from "thuggery." Viewing his position as morally absolute, Holdom lambasted the judges who disagreed as corrupt partisans.[24]

conspiracy law, but also because it invalidated an 1893 amendment requiring corporations (but not other firms) to file affidavits denying participation in pools or trusts. *People ex rel. Akin v. Butler Street Foundry*, 201 Ill. 236 (1903). For other decisions regarding the exception, see, *People v. Richards and Kelly Manufacturing Co.* 1 Ill.C.C. 171 (1900); *Union Sewer Pipe Co. v. Connelly* 99 F. 354 (1900); *Connolly v. Union Sewer Pipe Co.* 184 U.S. 540 (1902); Beckner, 17–8; IC, *Reports*, v.8, 74.
[23] "Judge Jesse Holdom, Dean of City's Jurists, Dies at 78," *CDT*, July 15, 1930, 3; Martin, *The Role of the Bar in Electing the Bench in Chicago*, 253.
[24] "Address of Jesse Holdom Before the Law Club of Chicago at the University Club, September 29, 1905," *Chicago Legal News* 38 (1905–1906): 70, 71;

Products of an elite bar that claimed close ties to both progressive politics and the corporate economy, most judges saw the open shop as a real expression of their reform values. For example, federal judge Christian Cecil Kohlsaat had served in 1896 as president of the elite Chicago Urban League Club. His brother, Herman Henry Kohlsaat, was a liberal Republican, close friends with Theodore Roosevelt, a merchant baker, and the publisher of reform newspapers such as the *Chicago Record-Herald*, the *Evening Post*, and the *Inter-Ocean*. Herman's firm defied rules established by drivers, team owners, waiters, and bakers of every rank, precipitating a major strike in 1903. Herman's son-in-law was Potter Palmer, Jr., heir to one of the city's largest fortunes.[25]

Judge Kohlsaat's understanding of the public interest naturally never strayed too very far from the private interests of his friends and family. Like Taft, Kohlsaat balanced the forces working upon him by arguing that the law should constrain trusts in labor and capital equally. In 1900, the judge voided the Illinois Anti-Trust Act of 1893, charging that the law discriminated against manufacturers by exempting farmers and workers. In 1904, he stated his feelings about organized labor:

> The labor union is as much a menace to the community at this time as is the man who will corner some necessity of life and fix the price to suit himself regardless of the people . . . I do not mean to deny the union laborer the right to strike, but I do say he has no right by force to prevent another man earning a living for his family. This is a species of anarchy that labor unions must eliminate, and with the ascension of conservative men to the heads of various organizations this great problem will solve itself.

Kohlsaat's statement mirrored the open shop sentiments of men like EA secretary Frederick Job. He defined a public interest, but located it in the free market. The judge decried monopoly, but largely to undermine the legitimacy of trade agreements. Kohlsaat acknowledged the unionist's right to strike, but he held it inferior to the liberty of the nonunion employee to work without interference.[26]

"Judges Hit By Judge," *CRH*, February 16, 1905, 7; "Justice Put at Naught By Politics on Bench," *CRH*, February 17, 1905, 1.

[25] Albert Nelson Marquis, ed., *Book of Chicagoans* (Chicago: A.N. Marquis, 1911), 396–97; "Federal Judges for Chicago," *Chicago Legal News* 37 (1904–1905): 256 (504); "'To My Dear Little Pauline,'" *NYT*, June 26, 1908, 7.

[26] *Union Sewer Pipe Co. v. Connelly*, 99 F. 354 (1900); *Connolly v. Union Sewer Pipe Co.*, 184 U.S. 540 (1902); "Makes Antitrust Law Void," *NYT*, January 30, 1900, 3; "Judge Kohlsaat on Unions," *NYT*, March 9, 1904, 2.

The structure of local justice enabled public officials like Kohlsaat to enforce their biases. First, judges had tremendous job security in Chicago. Federal appointees had lifetime tenure, while the power of the local bar and the strength of certain ethnic constituencies guaranteed the continued election of judges like Holdom. Second, attorneys could choose which arbiter heard their petitions for injunction, a fact generally guaranteeing a favorable ruling. But in any case, the law required defendants to obey any injunction until a higher court decided its fate. Unions lost strikes while waiting to learn the results of their appeals. And a favorable ruling meant little, as the courts upheld the punishment of workers who violated faulty injunctions. Judges issued orders as they wished, knowing that they carried the weight of law for months and even years.[27]

Judges shared power over criminal justice with the Cook County State's Attorney, the official with authority to investigate, indict, and bring people to trial. Though an elected position, the State's Attorney was one of the few offices the business elite made absolutely certain they controlled. Republican prosecutors like Charles Deneen were closely tied to Chicago's upper class. Democratic prosecutors such as John Healy, MacClay Hoyne, and John E.W. Weyman, faced persistent pressure from the Republican press and the business community to control labor militancy. The Employers Association developed financial relationships with assistant state's attorneys, creating a revolving door between the prosecutors' office and that organization.[28]

The grand jury, the body responsible for issuing indictments, was also an elite institution. Newspaper headlines announced: "Business Men on Grand Jury." One panel contained chewing-gum magnate William Wrigley, Jr. and three other well-known employers. Grand jury foremen were professionals like Solon Spencer Beman, the architect who designed the town of Pullman or businessmen like Watson F. Blair, a self-described "capitalist," a director of the Corn Exchange National Bank, and a grain dealer on the Board of Trade, who retired at the age of forty to enjoy travel and club life. The jury commissioners chose panelists from an incomplete record of all the male voters in Cook County, the Chicago city directory, which contained few of the city's poorest residents. By 1907, the situation had become so blatant that Chicago mayor and former judge Edward Dunne pronounced the

---

[27] Gosnell, *Machine Politics*, 29; Martin, *Bar and Bench*, 75–85; *O'Brien v. People*, 216 Ill. 355, 365 (1905).

[28] "Don't Cloud the Main Issue," *Daily Labor Bulletin*, June 5, 1905, 2; "Call for Books," *Daily Labor Bulletin*, June 5, 1905, 1.

Craftsmen reviled British-born Cook County Superior Court Judge Jesse Holdom for issuing a series of injunctions restraining pickets and boycotts during the first decades of the century. His heated defenses of property belied his mild appearance. Courtesy of Chicago Historical Society (DN-003025).

grand jury a "laughing stock . . . selected by the vested interests and the privileged classes."[29]

The reorganization of Chicago's criminal justice system in 1906 raised the workers hopes but eventually empowered the elite. In 1904, the Illinois State Federation of Labor endorsed a new city charter, in part because it empowered Chicago to replace the corrupt, arbitrary, and oppressive magistrate system with a gleaming new Municipal Court. But corporations also supported the revised court, projecting it as a bulwark against insurgent tradesmen, who seemed to escape justice all too often. The police, once brutal in crushing strikes, increasingly declined to arrest politically powerful unionists. The sheriffs who enforced judicial writs were understaffed and corrupt, demanding tips for serving summonses, posting injunctions, and arresting picketers. Justices of the peace lacked the time and staff to punish unionists flooding into the police courts. Executives favored the Municipal Court in part because they believed that a professional, scientific, and modern justice system could more effectively enforce property rights. And when the reform faction of the Republican Party took control over the court, corporations found their ambitions vindicated.[30]

Judgment Days

Stacked with upper class reformers and reactionaries, the judiciary overwhelmingly endorsed the open shop vision. In August 1903, near

---

[29] "Business Men on Grand Jury," *CRH*, February 2, 1912, 9; *Book of Chicagoans, 1911*, 54; True Bill, July 3, 1903, *People v. Egger*, case #69701, Crim.C.C., IR 134, 97; *Book of Chicagoans, 1911*, 66; "Watson F. Blair, Who Recommends a Special Grand Jury for Labor Lawlessness," *CRH*, February 1, 1904, 7 "Danger in Union Idea," *CRH*, February 1, 1904, 7; True Bill, January 26, 1904, *People v. Obermeyer*, case #72033, Crim.C.C., IR 134, 137; True Bill, January 28, 1904, *People v. Lindemann*, case #72078, Crim.C.C., IR 134, 138. Other foremen listed in *Who's Who* included real estate investor Wyllys Baird, manufacturing executive John C. Cannon, banker William Edens, grain dealer William W. Hunter, insurance executive James Nye, terracotta manufacturer John R. True, nonunion brick manufacturer Bernard Weber, and insurance underwriter William Wyman. *Book of Chicagoans, 1905*, 305, 577, 631; *Book of Chicagoans, 1911*, 28, 116, 208, 511, 704; *People v. Walsh*, 322 Ill. 197 (1926); "True Bills Bury 'Books' and Bars: Mayor Censured," *CDT*, February 3, 1907, 1.

[30] Michael Willrich, *City of Courts: Socializing Justice in Progressive Era Chicago* (New York: Cambridge University Press, 2003), 25–7, 33–44; Staley, *History of the Illinois State Federation*, 297; Lindberg, *To Serve and Collect*, 64–6; Miller, "Coercive Trade Unionism," 336; IC, *Reports*, v. 8., 37, 323, 372; Forbath, *Law and the Shaping*, 111.

the beginning of the corporate crusade, labor leaders expressed a good deal of optimism about their chances in court. R.C. Wall, secretary of the CFL Defense Fund Committee stated:

> Evidently the employers have changed the battlefield from the open arena when it previously existed to that of the courts where they believe they have some prestige, can bring some influence to bear and where their chances for success are enhanced, but believing that the laws of this country are fair and equitable and that all we need is to have an equally good talent to defend our cases as they have on their side, justice will eventually crown the side which it rightfully belongs to, that of the wage earner."[31]

But within months, experience led union officials to dismiss the law as a repressive institution. In December 1903, after seeing his striking constituents hobbled by injunctions and scrutinized by the grand jury, Timothy P. Quinn, the fiery leader of the Street Car Workers noted:

> The greatest superstition of the age is the law. We used to bow down to the church; now it is the law. I wish every wage worker in the city could be buttonholed into jail by such a grand jury, for it would be a warning and an education. The greatest handicap to the progress and development of justice is the judiciary. Any action by the grand jury would merely hasten a revolt against the judges and their renditions of the laws.

At the 1904 Illinois State Federation of Labor convention, steamfitter Martin B. "Skinny" Madden and two other CFL officials introduced a resolution demanding a more egalitarian system of selecting grand jurors and stating, "corporations are using the grand jury to coerce the union men of Chicago."[32]

The courts routinely intervened in the craftsmen's attempts at enforcing their rules and agreements. Criminal courts punished craft unions and associations for boycotting nonmembers and controlling competition. In 1905, the court fined six brewers and two barbers $100 each (over $2,000 in current dollars), for conspiracy to boycott when these craftsmen printed flyers asking the public not to patronize nonunion workplaces. That same year, a judge sentenced three brick corporations, four businessmen, and two teamsters' union officers to

[31] Minutes, August 16, 1903, *Chicago Federation of Labor Meetings*, 12, CFL Papers, microfilm in CHS.
[32] "Grand Jury Decried," *CRH*, December 21, 1903, 2; True Bill, December 24, 1904, *People v. Conn*, case #71812, Crim.C.C., IR 135, 135; True Bill, January 20, 1904, *People v. Foster*, case #71884, Crim.C.C., IR 135, 142; Beckner, 296.

fines of $2,000 each ($40,500 in current dollars) for a conspiracy to restrain trade, punishing them for using an arbitration agreement to fix prices.[33]

Open shoppers successfully pressed judges to limit not only picketing, but also more abstract forms of interference. For example, in 1903, nonunion painting contractor John Stiles asked Judge Chytraus to enjoin the Brotherhood of Painters from interfering with his business. Stiles told the judge how the union had pressured a general contractor, Clark Construction, to fire him. The judge initially dismissed Stiles' petition, telling him to sue Clark for breach of contract, a ruling upheld by the Illinois Appellate Court. But, in 1904, Stiles and his AABA attorneys returned to court and showed that the painters were engaged in a continuing boycott. This time, Chytraus held the union to be acting as a conspiracy and issued a writ enjoining five of its officials.

With slight reluctance, judges interfered in union discipline. Three times between 1904 and 1905, judges enjoined the Chicago Federation of Musicians from enforcing its by-laws, including one provision requiring members to wear special union uniforms. In 1901, former bricklayers' union member James Gavin asked the Superior Court Judge Jesse Holdom to enjoin his fellow tradesmen from impeding his employment. Holdom was more conciliatory than usual, encouraging Gavin and the unions to come to agreement in open court. But eight months later, the plaintiff returned, alleging the president of the local had broken the deal, commenting "to hell with the agreement and Holdom." Faced with the union's ongoing boycott and purported contempt for the judge's authority, Holdom finally issued the writ.[34]

---

33 True Bill, January 26, 1904, *People v. Obermeyer*, case #72033, Crim.C.C., IR 134, 137; Entry, August 24, 1905, *People v. Obermeyer*, case #72033, Crim.C.C., Docket 34A, 353; "Jury Undecided in Labor Trial," *CDT*, August 25, 1905, 5; True Bill, September 30, 1904, *People v. Bausk*, case #74791, Crim.C.C., IR 134, 169; Entry, November 15, 1904, *People v. Bausk*, case #75791, Crim.C.C., Docket 35A, 110; True Bill, July 1, 1905, *People v. Prussing*, case #s 77368–77372, Crim.C.C., IR 134, 264–78; True Bill, December 2, 1905, *People v. Illinois Brick Co.*, case #s 79340–79341, Crim.C.C., IR 134, 290–308; Entry, December 18,1905, *People v. Illinois Brick Co.*, case #79340, Crim.C.C., Docket 35B, 115; "'Brick Trust' Hit by Heavy Fines," *CDT*, December 19, 1905, 7.

34 *Brindley v. Chicago Federation of Musicians*, case #255626, Circ.C.C. (1904); *Doehne v. Chicago Federation of Musicians*, case #255329, Circ.C.C. (1905); *Weldon v. Chicago Federation of Musicians*, case #263907, Circ.C.C. (1905); *Advisory Board Building Trades v. Builders Painting and Decorating Company*, case #227537, Sup.C.C. (1903); *Builders Painting and Decorating Company v. Advisory Board Building Trades of Chicago*, 116 Ill. App. 264 (1904); Decree,

Judges prohibited unionists from engaging in sympathy strikes in aid of workers outside their "natural jurisdiction." Following the logic of the new progressive doctrines, courts held such walkouts intentionally harmful and therefore conspiratorial. In 1906, Judge Julian Mack of the Cook County Circuit Court enjoined the city's building-trades unions from aiding the Journeymen Stone Cutters Association in its efforts at absorbing the National Stone Cutters Society, an independent union, ruling that they aimed "not to better the condition of the striker himself, but to assist his friend by injuring that friend's opponent." Mack continued: "There is no legal justification for such injury when the purpose is not self-preservation but to aid another." A reformer closely associated with Hull House, a friend of Louis Brandeis, and later an advisor to Franklin Roosevelt, Mack was no hoary-headed conservative. Rather, the judge's ruling reflected contemporary progressive legal thought, which was quite hostile to craft governance.[35]

Courts treated pickets especially harshly. The courts restrained bakers, piano makers, and metal workers from protesting, holding workers who persisted in contempt, fining them as much as $100 and sending them to jail for months.[36] Between 1900 and 1904, the grand jury indicted representatives of the brass molders, piano workers, electrical workers, and machinists for conspiring to interfere with replacement workers. Prosecutors used such conspiracy prosecutions to implicate union officials in the acts of their constituents. In 1905, the states' attorney prosecuted officers of Carriage and Wagon Workers Union #4 for conspiracy to assault, charging them with paying a "professional slugging committee" fifty dollars to assault eight "scabs," one of whom,

---

July 5, 1905, *Stiles v. Brotherhood of Painters*, case #232122, Sup.C.C. (1903); *Stiles v. Brotherhood of Painters*, case #231675, Sup.C.C. (1903); "Bar Sympathy Strike," *CDT*, January 13, 1903, 10; "Shake off Union Nemesis, *CDT*, September 10, 1903, 4; Supplemental Bill to 2nd Bill, October 9, 1903, *Gavin v. Bricklayers*, case #227562, Sup.C.C. (1903); Order, October 23, 1903, *Gavin v. Bricklayers*, case #227562, Sup.C.C. (1903); Order, June 28, 1904, *Gavin v. Bricklayers*, case #227562, Sup.C.C. (1903); Decree, March 7, 1905, *Gavin v. Bricklayers*, case #227562, Sup.C.C. (1903).

[35] *Chicago and Cook County Branch National Stonecutters Society v. Journeymen Stonecutters Association*, 2 Ill. C.C. 118, 120 (1906); "Let Partisan Jurors Go," *NYT*, March 24, 1904, 1; "Julian Mack Dies; 40 Years on Bench," *NYT*, September 6, 1943, 17; *Moores v. Bricklayers Union #1*, 23 Weekly Law Bulletin 48 (Ohio Supreme Court 1890); Ernst, *Lawyers Against Labor*, 191–213.

[36] *Bent v. Piano and Organ Workers Union*, case #204497, Sup.C.C. (1900); *Piano and Organ Supply Co. v. Piano and Organ Workers Union*, 124 Ill. App. 353 (1906); *Christensen v. Kellogg Switchboard*, 110 Ill. App. 61 (1903); *O'Brien v. People ex rel Kellogg Switchboard*, 216 Ill. 354 (1905); Ernst, *Lawyers Against Labor*, 95–9.

Christ Carlstrom, later died. The EA stood behind the prosecution, allegedly influencing a witness and paying lawyers Frederick Fake and James Wilkerson to assist the state's attorney. After three months, the jury convicted the seven defendants to sentences of one to five years in prison and fines up to $2,000.[37]

A sympathetic boycott begun in aid of manufacturing workers featuring extensive picketing, the Teamsters' Strike of 1905 attracted the court's full censure. On April 20, three weeks after the teamsters' union decided to honor the garment workers' strike against Montgomery Ward, Superior Court judge Theodore Brentano granted the mail-order giant an injunction restraining the drivers from interfering with its business. To gain federal jurisdiction, the EA incorporated the Employers' Teaming Company (ETC) in West Virginia. On April 28, U.S. District Court Judge Kohlsaat issued a temporary injunction protecting ETC wagons and assigned E.B. Sherman, a Republican master in chancery, to investigate the matter. Upon Sherman's recommendation, Kohlsaat issued a permanent order prohibiting anyone from blocking the streets and harassing ETC employees. Federal marshals enforced this injunction, jailing a fireman named Daniel Garrigan for throwing stones at replacements.[38]

Corporations experimented, using other legal forms to restrain the drivers. On May 3, 1905, Thomas Platt, the president of the United

37 True Bill, June 29, 1900, *People v. Dold*, case #59120, Crim.C.C., IR 133, 6–11; True Bill, August 7, 1902, *People v. Johnson*, case #66201, Crim.C.C., IR 134, 1–4; *Johnson v. People*, 124 Ill. App. 213 (1906); True Bill, December 24, 1903, *People v. Johnson*, case #71818, Crim.C.C., IR 134, 136; True Bill, May 23, 1905, *People v. Miller et al.*, case #77028, Crim.C.C., IR 134, 213–14; *Shields v. People*, 132 Ill. App. 109 (1907). These cases rebut the assertion that injunction replaced criminal conspiracy law in the twentieth century. Criminal cases were common if rarely appealed. Edwin E. Witte, *The Government in Labor Disputes* (New York: McGraw-Hill, 1932), 46; Hattam, *Labor Visions and State Power*, 161–62; Forbath, *Law and the Shaping*, 61–2; Herbert Hovenkamp, "Labor Conspiracies in American Law, 1880–1930," *Texas Law Review* 66:5 (1988): 919–65; Daniel Ernst, "Free Labor, the Consumer Interest, and the Law of Industrial Disputes, 1885–1900," *American Journal of Legal History* 36 (1992): 19–37; Daniel Ernst, "The Closed Shop, the Proprietary Capitalist, and the Law, 1897–1915," in *Masters to Managers*, Sanford Jacoby, ed., (New York: Columbia University Press, 1991), 132–48 esp. 136.
38 Grant, "Rights and Wrongs," 890; *Montgomery Ward and Company v. International Brotherhood of Teamsters*, case File #243939, Sup.C.C. (1905); *Employers' Teaming Co. v. Teamsters Joint Council*, 141 F. 679 (1905); *Garrigan v. United States*, 163 F. 16 (1908); John J. Flynn, ed., *Handbook of Chicago Biography* (Chicago: Standard Guide Co., 1893), 321–22; *Daily Labor Bulletin*, May 23–31, 1905.

States Express Company and a U.S. Senator from New York, sued both teamsters' president Cornelius Shea and express drivers' official James B. Barry for $25,000 in damages, alleging they had ordered workers to boycott his company. When former teamsters' president Albert Young told the grand jury that Robert J. Thorne, the president of the EA and the general manager of Montgomery Ward, had offered him a bribe to order a strike against Sears, Roebuck, Thorne accused Young of libel, and sued him for $25,000. Neither case was successful, but both hung over the unions, distracting them from their objectives.[39]

The ETC appealed to the criminal courts, which hammered the union teamsters. Justices of the Peace fined or jailed many drivers for assault, interference, disorderly conduct, failing to move their wagons, and using abusive language. Felony courts blamed the union officials for the more serious acts of violence. For instance, the grand jury indicted Edward Mullen, the vice-president of the CFL, for injuring Special Policeman Smith, even though Mullen himself had been shot in the fracas. To insure his appearance, the court demanded Mullen pay a $2,000 bond.[40]

The grand jury considered the strike itself a criminal act. With Alexander A. McCormick, the publisher of the *Chicago Evening Post* and the sitting Union League Club president, as foreman, the grand jury heard testimony regarding the teaming trade. The panel was explosive, for witnesses testified to graft within the union, causing the teamsters to lose much of their public support. But the grand jury also used its power to pressure the drivers to return to work, indicting the teamsters' officers on April 29 for conspiracy to commit illegal acts injurious to the public trade, morals, and police. The true bills accused the union of boycotting Montgomery Ward, interfering with its employees, and threatening to deny supplies to hotels and other businesses serving the mail-order house.[41]

Judges even forced teaming companies to serve Montgomery Ward and the ETC, barring the cross-class alliances essential to craft governance. The strike had divided the express delivery trade. The larger

---

[39] Declaration, June 21, 1905, *Platt v. Barry*, case #244201, Sup.C.C. (1905); Declaration, June 21, 1905, *Platt v. Shea*, case #244200, Sup.C.C. (1905); Harold F. Gosnell, *Boss Platt and His New York Machine* (Chicago: University of Chicago Press, 1924); Capias Affidavit, June 3, 1905, *Thorne v. Young*, case #244976, Sup.C.C. (1905).

[40] "Shot by Special Policeman," *CRH*, June 15, 1905, 2; "Shot in a Strike Riot," *CRH*, June 16, 1905, 2.

[41] Witwer, 88; True Bill, April 29, 1904, *People v. Shea*, case #76994, Crim.C.C., IR 134, 206–12; "Indict Leaders of the Strikers," *CDT*, April 30, 1905, 1, 3.

firms, which controlled package shipping at that time, sided with the mail-order house, causing their union workers to quit. But the smaller companies like Becklenberg Express Co. tried to retain friendly relations with the teamsters by staying out of the dispute. The EA objected and asked the court for help. On July 6, upon the petition of Marshall Field & Co. and eight other complainants, Judge Holdom ruled that Becklenberg and his peers were common carriers required by customary law and by municipal ordinance to serve clients without discrimination. The judge issued an injunction forcing all express delivery companies to cross picket lines and cart goods to and from the struck houses. Shortly thereafter, on August 1, the teamsters ended their strike.

Even more than Brentano and Kohlsaat's injunctions, Holdom's ruling in *Marshall Field & Co. v. Becklenberg* perfectly illustrated how judicial understandings of public and private, the sovereignty of law and individual rights, aided the EA. Just four years earlier, in *City of Chicago v. Forbes Cartage* (1901), Holdom had freed teaming companies that worked solely for massive wholesale houses like Hibbard, Spencer, Bartlett, & Co. (whose owner was a founding member of the EA) from municipal license laws. The judge concluded that such teaming firms were private corporations, not common carriers affected with a public interest. Combined with his ruling in *Becklenberg*, Holdom offered team owners a stark choice: join the corporate order and gain immunity from regulation, or remain independent and be forced by the state to serve the elite.[42]

The law shadowed the leaders of Chicago's unions. Indictments loomed, a hedge against craft militancy, as prosecutors dropped charges only after complaints became irrelevant. Officers of the piano workers' union remained in jeopardy for seven years before the state's attorney struck their indictments. Prosecutors lifted the charges against the metal workers only after the Kellogg Switchboard Co. had won its dispute and the Illinois Supreme Court had affirmed contempt citations. The plumbing and roofing contractors' indictments sat on the criminal docket for five years before being quashed. These true bills strongly discouraged defendants from enforcing their rules.[43]

---

[42] "Strike Aid Held Back," *CRH*, June 15, 1905, 2; *Marshall Field and Co. v. Becklenberg*, 1 Ill. C.C. 59 (1905); *City of Chicago v. Forbes Cartage Co.*, 1 Ill. C.C. 473 (1901).

[43] True Bill, June 29, 1900, *People v. Dold*, case #59120, Crim.C.C., IR 133, 6–11; Entry, May 21, 1907, *People v. Dold*, case #59120, Crim.C.C., Docket 36A, 5; Entry, June 10, 1907, *People v. Johnson*, case #71818, Crim.C.C., Docket 36A, 16. For sheet metal and plumbing, see True Bill, October 3, 1903, *People v.*

Constant fines and the costs of quality representation placed crafts-men under intense financial strain. During the teamsters strike, the courts convicted 726 men of various crimes, fining them $11,000. Some were able to pay the costs. The brickmakers and teamsters paid the court clerk $4,000 in cash within two minutes of their 1905 conspiracy conviction. But most unions struggled to finance their legal battles. Union members paid special assessments or turned to central bodies like the CFL. In the summer of 1905, the CFL spent over $12,000 per month on legal bills, leaving it unable to help the carriage workers pay their lawyers in December.[44]

The Failure of Progressive Law

If turn-of-the-century courts embraced the open shop progressivism of men like Paul Blatchford, they rejected the vision of "responsi-ble" unionism imagined by Ray Stannard Baker and Louis Brandeis. Brandeis had argued that incorporation would give unions the ability to sign and enforce written contracts. Though state-chartered unions would be subject to suits for damages, Brandeis contended that they would be less vulnerable to injunctions, since the rules of equity for-bade courts from issuing orders when plaintiffs had a remedy at-law. But the experience of the unions that did incorporate shows Bran-deis' doctrinal argument to be speculative. Judges actually grew more intrusive in their use of injunctions, while never quite accepting law-suits against unions. Offering few benefits and many disadvantages, incorporation provided craftsmen with a cautionary example of the dangers of following middle-class reformers.

Miller, case #70799, Crim.C.C., IR 134, 104–9; "Unions with Slocum," *CRH*, June 5, 1903, 3; "Expose Pools to Grand Jury," *CDT*, October 3, 1903, 7; "Pool Secrets Bared," October 3, 1903, 9; "Indictments for 19 Contractors," *CDT*, October 4, 1903, 4; True Bill, October 3, 1905, *People v. Sanitary Specialty Manufacturing*, case #71392, Crim.C.C., IR 134, 131; "Docket Charges Grist of Crimes," *CDT*, September 6, 1903, 7; Entry, May 25, 1908, *People v. Miller*, case #70799, Crim.C.C., Docket 37A, 4; Forbath, *Law and the Shaping*, 108.
[44] Entry, August 24, 1905, *People v. Obermeyer*, case #72033, Crim.C.C., Docket 34A, 353; "Jury Undecided in Labor Trial," *CDT*, August 25, 1905, 5; Entry, November 15, 1904, *People v. Bausk*, case #75791, Crim.C.C., Docket 35A, 110; Entry, December 18, 1905, *People v. Illinois Brick Co.*, case #79340, Crim.C.C., Docket 35B, 115; "'Brick Trust' Hit by Heavy Fines," *CDT*, December 19, 1905, 7; "Labor's 'Big Stick' is the Strike, He Says," *NYT*, December 18, 1905, 4; "Court Bills 'Break' Labor," *CDT*, December 2, 1905, 1; "Carpenters at Peace," *CRH*, March 4, 1909, 9.

Unlike unincorporated associations, which were considered private
bodies, state-chartered unions were susceptible to judicial supervision
of their disciplinary proceedings. In *F.J. Beesley v. Chicago Journeymen
Plumbers* (1892), the Illinois Appellate Court ruled corporate unions
subject to judicial scrutiny. The membership of the plumbers union
voted to expel Beesley after concluding that he was a bricklayer by
trade who had never served an apprenticeship as a plumber and had
lied about his credentials. Seeking reinstatement, Beesley petitioned
the Circuit Court of Cook County for a court order commanding a
corporation to obey its constitution, which would force the union to
reverse its decision. The Circuit Court refused. Illinois Appellate Court
Judge Shepard affirmed the lower court's decision, but only because
he concluded that plumbers had acted fairly. Though Judge Joseph
Gary, who had presided over the infamous Haymarket trial in 1886,
rejected the implication that the court might interfere with the operation of worker organizations "under any circumstances," the larger
panel proved willing to involve itself in the internal affairs of incorporated unions.[45]

Unaware of Brandeis' interpretation of equity jurisdiction, judges
frequently restrained incorporated unions. Indeed, in the musicians,
painters, and bricklayers' cases mentioned above, the judges never
even considered the fact that unions involved held state charters. In
no case did the courts endorse Brandeis' contention that such unions
were immune to injunction. And only once did the courts uphold
this logic with regard to a trade association. In 1906, Richard Allen
violated the by-laws of the Chicago Undertakers' Association (CUA),
which threatened to suspend his membership, making it impossible
for him to obtain the services of any hearses, carriages, or liverymen.
Allen obtained a temporary restraining order from the Superior Court,
which Judge McEwen quickly dissolved. The next year, the Illinois
Supreme Court affirmed McEwen's decision, ruling that, "the power
to expel is essential to the healthful existence of a corporate body,"
and recommending the plaintiff sue the CUA for damages.[46]

[45] *Beesley v. Chicago Journeymen Plumbers' Association*, 44 Ill. App. 278 (1892);
*International Freight Handlers Union, Local #4 v. International Freight Han-
dlers Union*, case #254260, Sup.C.C. (1906); Ray Ginger, *Altgeld's America* (Chicago: Quadrangle Books, 1965), 52. For the doctrine of non-
interference, see *Green v. Board of Trade*, 174 Ill. 585 (1898); *Engel v. Walsh*,
258 Ill. 98, 103 (1913); Ernst, *Lawyers Against Labor*, 156. The courts eventually reversed Beesley, suggesting the courts reluctance to diverge from
precedent. *Clifford v. Hedrick*, 159 Ill. App. 63 (1910).
[46] *Brindley v. Chicago Federation of Musicians*, case #255626, Circ.C.C. (1904);
Doehne v. Chicago Federation of Musicians, case #255329, Circ.C.C. (1905);
Weldon v. Chicago Federation of Musicians, case #263907, Circ.C.C. (1905);

Hopes for using common law to promote union responsibility proved similarly unrealistic, as few lawsuits against chartered unions succeeded. Having obtained injunctions, neither John Stiles nor James Gavin seemed to push their suits to trial. The craftsmen managed to cloak themselves and their organizations in the rhetoric of voluntarism. Paperhanger John Burgher's lawyer, Simeon Shope, showed that the painters' union had expelled his client, that its members shunned him, and that contractors refused to employ him for fear of walkouts. But Shope was unable to prove that the union had maliciously ordered strikes, making the organization responsible for $35,000 in damages. Defending the worker's right to choose his friends and the union's right to enforce its rules, Judge Joseph Gary instructed the jury to find for the defendants, stating, "No set of men can be compelled to associate, and there is no wrong done by saying 'We will not have a certain man associated with us.'"[47]

Lawsuits seemed to hinge more upon the relative power of parties than their corporate status. For example, juries forced some the Chicago Laundrymen to compensate washerwoman Mary Hennessey to the tune of $6,000. Boycotted brick manufacturer George Hinchliff won $7,000 from the Brick Manufacturers Association and the Chicago Masons and Builders.[48] Widows and heirs were invariably successful when they sued incorporated unions for death benefits. But in these cases, juries held for the plaintiffs regardless of the union's legal status. In 1904, W.E. Klapetzky, the secretary-treasurer of the unincorporated Journeymen Barbers' International Union, described a week without a benefits lawsuit as "rare." In 1901, Louise Huecker sued the Cigar Makers International Union (CMIU) for her husband's $550 death benefit. When the CMIU protested that it was unincorporated, and thus without legal standing, the plaintiffs responded that Huecker belonged to CMIU Local #14, which was chartered by the State of Illinois.

Advisory Board Building Trades v. Builders Painting and Decorating Company, case #227537, Sup.C.C. (1903); *Gavin v. Bricklayers,* case #227562, Sup.C.C. (1903); *Allen v. Chicago Undertakers' Association,* 232 Ill. 458 (1908).

[47] Narr., September 8 ,1901, *Gavin v. Bricklayers,* case #218594, Circ.C.C. (1901); *Gavin v. Bricklayers,* case #243717, Sup.C.C. (1905); *Gavin v. Bricklayers,* case #266991, Sup.C.C. (1908). Bill of Exceptions, December 20, 1905, *Burgher v. Painters,* case #234118, Sup.C.C. (1903), 51–4, 23–4.

[48] *Doremus v. Hennessey* 176 Ill. 613 (1898). The court reduced Hinchliff's jury award of $22,000 to $7,000. *Purington v. Hunchliff,* 219 Ill. 159 (1905); *Purington v. Hinchliff,* 120 Ill. App. 528, 535 (1905). Martin Emerich "amicably adjusted" his $100,000 suit against the brick interests. Stipulation to Dismiss Without Costs, August 16, 1901, *Union Pressed Brick Co. v. Chicago Hydraulic Pressed Brick Co.,* case #216762, Circ.C.C. (1901); Ernst, *Lawyers Against Labor,* 147–64.

Moreover, by offering financial services, the international acted like a corporation. The jury ruled in favor of the plaintiffs for $646.31.[49]

Nonetheless, incorporated unions were financially vulnerable to other forms of legal action, as became apparent during the 1904 print feeders' strike. As their name suggests, print feeders filled the presses with paper, an occupation created by the mechanization of Chicago's publishing industry in the late nineteenth century. Although less skilled than the other unionized print workers, the feeders occupied a strategic position in the publishing process, for without paper the machines ground to halt. Founded in 1887, their organization, Franklin Union #4 (FUNF), had twelve hundred members by 1899. In 1894, after a brief flirtation with the International Typographical Union, the feeders decided they did not need outside assistance from other labor organizations. Instead, the union became a corporate person under Illinois law, capable of signing contracts on behalf of its members.[50]

For a decade, FUNF was successful as an independent union, obtaining a series of wage advances for its workers and beginning a campaign to organize all the semi-skilled print workers. Yet this growth created a rivalry between FUNF and the International Printing Pressmen and Assistants' Union (IPPU), which exploded in 1903 when the former union demanded that employers discharge an apprentice feeder belonging to the latter. Fearing the highly skilled pressmen and desiring an end to the feeders' demands, the Chicago Typothetae, a group of the most powerful printers, refused to fire the worker. The contract stipulated arbitration, but when the umpire decided in favor of the employers, FUNF abrogated the agreement and went on strike. The Typothetae reacted by withdrawing recognition of the union. The pressmen offered to assist the Franklin Union if they ended their independence, but with $30,000 in their treasury from dues and initiation fees, the confident feeders refused. When the employers hired young female replacements, the IPPU created their own Local #57, which organized two hundred of the new workers.

---

49 *Report of Proceedings of the Eleventh Convention of the Journeymen Barbers' International Union of America* (Indianapolis: J.B.I.U.A., 1904), 46–7; *Huecker v. Cigar Makers International Union*, case #211775, Sup.C.C. (1901). See also, *Tischler v. Cigar Makers International Union*, case #265964, Circ.C.C. (1905); *Sherman v. Chicago Federation of Musicians*, case #206264, Sup.C.C. (1900); *Guthrie v. Chicago Federation of Musicians*, case #220809, Sup.C.C. (1902); *Prucha v. United Order of American Bricklayers*, case #207992, Circ.C.C. (1900); *Rili v. United Order of American Bricklayers*, case #246928, Circ.C.C. (1903).

50 Brown, *Book and Job Printing in Chicago*, 77–8.

Violent confrontations followed. Picketing ensued around Typothetae plants, and, by most accounts, intimidation was its intent. FUNF allegedly hired women to spy on the replacement feeders then threatened and assaulted these "scabs" outside the workplace. In one case in January 1904, a union officer, Louis Lindermann, and three other feeders were accused of throwing "a certain compound" on three members of the Thomma family – Catherine, Frances, and Verena – to damage their clothing. Other cases were more serious, and one replacement worker died as a result of an assault.[51]

In the last three months of 1903, the Typothetae pursued three legal avenues. First, the printers filed bills of injunction in the name of the individual corporations and in the name of the trade association. Charging a conspiracy to interfere with the business of the members of the Typothetae, these bills requested a court order restraining the union and its members. Second, four major employers – R. R. Donnelley and Sons, Rand McNally, Childs and Company, and Gustave Ouclay – sued the incorporated union for damages ranging from $18,000 to $20,000, charging breach of contract and a conspiracy to destroy their business. Finally, testifying before the grand jury, the employers encouraged the state to charge the leaders of FUNF with conspiring to injure a nonunion worker named Charles M. Elliot.[52]

Because the union was incorporated, the Typothetae saw particular promise in the suits for damages. Rand McNally attorney Adolph Wesemann commented, "We believe a union can be held responsible for its acts." Unconcerned, FUNF secretary John Shea replied, "We are losing no sleep over this suit." Shea's confidence proved justifiable. Although the damage suits and the conspiracy charges remained on their respective dockets for years, neither went beyond the first stages. Judge Holdom dismissed one of the suits in 1903, when the plaintiff, Gustave Ouclay, failed to file a declaration. Two others were dismissed by stipulation of the parties in 1905. Rand McNally's $20,000 suit

---

[51] Brown, *Book and Job Printing in Chicago*, 83–7; *Typothetae v. Franklin Union #4*, case #232708, Sup.C.C. (1903); True Bill, January 28, 1904, *People v. Lindemann*, case #72078, Crim.C.C., IR 134, 133–34. Also see True Bill, October 16, 1903, *People v. Woerner*, case #71762, Crim.C.C., IR 134, 133–34; Myers, "Policing of Labor Disputes in Chicago," 464–67.

[52] *Typothetae v. Franklin Union #4*, case #232708, Sup.C.C. (1903); *Rand McNally v. Franklin Union #4*, case #232947, Sup.C.C. (1903); *Donnelley v. Franklin Union #4*, case #234015, Sup.C.C. (1903); *Rand McNally v. Franklin Union #4*, case #233046, Sup.C.C. (1903); *Childs v. Franklin Union #4*, case #234227, Sup.C.C. (1903); *Ouclay v. Franklin Union #4*, case #232812, Sup.C.C. (1903); True Bill, October 16, 1903, *People v. Woerner*, case #71762, Crim.C.C., IR 134, 133–34.

remained active until May 1906 when it was dismissed without costs. One month later, the criminal charges against the leaders of FUNF were also stricken off the record.[53]

The plaintiffs continued, however, to seek an injunction. On October 10, 1903, Judge Holdom issued a broad and restrictive order. Holdom ruled that, although it had a right to exist and even to strike, the union, as a corporate person, had conspired with its own members to injure the printers' business. Within a month, a member of the union was sentenced to thirty days in jail and a $100 fine for contempt of court. And on December 12, 1903, Holdom ruled that the union itself had violated his order and sentenced its corporate person to fines totaling $2,000.[54]

The union responded by immediately dissolving the corporation and distributing its assets among the corporate officers. Neither the county sheriff, nor the Typothetae, acted rapidly enough to stop the purposeful disintegration of the union. Arriving at the union office, the sheriff could find nothing of value to attach. And when the Typothetae obtained a court order prohibiting further distribution of property and placing the union in receivership, the receiver found nothing but aging office furniture and less than $40 in stamps and small change.[55]

The feeders then took the multiple contempt citations to the Supreme Court of Illinois. One by one, the high court dismissed their objections, in the process creating a new and highly repressive labor law

[53] "Union Sued for Damages," *CDT*, October 24, 1903, 3. Prosecutors probably dropped these indictments because the appellate courts had recently upheld contempt citations against the union. *Franklin Union #4 v. People*, 121 Ill. App. 647 (1905); *Franklin Union #4 v. People*, 220 Ill. 355 (1906); *Flannery v. People*, 127 Ill. App. 526 (1906); *Flannery v. People*, 225 Ill. 62 (1907); *Donnelley v. Franklin Union #4*, case #234015, Sup.C.C. (1903); *Rand McNally v. Franklin Union #4*, case #233046, Sup.C.C. (1903); *Childs v. Franklin Union #4*, case #234227, Sup.C.C. (1903); *Ouclay v. Franklin Union #4*, case #232812, Sup.C.C. (1903); Myers, "Policing," 467. The criminal case was stricken off on June 5, 1906. Entry, June 5, 1906, *People v. Woerner*, case #71762, Crim.C.C., Docket 35A, 44.

[54] Myers, "Policing," 468–69; *Franklin Union v. People*, 362–63 (1906). This decision was consistent with a 1905 decision holding that corporations could be tried for criminal conspiracy. *Chicago, Wilmington and Vermillion Coal Co. v. People*, 214 Ill. 421 (1905).

[55] The dissolution of the corporation was proposed on the 12th, but the union did not file papers until December 23, 1903. *Flannery v. People*, 527 (1906); Brown, *Book and Job Printing in Chicago*, 88; Myers, "Policing of Labor Disputes," 471–72.

for the State of Illinois. When the counsel for the union, John Bloom-ingston, challenged Judge Holdom's ability to cite a corporation for contempt, the high court upheld Holdom's decision. Further, Bloom-ingston noted that the bill for injunction was erroneous, since the Typothetae, an unincorporated voluntary association with no stand-ing in court, had brought the suit. Ironically, in this case, a union had capacity while the employers did not. Unconvinced, the court ruled this a minor defect that should have been raised by demurrer before Judge Holdom. Moreover, the court held that even if the order had been defective, the union was obliged to obey. In other words, faced with an unlawful and unreasonable injunction, unions were obliged to obey the order, postpone their strike, and wait over two years for the appellate courts to rule.

Most importantly, the higher court took this opportunity to pro-hibit picketing, ruling that, "There can be no such thing as peace-ful 'polite and gentlemanly' picketing, any more than there can be chaste 'polite and gentlemanly' vulgarity, or peaceful mobbing or law-ful lynching." The Supreme Court, despite two vehement dissents, essentially affirmed this principle, grouping together picketing, force, threats, and intimidation without any legal distinction. This modifica-tion meant that picketing workers were conspiracies, a group seeking a lawful goal by unlawful means. Moreover, the Illinois Supreme Court held unions and their officers liable for the acts of members, even when unknown to and unsanctioned by the organization. The court upheld the fine against FUNF even though it had publicly urged its member to eschew violence, charging that its meetings, its strike fund, and visiting committees had "naturally" resulted in bloodshed.[56]

As the judge opined, the striking members of Franklin Union #4 faced grim defeat. While the employers failed to destroy the union entirely, they succeeded in limiting its size and power. Less than half of Typothetae plants employed members of FUNF, and the trade as-sociation refused to bargain collectively with the union. While the union maintained strong in non-Typothetae plants, its was reduced to 1,000 members by the end of 1904. Faced with the continuing hos-tility of the employers, the union attempted to resolve its differences with the pressmen, which had unsuccessfully attempted to take the feeders' jurisdiction during the strike. In 1907, the two unions agreed to join forces. IPPU disbanded Local #57, and issued a charter to Local #4. Defeated in industrial warfare, its corporate status dissolved,

---

[56] *Franklin Union v. People*, 364–73, 376–81, 384–93 (1906); Myers, "Policing of Labor Disputes," 472–73. The judges reaffirmed the prohibition of peaceful picketing in *Barnes v. Typographical Union*, 232 Ill. 424 (1908).

subordinate to the pressmen and the AFL, FUNF had "joined the ranks of orthodox trade unionism."[57]

Louis Brandeis' vision of legally enforceable collective bargaining through union incorporation remained entirely unrealized. Incorporation had not made the Franklin Union responsible; its members had violated their contract with the Typothetae and assaulted replacement workers. Nor did a corporate charter change the legal status of the union appreciably. Picket-line violence gave the grand jury pretext with which to charge leaders with criminal conspiracy. The courts ignored the rules of equity jurisprudence, central to Brandeis' argument, granting employers who had a valid remedy at common law their requests for injunctions. Overall, judges undermined the progressive model of industrial relations, pushing FUNF to abandon its Illinois charter and discouraging even reform-minded craft unionists like CFL secretary Edward Nockles, who stated, "I do not believe in labor unions incorporating. The experience of Franklin Union demonstrates that. Through incorporation you are taken into court and your money is burned, whether you are right or wrong." The demands of responsibility simply outweighed the privileges of legitimacy.[58]

Corruption Becomes a Crime

The citizenry embraced the progressive critique of union administration, but the courts lagged behind, only slowly developing a means of prosecuting labor leaders for misuse of office. For example, during the Teamsters' Strike of 1905, John Driscoll's charges of widespread graft turned public opinion against the workers. Yet the prosecutors ignored allegations of bribery, indicting union officers instead for boycotting Montgomery Ward & Co. The first trial was the longest in Cook County history to that point, beginning on September 13, 1906 and ending on January 19, 1907 with a hung jury. The second trial was hastier, lasting less than three weeks and ending in acquittal. In both trials, defense attorneys successfully played upon the jury's sympathy for workers by asserting the legality of strikes and boycotts.[59]

State's attorneys declined to charge graft partly because their backers wanted to establish the illegality of sympathetic strikes. A graft trial could have had the opposite effect, legitimizing properly administered unions and trade agreements. For the EA, charging Con Shea with fraud was like accusing an insurrectionist of embezzlement; it

---

57 Brown, *Book and Job Printing in Chicago*, 89–90.
58 "Powderly in Error Say Labor Leaders," *CRH*, April 27, 1904, 3.
59 *CDN Almanac* 24 (1908): 78; Myers, "Policing of Labor Disputes," 581, 636–37.

presumed one could strike (or conspire) in an honest, businesslike fashion. Further, a thorough investigation of the teamsters would have revealed that employers willingly paid to prevent walkouts, or worse, to initiate strikes in competing concerns. Though executives like Robert Thorne either denied such allegations or claimed to be victims of union extortion, a corruption trial would have sullied their reputations, since they chose to pay rather than notifying the proper authorities.[60]

Prosecutors also ignored the issue of corruption because no law specifically banned graft and extortion in industrial relations. This legal vacuum existed because neither corporations nor unions accepted the reformers understanding of union legitimacy. Open shop employers had never demanded such a law, perhaps because such laws presumed that union officials were permitted to police the economy. Instead, in 1909, the CFL proposed the first bill in Illinois banning the bribery of union officials. The federation even hired reform journalist Luke Grant to draft the law, but when Grant made both the unionist and the employer responsible for the crime, the CFL altered the bill to place all liability on the employer. By blaming business alone, the CFL claimed for walking delegates a presumption of legitimacy that even elected officials did not possess. This version unsurprisingly failed in the legislature, and the state remained without a labor corruption law until 1920.[61]

When state's attorneys did try craftsmen for graft, they used conspiracy laws that made coercion the *gravamen* of the offense. The prosecutor tried union officials for demanding money, regardless of their intent or its dispensation. A fine was no different from a bribe. For example, during the massive restaurant strike of May 1903, the Hotel and Restaurant Workers International Alliance and the CFL boycotted the *Chicago Record-Herald*, after the paper criticized the Waiters Union Local #336. Two months later, the grand jury indicted Frank A. Egger and Edward W. Parlee, two union officials, for offering to use their influence to lift the boycott in exchange for "$225 in treasury notes." But rather than alleging graft, per se, the indictment imputed a conspiracy to injure the business of the *Record-Herald*. The case never went to trial, but it raised the possibility of prosecuting craftsmen for bribery.[62]

[60] *Thorne v. Young*, case #244976, Sup.C.C. (1905); "Graft Probe Held Up," *CRH*, June 20, 1905, 3.

[61] Beckner, 28; "To Make Bribery of Labor Leaders a Crime," *CRH*, April 13, 1904, 6; "Labor Dodges Graft," *CRH*, March 8, 1909, 3.

[62] True Bill, July 3, 1903, *People v. Egger*, case #69701, Crim.C.C., IR 134, 97–9; Entry, August 7, 1906, *People v. Egger*, case #69701, Crim.C.C., Docket Book 35A, 28; Matthew Josephson, *Union House, Union Bar: A History of the*

The first prosecutions focused not on corruption, but on the use of cash fines to punish employers. In 1905, the grand jury indicted three walking delegates for Plumbers' Union Local #130, including eventual BTC president Simon O'Donnell, for interfering with the employees of William Downs. Downs had refused to pay $200 in fines for unspecified rule violations, so plumbers' union officials asked his employees to walk out, proffered charges within the union against four who refused, and finally attempted to block their access to work. Prosecutors seemed ready to charge extortion, but instead followed familiar patterns, with dismissal the result.[63]

The prosecutors' continuing attacks on trade agreements undermined their pursuit of corrupt union officials. In the summer of 1909, William H. Schrontz [or Scromtz], a union lather from Cleveland came to Chicago. Upon his arrival, local officers informed him that he needed to pay a $50 fee to work in the city. When he protested that the national union had forbidden such local initiation fees, the union granted him a three-day "permit." Schrontz took a job with a contractor C.A. Budge, but when he exceeded the time limit, the union summoned him before its examining board, fined him $300, and declared Budge's workers on strike. Budge and Schrontz complained to the grand jury, leading that body to indict the executive committee of the lathers for conspiracy. While a *Chicago Record-Herald* article on the Schrontz case blared, "Extortion is Charged," the prosecutor again focused on coercive rules rather than the integrity of officials, resulting in another acquittal.[64]

Only at the end of the decade did prosecutors change their tactics. The trial of Martin B. "Skinny" Madden represented a sea change in the courts attitude towards alleged union corruption. For years,

---

Hotel and Restaurant Workers International Union (New York: Random House, 1956), 19–30.

[63] True Bill, May 29, 1905, *People v. Carney*, case #76979, Crim.C.C., IR 134, 193–98; Entry, October 3, 1905, *People v. Carney*, case #76979, Crim.C.C., Docket Book 35A, 233; True Bill, September 28, 1905, *People v. Carney*, case #78365, Crim.C.C., IR 134, 251–55; Entry, November 23, 1906, *People v. Carney*, case #78365, Crim.C.C., 36A, 149.

[64] True Bill, June 29, 1909, *People v. Ruth*, case #91386, Crim.C.C., IR 149, 307–11; Entry, November 21, 1910, *People v. Ruth*, case #91386, Crim.C.C., Docket Book 40A, n.p; "New Labor True Bills," *CRH*, June 30, 1909, 3. Just four days later, the grand jury issued a very similar indictment charging members of the sailors' union with interference. The convicted workers paid fines between $25 and $50. True Bill, July 3, 1909, *People v. Haley*, case #91483, Crim.C.C., IR 149, 312–14; Entry, May 24, 1910, *People v. Haley*, case #91483, Crim.C.C., Docket Book 39A, n.p.

Madden had been the "Knight Errant" of the Chicago labor movement. After Madden's defeat in the Building Trades' Lockout of 1899, he rebounded quickly, retaining his position as business agent of the Junior Steamfitters and founding two new bodies, the Associated Building Trades and the Board of Business Agents, to replace the defunct BTC. His popularity and political connections made him the most powerful workingman in the construction industry, if not in the city's labor movement as a whole. But by the end of the decade, Madden had worn out his welcome entirely. In 1905, the CFL expelled him, and many building tradesmen including John Metz, president of the Carpenters' District Council, the city's largest construction union, decided Madden had to go.

In 1909, with the support of a reform coalition including the Brotherhood of Carpenters, State's Attorney John E.W. Weyman prosecuted Madden, electrical workers' business agent Michael Boyle, and sheetmetal workers' business agent Fred A. Pouchot for conspiracy to obtain money under false pretenses. As in earlier cases, the indictment flowed from labor's attempts at governing commerce. The grand jury alleged that the three unionists had declared a work stoppage on a building being constructed by nonunion contractors, hiring nonunion workers, and using nonunion materials. Madden, Boyle, and Pouchot agreed to end the dispute if the builder, the Joseph Klicka Company, hired union contractors and paid a fine of $1,500. Klicka offered the officials $1,000, but later changed his mind and testified before the grand jury. After a long trial, the jury convicted the men and sentenced each to a $500 fine.[65]

The focus on Madden's honesty was as notable as labor's support for the prosecution. Unlike past conspiracy cases, the trial focused not on the Klicka strike itself, but on the misuse of the money. The case presumed that "Skinny" had a legal right to fine employers as long as he did so "in the interest of union labor" and not for a "corrupt purpose." Consequently, the court questioned whether the leaders had fined Klicka on the authority of the union or kept the money for themselves. In other words, the jury considered whether they had deceived the contractors about their purpose and the workers about

[65] *People v. Pouchot*, 174 Ill. App. 1 (1912). True Bill, February 20, 1909, *People v. Madden*, case #90527, Crim.C.C., IR 149, 221–31. See also, case #s 90528–90530, 90577, 90579, 91317, Crim.C.C., IR 149, 231–55, 261–92, 296–306; *People v. Madden*, case #90530, Crim.C.C., Docket 42A, 11; "Madden's a Grafter; Trio is Held Guilty; Fines, but No Cell," *CRH*, May 30, 1909, 1, 3; "Rise and Fall of Skinny," *CRH*, May 30, 1909, 3; "Skinny Scotched by Jury Verdict," *CDT*, May 30, 1909, 1.

the dispensation of the money. Though prosecutors could not prove intent, Madden's scandalous reputation led the jury and the appellate judges to believe allegations of deceit and theft.[66]

The affirmation of Madden's conviction established the court's role in policing union administration, showing that public anxiety about graft had overtaken concern regarding unions themselves. Yet the Madden case revealed the inadequacy of existing laws for corruption cases. The jury convicted Boyle and Pouchot on the basis of guilty knowledge, not for any direct evidentiary connection to the payoff. The judge sentenced them to relatively small fines in part because he sensed that they had been indicted to satisfy the conspiracy doctrine, which required multiple defendants, not because of their actions. To stop graft and extortion, prosecutors would need new laws targeting individual dishonesty and acknowledging the legitimacy of craft governance.

The Great Disappointment

Though the law seemed the stalwart guardian of the corporate vision, craft governance survived this period. The courts largely validated the principles of open shop and blocked the growth of unions in manufacturing, but the law failed to establish open shop conditions in trades like construction, trucking, barbering, and baking. Believing in voluntarism, even judges like Jesse Holdom showed reluctance to interfere in unincorporated associations and their contracts. In other cases, craftsmen found ways to circumvent the law, and the state proved too weak to overcome their unified will. But most importantly, the public showed increasing sympathy for organized craftsmen, and juries showed declining interest in punishing them for strikes and boycotts. Public concern about corruption grew, but corporations remained committed to invalidating craft governance itself, so no statute emerged to address the problem.

In trades where craft governance was popular and accepted, plaintiffs had difficulty enforcing injunctions, which granted formal protection but little outright defense. County sheriffs, the men responsible

---

[66] *People v. Pouchot*, 174 Ill. App. 9, 16–7 (1912). "Wayman to Push Other Madden Cases," *CRH*, May 31, 1909, 4. By the time of the appeal, Madden had died of tuberculosis. Boyle remained an infamous but powerful labor leader until his death in 1958. "Michael J. Boyle, Labor Leader, 77," *NYT*, May 19, 1958, 25; Graham Taylor, "The End of an Industrial Brigand," *The Survey* 22 (June 12, 1909): 401–2; "Rise and Fall of Skinny," *CRH*, May 30, 1909, 3.

for enforcing writs, often lacked the staff to adequately police their stipulations. Before issuing contempt citations, courts required plaintiffs to pay costs and supply proof of culpability. As a consequence, injunctions were largely ineffective without an affluent employer behind them. For instance, bricklayers ignored Judge Holdom's 1903 injunction prohibiting them from interfering with James Gavin's employment. Though Judge Brentano threatened them with jail, they continued to obstruct Gavin as late as 1908.[67]

As experienced political actors in a city famous for corruption, craftsmen proved adept at circumventing criminal justice by surreptitious methods. In 1902, the grand jury indicted John Gallagher for destroying electrical equipment belonging to Lakeside Electrical Construction Co. during a strike against that firm. Gallagher allegedly demanded $300 from Electrical Workers' Local #134 to pay court clerk, Harry L. Pelkus, to remove the case from the docket before the trial. Pelkus was one of a group of court employees engaged in fixing cases, with connections not only to labor unions, but also to streetcar companies, Republican politicians like Nathaniel Sears, and labor lawyers like Clarence Darrow. When State's Attorney Deneen put Pelkus on trial in 1903, union men allegedly secreted the sole witness out of the state. Electricians' union official Michael Boyle became so expert in jury bribery during this period that Illinois Governor Len Small allegedly turned to him for help fixing his own trial during the next decade.[68]

The attempted suppression of craft governance prompted not obedience, but angry defiance. In June 1904, unknown assailants assaulted Alexander C. Allen, the local counsel for the AABA, striking him in the head, knocking him unconscious, and leaving him with "severe scalp wounds." Few doubted the perpetrators or their rationale. Rather than putting unions, associations, and agreements on a legitimate footing, the courts inspired the tradesmen's hatred, brutality, and defensiveness. As local unions and associations grew more powerful and violent in the ensuing decades, corporations struggle to invent new ideas and new laws to contain them.[69]

[67] Order, March 29, 1905, *Gavin v. Bricklayers,* case #227562, Sup.C.C. (1903); *Gavin v. Bricklayers,* case #266991, Sup.C.C. (1908).
[68] True Bill, December 5, 1903, *People v. Wilson,* Case #71395, Crim.C.C., IR 134, 132; "Court Clerk Bribed," *CRH,* April 22, 1903, 2; *O'Donnell et al. v. People,* 110 Ill. App. 250 (1903); *Sullivan v. People,* 108 Ill. App. 328 (1903); *People ex rel. Deneen v. Sullivan,* 218 Ill. 419 (1905); "Pardons Labor Men," *NYT,* October 23, 1923, 29.
[69] "Attorney Assaulted," *WP,* June 26, 1904, 5; Ernst, *Lawyers Against Labor,* 58.

Water Street Market, 1922. What often appeared to be a chaotic mix of truckers, commission merchants, and buyers was in fact regulated by a set of private agreements between unions and associations. This governance took a violent turn in the 1920s. Courtesy of Chicago Historical Society (DN-075186).

6

Containing Mass Society and the Problem of Corruption

Despite losing major strikes, public opinion, and court battles, Chicago craftsmen continued to set practical limits on technology, the national market, and mass culture in their city from the 1910s through the 1920s. The era of the humble workshop had ended; most manufacturing was now corporate, and industrial production in massive steel plants and stockyards drew thousands of migrants to the city. The city's geography – its centrality, its train depots, rivers, lakes, and canals – made it the crux of a developing national economy, a hub for the wholesale distribution of goods produced elsewhere. Yet once the boxcars entered the city, they still entered a relatively immodern world of hustling entrepreneurs and craft workers, commission merchants and haulers, freight handlers and teamsters. Despite the hostility of the courts and the fierce opposition of the city's wealthiest businessmen, tradesmen organized unions and associations that denied corporations their competitive advantages and chased many potential investors out of the city altogether.

Looking back today, this highly combustable world is nearly invisible. In the literature, the 1910s begin with moderate reform and end with political conservatism and economic consolidation. President Woodrow Wilson prodded Congress into passing a series of federal laws regulating business and protecting selected workers. During World War I, the progressive impulse became increasingly coercive and ethnocentric as the effort to force support for the war depleted the movement's strength. After the armistice, self-consciously inactive politicians like Warren Harding and Calvin Coolidge replaced Wilson. Under these presidents, the federal government abandoned its opposition to corporate power, adopting policies that aided the largest firms and encouraged trusts, mergers, and national trade associations.[1]

Scholars see organized labor as particularly dormant, beleaguered, and shortsighted during the latter part of this period. In 1916, under pressure from the Wilson administration, the AFL endorsed the Democrats, abandoning the possibility of an autonomous labor party. Though wartime laws permitted workers to participate in governing the economy – to organize new unions, gain higher wages, and obtain shorter hours – these schemes of "industrial democracy" proved temporary. Meanwhile, AFL leaders chose sectarian advantage over the health of the movement, using their political muscle to crush their own left wing. Labor showed bursts of energy between 1919 and 1922, but these failed surges only highlight the movement's relative lack of ambition in the following years. Chastened by postwar defeats in steel, meat, and railway shops, committed to craft jurisdictions, lacking political power, and hesitant to gamble on immigrant, black, and female industrial workers, the AFL declined to mount another prolonged drive to organize America's factories until the 1930s.[2]

By contrast, historians see the cultural world as vibrant and contested. During the teens and twenties, women gained the suffrage and shed the binding clothes and coiffures of the past for the liberating short dresses and hairdos of the flapper. New forms of communication like radio and film permitted the distribution of preproduced art for a national audience, thus shattering the dominance of local live entertainment and slowly melting cultural differences. Mass production of the automobile shortened distances, allowing the development of suburbs. Americans danced to jazz, a new music composed and performed by African-Americans, who themselves had found freedom of expression after fleeing Southern hamlets for cities like New Orleans

---

[1] See for example, Arthur Schlesinger, Jr., *The Crisis of the Old Order, 1919–1933* (New York: Houghton Mifflin, 1957).

[2] Barbara Warne Newell, *Chicago and the Labor Movement: Metropolitan Unionism in the 1930s* (Urbana: University of Illinois Press, 1961), 24–9; Cohen, *Making a New Deal*, 48–52; Gordon, *New Deals*, 13; Irving Bernstein, *The Lean Years: A History of the American Worker 1920–1933* (Boston: Houghton Mifflin, 1960), 83–143; Montgomery, *Fall of the House of Labor*, 375, 452–64; Melvyn Dubofsky, *The State and Labor in Modern America* (Chapel Hill: University of North Carolina Press, 1994), 83–106; Joseph McCartin, *Labor's Great War: The Struggle for Industrial Democracy and the Origins of Modern American Labor Relations, 1912–1921* (Chapel Hill: University of North Carolina Press, 1997); Greene, *Pure and Simple Politics*, 274–86; Elizabeth McKillen, *Chicago Labor and the Quest for a Diplomatic Diplomacy, 1914–1924* (Ithaca, NY: Cornell University Press, 1995), 214–23.

and Chicago. Innovations in advertising, branding, and distribution helped create a mass market for new products and services. Even the most vital political issue of the day – the explosion in lethal gang violence prompted by the prohibition of alcoholic beverages – hinged upon questions of leisure, consumption, and religion.[3]

Lower-middle-class shopkeepers, musicians, carpenters, and teamsters sought to resist and even control this rising tide. Though conservative, craftsmen staunchly defended their place in Chicago's economy against the transformative effects of the new mass production – mass consumption society. They organized to maintain localism and control new technologies of production, modes of distribution such as chain stores, and cultural forms including films, sound recording, and radio. Though craftsmen actively rejected radical schemes for regulating business and eliminating private property, they did empower their own private organizations to place practical limits on local commerce.

Over time, the dark side of their antimodernism grew more evident. The craftsmen enforced regulations for their own benefit, often brutally so. Craftsmen not only inhibited ambitious corporate employers, they also denied consumers access to a full range of choices. They viewed the economic equality of African-Americans and women with some of the same resentment they expressed towards corporate capitalism, and they made rules setting practical limits on the freedom of these newly liberated populations. Further, craft organizations were plagued by factionalism, violence, and embezzlement. As the 1920s wore on, their methods grew more brutal and their leaders more mercenary, while their wealth made them attractive targets for outsiders like bootlegger Alphonse Capone.

Controlling Mass Culture

Chicago's craftsmen asserted control over the explosion in consumer spending that is this period's most distinctive innovation. A wave of invention allowed Americans to enjoy new entertainments such as film and radio and communicate using new technologies like the telephone. As the second wave of immigration to Chicago ended,

[3] Cohen, *Making a New Deal*, 51–52, 99–158; William Leach, *Land of Desire: Merchants, Power, and the Rise of a New American Culture* (New York: Vintage, 1994), 263–378; *Crabgrass Frontier: The Suburbanization of the United States* (New York: Oxford University Press, 1987); James R. Grossman, *Land of Hope: Chicago, Black Southerners, and the Great Migration* (Chicago: University of Chicago Press, 1989); Stewart Ewen, *Captains of Consciousness: Advertising and the Roots of the Consumer Culture* (New York: McGraw-Hill, 1976).

residents demanded more plentiful and higher quality housing. Ordinary laborers took advantage of rising wages and falling prices, buying products such as meat, tobacco, and candy in far greater quantities than ever before. Clothes washing moved from the home to laundries and drycleaners. Though workers earned their wages in a maturing corporate economy, their consumption often transpired in the city's craft economy, under the gaze of unions and associations. Craftsmen policed the development of mass culture in Chicago, trying to create public demand for new goods and services while stopping new competitors from capturing these desires.

As much as traditional spending habits, these institutional limits on retail, service, and entertainment obstructed the development of a broad-based consumer culture. Historians like Lizabeth Cohen show that ethnic workers often declined to patronize corporate firms or purchase name brands, choosing instead to shop in small neighborhood stores where they could socialize with their countrymen, find familiar products, and obtain credit. But craft governance defined the available options, making it hard to discern real preferences. Unions and associations regulated the location of stores, the hours they opened and closed, the prices they charged, the wholesalers they used, and the products they sold. These strict rules, often backed by violence, strongly discouraged corporations and ambitious entrepreneurs from entering and transforming retail, service, and entertainment trades.[4]

The trade in kosher bread, meat, and poultry among Jewish residents best exemplifies the cultural and economic forces that guided consumer spending. On one level, the persistence of religious laws regulating the production of certain foods illustrated the stubbornness of traditional identities. By eating kosher meat, a Jewish consumer demonstrated not only obedience to God's law, but also a dedication

---

[4] Robert and Helen Lynd found wide disparities of wealth in 1920s Muncie, Indiana, but they argued that the easy availability of consumer products deradicalized workers. Others contend that workers of the 1920s participated in the consumer revolution on their own culturally constructed terms and used new desires to justify radical action. But few note how skilled craftsmen circumscribed the options available to consumers. Robert and Helen Lynd, *Middletown: A Study in Modern American Culture* (New York: Harcourt Brace Jovanovich, 1929), 89; Daniel Bell, *The End of Ideology* (New York: The Free Press, 1962), 21–39; Cohen, *Making a New Deal*, 100–1, 398–99; Roy Rosenzweig, *"Eight Hours for What We Will": Workers and Leisure in Worcester Massachusetts, 1870–1930* (New York: Cambridge University Press, 1984); Dana Frank, *Purchasing Power: Consumer Organizing, Gender, and the Seattle Labor Movement, 1919–1929* (New York: Cambridge University Press, 1994).

to Old World culture and a reluctance to assimilate. Butchers and bakers were immigrant craftsmen, preparing food in an ancient manner seemingly antithetical to mass production. Consumers patronized shopkeepers they trusted would not mislabel *chazerai* (unclean food) as kosher. Yet none of these factors can entirely explain why observant Jews would prefer to shop at smaller concerns. Consumers might have purchased mass-produced specialty products in chain stores or larger kosher markets without violating the laws of *kashruth*. The traditional skill of the *schochet* (or kosher butcher) did not preclude improvements in management, investment, and distribution. The fear of fraud probably encouraged some shoppers to patronize trusted local tradesmen, but contemporary economists use the same impulse to explain the rise of brand names, which promise consistency and quality control.[5]

In fact, large-scale production and distribution of kosher foods developed slowly during the 1910s and 1920s because a variety of unions and associations governed that industry in Chicago, New York, and other cities. Kosher bakers enforced standard prices in a number of ways. In 1912, the Jewish Master Bakers Association set up a phony store, which sold bread at prices far below market, to undercut a baker named Morris Abrams, who refused to join their group. Journeymen bakers belonged to special union locals, and these groups aided the masters. In 1923, Sam and Abraham Cohen owned a Southwest Side wholesale and retail bakery at 3615 West Roosevelt Road, which employed union bakers and paid the union scale. But when the Cohens lowered their prices, two nearby bakers complained to Harry Lipkin and Sam Mossler, officers of Bakers and Confectioners Local #237. The business agents demanded the Cohens accept the association price and pulled the union workers off the job, causing the firm to lose $300 per week. Lipkin and Mossler allegedly threatened to bomb the Cohen Brothers' bakery, should they persist in price-cutting.[6]

Kosher butchers regulated their trade even more closely. Associations pressured retailers into joining and adopting standard prices. In 1920, Jacob Weller and David Trabish, two butchers on the near

[5] Cohen, *Making a New Deal*, 110–11; Susan Fournier, "Consumers and their Brands: Developing Relationship Theory in Consumer Research," *Journal of Consumer Research* 24:4 (March 1998): 350–51.

[6] Bill, May 4, 1912, *Abrams v. Master Bakers Association*, case #294250, Sup.C.C. (1912); Bill for Injunction, December 22, 1923, *Cohen v. Bakers and Confectioners No. 237*, Circ.C.C. 105070 (1923), 2–5; "War to Death of Beef Trust," *Atlanta Constitution*, April 20, 1902, 19; "Jews Without Bread," *WP*, August 8, 1905, 1; "Kosher Bakers Strike," *Atlanta Constitution*, April 21, 1913, 4; "4,000 Kosher Butchers Striking in New York," *WP*, November 23, 1924, 3.

southwest side, tested the rule of the Chicago Hebrew Master Butchers Beneficial Association. When Weller and Trabish refused to enlist in the association, the officers allegedly asked Joseph Etkin, the business agent of Local #598, Amalgamated Meat Cutters, to pressure them to join and buy stock in the United Kosher Sausage Factory. Etkin allegedly called their employees on strike, hired a "gang of sluggers" to brandish revolvers, throw stink bombs, break windows, intimidate drivers from Armour & Co., and use "vile and approbious [*sic*] language" in front of customers.[7]

In the mid-1920s, Maxie Eisen took the reins of the Hebrew Master Butchers' Association. Eisen ran at least two other associations of kosher food dealers – the Master Bakers (northwest side) and the Wholesale and Retail Fish Dealers – and his methods of governing trade were more brutal than those of his predecessors. For instance, in 1927, David Trabish refused to adopt standard prices. The Master Butchers sent a woman undercover to his store at 1224 S. Kedzie to buy a chicken. When she reported that Trabish was undercutting his peers, the association fined him $50. Trabish refused to pay, and, on October 8, 1927, Eisen and his aide Jack "Knuckles" Cito clubbed the butcher senseless with a revolver butt and an iron bar, creating a gash requiring sixteen stitches.

In addition to setting prices, Eisen forcefully limited entry into the kosher food business, terrifying potential competitors. In 1926, David Elkins, a fish dealer, accused Eisen of throwing kerosene into his stock. In 1927, Eisen allegedly shot a fish dealer in the leg when he refused to quit to relieve competition. Judge and mayoral candidate John Lyle claimed that Eisen demanded a widow pay the association $3,000 for permission to open a fish market with her husband's life insurance. Though most of those punished were small operators, Eisen was not afraid to pressure the largest kosher dealers and packinghouses. In 1927, the United Kosher Sausage Factory – a concern that the Master Butchers had promoted in 1920 – claimed that Maxie had hurled poison into stores selling their merchandise, damaging their business to the tune of $180,000.[8]

Consumers felt the effects of such rules, which increased the cost of food and limited the range of purchasing options. Many historians describe the "food riots" of the early twentieth century, in which Jewish

---

7 Bill of Complaint, May 8, 1920, *Weller v. Chicago Hebrew Butchers*, USDC, ND, E. IL, Equity case #1447 in NARA-GL (1920).

8 John Landesco, *Organized Crime in Chicago, Part III of the Illinois Crime Survey, 1929* (Chicago: University of Chicago, 1968), 160–61; Lyle, *Dry and Lawless Years*, 189.

women protested inflation in New York, Chicago, and other cities. Yet these scholars tend to be vague about the relationship between various craft organizations and high prices, a connection that was clear in the contemporary press. In 1912, the Jewish women of Chicago's southwest side boycotted members of the kosher butchers' association. Their leader, Clara Friedman, demanded cooperative stores, calling the dealers "Egyptians . . . in league against the people of God" who cared "not for us but for our money." The president of the Peddlers' Protective Association, Ben Liffshitz, suggested Jews cease eating kosher food and declared his desire to eliminate the wholesale butchers altogether and deal directly with the meatpacking trusts.[9]

Similar protests occurred again in 1917, a year in which wartime food shortages inspired violence in many American cities. The local Yiddish language newspaper, *The World*, again described consumer resentment:

> A representative of *The World* succeeded yesterday in unveiling a horrible conspiracy by the local Jewish baker bosses, under the name "Jewish Master Bakers' Association" in order to extort more money from the poor working families by raising the prices on bread and filling themselves with immense profits by doing so.[10]

The development of mass culture thus divided immigrants. A radical Jewish public defended their right to consume. Some, like Ben Liffshitz, proposed abandoning craft production and religious tradition in favor of corporations and American culture. Others, like Clara Friedman, believed that cooperative stores would allow them to

[9] "Women Start Riot," *CRH*, June 11, 1912, 7; "Markets to Reopen; Meat at Old Prices," *CRH*, June 13, 1912, 1; Dana Frank, "Housewives, Socialists, and the Politics of Food: The 1917 New York Cost-of-Living Protests," *Feminist Studies* 11:2 (Summer 1985): 255–85; Paula Hyman, "Immigrant Women And Consumer Protest: The New York City Kosher Meat Boycott Of 1902," *American Jewish History* 70 (1980): 91–105; "Kosher Shops All Closed," *Atlanta Constitution*, July 27, 1907, 8; "Women Lead Riots," *WP*, July 26, 1907, 1; "The Jewish Housekeepers," *Trenton Evening Times*, November 14, 1907, 6; "Boycott of Detroit Kosher Meat Goes On," *WP*, March 11, 1927, 5.

[10] "Jewish Quarter Terrorized by Baker Boss Association," *The World*, October 19, 1917 in Chicago Foreign Language Press Survey, Box 26, II E 1, University of Chicago Special Collections; "Police Out to Stop Chicago Food Rioting," *Fort Wayne Sentinal*, March 30, 1917, 1. In 1932, Jewish leaders successfully ousted Eisen by threatening to boycott the Hebrew Butchers. The violence continued, while Eisen moved into other criminal activities, such as counterfitting. "Head of Butchers Held in Two Bombings," *CDT*, September 4, 1932; "Nab Five Accused Counterfeiters," *Charleston Daily Mail*, July 7, 1935, 1.

preserve rituals and lower prices while rejecting both corporate capitalism and local craft governance. But the bakers and butchers saw the mass production–mass consumption economy as a thing to be controlled and perhaps even exploited.

Craftsmen regulated consumer options, prices, routes, distributors, and wages in many service and retail trades, including milk, laundry, barbering, shoeshining, ice delivery, building maintenance, and advertising. Since the first decade in the century, three organizations governed the milk trade, the Chicago Milk Dealers Association (CMDA), the Milk Producers' Association (MPA), and the Milk Drivers' Union, Local #753 (MDU). Between 1907 and 1920, they expended most of their energy trying to crush the large dairies, such as Borden Condensed Milk Co., a New Jersey corporation that defied both the producers and the dealers by refusing to accept standard wholesale rates and retail prices. In 1907, they pressured the state's attorney to indict Borden and four other large dairies for price fixing, a charge the five firms successfully rebutted. Failing to stop Borden had a dramatic effect on the small producers. In 1911, over 1,200 milk dealers operated in Chicago; by 1917, the number had dropped to 668. In reaction, local associations attempted to bankrupt the national firm. In April 1916, when dairy farmer and MPA member, Fred Secore, began selling to Borden, a crowd allegedly stopped his truck, took possession of his cargo, and dumped his milk on the highway.[11]

By 1919, the dairymen had more or less enlisted Borden in their cause, taming the large corporation with the promise of profits. In 1924, the milk producers asked the CFL to help them form a union, hoping to improve their leverage with the dealers. The resulting agreements offered drivers a closed shop and massive wages increases (163 percent between 1914 and 1929), while the teamsters agreed not to challenge standard prices or assigned routes. Just as importantly, the teamsters policed the boundaries of the membership of the milk dealers' association by boycotting and physically threatening non-members. Unions agreed to protest the importation of milk from outside the fifty-mile inspection zone set by health commissioner Herman Bundesen. In 1925, Cook County State's Attorney Robert Crowe

---

[11] True Bill, December 21, 1907, *People v. Ira J. Mix*, Crim.C.C., case #86389, IR 149, 131–37; "No 'Milk Trust' Seen," *CRH*, March 4, 1909, 16; "Defi for 'Milk Trust,'" *CRH*, February 8, 1910, 3; Christenson, *Collective Bargaining in Chicago*, 179; Bill for Injunction, April 6, 1916, *Borden's Condensed Milk v. Milk Producers' Association*, USDC, ND, E. IL, Equity case #636 in NARA-GL (1916); "Milk Producers Ask Charge Be Explained," *CDN*, April 21, 1919, 4.

accused five union officials of bombing an independent dairy owned
by a Mrs. Jaroez. Freed from competition, the dealers raised prices
from 8 to 14 cents per quart between 1914 and 1927, a boost they split
with the teamsters.[12]

Though the dealers had accepted Borden, they still fought to preserve traditional modes of retail distribution and limit consumer
choices. In the early twentieth century, Chicagoans purchased food,
coal, and clothes from commission salesmen who traveled door-to-
door, and these tradesmen feared the advent of direct retailers, who
shucked older purchasing patterns, choosing instead to attract consumers through advertising and price competition. Door-to-door milk
delivery was mandated by the teamsters, who wanted to protect their
jobs, and by the dairies, which needed the drivers to enforce price
and route restrictions. The teamsters and the flat janitors union
agreed that members of the former would refuse to deliver milk
to nonunion apartment buildings and members of the latter union
would not permit deliveries from nonunion milk drivers. The union
then proceeded to assault any retailer who sold milk directly to the
consumer.[13]

Other local tradesmen sought to ride the revolution in spending
habits. Consumption of candy grew wildly in the twenties – by 1927,
the wholesale candy market was $7 million dollars – but such spend-
ing also occurred within a locally controlled market. The Chicago
Association of Candy Jobbers and its subordinate group, the Jewish
Benevolent Association, fixed prices and set distribution routes. In
1925, the association and its 295 member firms hired James Boyle to
investigate jobbers suspected of cutting prices, "stealing" customers, or
selling without joining the association and paying a $250 initiation fee.
They employed a business manager, Vincent Pastor, to enforce these

[12] Landesco, *Organized Crime*, 141, 144; Christenson, *Collective Bargaining*, 178–
83. This is not to say that consensus reigned among the various milk interests. And even after Borden signed price agreements, similar protests
plagued other large dairies. "Milk Producers May Push Fight as Labor
Union," *CDT*, January 10, 1924, 5; "Complaints of Bad Milk Stir City to
Action," *CDT*, January 11, 1924, 12.

[13] Declaration, November 22, 1932, *Meadowmoor Dairy v. Chicago Milk Dealers Assn. et al.*, USDC, ND, E. IL, Equity case #41533 in NARA-GL; Bill of
Complaint, January 29, 1934, *Meadowmoor Dairy v. Borden Farm Products*,
USDC, ND, E. IL, Equity case #13697 in NARA-GL; Bill for injunction,
March 31, 1927, *Martin v. Chicago Flat Janitors Union*, Circ.C.C. case #143895
(1927); John Jentz, "Labor, the Law, and Economics: The Organization
of the Chicago Flat Janitors' Union, 1902–1917," *Labor History* 38:4 (Fall
1997): 417.

provisions. Meeting with the Salesmen's Club and the Manufacturers' Welfare Club, Pastor arranged a mutual boycott system that denied independent jobbers access to products and pressured manufacturers to deal exclusively with his association. When tobacco wholesalers, who had their own powerful organization, circumvented these boycotts, the association told Pastor to use force. He met an unnamed man in City Hall and hired him to smash windows and throw stink bombs at a rate of $25 per window.[14]

During the teens, an entertainment industry emerged in Chicago, and residents gained access to mass culture via new technologies such as film and radio. Yet local organizations also mediated the production and distribution of popular art forms. Over two thousand projectionists, stage employees, ticket takers, ushers, opera singers, and actors belonged to unions. But the most powerful union was the Chicago Federation of Musicians (CFM), a body with 8,300 members in two racially segregated locals. These organizations controlled more than 90 percent of all professional working musicians in Cook and DuPage Counties. The CFM had contracts with the Chicago Broadcasters' Association, various operas and symphonies, cafes, dance halls, and the Exhibitors' Association. Even in 1930, with unemployment rising in the aftermath of the stock market crash, every theater in the city but one, located in the so-called Black Belt, employed exclusively CFM members.

These unions obtained effective control over entry into their trades and forced employers' associations to engage in regular collective bargaining during the 1920s. As they had for decades, musicians operated an independent court system to discipline members who violated union rules. Having established their dominance in the previous years, their authority was self-sustaining. Union members knew that they would lose their ability to work altogether if they worked with nonunionists. The Motion Picture Operators' Union barred all outsiders. Between 1921 and 1929, apprentices never exceeded 3.1 percent of the workforce, and most years saw fewer than ten new projectionists (out of between 600 and 1000 total). Since unlike music, projection required no particular skill, the projectionists depended upon their political connections. Through party ties, Tommy Malloy, the union president, managed to place his brother

[14] Records and Briefs, *James Boyle et al. v. United States*, United States Court of Appeals (henceforth USCA), 7th Circuit, case #4207 (1928), 11–3, 27–107, 286–89; M. H. Zimmerman, "The How and Why of Chain Growth in Various Trades," *Printers' Ink* 153:2 (October 9, 1930): 130.

Joseph in the job of the chief inspector for the city licensing board.[15]

Members used this exclusivity to obtain high wages and soften the effects of technology. A musician working at an amusement park in 1929 earned $80 for a forty-four-hour week, plus extra charges for working short engagements ($14.00), wearing a tuxedo ($3.50), or appearing in blackface ($7.00). Projectionists in the deluxe houses might earn $3.25 per hour, or $137.50 for a forty-two-hour week – staggering sums in an era where the best paid manufacturing workers made $5.00 to $10.00 per day. Both groups also attempted to control mechanization. Though the operators had their contract amended to give them the formal power to veto new technology, they basically accepted new machines. By contrast, in 1928, the CFM went on strike, demanding that any new theater with 800 seats employ a four-piece orchestra for forty-four weeks a year, and that any exhibitor "which instals [*sic*] Vitaphone, Movietone, or any other mechanical instrument which carries with it orchestral music . . . must employ at all times this instrument is in operation, a minimum of six men exclusive of organist." The exhibitors rejected any restrictions on the use of prerecorded sound but agreed to hire four-piece orchestras.

Unlike the dairies, smaller film exhibitors were never able to use craft governance to their advantage because they never found any common interest with their workers besides the desire for uninterrupted operation. High labor costs frustrated entertainment corporations, as musicians consumed as much as 15 percent of the budget for a deluxe movie theater, but they hardly dulled their competitive edge. More than other businesses, movie theaters vied for the most sumptuous surroundings and the highest quality films in an effort at attracting respectable middle-class patrons to theaters. Musicians' unions could do little stem this competition. Moreover, the technological leaps affecting the business were quantum – e.g., the introduction of sound – rather than small and continuous. While construction workers might appeal to smaller contractors by stemming an incremental improvement in production that favored the leading firms, musicians could not. No exhibitor could afford to reject the qualitative improvement represented by talking pictures like *The Jazz Singer*, so restrictions on prerecorded music were simply impossible.[16]

[15] Christenson, *Collective Bargaining in Chicago*, 239, 248; Lyle, *Dry and Lawless Years*, 193.
[16] Christenson, *Collective Bargaining in Chicago*, 215, 218, 222–23, 231, 226.

Indeed, elite film exhibitors showed that corporations could bend craft governance, even at its most militant, to their own interests. Like any large concern, chains of film exhibitors held significant amounts of invested capital, making labor troubles very expensive. But while other corporations crushed unions for this reason, the theaters chose to negotiate. This attitude was partly cultural. Balaban & Katz, the theater chain, was both a vertically integrated firm linked to Hollywood film producers and the creation of recent immigrants with experience in the unionized economy. A. J. Balaban had been a factory laborer before entering film exhibition. His eventual partner, Adolph Zukor of Paramount Studios (a.k.a. Famous Players-Lasky), was a former furrier. Perhaps because of their personal histories, these men proved proficient at using union rules to their advantage. They pressured the CFM to accept talking film technology in exchange for "make work" rules giving them job security. Such agreements eventually encouraged the growth of chains at the expense of the independent theater owners, for the former were able both to support an orchestra and purchase the necessary sound equipment, while the latter could not.[17]

Corporations, Technology, and the National Market

In construction and transportation, craftsmen continued to inhibit the national firms and ambitious modernizers who threatened their economic position by introducing machines, restructuring work, and using nonunion labor. During an era when the U.S. Supreme Court held that the constitution forbade legislators from passing laws interfering in the economic decisions of individuals, craftsmen in Chicago gave themselves the authority to regulate commerce through trade agreements. This assertion was more than bluster. In trades like construction, unions and associations jointly exercised extraordinary control not only of the work process, but also of prices, materials, and access to jobs.

The context for their efforts was the transformation of the American economy, which began over a century earlier, but reached a particular zenith during the years before and after World War I. Famed automobile manufacturer Henry Ford personally embodied the threat to craftsmen in this period. Ford made his fortune by standardizing the mode of production, the producer, and the product. He took

---

[17] Lary May, *Screening Out the Past: The Birth of Mass Culture and the Motion Picture Industry* (Chicago: University of Chicago Press, 1983), 148–49, 157; Christenson, *Collective Bargaining in Chicago*, 225–31.

the idea of the assembly line, developed in the meatpacking industry, and adapted it to the manufacture of cars, breaking down the
work process into a series of tiny tasks. For his workers, Ford hired
African-Americans, farm boys, and immigrants, men who undoubtedly possessed many different skills, few of which he actually needed.
Ford wanted these workers to be interchangeable, and he tried to ho-
mogenize them by offering higher wages to those who accepted an
American identity and middle class values such as thrift, sobriety, and
a stable home life. Ford's only product was the Model T, a no frills vehicle that came in only one color, but which was inexpensive enough
for ordinary Americans to buy. In sum, Ford was in the vanguard of
a new economic world, in which huge corporations, hiring thousands
of semi-skilled workers, manufactured complex but identical products
for a national mass market.[18]

Ford's economic vision terrified Chicago's craft workers and employers, who favored an economy composed of many local producers,
employing skilled labor, governed by trade agreements. In their view,
high wages depended not on sales volume, productivity, and the benef-
icent patronage of the employer, but on high prices, scarce talents,
unique products, and the ability to negotiate a local regulatory apparatus. The craftsmen's fears were magnified by Ford's immense success.
They had witnessed Ford's system utterly eradicate craft production of
carriages, a luxury good once produced in many small workshops by
skilled carpenters and metal workers. So, when Chicago's own Sears,
Roebuck catalog began offering consumers the ability to buy prefabricated homes through the mail, craftsmen were aware of the devastating
implications.[19]

In a few cases, tradesmen directly battled against machines that undermined workers' skills and eliminated existing jobs. Construction
workers were particularly vehement in their opposition to labor saving equipment, such as the mechanical stone planer. But other craft

---

[18] Allen Nevins and Frank Ernest Hill, *Ford: Expansion and Challenge 1915–
1932* (New York: Charles Scribner's Sons, 1957); Daniel Nelson, *Managers
and Workers: Origins of the Factory System in the United States, 1880–1920* (Madison: University of Wisconsin Press, 1975), 140–64; Olivier Zunz, *The Changing Face of Inequality: Urbanization, Industrial Development, and Immigrants in
Detroit, 1880–1920* (Chicago: University of Chicago, 1982); Antonio Gram-
sci, "Americanism and Fordism," in *Selections from the Prison Notebooks*, ed.,
Quintin Hoare and Geoffrey Nowell Smith (New York: International Publishers, 1992), 286.

[19] "In Home Building Field," *NYT*, June 9, 1929, RE4; Rosemary Thornton,
*The Houses That Sears Built; Everything You Ever Wanted To Know About Sears
Catalog Homes* (Alton, IL: Gentle Beam Publications, 2002).

workers also protested technological innovation. In 1912, for example, thirty teamsters walked off their jobs, when their employer, Consolidated Bottling Company, introduced "six large auto trucks, each of which will do the work of two teams." This, the first teamsters' protest against the introduction of motorized vehicles, caused concern among many employers, who embraced the technology as "a logical development in the transportation problem."[20] The teamsters' initial resistance gave way to acceptance, and gas and electric trucks became standard by the 1920s, but only because the job losses were so small and the efficiency gains so great.

Craftsmen opposed new and potentially popular consumer products that altered habitual work patterns. In 1929, Julius Rosenwald, a noted philanthropist and the president of Sears, Roebuck built a "model tenement" that he hoped would set the standard for reasonably priced housing in the city. One of the key features of the 400 apartments in the $2.5 million building was the introduction of electric refrigerators, machines replacing iceboxes that required both daily ice delivery and drains to collect the water produced by melting. When Rosenwald informed the plumbers that he did not need them to build drains, a job that had previously provided many hours of labor in the past, they demanded that he pay them anyway. Rosenwald declined, so the plumbers' union initiated an unsuccessful two-week strike.[21]

Anxiety about looming economic transformation helps explain labor's obsession with the jurisdictional boundaries that separated different crafts. Workers, especially in the building trades, initiated strikes when an employer hired members of one union to perform the tasks traditionally performed by the members of another. For example, in 1925, the George A. Fuller Co., a national firm owned by the Rockefeller family, hired the Dahlstrom Metallic Door Company, a

[20] "Autos Cause Drivers Strike," *CRH*, October 4, 12, 17; Clay McShane and Joel Tarr, "The Centrality of the Horse in the Nineteenth-Century American City," in *The Making of Urban America*, ed., Mohl (Wilmington: Scholarly Resources, 1997), 124.

[21] Typescript on the building trades (nd, probably 1932), 1 in Gerhard F. Meyne Papers, Folder 6 in CHS. This unidentified "model tenement" was almost certainly the Michigan Boulevard Garden Apartments, which Rosenwald built for African-American migrants to the city. The plumbers' union was racially exclusive, suggesting again the perceived connection between the open labor market, racial egalitarianism, consumerism, and the decline of the craftsmen's status. Peter Dreier, "Philanthropy and the Housing Crisis: The Dilemmas of Private Charity and Public Policy," *Housing Policy Update* 8:1 (1997), 242; Herbert Hill, *Black Labor and the American Legal System: Race, Work, and the Law* (Madison: University of Wisconsin Press, 1985), 237–39.

New York corporation, to install 600 doors for stairwells and fire escapes in buildings owned by the Stephens Hotel Company – an $80,000 job. In 1926, Dahlstrom hired members of the United Brotherhood of Carpenters to hang the doors, only to face protests from the Bridge, Structural, and Ornamental Iron Workers Local #63 (BSOIW) and an allied union, Electrical Workers Local #1.

The BSOIW claimed that the National Board of Jurisdictional Disputes, a private group that unions and contractors created to arbitrate craft boundaries, had ordered employers to give these jobs to iron-workers. The iron contractors working on the site, A. E. Coleman and Wetzel Iron, also rebuked the manufacturer. Wetzel's manager allegedly told Dahlstrom's erecting superintendent, Ernest Dion, "You will get off this job a lot quicker than you got on." Under pressure from the general contractor, Dahlstrom agreed to hire some ironworkers for the job, but the unions refused to end their walkouts until the firm fired all the carpenters.

Jurisdictional disputes could be petty, indicating the selfish desire for work, but they could be profound, expressing a fear of technological change and a desire for local control. As economist Robert Christie notes, the carpenters poached the ironworkers' jurisdiction in an effort to preserve their traditional right to hang doors, which dated back to the era when carpenters constructed wood doors at the building site itself. The invention of steel doors, manufactured off-site, provided superior fire protection for taller buildings, but threatened the carpenters' livelihood. Meanwhile, the BSOIW and the small contractors that employed them saw an arrogant out-of-state corporation trying to override local conditions and the will of the industry's private (though admittedly national) governing body. Thus, even at their most conflicted and ambiguous, craftsmen used jurisdiction in varying ways to protect themselves against economic transformation.[22]

Similarly, building tradesmen continued to oppose the installation of prefabricated building materials that undermined their skills and

---

[22] Bill of Complaint, March 30, 1926, *Dahlstrom Metallic Door Co. v. Iron Workers Local #63*, United States District Court (henceforth USDC), Northern District (henceforth ND), Eastern Illinois (henceforth E. IL), case #5724 in National Archives Research Administration, Great Lakes Division (henceforth NARA-GL); Affidavit of Ernest Dion, April 17, 1926, *Dahlstrom Metallic Door Co. v. Iron Workers Local #63*, USDC, ND, E. IL, case #5724 in NARA-GL; Bernstein, *The Lean Years*, 115–17; Montgomery, *Fall of the House of Labor*, 453–54; Robert A. Christie, *Empire in Wood: A History of the Carpenters Union* (Ithaca, NY: Cornell University, 1956), 171, 269–70.

shifted jobs outside the city. In 1927, a number of out-of-state firms, such as the Wasmuth Endicott Co., began manufacturing "built-in" kitchen cabinets with hard enamel finishes, created by mechanically spaying paint on the surface and baking the finished product. These cabinets were in demand because of their smooth ornamental appearance and low cost. Yet the members of Painters' District Council #14 of Chicago, which represented over twenty local unions, saw them as a terrible threat, for they replaced the labor of local painters with the out-of-state labor of factory workers and, worse yet, machines. The painters determined not to work on building sites where contractors installed the Wasmuth Endicott cabinets unless either the manufacturer shipped the cabinets with only a coat of primer (creating work for painters but destroying the appeal of the product), or the contractor paid the union $2 per kitchen and employed union members to stand and watch the installations. Needing to complete the other necessary painting work, the local contractors agreed to these terms, severely increasing the cost and decreasing the success of the product.[23]

Opposition to technology worked hand in hand with localism, as journeymen controlled mechanization by closing the city to nonunion, out-of-state manufacturers. Contractors had obtained the right to use prefabricated stone, electrical fixtures, doors, and windows during the pivotal Building Trades Lockout of 1899, but around 1910, the two sides achieved a stable compromise; the unions were given exclusive contracts and, in exchange, they promised to protect local businesses from competition with national firms. Contractors, manufacturers, and workers in plumbing, steam fitting, terracotta, and sheet metal established rules limiting the employment of nonunion workers, the operation of independent contractors, and the use of out-of-state materials. As they had for decades, the participants enforced self-styled laws through a series of interlocking boycotts. Local sheet metal manufacturers agreed to hire only union workers, and sheet metal workers passed rules banning materials produced out-of-state by corporations like Carrier Air Conditioning of Buffalo. The Chicago Master Steam Fitters' Association, a group of local contractors and suppliers, granted the Chicago Journeymen Steam Fitters' Protective Association a closed shop. In return, members of the union refused to work for contractors who were not members of the association. Firms that tried to sell steam equipment in the city, such as Sears,

[23] Petition, August 22, 1928, *U.S. v. Painters District Council No 14*, USDC, ND, E. IL, case #8556 in NARA-GL; Typescript on the building trades (nd, probably 1932), 1 in Gerhard Meyne Papers, Folder 6 in CHS.

Roebuck, found that none of the city's contractors would buy their wares.[24]

Craftsmen used geographic restrictions to place technologically sophisticated manufacturing under the penumbra of the craft economy. For instance, the International Brotherhood of Electrical Workers (IBEW) always accepted factory-made switchboards and wiring; to prohibit such equipment would have been impossible, for workers could not fashion switchboards at a worksite. But electrical workers did insist on the use of gear made in Chicago by local firms employing solely union labor. On April 1, 1911, IBEW Local #376 signed an agreement with the Chicago Switchboard Manufacturers Association in which the employers agreed to hire only union workers and adopted a fixed wage scale, which would go into effect once the union "succeeded before October 1, 1911, in bringing about a condition which will permit of none but Union label switchboard work to be installed in the City of Chicago." In other words, employers allowed wage increases if and only if the union excluded foreign and nonunion competition, including major firms like General Electric. The Chicago Lighting Fixture Association, led by secretary treasurer William J. Feeney, signed a similar agreement with Local #376, barring out-of-state manufacturers from the Chicago market.[25]

Electricians' unions worked with Chicago-based corporations to ruin national competitors or force them to adopt local standards. After making an alliance with the Chicago Telephone Company during the war, IBEW Local #134 focused on Western Union, the nonunion telegraph giant. Union electricians harassed the firm's installers, picketed their buildings, drove nails into their cables, removed bulbs from sockets, and pulled out wires. In 1920, the Republican Party decided to hold its presidential convention in Chicago's Coliseum, hiring Western Union to install the telegraph and telephone wiring. BTC head

---

[24] *United States v. Chicago Mosaic Tiling Co. et al.*, USDC, ND, E. IL, Criminal case #6068 in NARA-GL (1917); *United States v. James Clow & Sons et al.*, USDC, ND, E. IL, Criminal case #7788 in NARA-GL (1921); *United States v. Louis Biegler Co. et al.*, USDC, ND, E. IL, Criminal case #7901 in NARA-GL (1921); *United States v. Chicago Master Steam Fitters' Association et al.*, USDC, ND, E. IL, Criminal case #7902 in NARA-GL (1921); *United States v. Lehigh Portland Cement Co. et al.*, USDC, ND, E. IL, Criminal case #9312 in NARA-GL (1922); *United States American v. Terra Cotta and Ceramic Co. et al.*, USDC, ND, E. IL, Criminal case #9333 in NARA-GL (1922).

[25] Indictment, April 27, 1915, *United States v. Michael Boyle*, USDC, ND, E. IL, Criminal case #5648 in NARA-GL (1915), 22; Indictment, April 27, 1915, *United States v. William J. Feeney*, USDC, ND, E. IL, Criminal case #5652 in NARA-GL (1915), 7.

Simon O'Donnell refused to allow this, charging that the corporation had "double-crossed" the building tradesmen in the past by promising to abide by local standards, then reneging by using "scab labor." Only a 1924 federal injunction allowed the corporation access to the city. The message was clear – national firms could not enter the Chicago market without cost and risk.[26]

Perhaps the most potent rules preserving localism existed in the carpentry, millwork, and lumber trade. For years, the United Brotherhood of Carpenters (UBC) had opposed millwork altogether, but during the teens they ended their ban on factory trim and experimented with organizing the mill workers. Millions of dollars in factory trim flowed from Wisconsin into Chicago until the labor shortage of World War I, when the union reasserted its authority. The Carpenters' District Council (CDC) boycotted all materials produced by men who declined to join the UBC, and they convinced local contractors to avoid nonunion material by agreeing to eschew lumber produced outside of the state as well, effectively excluding firms located in Oshkosh, Wisconsin. The CDC then endeavored to organize the Illinois mill workers. For example, CDC president William Brims asked Anderson & Lind Manufacturing Co. (A&L), an open shop firm with a plant in Chicago, to sign an exclusive contract with the union. When the firm insisted on hiring nonunion workers, the CDC barred them from selling in the city. In 1919, a contractor named Robert Pottinger purchased A&L millwork for a large apartment building, only to have Brims and other union officials call his employees on strike twenty times during the next year. Fearing such work stoppages, other contractors refused to purchase A&L material.[27]

Teamsters worked at the hubs of the American transportation network, and they also used their power to tame the developing national economy. Between 1912 and 1928, the machinery movers' union, an

[26] Radical union organizer William Z. Foster claimed that the Chicago Telephone Company paid IBEW officer Michael Boyle a bribe of $10,000 for his allegiance. In return, Boyle also agreed not to organize the workers in CTC switching facilities. Foster, *Misleaders of Labor*, 170; "Labor Unyielding on Coliseum Wires," *NYT*, May 30, 1920, 1; Notice, Motion for Injunction, and Supporting Affidavits, June 9, 1924, *Western Union v. IBEW #134 et al.*, USDC, ND, E. IL, Equity case #4047 in NARA-GL (1924).

[27] *U.S. v. Andrews Lumber, et al.*, USDC, ND, E. IL, Criminal case #7518 in NARA-GL (1918); *U.S. v. Andrews Lumber, et al.*, USDC, ND, E. IL, Criminal case #8302 in NARA-GL (1921); *U.S. v. Brims*, USCA, 7th Circuit, case #3436 (1923); *Brims v. U.S.*, 6 F.2d 99; *U.S. v. Brims*, 272 U.S. 549 (1926); *Anderson & Lind v. Carpenters' District Council*, 308 IL. 488 (1923); Ernst, *Lawyers Against Labor*, 191–213.

affiliate of the independent Chicago Teamsters Union, was the primary obstacle standing between out-of-state manufacturers and the lucrative Chicago market. Union President Mike Artery repeatedly ordered his constituents not to haul ice machines and boilers produced by companies like York Manufacturing of Pennsylvania and Babcock & Wilcox of New Jersey, from the rail yard to their purchasers. Again, once goods entered the city, they fell into the hands of men hostile to corporate commerce, the national market, and nonunion labor.[28]

The truckers who carted fruits, vegetables, meats, and cheeses to the wholesalers at the Water Street Market joined with commission team owners and merchants to set rates for interstate grocery hauling. In July 1924, three union shipping firms, C. B. Williams, H. M. Stephens, and Coyne Brothers reduced their hauling rates, incurring the wrath of the Chicago Commission Team Owners' Association and its president, John Quirk. Quirk told the teamsters and teaming contractors not to unload the shippers' chicken coops and other merchandise. Though the poultry merchants sided with Coyne and refused to go along with the boycott, the Poultry Handlers Union Local #17177 supported the commission teaming interests. On July 19, 1924, drivers Mike Doyle and George Vinton prevented Frank Quackenbush from unloading chicken coops from Coyne Brothers' wagons at the Peoria Street railway station.[29]

Teamsters' locals forcefully set interstate transportation rates not only by boycotting dissidents, but also by threatening violence and financial ruin. In 1928, A. J. "Smiles" Paglinghi, the business agent of IBT Local #703, allegedly had the following conversation with D. W. Lamson, a Michigan hauler working between that state, Wisconsin, Illinois, Indiana, and Ohio:

[28] *United States v. Michael Artery*, USDC, ND, E. IL, Criminal case #5545 in NARA-GL (1915); *United States v. Michael Artery*, USDC, ND, E. IL, Criminal case #5546 in NARA-GL (1915); *United States v. Michael Artery*, USDC, ND, E. IL, Criminal case #5547 in NARA-GL (1915); *United States v. John Dohney*, USDC, ND, E. IL, Criminal case #5649 in NARA-GL (1915); *United States v. John Dohney*, USDC, ND, E. IL, Criminal case #5650 in NARA-GL (1915); *United States v. John Dohney*, USDC, ND, E. IL, Criminal case #5651 in NARA-GL (1915); *United States v. John F. Stretch*, USDC, ND, E. IL, Criminal case #5653 in NARA-GL (1915); *Babcock and Wilcox Co. v. Boilermakers et al.*, USDC, ND, E. IL, Equity case #9360 in NARA-GL (1929).

[29] Bill of Complaint, July 23, 1924, *Coyne Brothers et al. v. International Brotherhood of Teamsters et al.*, 4183 (1924). Information for Contempt and Affidavit, July 21, 1924, *Chicago Poultry Merchants Association v. Chicago Poultry Handlers' Union Local No. 17,177*, USDC, ND, E. IL, Equity case #4176 in NARA-GL (1924).

PAGLINGHI: "You are cutting rates on the Milwaukee haul – you got to quit it."

LAMSON: "What will happen if I don't?"

PAGLINGHI: "We will put you out of business."

LAMSON: "What rate do you want me to charge?"

PAGLINGHI: "Forty-seven cents, and not a damned cent less."

LAMSON: "I guess I will have to charge that."

PAGLINGHI: "Don't let us catch you charging less."

Whether or not Lamson then began complying with the rules, he had earned the wrath of the union officials, who began physically intimidating his workers and pressuring merchants to give his contracts to a better-connected firm, Reliable Transit Co. When Lamson allegedly begged the union president, James Langudora, for forgiveness, Langudora replied, "It's the end for you – you are through on the Street."[30]

Langudora's alleged actions suggest a less than ideal unionism, but they do rebut the characterization of labor as dormant in Chicago before the Great Depression. These men battled not only humble teamsters like Lamson, but large corporations like General Electric and Western Union. Moreover, the context for, if not the cause of, their aggression was competitive pressure wrought by the growth of integrated corporations, improvements in production and the creation of national networks of commerce. By protecting their own self-interest, they attacked a modern order in which technological innovation and market forces were the only sovereigns.

Restricting New Workers

The same rules that impeded corporate competition also limited the rights of new workers and entrepreneurs, many of them black and female. Before 1911, the relative paucity of African Americans and women seeking to enter Chicago's craft economy made the rules restricting them subsidiary to a larger craft governance that impeded corporations, price cutters, unaffiliated workers, and even rival unions. The explosive growth of the city's black population and changing attitudes towards femininity magnified the significance of preexisting racial and sexual restrictions, setting in motion a cycle of white male privilege, resentment, and violence that strengthened the craftsmen's equation of equal opportunity with corporate domination and hardened the segregation of the city's economy.

[30] *Lamson v. Reliable Transit Co.*, USDC, ND, E. IL, Equity case #8060 in NARA-GL (1928).

The broad context for racial violence in the craft economy was black migration to cities like Chicago. During and after World War I, thousands of African-Americans experienced a new freedom as they moved from the South to northern cities to work in war factories. Black artists and intellectuals experienced a "renaissance" in cities like New York and Chicago, producing music, literature, and scholarship that defiantly trumpeted the arrival of the black communities and the experiences of its denizens. But the anxious anticipation black migrants felt departing the Jim Crow South was muted by the hostile greeting they received from many Northern whites. During the 1920s, a reconstituted Ku Klux Klan, riots, lynchings, segregation, and a growing belief in scientific racism combined to contain black advancement and even crush black ambition in cities like Chicago.[31]

Skilled black tradesmen who came to the city found institutional barriers to their employment, as craft organizations controlled access to jobs by passing union membership from father to son. For instance, in 1915, a Chicago teenager named LeRoy Boyd decided he wanted to be an electrician. Because of his mother's death and his father's migration to Florida, LeRoy lived with his older sister and her husband, Matthew G. Lenehan, a member of the IBEW. With Linehan's backing, LeRoy requested admission to the union, but the officials rejected him, reserving cards for the sons of current members. The IBEW relented only when the Lenehans legally adopted LeRoy, making the teen, the *Tribune* jested, "his own nephew." Though too restrictive to be considered solely an expression of negrophobia, such rules barred most African-American workers from the trade.[32]

After 1915, craftsmen increasingly found themselves battling for white privilege, and barriers on entry grew increasingly racist in both principle and effect. The migration of over 50,000 new African-American workers to Chicago during the war meant that ordinary efforts at maintaining exclusivity disproportionately affected black newcomers. At the same time, the migration also inflamed longstanding racial prejudices, leading to new rules barring nonwhites. The teamsters, painters, plasterers, bricklayers, and laborers unions admitted black workers, and as a consequence African American workers made

---

[31] James R. Grossman, *Land of Hope: Chicago, Black Southerners, and the Great Migration* (Chicago: University of Chicago Press, 1989), 98–160; William M. Tuttle, *Race Riot: Chicago in the Red Summer of 1919* (New York: Atheneum, 1970), 77–102; Arvarh E. Strickland, *History of the Chicago Urban League* (Columbia, MO: University of Missouri Press, 1966), 25.

[32] "Becomes His Own Nephew to Put One Over on the Union," *CDT*, December 22, 1915, 13.

some inroads in these trades. In 1920, black men constituted 4.91 percent of the city's workforce and 10 percent of the laborers, 5.7 percent of the plasterers, 2.8 percent of the teamsters, 2.5 percent of the painters, and 2.4 percent of the masons. But many other unions – the plumbers and the electricians to name two – totally thwarted black opportunity, and the effects there were equally obvious: only 0.8 percent of electricians and 1.3 percent of plumbers claimed African ancestry in 1920.[33]

A cycle of exclusion, rivalry, and violence hardened racial prejudices. On March 6, 1915, the lathers – the building tradesmen who hammered wood superstructures for plaster walls – quit work to protest their employers' decision to form a new association. Rather than settling the matter with the union, the bosses hired, "good husky young men from both in and outside the city," including a number of black workers, as replacements. The strikers reacted by searching for the substitute lathers, demanding they cease working, and assaulting those that resisted. According to Edward M. Craig, an employers' representative: "brick bats were thrown into windows . . . many men were taken to the hospital."

One week later, a union posse found David A. Johnson, a "colored" lather who had held union cards in Atlanta, Georgia and Gary, Indiana, working on a new building at 3200 Chicago Avenue. The leader of the group cried, "beat it out of here, you cheap skates, or you'll all be croaked." When Johnson refused, the man pushed a revolver through the door and shot him in the left leg. Though the strike ended on July 17, the rivalry continued. On December 16, lathers' official Axel Alex passed a new building at 96th Street and Calumet Avenue. When David Johnson's brother, Robert, saw Alex, he allegedly left his work, ran into the street, and fired four bullets, shouting, "You shot my brother, and I'm going to shoot you." As Alex bled to death, Robert fled to his home at 104 W. 95th Street then hopped an eastbound freight train, leading the police on a high-speed chase. Taken into custody, Johnson stated that Alex had brandished a gun first. Despite his claims to self-defense, Robert was convicted of murder, only to be pardoned by Republican Governor Len Small. The Lathers' Union was less generous. For decades, they refused to admit another black worker.[34]

---

[33] Department of Commerce, Bureau of the Census, *14th Census of the United States, v. IV, Population 1920: Occupations* (Washington, DC: Government Printing Office, 1923), 1076–80.

[34] "Autobiography of E. M. Craig" (nd) in Gerhardt Meyne Papers, Folder 7 in CHS; Chicago Police Department Homicide Record Index, 2: 4A; "Nonunion Worker Shot in Lathers' Lockout War," *CDT*, March 14, 1915,

The story of Alex and the Johnson brothers suggests the complex interaction between localism and race, "scabbing" and exclusion, violence and politics. Though the Lathers' International Union forbade large local initiation fees, the White City Lathers' District Council refused to recognize members from other cities unless they paid $50 or more. This financial barrier probably combined with official racism to keep black migrants like David and Robert Johnson from practicing their trade in the City of Chicago. Needing to earn a living, the Johnsons crossed picket lines to work during the 1915 strike, which gave Alex a rationale for excluding them and eventually all African-Americans. Strike violence became racial violence, as the union forcibly removed black workers, who defended themselves and even gained revenge. Finally, this brutal cycle pushed African-American migrants deeper into their relationships with corporations and the Thompson–Crowe–Small Republican political machine.[35]

Craft governance also provides a context for the Race Riot of 1919. Though official investigators downplayed the role of organized labor in the tragedy, historian William Tuttle convincingly argues that racial antagonism flowed from black anger at the racial exclusivity of many craft unions, the white memory of the southern African-Americans breaking the Teamsters' Strike of 1905, and the hesitance of African-American steel and packinghouse workers during the strikes of 1919. Certainly, Ragan's Colts, the South Side political club and youth organization that allegedly instigated the riot, claimed close ties to craft unions. James Ragen, whose brother Frank was the eponymous club president, worked as a business agent and slugger for the United Association of Plumbers, one of the city's most racially exclusive unions. Frank Ragen's successor, Hugh Mulligan, was the president of the Asbestos Workers' Union.[36]

part II, 1; "Union Labor Agent is Shot and Killed," *CDN*, December 16, 1915, 1; "Labor Slugger Slain by Negro to Avenge Kin," *CDT*, Decemebr 17, 1915, 15; "Business Agent Shot to Death in Labor Feud, *CDT*, December 17, 1915; "Alex Dual Life Comes to Light at Inquest," *CDT*, December 18, 1915, 4; "Johnson Hounded by Labor Agent," *Chicago Defender*, December 25, 1915, 1, 4.

[35] "New Labor True Bills," *CRH*, June 30, 1909, 3.

[36] Tuttle, *Race Riot*, 32–3, 54–5, 120–23, 199–200; Landesco, *Organized Crime*, 172; True Bills, *People v. Eisenlord*, March 29, 1906, case #s 80445–80447, Crim.C.C., IR 149, 47–9; "Shooting Case to Jury," *CRH*, July 10, 1908, 11; "Special Grand Jury for Labor Sluggers," *CRH*, August 6, 1911, 1; "Ragen Case Dismissed," *CRH*, June 29, 1912, 9; John Landesco, "Interview with

Partly for this reason, racial violence resembled the labor violence of the same period. For example, on March 20, 1919, four months before the riot, a bomb exploded at the office of African-American banker and real estate entrepreneur Jesse Binga. Observers disagreed as to the cause of the explosion. Some believed the bombers sought to intimidate blacks into accepting residential segregation, but others claimed the Flat Janitors' Union a powerful mixed-race union, had punished Binga for using nonunion help. Some groups sought to intimidate blacks, while others sought to channel their asperations. But the means were the same, leading to substantial confusion.[37]

Within these bounds, some black workers nevertheless managed to negotiate a place for themselves. As their numbers grew, African-Americans swiftly became part of the Republican political machine, controlled by Mayor William Hale Thompson, Congressman Martin Barnaby Madden (no relation to "Skinny" Madden), and Governor Len Small. In exchange for votes, this political organization provided black craftsmen with access to union jobs in government and utility corporations. By 1930, in a city that was 7 percent black, 4.4 percent of the plumbers, 5.7 percent of the teamsters, 3.3 percent of the crane men, 8.2 percent of elevator tenders, and 27 percent of the janitors working in the government service claimed African-American backgrounds. Similarly, when a streetcar company hired white drivers to run a line servicing an African-American neighborhood, the residents formed the John Brown Political Club, which picketed until the corporation hired black operators.[38]

Black craftsmen also formed their own unions and associations in response to discrimination. In 1914, an African-American named Edward L. Doty took a job as a pipefitter's helper at Armour & Co., the giant meatpacker. When the Steamfitters' Protective Association began organizing the stockyards, Doty and his coworkers tried to join, but they were refused – the union officials "saw our faces and they slammed the door." In 1917, Armour promoted Doty to fitter, but he wanted to be a foreman, and the packinghouse refused to promote any black worker to that position. So Doty left the Yards, taking his trade to the public.

Doty had little initial success as an unlicensed, self-employed, nonunion plumber. The unions and the contractors refused to let him work, and the police arrested him when they saw him carrying plumbers' tools. In 1921, Doty obtained a license from the Illinois

John Shields, August 23, 1927," 7 in Box 34, Folder 9, Burgess Papers, University of Chicago Special Collections.
[37] Tuttle, *Race Riot*, 168–76; Landesco, *Organized Crime*, 130.
[38] Gosnell, *Negro Politicians*, 377, 141–42.

Board of Examiners – one of the first black men to do so – but without a union card, he remained unemployable. Finally, in 1926, a frustrated Doty obtained a charter from the State of Illinois for his own union, the Chicago Colored Plumbers Protective Association (CPPA). The CPPA signed an agreement with the New Era Plumbing Contractors Association, an organization of African-American contractors who confined their business to the growing Black Belt. In 1928, Doty ran for office, seeking to become the first African-American in the United States Congress since Reconstruction. Running on the new Communist Party ticket, Doty lost badly to Republican Oscar DePriest, himself a successful black building tradesman.

Doty's story illuminates the racial order of the craft economy. Black workers found employment – though limited advancement – at corporations like Armour & Co. Because such firms hired African-Americans, white tradesmen often equated corporate ownership, racial inclusivity, and the permanent subordination of workers. Perhaps for this reason, racial restrictions appealed to both white workers and smaller employers, who either endorsed a lily-white trade or declined to question the union's control over the labor market. Finally, Doty survived by playing the white craftsmen's game, forming his own union and signing agreements with an association of black employers. Though the white pipefitters doubtless disapproved of the Colored Plumbers, they could not deny Doty's logic. Even when craftsmen did not recognize a worker's individual right to practice a trade, they did acknowledge an organization's authority over work and workers in a particular precinct, when backed by sufficient force.[39]

The craftsmen also rejected equal opportunity for women. During the war, women worked temporarily in war factories, and, after the armistice, they obtained the national suffrage, overthrew traditional attitudes toward fashion and sexuality, and made new inroads into the labor market. These women faced similar obstacles to African-American men, but because they seldom tried to take jobs in the masculine trades like construction, they generally avoided the cycle of antagonism that had placed black workers at risk. Indeed, an AFL poll revealed the unions that most staunchly opposed female membership were those least threatened by its prospect: the teamsters, the blacksmiths, and the miners. In 1926, labor economist Theresa Wolfson argued that official bars on female membership only existed

---

[39] Strickland, *History of the Chicago Urban League*, 58–9, 65, 69; Hill, *Black Labor and the American Legal System.*, 237–39. Doty received only one hundred votes, less than 0.2 percent of the total. Gosnell, *Negro Politicians*, 350, 168–69, 182–83.

in trades where women were not yet employed, and that restrictive unions would necessarily succumb to practical realities once women entered these fields. Wolfson implied the ideological connection between feminization and de-skilling in the minds of many craftsmen. By opposing women, craftsmen believed they could preserve craft labor and social mobility.[40]

Such attitudes were hardly unique to craftsmen; contempt for women's capabilities was a major component of the new consumer culture being promoted by corporations. At a 1911 convention, Paul Schulze, the wealthy owner of a Chicago-based bakery chain and the president of the National Association of Master Bakers, chided housewives for the "mistaken sense of duty" that led them to bake bread at home, positioning his firm as the protector of the nation's "long suffering stomachs." Schulze told his constituents about a woman who sold a homemade health bread and offered to sell him the recipe. Purportedly finding uncooked dough in the loaf, Schulze jokingly accused her of "murder," speculating that her product had raised the death rate in Chicago. Corporate bakers tried to promote mass-produced bread by portraying baking as a profession requiring sophisticated equipment and manly expertise.[41]

But if craftsmen were unexceptional in their misogyny, they were distinctive in their attempts to limit the participation of women in many trades. In 1920, the Whitestone Company began construction of the luxury Drake Hotel, and the builder let the contract for 2,000 bedside lamps to the Women's Exchange, a charitable organization led by Narcissa Thorne, the wife of an heir to the Montgomery Ward fortune. Housewives affiliated with the Women's Exchange earned wages for producing the shades at home, while the organization subcontracted the manufacturing of the lamps themselves to a nonunion firm. Fred "Frenchy" Mader, business agent for the Fixture Hangers union, threatened to call all the workers off the hotel unless the women paid a $2,000 fine and hired a union firm to rewire the lamps. Though the Women's Exchange declined to pay the fine, they did agree to pay

[40] Alice Kessler-Harris, *Out to Work: A History of Wage Earning Women in the United States* (New York, Oxford University Press, 1982), 219–30; Theresa Wolfson, *The Woman Worker and the Trade Unions* (New York: International Publishers, 1926), 69, 75.

[41] "Home-Made Bread Kills," *WP*, August 23, 1911, 10; "The Murdering Housewife," *NYT*, August 24, 1911, 6; "Purity Bakeries," *WSJ*, December 14, 1926, 2; Paul Schulze household, 1930 U. S. census, Cook County, Illinois, population schedule, city of Chicago, enumeration district 1656, supervisor's district 5, sheet 3A, dwelling 19, family 37, National Archives micropublication T626, roll 486.

an exorbitant $1,418 to rewire the lamps – over half received by the union official.

As this story suggests, craftsmen like Mader considered a woman's assumptions about the proper operation of the economy as important as her gender. On the surface, sexual politics barely figured in the incident; Mader was less concerned with the housewives who produced the shades than with the nonunion workers who wired the lamps and the money he would get to adjust the dispute. But the story shows the vast ideological chasm that separated the fixture hangers like Mader from wealthy women like Narcissa Thorne. The Women's Exchange was an odd amalgam of business and charity that gave middle and working-class women a chance to express their creativity while earning money in the market economy. Its wealthy leaders saw no reason either to use a union manufacturer or to pay a union fine. By contrast, building tradesmen like Mader believed that union men needed exclusive access to the lamp work to provide for their families. Mader assumed that women should recognize male privilege if they wished to participate in the craft economy.[42]

The women who accepted job segregation and male authority were allowed a limited place in local craft organizations. International unions did admit women to separate locals with lower benefits but also lower dues and initiation fees, and, in 1922, the AFL passed nonbinding resolutions recommending an end to gender restrictions. Once permitted to join unions, women did so. For example, 12,000 women – mostly telephone operators – belonged to the International Brotherhood of Electrical Workers, a union notorious for its racial exclusivity. These workers organized themselves, and then petitioned the IBEW for a union charter, which was granted. Waitresses formed and ran a union that worked closely with the male bakers and cooks in the drive to organize the city's restaurant industry. These same women led drives to organize retail clerks working in Chicago department stores, one of the largest blocks of female workers in the city. Such organizations allowed women to participate in local craft governance, though rarely on the same terms as men.[43]

---

[42] *People v. Mader*, 313 Ill. 277 (1924); Kathleen Waters Sanders, *The Business of Charity: The Woman's Exchange Movement, 1832–1900* (Chicago: University of Illinois Press, 1998), 84–7.

[43] Wolfson, *The Woman Worker*, 86, 114–15, 118; *Boston Store of Chicago v. Retail Clerks Local 226*, 216 Ill. App. 428 (1920); Dorothy Sue Cobble, "'Drawing the Line': The Construction of a Gendered Work Force in the Food Service Industry," *Work Engendered: Towards a New History of American Labor*, ed., Ava Baron (Ithaca: Cornell University Press, 1991), 224–25.

The human costs. Plumbers' Union business agent Maurice "Mossie" Enright allegedly murdered Steamfitters' Union business agent William "Dutch" Gentleman in 1910, one duel in the long feud between the two rival unions. The assassination left Mrs. Gentleman (above) a widow. Courtesy of Chicago Historical Society (DN-057124).

The craftsmen's anxieties became acute in service trades like haircutting, where the assumptions regarding feminine weakness bore no weight. For decades, the Journeyman Barbers' International Union (JBIU) had declined to admit any of the women who regularly petitioned for membership in their fraternity. Yet the issue festered as women challenged these barriers. At the 1924 JBIU convention, one opponent of open membership argued that women not only lacked skill, but also undermined craft governance. The "real reason," he suggested, "for employing women in barber shops is the questionable worth or drawing power as a physical attraction," not "their workmanship." The speaker then alleged that women did not possess a "sense of honour from a pecuniary standpoint" that would prompt them to protest wage cuts. A woman who was "comely to look at" threatened discipline, created "discord" among "real working brothers," and eventually became a "blithering liability" at "forty-five or fifty, with her drawing power limited, and her attractiveness practically gone." Unable to imagine a trained female barber, the craftsmen saw women as agents of the ubiquitous consumer revolution, transforming their trade by substituting advertising and sexualized promotion for ability.[44]

Though female barbers found such intransigence frustrating, sexual segregation offered them a workplace that the JBIU could not control: the beauty shop. Denied access to male heads, women served other women, taking positions in distinctly feminine spaces. The rise of the short "bob" style in the 1920s prompted a boom in the cosmetology business and an explosion in the number of women who actually cut hair, as opposed to arranging it. When the barbers tried to capture this business by demanding inspectors enforce laws that made cutting hair without a license a misdemeanor, the stylists established affiliations with trade associations and corporate franchises, such as Martha Matilda Harper's "beauty system." With the power of these groups behind them, they obtained their own licensing laws and successfully used the courts to force inspectors to recognize their credentials.[45]

Corruption and Violence

On December 17, 1915, the Cook County Criminal Court held an inquest to investigate Robert Johnson's murder of lathers' business agent Axel Alex. Officials rapidly discovered that Alex had lived a double life. His real name was Armien Luettich. The name Axel Alex – used in both newspaper articles and criminal indictments – was actually an alias born of a mispronunciation, followed by a misunderstanding. Born in Milwaukee to a German-American artist who migrated to Chicago in 1882, Luettich came from a family of respectable tradesmen, who denied the common newspaper allegation that their dead kinsman was a gunman from New York City. Revealed to be a Midwestern family man, from a hardworking and fairly educated background, Luettich showed the divide between journalistic representations and the rather more complex reality.[46]

---

[44] *Proceedings of the Journeyman Barbers' International Union, 1924*, in Wolfson, *The Woman Worker*, 77–8.

[45] Wolfson, *The Woman Worker*, 76; Jane Plitt, *Mabel Matilda Harper and the American Dream: How One Woman Changed the Face of American Business* (Syracuse: Syracuse University Press, 2000), 105–07; *Banghart v. Walsh*, 339 Ill. 132 (1930); Earl Beckner, *A History of Illinois Labor Legislation* (Chicago: University of Chicago Press, 1929), 382, ft. 2.

[46] "Alex Dual Life Comes to Light at Inquest," *CDT*, December 18, 1915, 4; "F. A. Luettich," *History of Cook County, Illinois: From the Earliest Period to the Present Time* (Chicago: A. T. Andreas, 1884).

But Luettich's life and death also suggested the changing character of union officials in this period. As labor leaders served the needs of the rank-and-file tradesmen, they faced new temptations and physical demands. Competition seemed to encourage impropriety. As consumer demand expanded, drawing hundreds of new actors into the marketplace, bribery became cheaper than compliance. Enforcement also became more brutal; bombing and murder replaced strikes, fines, and boycotts. And finally, gangsters, lured by profit, empowered by their willingness to kill, and uninterested in the rank and file, began turning unions and associations to their own ends.

During the 1910s, violence became even more routine and systematic. In the middle of the decade, four construction unions – the Painters, the Glaziers, the Wood Finishers, and the Fixture Hangers – divided the city into zones, each patrolled by a business agent. Officials, led by Luettich and Frank "Doc" Curran of the painters' union, noted the businesses that hired nonunion workers or installed banned glass, wood-trim, and electrical fixtures. Every day, the Board of Business Agents (BBA) updated the "glass list" – so called because the BBA hired men to throw bottles, bricks, and stones at the windows of the "unfair" firms thereon. The BBA gave copies to the city's glass dealers, who boycotted the offenders, leaving disciplined firms with no choice but to meet the delegates at Johnson's Saloon at 333 W. Madison Street, where they could pay fines and purchase new windows.

Relatively minor violations demanded payments. In 1915, Isadore Hoffman had some electrical work done on his North Side store by Philip Goldstein, a member of the switchboard workers' union, IBEW Local #376. Unfortunately for Hoffman, Local #376 was involved in a heated rivalry with IBEW Local #134, and Goldstein was not a "legitimate" worker in the eyes of officials. Three delegates, including Fred Mader, came to Hoffman and told him that he would "be square" if he paid them $300. Hoffman refused, so men came and smashed his windows. Hoffman obtained glass for his storefront only after going to Johnson's Saloon and paying Mader $400. In 1920, Mark Solomon and Frank P. Reger were building the Versailles, an apartment building on Dorchester Street in Hyde Park. One day in October, Frank Hayes and Thomas Walsh of the Sheet Metal Workers complained to Solomon that he had used Ornamental Iron Workers rather than sheet metal workers to install the trim around the elevator doors. The two BAs called their constituents off the site until Solomon removed the trim, paid $1,000, and hired their men to reinstall the frames. Solomon asked what he could do to resolve the matter, but

Walsh replied: "not a damned thing; take them out." After four days of negotiation, Hayes relented, but only after receiving $500 from Solomon.[47]

This steady flow of cash made these organizations vulnerable to real and perceived corruption. By 1929, many unions accumulated large funds for pensions, death benefits, and strike relief. For example, the Milk Wagon Drivers had a treasury worth more than $1 million and yearly inflows of $250,000. Because no laws existed regulating the finances of labor organizations, officers could steal funds without any external scrutiny. Many unions did not even have bank accounts; rather they kept cash and bonds in a safety deposit box or – even worse – in a safe at their headquarters. Business agents could steal these treasuries, or they could appropriate the fines they collected from rule violators as so-called "strike insurance." The master of this technique was Michael Boyle of the electrical workers. "Umbrella Mike" was famous for sitting in Johnson's Saloon with his parasol hanging from the bar. Contractors seeking to adjudicate disputes dropped cash into the umbrella, thus allowing Boyle to deny in court that he had knowingly received any money.[48]

Though frustrated by these demands, employers paid the fines and practiced these methods themselves. The glass dealers who aided the downtown building trades' unions in 1915 were perhaps unusually involved in the machinery of enforcement, but many employers saw fines as a straightforward – if potentially fraudulent – method of resolving labor disputes, far preferable to strikes and boycotts. Moreover, many trade associations also engaged in fines, extortion, and graft. For instance, observers like Judge John Lyle presumed kosher food czar Maxie Eisen kept the $3,000 fee he collected from a widow for permission to open a fish market.

---

[47] *People v. Curran*, 286 Illinois 309–11 (1919); True Bill, December 3, 1915, *People v. Cleary*, IR 217, 6–7, Crim.CC #7793 (1915); "54 Indicted as Labor Graft Ring Leaders," *CDT*, December 4, 1915, 1–2; *People v. Walsh*, 322 Ill. 205–6.

[48] "Umbrella His Graft Bag," *NYT*, July 5, 1914, 6; Foster, *Misleaders of Labor*, 169–71. Touhy, *The Stolen Years*, 84–8; Lyle, *Dry and Lawless Years*, 194–96. One union held $34,000 in a safety deposit box, nearly $10,000 of it in cash. *Chicago German Hod Carriers Union v. Security Trust*, 315 Ill. 204 (1924). It is possible that unions believed that bank accounts were more vulnerable to the interference of courts. *First Trust and Savings Bank v. Brotherhood of Painters*, Sup.C.C. case #278195 (1910). Such practices extended well beyond the building trades. See *People v. Walczak et al.*, 315 Ill. 54–5 (1924).

Some officials resisted this temptation, but many clearly accumulated property and lived as wealthy gentlemen, despite salaries of around $40 per week. Michael Boyle invested cash left in his umbrella in a real estate firm and a valve manufacturing company, businesses that could profit from his connections. As early as 1914, Boyle had allegedly accumulated $350,000; by 1927, this had grown to a cool million. When plumber and Building Trades Council President Simon O'Donnell died in 1927, he purportedly left an estate worth over $500,000. A 1923 burglary illustrated O'Donnell's lifestyle. The newspapers reported that thieves broke into his home and stole a mink coat, a diamond pin, pearls, silver cigarette cases, and other luxuries. Nor was O'Donnell the only labor tycoon. Tom Kearney, O'Donnell's successor as BTC president, left an estate worth $200,000 including real estate and stock, while Machinery Movers' Union officer Michael Artery owned real estate worth $500,000.[49]

These officials viewed their personal comfort as their reward for preserving the well being of their constituents. Confronting extreme physical danger and the very real possibility of prison, officials easily rationalized their incomes and saw themselves as dedicated and even self-sacrificing. Business agent Fred Mader played the martyr after the Fixture Hangers' Union suspended him in 1923 on charges of extortion. He lamented wasting his time in the labor movement, projecting that he "would be worth $500,000 today" not $100,000 had he focused on his real estate business. Though graft remained disreputable, union officers saw their informal salary as compensation for the risks they took on behalf of their members. Even radical William Z. Foster admitted that William Quesse, president of the Chicago Flat Janitors Union, was an effective organizer who obtained benefits for his constituents. Quesse presumably believed that his service, which included the continual threat of injury and imprisonment, granted him ownership of his office and the right to a comfortable life. Thus, when Quesse died, his heirs inherited $200,000, and his son in-law, William McFetridge, took over the union.[50]

[49] Lyle, *Dry and Lawless Years*, 189; Foster, *Misleaders of Labor*, 165–71, 176–77; "Gag Maid and Steal Union Leader's Gems," *NYT*, August 15, 1923, 10; "Boyle's Record Long Clouded by Graft Charges," *CDT*, April 28, 1915, 2; "Michael J. Boyle, Labor Leader, 77," *NYT*, May 19, 1958, 25; "Politicians and Labor Heads Pay Kearney Honor," *CDT*, January 10, 1924, 8; John Landesco, "Interview with John Shields, August 23, 1927," 7 in Box 34, Folder 9, Burgess Papers, University of Chicago Special Collections.
[50] Foster, *Misleaders of Labor*, 176, 179–80; Jentz, "Labor, the Law . . ." 416, 419.

Meanwhile, a variety of factors combined to make the administration of craft governance itself more violent. Before 1910, administrators enforced craft rules by smashing windows and assaulting bodies. Though sluggers injured some of their victims for life, they seldom killed except by accident. After 1910, bombings, shootings, and murder almost became routine. This context for this escalation was an overall explosion in homicide rates during this period in American history. Social scientists often blame this trend on the prohibition of alcoholic beverages in 1919, which led to heated competition among gangs selling illegal booze. But the violence began earlier and occurred in other areas of Chicago life. Bombs greeted African-Americans who moved outside the bounds of the so-called Black Belt, while politics provoked rivalries that turned elections into armed engagements.[51]

Tradesmen grew desperate as they tried to control prices in a rapidly expanding economy. In 1926, the Chicago Association of Candy Jobbers hired Vincent Pastor, an Italian-American, as business manager, believing stereotypically that he would have "Black Hand" connections that would allow him to suppress renegade candy dealers. The association gave Pastor $1,500 for "educational work," with which he hired men to smash windows and throw stink bombs, but his ethnicity granted him no special talent for mayhem, and the price-cutting continued. The frustrated president of the jobbers, Albert A. Hoffman, allegedly told business manager, "the only way to get the bastards is bust their windows, cripple them or something." Pastor hired men to smash windows, but grew nervous about the escalating violence. So Hoffman replaced him with John Hand, an officer of Laundry Workers' Union #32 and a protégé of drycleaning boss Simon Gorman. Well known for his skill with a gun, Hand promptly began assaulting candy jobbers who refused to join the association, to pay dues, or to abide by standard prices. Hand continued in this role until 1929, when he himself was murdered.[52]

Gunmen like Hand eagerly accepted official positions with unions and associations, seeing opportunities for personal profit. Another

---

[51] Landesco, *Organized Crime*, 98–147; Carroll Hill Wooddy, *The Chicago Primary of 1926: A Study in Election Methods* (Chicago: University of Chicago Press, 1926); Willrich, *City of Courts*, 287.

[52] The Black Hand was a Sicilian form of extortion found among Italian-American immigrants. Landesco, *Organized Crime*, 109–10; Humbert Nelli, *The Business of Crime: Italians and Syndicate Crime in the United States* (New York: Oxford University Press, 1976), 69–100; Records and Briefs, *James Boyle et al. v. United States*, USCA, 7th Circ., case #4207 (1928), 61, 73, 77–8, 84, 167–72, 264–69.

such official was "Big Tim" Murphy, a ward politician and crime im-
presario who bounced from one lucrative scheme to another before
finally landing in the labor movement. A former state legislator from
the Irish Back-of-the-Yards district, Murphy organized the men laboring for the city or local utilities, including gas workers, bridge laborers, street cleaners, street foremen, asphalt layers, garbage handlers,
bootblacks, window washers, and drycleaners, during World War I.
In 1920, Murphy was indicted for the murder of his former mentor,
Maurice "Mossie" Enright, and, in 1922, he stood trial for the killing
of a policeman named Thomas Clark. That same year, he was convicted of robbing a mail shipment at Dearborn Street Station and sentenced to six years in Leavenworth federal prison. There he met Nicky
Arnstein, the infamous gambler and husband of singer Fanny Brice,
and together they opened a Gold Coast casino.

Though Murphy's moonlighting casts a shadow on his stewardship,
he was an aggressive union official popular with his constituents. As
his rap sheet suggests, "Big Tim" had "muscle," which served some
workers' desire for physically forceful administrators. Upon one of
his releases from jail in 1920, he reviled those who would run his
union "on a Sunday school basis," that would "hand out stogies and
punch the bag and don't accomplish anything." Murphy explained
that, "A man that can't fight don't amount to much" because "they
don't use boxing gloves in the labor movement, they use Smith and
Wessons." Some saw Murphy as a grafting usurper, but he apparently
forged a bond with rank-and-file workers. After prosecutors dropped
his indictment for the 1920 Enright murder, a "troop of admirers"
greeted the "hero to thousands" at City Hall. During Murphy's six-year
term in federal prison, the gas workers' union repeatedly elected him
president, paying his $100 per week salary to his "buxom blonde" wife,
Florence. After his 1928 assassination, thousands filed into his house
to attend his wake, forcing the city to station policemen to direct that
traffic.[53]

As Murphy's murder suggests, gunmen were themselves vulnerable
to violence, especially from the new style of criminals bred by prohibition. Unlike "Big Tim," Al Capone viewed the craftsmen as little more than blobs of cash, and he showed his indifference to craft

---

[53] Murphy's critics simplified his biography. William Z. Foster claimed that
Murphy passively accepted the massive wage cuts of 1921, when Tim actually
led the most violent resistance to that ruling, though possibly to extort cash
to settle the matter. Foster, *Misleaders*, 171–75, esp. 174; Lyle, *Dry and Lawless
Years*, 54–69, esp. 57, 62; Landesco, *Organized Crime*, 134–40, 203–4; "'Tim'
and 'Mike,' in Cells, Call Strike on City," *CDT*, May 18, 20, 1; "Seek Murphy
Slayers," *Federation News*, June 30, 1928, 1.

governance by murdering union executives and aiding price cutters. For example, in 1928, Capone set his sights upon Chicago's $35 million per year drycleaning trade. A young industry, technologically sophisticated and catering to the aspirations of the growing urban middle class, drycleaning typified the new service economy. Yet as early as 1920, three groups – the Master Cleaners' Association (MCA), the Retail Cleaners and Dyers Union Local #20077 (later #17792), an AFL union of the storefront tailors, and the Laundry Drivers' Union, Local #712 – established strict rules bounding the expansion of this trade. If, for example, a new drycleaning shop opened near an established firm, deviated from the standard price, or failed to pay its dues, then the retail cleaners picketed that store. If a plant reduced its wholesale rates or solicited clients (called "stops") from its competitors, the teamsters refused to cart its clothes and its inside employees went on strike.[54]

During the 1920s, increasingly violent price wars had gripped the cleaning business. As the market for the service grew, hundreds of firms scrambled for trade, challenging the wages and prices. In 1921, Eagle Cleaning and Dyeing Co. contended that the association had hired Harry Berger, a man allegedly without "lawful or useful occupation," to lead a group of "thugs, sluggers, and gunmen" to pressure the independent firm to join the ranks. Conditions worsened as the decade wore on. Nicholas Georgson, a disabled war veteran who owned a South Side cleaning shop, testified that the association had fined him for violating its rules, then broke his windows, then finally "wrecked" his store. In 1928, the cleaning interests targeted the Central Cleaners and Dyers, a nonunion plant. MCA boss Simon J. Gorman allegedly paid Samuel Weiss to secure a job at Central and put acid in their cleaning solution. The associations sent suits for cleaning with hidden explosives sewn into the hems, allegedly causing Central $15,000 in damage. Again, the violence escalated. In April 1928, men in the association's employ stopped one of Central's trucks, beat its drivers, and set their cargo aflame, causing one driver to receive serious burns.

Capone saw gold in this mayhem, and he angled for access to the trade. His passkey was a stubborn and idealistic cleaning tycoon named Morris Becker. Over the previous two decades, Becker had gained competitive advantage by removing the middleman. He owned both a wholesale plant and a retail chain of storefronts, and he introduced cash-and-carry service, which allowed him to eliminate door-to-door

[54] Morrison Handsaker, "The Chicago Cleaning and Dyeing Industry: A Case Study in 'Controlled Competition'" (Ph.D. diss., University of Chicago, 1939), 102–73, esp. 115–20.

salesmen belonging to the teamsters' union. Upsetting conventional business methods and defying price regulations, Becker enraged his peers, who had successfully deflected past chains. One day, Sam Rubin, the president of the RCU, came to Becker's facility and demanded he raise his rates. When Becker refused, citing his constitutional rights, Rubin allegedly thundered, "To hell with the Constitution. I am a damned sight bigger than the Constitution." Three days later, Becker's plant was bombed. When Becker still refused to budge, Benjamin Abrams, the president of the cleaning workers' union, informed him that he would be "bumped off" if he did not raise prices. He demurred. Then Arthur Berg, the president of the MCA, approached him; Becker still declined.[55]

Becker instead searched for a protector. First, he went to the grand jury, which indicted and tried the cleaners for conspiracy to restrain trade. Unenthusiastic about prosecuting the well-connected business-men, the state's attorney called few witnesses, allowing the cleaners' at-torney, Clarence Darrow, to swiftly secure an acquittal. In 1927, Becker merged his firm with a national corporation, Baxter Laundries, Inc., which claimed to be large enough to resist the MCA. But when Baxter caved in to the masters and began raising prices, a frustrated Becker ended his relationship with the corporation. On May 28, 1928, he announced that he had made Al Capone a partner in his new firm, Sanitary Cleaning Shops Inc, stating, "I could get no help from the po-lice, the courts or the state's attorney. Now I have the best protection in the world." With the bootlegger behind him, Becker proceeded to lower cleaning prices 25 percent.[56]

---

[55] Bill, October 5, 1921, *Eagle Cleaning and Dying v. Master Cleaners and Dyers*, Sup.C.C. case #370500 (1921); Amended Bill for Injunction, September 12, 1921, *American Ideal Cleaning v. Master Cleaners and Dyers*, Sup.C.C. case #369807 (1921); Handsaker, "Chicago Cleaning and Dyeing Industry," 51–2; Landesco, *Organized Crime*, 157; M. H. Zimmerman, "The How and Why of Chain Growth in Various Trades," *Printers' Ink* 153:2 (October 9, 1930): 130.

[56] The Beckers signed a five-year noncompete agreement, under which Morris Becker became owner-manager of a dozen Baxter storefronts and used a Baxter plant, to be run by Morris' son Theodore. When Baxter capitulated to the MCA, the arrangement fell apart. Baxter fired Theodore for refusing to raise prices. So, Morris Becker constructed his own plant at 63rd and Prairie in violation of his contract. In 1928, Baxter unsuccessfully sued for injunction. Hostetter, *It's a Racket*, 37–41; Handsaker, "Chicago Cleaning and Dyeing Industry," 125–28; Landesco, *Organized Crime*, 157–59. Briefs for *Baxter Laundries Inc. v. Morris Becker*, case #s 8578 and 9078, USDC, N. IL, E. Div., in Box 37, Folder 4, Ernest Burgess Papers, University of Chicago Special Collections.

For perhaps the first time, Chicago's daily newspapers praised Capone, and for many years after the infamous bootlegger bragged about his defending the plucky Becker and the consumer's right to low prices. Capone's real ambitions were hardly so noble. He used his position as Becker's bodyguard to blackmail the organized cleaners and launderers. A wave of deaths and assassinations followed Capone's self-styled philanthropy: first Tim Murphy (June 26, 1928), then Retail Cleaners' Union president Sam Rubin (October 20, 1928), then beloved Laundry Drivers' Union officer John Clay (November 16, 1928), and finally laundry workers' official and candy industry enforcer, John Hand (May 21, 1929). The terrified cleaners had three options: disband their associations, pay tribute to Capone, or fight. Some, like Al Weinshank, who died in the infamous St. Valentine's Day Massacre, scrambled to find their own "protection," forging an alliance with North Side bootlegger George "Bugs" Moran that drew them into the broader gang wars of this period. Meanwhile, cleaning prices returned to their earlier level, but with the proceeds flowing to Capone and Moran rather than to the tradesmen. Becker had not freed the market; he had merely given it terrifying new masters.[57]

The debate over the legitimacy of craft governance grew more complicated as its administration became more exploitative. Before 1928, the violent price wars in dry cleaning ran parallel to the bloody turf battles in the illegal alcohol trade. After 1928, the underworld and the craft economy increasingly intersected, as bootleggers, pimps, and gamblers forced themselves into many trades, elbowing aside the gunmen of years past. The confluence of these two public issues deeply affected the legal landscape, prompting the invention of the term "racketeering" and a major shift in the status of labor unions.

[57] "Seek Murphy Slayers," *Federation News*, June 30, 1928, 1; "Will Hold Memorial Services for Samuel Rubin of Cleaners," *Federation News*, October 20, 1928, 1; "Mourn Killing of Racketeer Victim," *Federation News*, November 24, 1928, 1; "Deplores Besmirching of Organized Labor," *Federation News*, June 1, 1929, 5, 17; Lyle, *Dry and Lawless Years*, 65–6; Landesco, *Organized Crime*, 157–58; Philip Hauser, "Materials Re: Funerals of St. Valentines Day," 4, in Box 131, Folder 2, Ernest Burgess Papers, University of Chicago Special Collections.

Politician, gambler, and labor leader, Timothy "Big Tim" Murphy, shown with co-defendant, Vincent Cosmano (second from right), and attorneys Benjamin Epstein (first on right) and John Sbarbaro (far left) during his trial for robbing the Dearborn Street train station in 1921. Often running the gas workers' union from a jail cell, Murphy was a transitional figure. One of the first union officials implicated in crimes unrelated to industrial relations, "Big Tim" helped bring the brutality of the urban underworld to the labor movement. He nevertheless remained popular among his constituents, many of whom saw him as a legitimate unionist, not an exploitative interloper. Courtesy of Chicago Historical Society (DN-073687).

7

From Conspiracy to Racketeering

As local tradesmen battled the forces of modernization, national corporations campaigned to remake Chicago's commercial life, their drives distinguished by a new enthusiasm for organization. In the past, executives had attacked the principle of cooperation, charging tradesmen with conspiring against nonunionists, price cutters, innovators, and out-of-state businessmen. But during the 1910s, elite businessmen began promoting their own models of association. Their rhetoric still valorized the individuals who defied local craftsmen, but they no longer agitated for a society of independent small producers. Rather, corporations proposed an economy regulated by national trade associations acting in the public interest.

The law came to reflect the elite's new faith in governance. Most notably, the state began distinguishing between legitimate and criminal forms of association. While craftsmen gained new freedom to picket, their leaders faced charges of fraud, monopoly, bribery, and extortion. Such cases were relatively novel, for they proposed not to defend the employers' property rights, but rather to protect the general population against corrupt union officials and oppressive agreements. Nevertheless, these prosecutions struck at the heart of the tradesmen's ability to enforce their contracts, in part because executives used the law instrumentally, implicating those who defied the evolving corporate vision of industrial order.

The culmination of this strategy was the invention of the word "racketeering" during the Prohibition decade. In 1927, Employers' Association (EA) secretary Gordon L. Hostetter conceived the term to direct growing public concern about bootleggers like Al Capone against the officials who enforced prices and wages in trades like construction, laundry, and kosher foods. He sought not to expose the power of men like Capone within the labor movement, but rather to compare craft governance to extortion. Though racketeering's meaning changed after 1929, Hostetter's rhetorical innovation significantly shaped the legal status of collective action in the United States during the New Deal and after.

The New Corporate Ideal

In the waning years of the Progressive Era, America's business elite abandoned the lonely individual as the romantic protagonist of its ideology. Past corporations had organized against organization, forming groups like the National Association of Manufacturers (NAM) to champion the freedom of the independent entrepreneur. While granting workers a token right to unionize, they dismissed the authority of any governing body – public or private – to regulate economic conditions. For a number of reasons, businessmen reversed course in the 1910s. When the turn-of-the-century merger movement failed to stem competition, corporations looked for other ways of maintaining prices. A new generation of executives rejected the individualism of their fathers. Government regulation of business during World War I affirmed corporate doubts about state supervision, but also showed many employers that cooperation was not inimical to profitability. And finally, manufacturers proposed combinations of self-regulation, company unions, and welfare capitalism to forestall worker protest and instrusive new laws.[1]

The trade association movement also appealed to corporate businessmen seeking to regain control over the local economy. The intellectual progenitor of associationalism, Arthur Jerome Eddy, was himself a product of Chicago and a close friend of Mayor Carter H. Harrison II. A nonpracticing attorney and art collector reared in an affluent household, Eddy produced an incredible range of texts, from legal treatises to criticism, policy discussions, travelogues, novels, plays, and a farm encyclopedia. In 1912, at the age of fifty-three, Eddy published his landmark work, *The New Competition*, which argued that cooperation was the future of American capitalism.

---

[1] Ellis Hawley, *The Great War and the Search for a Modern Order: A History of the American People and Their Institutions, 1917–1933* (New York: St. Martin's Press, 1979); Ernst, *Lawyers Against Labor*, 214–35; Cohen, *Making a New Deal*, 181–83; Robert Himmelberg, *The Origins of the National Recovery Administration: Business, Government, and the Trade Association Issue, 1921–1933* (New York: Fordham University Press, 1993); Colin Gordon, *New Deals: Business, Labor, and Politics in America, 1920–1935* (New York: Cambridge University Press, 1994), 35–40.

Charging that the right organizations could balance individual rights and the public interest, *The New Competition* became extraordinarily popular among businessmen during the following years. Eddy the libertarian believed that associations should exercise only limited control over the decisions of each firm, distributing expert information, but not setting prices. But Eddy the progressive rejected laissez-faire. Using professional associations as his models, he imagined businessmen establishing ethical codes setting the terms for "fair" trade in each industry. As was clear in his 1908 novel, *Ganton & Co.*, Eddy saw this collegiality as protecting the public from excessive competition and, just as importantly, from unions. His protagonist, John Ganton, Jr., places his father's business on a proper footing by defeating the teamsters, befriending the other packers, and ending a cycle of destructive competition that had threatened to starve the city. As some professional groups achieved respectability by marginalizing ethnic practitioners, Eddy rationalized corporate associations as alternatives to corrupt, tyrannical craft governance.[2]

During the subsequent decade, corporate rhetoric followed Eddy's recipe. Open shoppers began using utilitarian arguments, noting the effect of trade agreements on prices and consumer choices and positioning themselves as the protectors of the public interest. Gerhardt Meyne, a prominent builder, avid open shopper, and opponent of the forty-hour workweek, told the Chicago Mortgage Bankers Association in 1926:

We of course have great difficulty to make <u>our employees see that their dollar is somebody elses cost of living. The builder realizes that he is the steward of the public in all labor</u> agreements because the public has no voice in these contracts. The builder stands between labor monopolies and the public in all labor agreements, and he realizes it is unfair to allow his employees to be parasites on the other fellows employees. [underlining in original]

[2] Arthur J. Eddy, *The New Competition* (New York: Appleton, 1912); *Book of Chicagoans* (Chicago: A. N. Marquis, 1917), 207; Robert Himmelberg, *The Origins of the National Recovery Administration*, 6–8; Gerald Berk, "Communities of Competitors: Open Price Associations and the American State, 1911–1929," *Social Science History* 20:3 (Fall 1996): 375–400; Ellis Hawley, "Herbert Hoover and Economic Stabilization," in *Herbert Hoover as Secretary of Commerce, 1921–1928: Studies in New Era Thought and Practice*, ed., Ellis Hawley (Iowa City: University of Iowa Press, 1981), 43–79; Jerrold Auerbach, *Unequal Justice: Lawyers and Social Change in Modern America* (New York: Oxford University Press, 1976), 102–29.

Even longstanding advocates of freedom of contract like NAM secretary James A. Emery began arguing that the open shop was not "a mere
issue of disagreement between employers and employees" but rather
a matter of "the public interest." NAM increasingly stressed the effect
of "combinations" on the average consumer, blaming unions for the
difference between prices in Chicago and other cities. Corporations argued that Chicagoans paid high rents because trade agreements raised
costs, inhibited technology, and prohibited the expansion of the city's
construction workforce.[3]

Executives promoted their ideals by stigmatizing the most aggressive
advocates of a regulated economy in this period – urban craftsmen. As
Robert Himmelberg notes, Secretary of Commerce Herbert Hoover
conceived his oft-discussed view of competition in reaction to revela-
tions of collusion and corruption in New York's construction industry.
In April 1922, in the midst of an open shop drive in the Chicago building trades, Hoover spoke to the National Federation of Construction
Industries. He charged that, "a small minority . . . smear with shame the
high standards of American business and labor." Hoover noted that
the state might "catch occasional crooks," but he called on "decent
men" to purify the industry themselves. The secretary saw associationalism as the key. He demanded, "cleaner organization of the trades,
not the destruction of trades organizations." Efficiency required not
individualism, but the extension of "individual initiative" through "cooperation between individuals."[4]

Inspired by Hoover and Eddy, the building trades became a trying ground for this vision of association. For example, in July 1922, a
group of general contractors, architects, and engineers founded the
American Construction Council (ACC). Led by defeated Democratic
vice-presidential candidate, Franklin Roosevelt, the ACC promised to
eradicate waste and corruption by establishing a code of ethics for
the industry. Walter Gordon Merritt, the chairman of the League for

3　"Address of Gerhardt F. Meyne before the Chicago Mortgage Bankers Asso-
　　ciation, April 27, 1926" in Gerhardt Meyne Papers, Folder 1, in CHS; "Calls
　　Open Shop an American Principle," *Chicago Commerce* 16:46 (February 5,
　　1921): 9–10, 42–4; Ernst, *Lawyers Against Labor*, 129–30; National Associ-
　　ation of Manufacturers, *Evidence in the Case for the Open Shop*, (New York:
　　Open Shop Department, National Association of Manufacturers, 1923);
　　Fine, *Without Blare of Trumpets*, 205, 212–13.
4　Himmelberg, *The Origins of the National Recovery Administration*, 6–21;
　　"Hoover Asks for Clean-up of Industries," *Chicago Commerce* 18:2 (April 8,
　　1922): 11; "Hoover Heads Move to Aid Construction," *Chicago Commerce*
　　18:1 (April 1, 1922): 5.

Industrial Rights, formerly known as the American Anti-Boycott Association (AABA), enthusiastically supported the new group, commenting that, "The evils of the construction industry are evils of organizations, not the evils of individuals." Merritt called for businessmen to abandon "selfish aims," and to "lay down a code of practice . . . in accord with the rules and principles" of the ACC. Rejecting the strict belief in individual rights, Merritt brought corporate industrial relations policy into line with Wilsonian progressivism.[5]

But if calls for ethical organization drew corporate executives into alliance with reformers, such calls were still intellectually consistent with opposition to craft unions. Though Merritt rejected the fierce anti-unionism of his predecessors, he never favored true collective bargaining. Rather, he hoped that company unions, subject to the authority of the employer, would replace independent craft unions as the representatives of the workers. Since its inception, corporations had acknowledged the right to organize in order to condemn boycotts, picketing, and sympathy strikes. As Finley Peter Dunne's Mr. Dooley observed, open shoppers favored unions "if properly conducted," meaning "No strike, no rules, no contracts, no scales, hardly any wages, an' dam' few members." In the 1910s and 1920s, these businessmen actually began promoting their own set of organizations by emphasizing the corruption of existing groups.[6]

This new utilitarianism had the potential to succeed where classical legal liberalism was failing. During lockouts, judges issued orders that protected strikebreakers and property from pickets, but they proved unwilling or unable to interfere with the enforcement of craft rules. In 1910, for instance, sheet metal worker Charles F. Engel asked the court to enjoin his union, Amalgamated Local #73, from inhibiting his employment. Unwilling to pay a $100 fine for using nonunion material, Local #73 suspended him, called strikes on the sites where he worked, and denied him access to the union label. The judge issued a temporary order, but dissolved it when the union argued that it had

---

5 F. W. Lord dedicated his 1918 work on ethics in construction to Arthur J. Eddy. Lord, *Ethics of Contracting and the Stabilizing of Profits* (Garden City, NY: The Country Life Press, 1918); "Construction Men Form Council which Aims to Put Industry on Higher Plane," *Chicago Commerce* 18:14 (July 1, 1922): 28.

6 Bernstein, *The Lean Years*, 116–17; Ernst, *Lawyers Against Labor*, 232–35; Montgomery, *Fall of the House of Labor*, 412; Finley Peter Dunne, "Mr. Dooley on the Open Shop," *Literary Digest*, November 27, 1920, reprinted in E. Wight Bakke and Clark Kerr, ed., *Unions, Management, and the Public* (New York: Harcourt, Brace and Company, 1948), 120–21.

the right to discipline its members. Both the Illinois Appellate and Supreme courts affirmed this judgment.

Injunctions proved ineffective against determined craftsmen. In 1914, for instance, the Chicago plastering contractors' association fined a member named Goldberg $500 after learning that he paid his workers less than the union scale. When Goldberg declined, union members boycotted him. The frustrated contractor obtained an injunction restraining both groups from interfering with his business, but Goldberg's union employees seldom stayed for more than a half-day before quitting. He tried hiring nonunion plasterers, but general contractors refused to call him, preferring not to anger the Building Trades Council. Economist Edwin Witte recalled that, "one week of such experiences was enough to show him that his injunction was valueless, and he then decided, as he put it, 'to lay low and take my medicine' – to drop his suit and pay the unlawful fine." Within the plastering trade, consensus overpowered the law.[7]

In response, corporations turned to other courts and jurisdictions. The Cook County Criminal Court offered businessmen some systemic advantages, leading EA general counsel Dudley Taylor to recommend its use in 1914. Criminal cases shifted the costs of legal action from employers onto the state, and a successful criminal prosecution could result in a long prison sentence, removing select administrators from the craft economy indefinitely. Executives also turned to the U. S. District Court (USD), whose jurors were former and whose judges were former white-shoe lawyers. The last Democrat to serve in the Northern Illinois district was Nathaniel Pope, an appointee of President James Monroe. Between 1912 and 1928, all four men who sat on the bench in Chicago – Kenesaw Landis, George Carpenter, James Wilkerson, and Adam Cliffe – were Republicans from educated, northern European, middle class or rural backgrounds.

Judge Wilkerson was perhaps the most extreme case. Born in Savannah, Missouri and educated at Indiana's DePauw University, Wilkerson began practicing law in Chicago in 1893. He became a partner in Tenney, Coffeen, Harding, & Wilkerson, the firm that helped the Kellogg Switchboard & Supply Co. withstand the strikes of 1903. Wilkerson served as an associate counsel to the AABA, and he continued to scourge labor organizations as United States Attorney for the Northern District of Illinois between 1911 and 1914, initiating an injunction under the Sherman Act restraining Michael Boyle and the electrical

---

[7] *Engel v. Walsh*, 258 Ill. 98 (1913); Witte, "Value of Injunctions in Labor Disputes," 340, 341, 335–37.

workers from interfering with telegraph giant Western Union. Shortly
after being nominated to the bench by President Harding in 1922,
Wilkerson enjoined striking railway shopmen, a famously burdensome
order that caused workers to call him "the injunction judge." Unlike
county court officials, Judge Wilkerson had lifetime tenure that insu-
lated him from public pressures; he could issue decisions that suited
his biases without fear of political reprisal.[8]

Though favorable to corporations, these courts encouraged them to
shed their liberal individualism and appeal to the public welfare. Federal judges increasingly considered social facts alongside formal doctrines and private rights. In cases like *Muller v. Oregon* (1908), the U. S.
Supreme Court rejected formalism for "sociological jurisprudence."
Upholding legislation guaranteeing women an eight-hour workday,
the court not only considered evidence regarding the effect of hard
labor on women, it granted legislatures the authority to subordinate
individual rights to the common good. By the 1920s, conservative reform jurists like William Howard Taft controlled the high court, speed-
ing this trend. Open shop employers swiftly learned to emphasize the
harm to the general population. In 1923, for instance, NAM entitled a
pamphlet, *Evidence in the Case for the Open Shop.* Framed as a legal brief,
the broadside presented statistics showing how unions raised prices in
various American cities.[9]

Utilitarian arguments were also necessary in criminal courts, which
were more sensitive to the popular will. The public had become reluctant to interfere in labor disputes, deeming them private matters, but
increasingly eager to regulate union government. For instance, while
two juries declined to convict union officials for boycotting Montgomery Ward, allegations of graft hobbled the Teamsters' Strike of
1905. Similarly, in 1921, unions marshaled forces in the Illinois legislature to defeat a restraint-of-trade bill that would have impeded
collective bargaining. Yet, in the same year, the state enacted a law
banning union officers from fining employers, a practice often linked

[8] Ernst, "The Closed Shop," 143–48, 136. For the threat of a "jury of farmers,"
see Records and Briefs, *Boyle v. U.S.*, USCA, 7th Circ., Case #4207 (1928),
72, 91, 264 in NARA-GL. The Republican Party controlled the White House
for all but sixteen years between 1860 and 1932, a fact that explains its
domination of the federal bench in Illinois. Federal Judicial Center Website
(**http://air.fjc.gov/history/judges frm.html**). Petition in Equity, February
2, 1913, *U.S. v. IBEW Local #9*, USDC, ND, E. IL, Equity case #14 in NARA-
GL. Ernst, *Lawyers Against Labor*, 175. For Wilkerson's railway injunction,
see Bernstein, *The Lean Years*, 149, 211–12.

[9] Ernst, *Lawyers Against Labor*, 1–9, 70; NAM, *Evidence in the Case*, 1; *Muller v.
Oregon*, 208 U.S. 412; Willrich, *City of Courts*, 98–114.

to bribery. To tap public opinion and convince criminal juries, corporations needed to cease opposing mundane protest and focus on crimes such as extortion, violence, and monopoly.[10]

Testing Ideas, Using the Law

Corporate executives tested their new faith in organization at the very center of craft governance: Chicago's construction industry. By 1911, the bonds that conjoined employers and employees in the building trades had been weakened by the increasing militancy of the contractors' central organization, the Building Construction Employers' Association (BCEA). Builders like BCEA president William O'Brien decried the erosion of concessions won in the Lockout of 1899, noting the reappearance of sympathy strikes, jurisdictional disputes, technological limitations, and material restrictions. In frustration, they began employing a muted version of the new corporate ideology. By crying extortion, they sought to bar inefficient practices, to limit labor's ability to govern trade, and to institute the rule of law.[11]

The first clash occurred in 1913, when construction employers locked out 27,000 journeymen, demanding fewer impromptu strikes. In January, marble setters quit their work on the Continental and Commercial Bank to protest the use of nonunion material from Vermont. The stonecutters, painters, and laborers followed, displaying solidarity in violation of their contracts. Under pressure from the BCEA, Simon O'Donnell, the president of the Building Trades Council (BTC), ordered his constituents to return to their jobs. But on June 12, electricians' officer Michael Boyle convinced nine unions – the bricklayers, sheet metal workers, steamfitters, ornamental ironworkers, hoisting engineers, machinery movers, machinists, derrickmen, and marble setters – to strike to protest another jurisdictional violation. Angry, the BCEA told its 150 members to fire these workers, founding a Wisconsin corporation, the Empire Construction Company, to continue operations on a nonunion basis.[12]

---

[10] "Report of Committee Appointed Under Senate Joint Resolution No. 9 of the Fifty-Second General Assembly of the State of Illinois, June 29, 1921," 3–4 in Folder 1, Landis Award Employers' Association papers, CHS. The extortion law was passed along with laws banning bribery of baseball players and laws increasing the penalty for bombing. Advance Sheets Hurd's Revised Statutes, 1921 in *Chicago Legal News*, July 28, 1921, 54.

[11] "Labor Finds Moses in Maze of Strikes," *CRH*, March 29, 1911, 1.

[12] "Autobiography of E. M. Craig," 136–37 in Gerhardt Meyne Papers, Folder 7, CHS; Montgomery, *Industrial Relations*, 70–2.

After four weeks and major financial losses on both sides, the employers rehired the strikers on unfavorable terms. In exchange for tokens, such as a small raise for the marble setters, the BTC agreed officially to abandon sympathy strikes and restrictions on material. They adopted a new administrative structure, creating a Joint Conference Board (JCB) with the authority to arbitrate any labor dispute involving more than one trade. In the past, unions stopped work on an entire building until the parties could agree which union's members would perform each job; now the BTC banned such strikes and required members to accept the JCB's decisions. The BTC also adopted the standard (or uniform) agreement in 1915. Citing a need to prevent graft, to improve the reputation of labor unions, and to protect workers from unnecessary strikes, O'Donnell pushed all BTC unions to sign contracts that contained provisions banning the sympathy strike, as well as restrictions on technology, output, and material.[13]

Unions immediately revolted against the new order and O'Donnell's leadership. The sheet metal workers were the first to rebel, initiating a series of strikes to protest the new regime in mid-July 1914. The BTC tried to maintain ranks by expelling them, but the defections continued. Between March 26 and April 1, 1915, the lathers, painters, machinists, glazers, and carpenters dropped their tools, attacking O'Donnell and his supporters as "union wreckers." The BCEA responded by locking out 30,000 workers, founding a rival lathers' union, and recruiting replacement workers, some African-American. The bloody, racially divisive, fight, which eventually resulted in the murder of Lathers' Union officer Armien Luettich (a.k.a. Axel Alex), ended on July 17, 1915, with members of the old body returning to work under conditions set by the BCEA.[14]

Pre-existing political factionalism divided the construction unions, setting the stage for this rebellion. For more than a decade, the jurisdictional dispute between the United Association of Plumbers (UA) and the International Association of Steam Fitters (IA) had divided Chicago labor. O'Donnell was an officer of UA, while Martin B. "Skinny" Madden, his predecessor as the leader of the BTC, was an IA delegate. In 1909, Madden's conviction on fraud charges led to a three-way power struggle between O'Donnell's plumbers, the carpenters, and an alliance of steamfitters, lathers, painters, sheet metal workers, and electricians. When O'Donnell won this fight, the UA-IA

[13] Montgomery, *Industrial Relations*, 72–8.
[14] "Autobiography of E. M. Craig," 137–40, 141–57 esp. 146 in Gerhardt Meyne Papers, Folder 7, CHS; Montgomery, *Industrial Relations*, 73–4, 81–2, 93–5, 96–100.

feud turned bitter, leading to multiple assaults and at least one murder in the year 1911. Even after Madden died of tuberculosis in 1912, the rivalry shaped the BTC's response to the employers' demands. O'Donnell supported the JCB because it could validate the plumbers' jurisdictional claims; the carpenters and other unions opposed the new order for the same reason.[15]

Economic assumptions and realities also divided the BTC. The unions that opposed the new order feared its effect on their operations. The lathers and machinists opposed giving the JCB power because they believed that the board would grant the carpenters and ironworkers their jurisdictions. The carpenters, electricians, fixture hangers, and sheet metal workers had successfully organized factory workers producing wood trim, electrical equipment, and metal doors, roofs, and smokestacks by promising manufacturers to ostracize non-union and out-of-state material. By refusing to carry non-union machinery and material from rail yards to construction sites, the teamsters gained the support of powerful building trades unions. By contrast, O'Donnell's plumbers had much to gain and little to lose from accepting a more rigid contractual system. They believed the JCB would affirm their right to steam-fitting work. And unlike the carpenters, the UA had no need for restrictions on material, as they had no desire to organize the factory workers producing pipes, valves, and sanitary equipment, who were not plumbers in any sense.[16]

But fear of the law was another factor determining support for the standard agreement. State's attorney Maclay Hoyne continually threatened Simon O'Donnell with prosecution for his participation in the violent feud between the UA and the IA. In July 1911, the grand jury indicted O'Donnell along with UA agent Maurice "Mossie" Enright for his alleged connection to the murder of IA delegate Vincent Altman. Hoyne obtained more leverage when Simon's brother Edward shot fisherman Peter DeRock on March 28, 1914. Though a coroner's jury rapidly exonerated Edward, ruling he had killed the drunken DeRock

[15] "Metz Loses Election," *CRH*, July 10, 1910, 2; "Madden's a Grafter; Trio Found Guilty; Fines but No Cell," *CRH*, May 30, 1909, 1; "Labor Thugs Elude 100 City Detectives," *CRH*, May 25, 1911, np; "Arrest Eleven Men As Labor Sluggers," *CRH*, May 27, 1911, np; "Grand Jury to Vote More Slugger Bills," *CRH*, June 12, 1911, np; "Enright Trial Near; 'Men Higher Up' Safe," *CRH*, July 22, 1911, 3; "War Between Trades Started by New Body," *CRH*, July 22, 1911, 3; "Special Grand Jury for Labor Sluggers," *CRH*, August 6, 1911, 1; "Life Sentence Given Enright; New Charge Up," *CRH*, October 29, 1911, 1; *People v. Enright*, 256 Ill. 221 (1912); *People v. Connors*, 253 Ill. 266 (1912); "Ragen Case Dismissed," *CRH*, 1912, 9.
[16] Montgomery, *Industrial Relations*, 80–2, 127, 132–39, 156–59, 199–206.

in self-defense, State's Attorney Hoyne insisted on arraigning him, leaving the door open to prosecution. In both cases, the state's attorney dropped the charges, but these indictments prompted O'Donnell's conservatism at a key moment.[17]

The union officials who rejected the uniform agreement faced criminal prosecutions. For example, the Chicago Teamsters Union refused to sign the uniform agreement or to transport nonunion goods, so a federal grand jury repeatedly indicted the truckers for restraining interstate commerce in building material. The Electrical Workers' Locals #376, #381 and #134 also declined, so the court charged them, along with members of the Chicago Switchboard Manufacturers Association and Chicago Lighting Fixture Association, with violating the Sherman Act. Assisted by the AABA, the prosecutors scored victories in both cases, forcing Simon O'Donnell, Michael Boyle, Fred Mader, and Michael Artery to pay fines from $100 to $5,000. In addition, Boyle received a year in prison.[18]

The pressure did not cease with the end of the lockout. On December 3, 1915, a Cook County grand jury indicted 54 individuals, including officers of the painters, glazers, electricians, sheet metal workers, and lathers' unions, for criminal conspiracy, malicious mischief, and extortion. Multiple indictments accused these men of placing businessmen using nonunion contractors on a "glass list," assessing them fines, and smashing the windows of those who did not pay. In 1916, fourteen of these defendants, including Fred Mader of the fixture hangers and

---

[17] "Enright Trial Near; 'Men Higher Up' Safe," *CRH*, July 22, 1911, 3; "O'Donnell Exonerated for Killing DeRock," *CRH*, April 3, 1914, 14.

[18] Indictment, January 8, 1915, *U.S. v. Artery*, USDC, ND, E. IL, case #5545 in NARA-GL; Indictment, January 12, 1915, *U.S. v. Norris*, USDC, ND, E. IL, case #5554 in NARA-GL; *U.S. v. Norris*, 255 F. 423 (1918); Indictment, April 27, 1915, *U.S. v. Artery*, USDC, ND, E. IL, case #5646 in NARA-GL; Indictment, April 27, 1915, *U.S. v. Artery*, USDC, ND, E. IL, case #5647 in NARA-GL; Indictment, April 27, 1915, *U.S. v. Dohney*, USDC, ND, E. IL, case #5649 in NARA-GL; Indictment, April 27, 1915, *U.S. v. Dohney*, USDC, ND, E. IL, case #5650 in NARA-GL; Indictment, April 27, 1915, *U.S. v. Dohney*, USDC, ND, E. IL, case #5651 in NARA-GL; Indictment, April 27, 1915, *U.S. v. Stretch*, USDC, ND, E. IL, case #5653 in NARA-GL; Indictment, April 27, 1915, *U.S. v. Boyle*, USDC, ND, E. IL, case #5648 in NARA-GL; Indictment, April 27, 1915, *U.S. v. Feeney*, USDC, ND, E. IL, case #5652 in NARA-GL; Montgomery, *Industrial Relations*, 202–5; "Government Trails Labor Union Trust," *NYT*, June 28, 1914, 11; "U.S. Indicts 100; Labor-Contractors' Conspiracy Charged," *CDT*, April 28, 1915, 1–2; "Ten Union Men Fined on Charge Four Years Old," *CDT*, March 9, 1919; Foster, *Misleaders of Labor*, 170; Ernst, *Lawyers Against Labor*, 175, 228; Criminal Docket Book 9, 361, 462–69, 507–9, 513 in NARA-GL.

Frank Curran of the painters, were convicted and sentenced to fines and imprisonment. The Illinois Supreme Court affirmed this judgment in 1919.[19]

By pushing craft workers to accept the new order, the law itself adopted emerging corporate values. The BCEA defined the standard agreement as the only alternative to extortion, turning private contractual disputes into public matters, subject to criminal law. Moreover, the cases showed how the legitimization of collective bargaining depended upon the emergence of new categories of criminal association. While section 20 of the Clayton Antitrust Act of 1914, "labor's Magna Carta," established the legality of labor unions under federal antitrust law, criminal antitrust prosecutions actually became more common after its enactment. The legitimacy of the JCB and the standard agreement depended on the illegitimacy of the old regime.[20]

In sharpening the line between legitimate and fraudulent association, the courts stemmed many practices essential to the administration of craft governance. For example, in *U.S. v. Norris* (1918), a federal judge affirmed the conviction of members of the Chicago Teamsters' Union for conspiring to restrain interstate commerce. The teamsters allegedly refused to carry a shipment of sand from the Chicago rail yards unless its owner paid the union a fine. Judge Arthur Loomis Sanborn, a Republican from the Western Wisconsin district, rejected the union's motion to set aside the verdict, accusing officials of "blackmailing" the material dealer. Sanborn noted that Congress intended the labor exemption "to legalize lawful strikes, and peaceful, lawful persuasion of workmen" not "dishonest and corrupt" walkouts, initiated for no stated reason. Sanborn held that the Clayton Act legalized an ideal of industrial relations not unionism per se. Even in county courts, where unions had no such statutory protection, judges held to this principle. The Illinois Supreme Court's decision in the "glass list" case, *People v. Curran* (1919), delineated between a "real and substantial controversy" and a "scheme to extort money." Judges placed craft governance in the latter category.[21]

---

[19] "54 Indicted as Labor Graft Ring Leaders," *CDT*, December 4, 1915, 1; True Bills, *People v. Cleary et al.*, case #s7793–7819, IR Vol. 217, 6–95; True Bills, *People v. Cleary et al.*, case #s 7810–7834, IR Vol. 218, 54–139; *People v. Curran*, 286 Ill. 302 (1919).

[20] Witte, *The Government in Labor Disputes*, 69–71.

[21] *U.S. v. Norris*, 255 F. 426, 424 (1918); Brief in Support of Motion in Arrest of Judgment, December 12, 1918, *U.S. v. Norris*, USDC, ND, E. IL, case #5554 in NARA-GL; Federal Judicial Center Website (**http://air.fjc.gov/history/judges frm.html**); Ernst, *Lawyers Against Labor*, 165–213; *People v. Curran*, 286 Ill. 309 (1919).

The AFL's new legitimacy came with a cost. The courts allowed the building tradesmen to bargain collectively but demanded they withdraw from the direct defense of their prerogatives, ceding power to arbitrators and judges. In *U.S. v. Norris* (1918) and *People v. Curran* (1919), judges defined a legitimate labor dispute, limiting private regulation. Strikes for higher wages and lower hours were lawful. Strikes to enforce a closed shop or jurisdictional boundaries were illegal restraints of trade at best and pretexts for extortion at worst. This tradeoff appealed to Simon O'Donnell (under duress) and his ally Samuel Gompers, but it frightened other union officials. For, as the tradesmen would discover, by ceding their own governing powers to the courts, they lost the ability to dictate the content of trade agreements.

The Landis Award and the Reorganization of the Building Trades

Labor's new responsibility soon seemed insufficient to Chicago's wealthiest businessmen, who demanded the total reorganization of the construction industry, pushing unions to permit the introduction of new technology, the use of out-of-state and factory-made material, and even the employment of nonunion workers. By presenting this open shop drive as a war against corruption, collusion, and inefficiency, executives cast themselves as representatives of the public interest. The elite advocated not the free market, but a corporate order, in which unions were subordinate to the citizenry, as defined by them.

The building trades crusade was one reaction to labor's recent gains. During World War I, a wave of labor radicalism swept the nation, as workers obtained union recognition, higher wages, and a shorter workweek. In 1919, the Chicago Federation of Labor (CFL) initiated campaigns to organize workers in the city's steel and meatpacking industries. Though led by radicals including organizer William Z. Foster, craft unionists like blacksmith John Fitzpatrick and steamfitter Ed Nockles endorsed this drive. Despite the initial unity of the local labor movement, employers won both strikes, splintering the participants along racial, ethnic, occupational, and ideological lines. By the end of 1921, corporate executives had gained the confidence to retaliate by initiating open shop drives in meat, construction, metalwork, printing, and transportation.[22]

---

[22] From the beginning, the craftsmen's support was tempered by doubts about steel workers' chances for victory. "Union Leader Doubts Success of Strike," *NYT*, September 24, 1919, 11; Montgomery, *Industrial Relations*, 235–36, ft. 3; Barrett, *Work and Community in the Jungle*, 191–268; Cohen, *Making a*

More than anything else, the elite sought to forge solidarity among employers. Three associations – the Chicago Association of Commerce (CAC), the Illinois Manufacturers' Association (IMA), and the Employers' Association (EA) – pushed businesses not to renew their union contracts. For example, in October 1921, the exclusive contract between the teamsters, the Chicago Cartage Exchange (CCE), and the merchants expired. With the wartime labor shortage over, the CCE first demanded a $6 per week wage reduction and then a $3 cut. Rejecting the offer, 6,000 men went on strike. The CCE accepted the backing of the EA and CAC, repudiating the teamsters' union and hiring replacements. The lockout faltered only when Hart, Schaffner, & Marx, the unionized men's clothing manufacturer, forced a settlement by defecting from the employers' ranks and canceling its contract with CCE president J. C. Zipperich.[23]

In construction, the open shop campaign was far more successful, dragging on through the decade. The context was an intense housing shortage caused by wartime increases in the price of building materials. As new construction stalled in 1917 and 1918, thousands of migrants moved to the city, creating overcrowding that was intensified by racial segregation. Facing a crisis, the Illinois State Legislature authorized a commission in 1921 to investigate the problem. Led by Representative John Dailey (R–Peoria), the commission revealed an industry governed by unions, trade associations, and exclusive agreements that thwarted meaningful competition in the city. Testimony also exposed the systematic use of payoffs and violence in the building trades.[24]

That year, the standard agreement expired, giving contractors a chance to negotiate new rules for the industry. When employers demanded a 20-percent wage reduction for skilled workers and

New Deal, 38–51; Tuttle, *Race Riot,* 124–56; McKillen, *Chicago Labor and the Quest,* 126–213.

[23] "'Open' Shop Drive Hit by Teamsters," *The New Majority* 6:21 (November 19, 1921): 1. Hart, Schaffner, & Marx acceded to the new Amalgamated Clothing Workers' Union in 1911, signing influential agreements that replaced strikes with arbitration. It is likely that dedication to these principles dictated their stance during the open shop drive of 1921. Amalgamated Clothing Workers' Union, "Chicago, 1911–1961: Fifty Years of Industrial Peace at Hart, Schaffner, & Marx" reprinted from *The Advance,* January 15, 1961.

[24] *Report of Illinois Building Investigation Commission,* 5, 45, 46, 47; Landesco, *Organized Crime,* 130–31; Tuttle, *Race Riot,* 157–83; Montgomery, *Industrial Relations,* 234. The Daley Commission resembled New York's Lockwood Commission. New York State Joint Committee on Housing, *Final Report of the Joint Committee on Housing* (Albany: J. B. Lyon Co., 1923).

30-percent cut for unskilled laborers, bargaining deadlocked. To break the jam, the parties chose Kenesaw Mountain Landis. A federal judge and newly hired commissioner of Major League Baseball, Landis seemed the perfect choice for arbitrator. The judge had proven himself no slave to corporate interests, fighting Standard Oil and issuing few labor injunctions. But Landis was a reformer of the Kohlsaat–Taft school, who hated corruption and monopoly but felt no special sympathy for workers. Shocked by the exposures of the Dailey Commission, and perhaps stung by the recent acquittal of the Chicago White Sox players charged with throwing the 1919 World Series, Landis took radical action against the unions. The judge banned work rules he saw as inefficient, restructured the wage scale, cut pay across the board, and awarded contractors the open shop, a concession they had not even requested.[25]

The workers were horrified. Though BTC president Thomas Kearney (a plumber, like his predecessor, Simon O'Donnell) urged his constituents to comply, believing that the unions could not defy a contractually mandated arbitrator, many unions saw the new conditions as unacceptable. The trades that had opposed the standard agreement in 1915 – the carpenters, fixture hangers, painters, sheet metal workers – rejected the arbitration on principle. More importantly, many did not believe (and the Illinois Supreme Court eventually supported their view) that the arbitration covered them. Landis only had legal authority to consider contracts that were being renewed; the carpenters, sheet metal workers, glaziers, elevator constructors, and fixture hangers had signed the standard agreement later than the more compliant unions, so their contracts had not yet expired. Having declined to accept arbitration from the start, the carpenters naturally refused to comply once they discovered the judge's opinions.

The Landis Award also divided the contractors. The leaders of the two umbrella groups – the Building Construction Employers' Association and the Associated Builders – saw how lucrative construction could be with wages reduced between 20 percent and 30 percent. But plumbing, steam fitting, and sheet metal contractors initially hesitated to buck the old order, which permitted friendly relations with their workers and provided them with both a relatively stable skilled

[25] David Pietrusza, *Judge and Jury: The Life and Times of Judge Kenesaw Mountain Landis* (South Bend, IN: Diamond Communications, 1998), 187–91; Montgomery, *Industrial Relations*, 237–269; "Judge Landis' Decision," *New Majority* 6:12 (September 17, 1921): 3; "Landis Soaks Workers," *New Majority* 6:12 (September 17, 1921): 1–2; "Read our Scoop; Landis Contract," *New Majority* 6:13 (September 24, 1921): 1–2.

workforce and protection against market forces. Many national firms also opposed the use of nonunion workers, fearing that unions would boycott them in other cities.[26]

The city fathers saw their window of opportunity closing. Should the contractors repudiate Landis or the carpenters defy him, unions would run the building trades for the term of the next agreement. In response, 176 manufacturers, merchants, and bankers, including nonunion publishing giant Thomas E. Donnelley, Sears and Roebuck president Julius Rosenwald, and utility magnate Samuel Insull, organized the Citizens' Committee to Enforce the Landis Award (CCLA). The group's name suggested its purpose. CCLA pushed employers to sign exclusive contracts with unions that accepted the wage reductions, but to declare open shops in the trades where unions refused to accept the new conditions. To replace the striking unionists, the CCLA imported 25,000 laborers into the city, operated an employment office, and founded a training school. They also formed a "protection department," led by a former army officer and staffed with 700 guards to serve at every worksite, as well as in a mobile "flying squadron" equipped with an automobile. The CCLA pressured bankers to refuse loans to contractors that continued to recognize "outlaw" unions. By 1925, these efforts had cost the CCLA nearly $2 million.[27]

The city's wealthiest businessmen chose the name "Citizen's Committee" to present themselves as representatives of the public. Their arguments focused on efficiency, utility, and honesty rather than on the rights of the nonunion employer and worker. Given ammunition by the Dailey Commission, the CCLA identified unions as the authors of the housing crisis and obstacles to mass consumption. The CCLA called the carpenters "outlaws," implying that the workers were somehow criminals for refusing to obey an agreement they had neither negotiated nor signed. Finally, CCLA members claimed to be reformers, whose goal was to eliminate graft and rout the "criminal element" in construction. The CCLA, like baseball owners after the Black Sox scandal of 1919, drew upon Landis' reputation as an enemy of corruption,

---

[26] Montgomery, *Industrial Relations*, 261, 264, 292–94; "Strike Fails to Impede Landis Drive," *Chicago Commerce*, January 7, 1921, 11; "Plumbing Contractors Agree to Work under Landis Award Requirements," *Chicago Commerce*, March 11, 1922, 16.

[27] Montgomery, *Industrial Relations*, 279–81; "Banks to Force Landis Wage Cut," *New Majority* 6:16 (October 15, 1921): 1; "Labor Smashers Named," *New Majority* 6:27 (December 31, 1921): 1; "The Following Are Names," Box 31, Folder 3, CFL Papers, CHS. To justify their claims to impartiality, the CCLA actually excluded all contractors. Fine, *Without Blare of Trumpets*, 217–18.

earned on the federal bench. Their desire for wage reductions, they claimed, was less important than their passion for "clean building."[28]

The open shop drive in construction demonstrated new corporate attitudes towards organization. Obviously, the CCLA was itself a powerful association, taking on all sorts of responsibilities beyond what nineteenth-century businessmen would have tolerated: collecting dues, hiring detectives, running schools, etc. The CCLA promoted the reorganization rather than the disaggregation of the construction industry, justifying its existence by making trade associations and craft unions obedient to the public interest (as defined by the city's elite). Finally, the CCLA and other open shop groups worked with the trade association movement to condemn corrupt behavior and promote a corporate pattern of organization. Both new groups, like the American Construction Council, and old, like the National Federation of Construction Industries, publicly supported the purification of the building trades, as did Herbert Hoover, the Secretary of Commerce and the nation's foremost advocate of cooperation.[29]

Building trades' unions resisted this logic, attempting to sway public opinion and push contractors to reject the Landis Award. On November 19, 1921, the CFL reframed high prices, corruption, and the public interest, calling members of the CCLA:

> Big business crooks, war profiteers who gouged millions out of the government or out of the public and then howled about patriotism for other people, dollar-a-year men, lining their own pockets, mortgage bankers who exact their toll out of the building of every structure that goes up in Chicago, building materials dealers who conspire to keep prices up, contractors who conspire to stifle competition, real estate sharks, lawyers and architects . . . The surest way to rid the Chicago building industry of graft and crookedness, would be to rid Chicago of themselves.

[28] "'Outlaw' Unions Profess They Will Yield," *Chicago Commerce*, June 10, 1922, 19; "Landis Body Gains in Outlaw Trades," *Chicago Commerce*, July 22, 1922, 13; "Landis Award Men Win Plumbing Jobs," *Chicago Commerce*, April 8, 1922, 15; "Criminal Rule in Unions is Attacked," *Chicago Commerce*, April 1, 1922, 13; "Oust Graft on Both Sides, Says Dailey," *Chicago Commerce*, September 17, 1921, 7; "Victory is Scored for Clean Building," *Chicago Commerce*, July 29, 1922, 13.

[29] "Hoover Asks for Clean-up of Industries," *Chicago Commerce* 18:2 (April 8, 1922): 11; "Hoover Heads Move to Aid Construction," *Chicago Commerce* 18:1 (April 1, 1922): 5. "Construction Men Form Council which Aims to Put Industry on Higher Plane," *Chicago Commerce* 18:14 (July 1, 1922): 28.

On April 30, 1922, new BTC president Fred "Frenchy" Mader of the fixture hangers led a parade of thousands to protest Landis's perceived condescension and the wealthy men's claim that they represented the public interest. Marchers held banners crying, "Would Landis work for 95 cents an hour?" and "Landis raised his salary to $50,000 a year and cut ours," referring to the judge's lucrative new job as baseball commissioner. Most potently, workers questioned whether one economic group could represent the public, proclaiming, "We are citizens, also able to form a Citizens Committee."[30]

Old habits die hard, and the building tradesmen responded by boycotting contractors and attacking worksites. Plumbers refused to work alongside men provided by the CCLA. A faction of the BTC allegedly bombed fifteen buildings during the year 1922. Blasts rocked a neighbor of CCLA president T. E. Donnelley, as well as the Tenth Church of Christ, Scientist in Hyde Park, a building decorated by Landis Award contractors. And, most extreme, on May 9, 1922, union officials allegedly shot two police officers while planting an explosive at an Orleans Street factory.[31]

Armed with utilitarian arguments, corporations appealed to the courts. During the war, corporate executives had established tighter control over the local criminal justice system. In 1917, the Chicago Association of Commerce (CAC) established the Chicago Crime Commission (CCC) to fight for improvements in the administration of criminal justice. The CCC was an elite reform organization that held its meetings in the Union League Club and focused on a broad array of criminal justice reforms, including increasing court efficiency, the appointment of judges, and improvements in the administration of bail. But its main function was to police the criminal justice system, forcing the state's attorney and federal prosecutor into a close relationship with the city's business community.[32]

[30] "Big Biz Prepares 'Open Shop' Drive," *New Majority* 6:21 (November 19, 1921): 1; Montgomery, *Industrial Relations*, 288.

[31] *Cahill v. United Association of Plumbers*, 238 Ill. App. 123; Montgomery, *Industrial Relations*, 288; Landesco, *Organized Crime*, 134–37; "City Joins Battle Against Terrorism," *Chicago Commerce*, May 20, 1922, 9; "Building Bombers Loose War on Crime," *Chicago Commerce*, May 13, 1922, 9; "Bombs Rouse Landis Award Committee to Seek the Men 'Higher Up,'" *Chicago Commerce*, April 15, 1922, 28.

[32] Andrew Wender Cohen, "The Chicago Crime Commission: Business Reform, Business Philanthropy, and Social Science in the 1920s," Unpublished paper in author's possession, 1991; David Johnson, "Crime Fighting Reform in Chicago: An Analysis of its Leadership, 1919–1927," Unpublished M.A. thesis, University of Chicago, 1966; Willrich, *City of Courts*, 281–84, 290–91.

The courts charged craftsmen with harming the public through monopoly, fraud, and extortion. In 1921, with the avid support of the EA, federal grand juries indicted poster advertisers, lumber dealers, carpenters, plumbing suppliers, steamfitters, as well as sheet metal, cement, and terracotta manufacturers for criminal violations of antitrust statutes. In many of these cases, prosecutors pursued craftsmen for impeding the consumer revolution. For example, the grand jury charged the Master Steam Fitters' Association of Chicago (MSFA) and the Journeymen Steam Fitters Protective Association with boycotting dealers that sold boilers, pipe, and radiators directly to city residents. This rule particularly stymied retailers like Sears, Roebuck, which found it could sell fixtures to customers around the world but not to anyone living in its own hometown. The Cook County Criminal Court was still more aggressive, issuing between eighty and one hundred indictments in the year 1921 charging building tradesmen, teamsters, flat janitors, and even waitresses, most of them charging conspiracy to extort money. And more indictments followed in 1922.[33]

The trial of Thomas Walsh was typical. The state's attorney contended that officers of the sheet metal workers, painters, and plumbers' unions – Walsh, Frank Hayes, Roy Shields, and Patrick Kane – had demanded cash to settle a series of strikes. For example, in January 1920, the court alleged they demanded $7,500 from Chicago United Theaters, Inc. to settle grievances regarding windows, doors, seats, carpentry, and electric work. The architect, William Kreig negotiated the number down to $3,000, to be paid in installments of $500. But when Krieg worried that Kane, the plumbers' business agent was not giving the cash to "the proper persons" (presumably the union treasurer), the architect declined to make the fifth payment. July saw a series of new disputes, which ceased only when Krieg agreed to give the final $1,000 to Shields. For this and other similar crimes, the judge sentenced the officers to one year in prison.

In principle, the state's attorney prosecuted union officials for graft; in practice, these cases aimed at undermining the basic operation of craft governance. When the Illinois Supreme Court affirmed the conviction above in *People v. Walsh* (1926), Justice Duncan struggled to distinguish the ordinary enforcement of rules from extortion. The

[33] Montgomery, *Industrial Relations*, 205–8; "Use Anti-Trust Law on Builders Taylor Urges," *CDT*, January 22, 1921, 2; "47 Building Men Indicted in U.S. Probe," *CDT*, January 22, 1921, 1–2; "Chicago Begins Active War on Crime," *Chicago Commerce*, March 25, 1922, 1; "Report of Committee Appointed under Senate Joint Resolution No. 9 . . . the State of Illinois, June 29, 1921," 5–6 in Folder 1, Landis Award Employers' Association Papers, CHS.

lawyers for the union delegates protested that they were merely fining contractors for legitimate rule violations, rather than "receiving
money for themselves or for any corrupt motives." They contended
that the builders willingly paid to retain their union employees; indeed, one developer testified he begged Walsh to accept money to
overlook a jurisdictional violation. But these arguments did not sway
the court. Despite the absence of evidence proving malfeasance, Justice Duncan saw the strikes as arbitrary impediments initiated solely
to provoke bribes, stating that, "an examination of the facts set forth
clearly establishes the guilt of the plaintiffs." The law barred union
officials from fining employers unless they could prove the workers
received the proceeds. In the informal world of union finance during
this period, this was a high standard.[34]

Though a new 1921 extortion law banned union officials from demanding payoffs, prosecutors continued to target organization themselves, choosing to charge craftsmen with conspiracy to demand money
under false pretenses. Perhaps the state's attorney hesitated to use an
unfamiliar law. Perhaps he disagreed with statutes that targeted the
maladministration of unions, leaving the organizations themselves un-
scathed. This continued reliance on older laws reached a troubling end
in 1922, when a jury found that Fred Mader of the fixture hangers had
conspired, alone, by himself, to extort money from the Woman's Exchange, a charity supplying lamps for the Drake Hotel. For this crime,
Mader received a sentence of one year in prison and a $1,000 fine. The
Illinois Supreme Court blocked this prosecutor's overreach in 1924,
freeing Mader and holding that a single defendant could not enact a
conspiracy.[35]

But legal doctrines were a means to an end. Workers who defied
the city fathers – be they teamsters, bartenders, waitresses, janitors, or
building tradesmen – faced charges of extortion. The courts prosecuted the opponents of the Landis Award for acts prior to the arbitrator's ruling. The defendants in *People v. Walsh* (1926) and *People v. Mader*

---

[34] *People v. Walsh*, 322 Ill. 206, 208 (1926). See also *People v. Seefeldt*, 310 Ill.
446, 449 (1923).
[35] The court tried Mader's coconspirator, Orrington Foster, separately. *People
v. Mader* 313 Ill. 277 (1924); Notes on *People v. Mader* in Book 6 (June 1922),
William Dever Papers, Box 10, CHS. The grand jury sometimes charged a
single defendant for conspiring with "other persons unknown." See True
Bill, June 29, 1921, *People v. Kearney*, case #25124, Crim. C.C., IR 272, 126–
27; True Bill, June 29, 1921, *People v. McCaffery*, case #25125, Crim.C.C., IR
272, 128; True Bill, November 17, 1921, *People v. Joseph Veltman*, case #26751,
Crim. C.C., IR 274, 202; True Bill, November 17, 1921, *People v. Wright*, case
#26752, Crim.C.C., IR 274, 203–4.

(1924) were officers of anti-Landis locals. Mader was the president of the BTC in its oppositional phase. The Carpenters' District Council (CDC), the largest of the so-called "outlaw" unions, was a particular target. In 1923, a Cook County court sentenced two CDC officials, Otto Seefeldt and William F. Brims, to seven months in jail for fining a contractor for a jurisdictional violation. Meanwhile, the federal courts persued Brims and other officers of the CDC, along with members of the Lumbermen's Association and Carpenter Contractors' Association.[36]

The government spared no expense to remove the most dangerous opponents of the new order. When prosecutors failed to convict Fred Mader, "Big Tim" Murphy, Con Shea, and "Dapper Dan" McCarthy for bombing CCLA buildings and murdering policemen Thomas Clark and Terrance Lyon, prosecutors looked for any means of getting them off the streets. In 1923, a federal grand jury indicted Murphy for robbing the Dearborn Street Rail Station of $385,000 in cash and bonds. "Big Tim" denied the charges, calling the trial a "frame-up," but the jury disagreed, sending him to Leavenworth Federal Penitentiary. Though Murphy's protest seemed the perfunctory cry of a skilled dissembler, a number of odd coincidences suggested the partiality of the proceedings. The court assigned Murphy's case to none other than Judge Landis, allowing him the opportunity to use his public authority to enforce his private arbitration. And only a few years later, the investigator who served as the prosecution's chief witness himself went to prison for mail robbery.[37]

---

[36] "Jury Disagrees in Extortion Case," *New Majority*, February 19, 1921, 9; "T. J. Vind Victim in War to Smash Labor," *New Majority*, July 8, 1922, 3; *People v. Walczak*, case #18895, Crim.C.C., June 28, 1922, Docket Book 51A, 720; *People v. Walczak*, 315 Ill. 49 (1924); "Brave Leader of Strike is Dead," *Federation News*, 1938, 1,3; Montgomery, *Industrial Relations*, 281–82; *People v. Walsh*, 322 Ill. 202 (1926); *People v. Mader*, 313 Ill. 277 (1924); *People v. Seefeldt*, Crim.C.C. Case #26946, January 9, 1924, Docket Book 51A, 308; *People v. Seefeldt*, 310 Ill. 441 (1923); "Many Convictions Are Obtained in Labor Cases," *Chicago Commerce*, June 29, 1922, 14; Indictment, January 21, 1921, *U.S. v. Andrews Lumber et al.*, USDC, ND, E. IL, case #7518 in NARA-GL; Indictment, 1921, *U.S. v. Andrews Lumber et al.*, USDC, ND, E. IL, case #8302 in NARA-GL; Records and Briefs, *Brims v. U.S.*, USCA, 7th Circ., case #3436 (1923); *U.S. v. Brims*, 6 F.2d 98 (1925); *U.S. v. Brims*, 272 U.S. 549 (1926); *U.S. v. Brims*, 21 F.2d 889 (1927).
[37] The second jury convicted plumbers' union officer John Miller. "Building Bombers Loose War on Crime," *Chicago Commerce*, May 13, 1922, 9; "Bombs Rouse Landis Award Committee to Seek the Men 'Higher Up,'" *Chicago Commerce*, April 15, 1922, 28; *People v. Miller*, Crim.C.C. case #28640, November 25, 1922, Docket 51A, 446, 723; Landesco, *Organized Crime*, 137–40, 204;

By contrast, prosecutors declined to press the indictments of those who complied with the CCLA. Among the businessmen charged by the federal grand jury, only the Carpenter Contractors were prosecuted. A federal grand jury indicted the master steamfitters and sheet contractors in 1921, but declined to pursue them after they agreed to accept the Landis Award in January 1922. While the terracotta and plumbing contractors pled guilty, they suffered only fines between $100 and $4,000.[38] State's Attorney Crowe also declined to try obedient union officials. For example, conservative BTC President Thomas Kearney was indicted five times in 1921 alone but never faced a jury. Crowe used indictments to force craftsmen to accept the arbitration, keeping the cases on the docket for years. On June 5, 1923, only five days after the BTC and the BCEA signed a new contract ratifying a modified version of Landis' ruling, Crowe struck the remaining true bills from the docket. The prosecutions occurred less to punish wrongs than to pressure craftsmen to accept the new order.[39]

The Invention of Racketeering

The criminal category "racketeering" emerged from these conflicts. Today, "racketeering" is a powerful but largely incoherent concept. While people commonly use the term as a synonym for "gangster," the courts have applied antiracketeering statutes to abortion protesters,

Lyle, *Dry and Lawless*, 58–9, 62–3; *U.S. v. Murphy*, USDC, ND, E. IL, case # 8330 (1921) in NARA-GL.

[38] Montgomery, *Industrial Relations*, 191–92, 199–202, 207–8; "Strike Fails to Impede Landis Drive," *Chicago Commerce*, 1921, 11; *U.S. v. Poster Advertising Association*, USDC, ND, E. IL, case #7648, 1921 in NARA-GL; *U.S. v. James Clow & Sons et al.*, USDC, ND, E. IL, case #7788, 1921 in NARA-GL; "Fine 16 Plumbing Concerns Under Antitrust Law," *CDT*, 1923; *U.S. v. Louis Biegler Co. et al.*, USDC, ND, E. IL, case #7901, 1921 in NARA-GL; *U.S. v. Chicago Master Steam Fitters' Association et al.*, USDC, ND, E. IL, case #7902, 1921 in NARA-GL; *U.S. v. Lehigh Portland Cement Co. et al.*, USDC, ND, E. IL, case #9312, 1922 in NARA-GL; *U.S. v. American Terra Cotta and Ceramic Co. et al.*, USDC, ND, E. IL, case #9333, 1922 in NARA-GL; in NARA-GL; "Six Terra Cotta Firms Fined on Plea of Guilty," *CDT*, August 5, 1923.

[39] *People v. Kearney*, case #24995, June 5, 1923, 51A, 224; *People v. Kearney*, case #25124, June 5, 1923, 51A, 230; *People v. Kearney*, case #26588, June 5, 1923, 51A, 289; *People v. Kearney*, case #27077, June 5, 1923, 51A, 316; *People v. Kearney*, case #27446, June 5, 1923, 51A, 346. Montgomery, *Industrial Relations*, 295. For the dispensations of the untried indictments, see Crim.C.C., Docket Book 51A, 252, 262–63, 266–67, 274, 277–78, 285, 289–90, 297–300, 302, 304–5, 307–9, 314–17, 319, 324, 328, 338, 346, 353, 364, 446.

figure skaters, and corporate executives. This indeterminacy is not new. Racketeering had no concrete meaning until the U.S. Congress passed the first antiracketeering law in 1934, and, even this did not settle definitional debates. In 1945, Harry Millis, a University of Chicago Economics Professor and the Chair of the National Labor Relations Board, commented that "racketeering has developed in labor organizations as well as in business and political affairs. The expression 'racket' is used so loosely as to include a great variety of things one does not like – graft, violence, monopolistic exactions, etc."[40]

This uncertainty dates back to the word's contested origins. Though scholars often write as if the word predates the labor movement, local debates over the legality of collective action produced the category of racketeering itself in the late 1920s. Open shop businessmen like Employers Association (EA) secretary Gordon L. Hostetter promoted racketeering in response to courtroom defeats during the second half of the 1920s. Conflating craft governance and gang violence, Hostetter appealed to a society obsessed with bootleggers and increasingly tolerant of unions.[41]

The EA hired Hostetter as its new secretary in 1923 to restore the group's position as the city's foremost open shop group. Founded in 1903 to tame organized teaming interests, the EA had been largely quiescent since its victory in 1905. A self-described "industrial relations engineer," Hostetter promised to restore the associations' vigor. Though his title suggested a scientific approach to labor, the thirty-year old's view of unions came not from any textbook, but from his experiences in the bloody coalfields of West Virginia, Kentucky, and Illinois. At a time when many businessmen were adopting the refined language of industrial relations, Hostetter ferociously painted unions and allied associations as criminal organizations that denied property

---

[40] Harry Millis and Royal Montgomery, *Organized Labor* (New York: McGraw Hill, 1945), 670.

[41] Irving Bernstein, *The Lean Years: A History of the American Worker 1920–1933* (Boston: Houghton Mifflin, 1960), 338–41; Philip Taft, *Corruption and Racketeering in the Labor Movement*, bulletin number 38, 2nd ed. (Ithaca, NY: New York State School of Industrial and Labor Relations, Cornell University, 1970); John Hutchinson, *The Imperfect Union: A History of Corruption in American Labor Unions* (New York: Dutton, 1972); David Scott Witwer, "Corruption and Reform in the Teamsters Union, 1898–1991" (Ph.D. diss. Brown University, 1994); Andrew W. Cohen, "The Racketeer's Progress: Commerce, Crime, and Law in Chicago, 1919–1929," *Journal of Urban History* 29:5 (July 2003): 574–97.

holders their rights, exploited workers, and mulcted the consuming public through monopolistic practices.[42]

Hostetter pushed the courts to supervise every area of the economy, from transportation to retail, from drycleaning to food services. In the EA newsletter, the *Employers' News*, he publicized the behavior of craft unions and associations, telling stories of violence, graft, and exploitation. Picked up by the newspapers, these tales aroused voters, and public opinion allowed Hostetter to place his employees in positions of authority. Employees of the EA such as Edwin J. Raber and Edward E. Wilson worked as Cook County prosecutors in certain cases. Walter Walker worked as an assistant state's attorney, general counsel for the EA, and later an investigator for the United States attorney.[43]

The EA lobbied for prosecutions in its monthly newsletter, the *Employers' News*, constructing with the help of the newspapers a rhetoric that implied that craft organizations were fronts for extortion rather than legitimate voluntary associations. In 1925, the EA issued a press release charging that union officials were "not content with holding the reins of the labor monopoly." They had "conspired with certain employers" and "set up organizations under harmless-sounding names" seeking blackmail from "a credulous public." He charged that the city was "in the clutches of this pernicious system of super-unions," that not only violated Illinois statutes, but also "confidently believe themselves stronger than the law." In 1926, the EA highlighted economic violence and the possibility that "criminals were "fastening themselves" onto the city's commerce. Such statements notably emphasized the illegality of craft governance rather than the involvement of gangsters in unions and associations.[44]

With some success, the EA convinced judges to enjoin craftsmen. Between 1923 and 1929, Cook County courts issued injunctions restraining, among others, janitors, teamsters, and bakers from interfering with nonunion employers and employees.[45] More significantly, between 1917 and 1927, the United States Supreme Court, led by

---

[42] Though Hostetter was twelve years younger than Walter Gordon Merritt, the secretary of the League for Industrial Rights, he showed little interest in Merritt's Ivy League reform rhetoric. *Employers' News*, April 1928, 6; Ernst, *Lawyers Against Labor*, 214–35; *Who's Who in Chicago* (Chicago: A. N. Marquis Co., 1931), v.5, 77–8, 476.

[43] *People v. Quesse*, 310 Ill. 467 (1924); Landesco, *Organized Crime*, 158–59, 204.

[44] Hostetter, *It's a Racket!*, 10–2.

[45] *Chmelik v. Teamsters*, case #163790, Circ.C.C. (1928); *Hartigan Brothers v. Teamsters*, Circ.C.C., case #177949 (1929); *Martin v. Chicago Flat Janitors' Union*, case #143895, Circ.C.C. (1927); *Cohen v. Bakers and Confectioners*, case #105070, Circ.C.C. (1923); *Stamos v. Chicago Bakers' Joint Council*, case #191865, Circ.C.C. (1929).

Chief Justice Taft, liberated the federal bench to enforce the court's definition of legitimate association. Judges who had issued orders only during major disputes now routinely defended interstate commerce against local craftsmen. Between 1920 and 1929, orders restrained kosher butchers, electrical workers, poultry handlers, teamsters, commission team owners, ironworkers, candy jobbers, painters, boilermakers, and the boiler manufacturers. With some limited effectiveness, these injunctions kept craftsmen from excluding out-of-state products from the Chicago market, from enforcing standard prices, from punishing members, and from harassing nonunion businesses.[46]

The EA gave special attention to the criminal courts. One list showed forty-three separate indictments naming union officials between 1923 and 1929. The targets were varied, ranging from idealistic labor organizers to the most cynical business agents, from union representatives to trade association secretaries, from peaceful protesters to bombers. The wave of indictments reached a peak in 1925, when State's Attorney Crowe simultaneously moved against milk drivers, kosher butchers, the retail fruit and vegetable dealers, the retail cleaners, and shoe repairers, charging them with price fixing, collusion, coercion, and violence. During the next four years, the courts also prosecuted barbers, bakers, bootblacks, florists, circular distributors, dental lab technicians, pop peddlers, garage workers, glaziers, butchers, machinery movers, waitresses, ice cream drivers, bakery drivers, and janitors for crimes ranging from conspiracy and to kidnapping, assault, murder and extortion.[47]

[46] *Hitchman Coal v. Mitchell,* 245 U.S. 229 (1917); *Duplex Printing Press v. Deering,* 254 U.S. 443 (1921); *American Steel Foundries v. Tri City Central Trades Council,* 257 U.S. 184 (1921); *United Mine Workers v. Coronado Coal,* 259 U.S. 344 (1922); *Bedford Cut Stone Co. v. Journeymen Stone Cutters,* 274 U.S. 37 (1927); Bernstein, *The Lean Years,* 190–215; *Weller v. Chicago Hebrew Butchers,* case #*1447,* USDC, ND, E. IL (1920); *Western Union v. IBEW #134 et al.,* case #*4047,* USDC, ND, E. IL (1924); *Chicago Poultry Merchants v. Chicago Poultry Handlers,* case #4176, USDC, ND, E. IL (1924); *Williams v. Teamsters,* case #4183, USDC, ND, E. IL (1924); *Dahlstrom Metallic Door Co. v. Iron Workers,* case #5724, USDC, ND, E. IL (1926); *U.S. v. Chicago Association of Candy Jobbers,* case #7906, USDC, ND, E. IL (1928); *Lamson v. Reliable Transit Co.,* case #8060, USDC, ND, E. IL (1928); *Peterson v. Teamsters,* case #8428, USDC, ND, E. IL (1928); *U.S. v. Painters District Council #14,* case #8556, USDC, ND, E. IL (1928); *Babcock and Wilcox Co. v. Boilermakers et al.,* case #9360, USDC, ND, E. IL (1929).

[47] Untitled list of criminal records of union officers, n.d. in Folder 6, Gerhardt Meyne Papers, CHS; "Women and Men Indicted as Bombers," *CDN,* December 1, 1925, 1; "Raid Bake Shops in Extortion Plots: Terrorists Levy on Small Trade Groups," *CDN,* December 3, 1925, 1; "Strike at Gang Rule Over Store Owners: Prices Fixed With Guns," *CDN,* December 4, 1925, 1;

Corporations and their associations used these indictments to protect themselves and to establish their own authority. Cook County grand juries indicted members of the Retail Cleaners and Dyers' Union Local #17792 for conspiracy three times between 1920 and 1929, charging them with forcing chain stores to abide by standard prices. National trade associations unsurprisingly reveled in the prosecution of such craftsmen. When a Cook County grand jury indicted the Kosher Master Butchers in 1925, the attorneys for the National Association of Retail Meat Dealers (NARM) – the German-Jewish firm of Sonnenschein, Berkman, Lautman, and Levinson – proudly denied any connection to "so-called 'Master Butchers' Associations.'" The prosecution of local groups allowed advocates of Arthur J. Eddy's "new competition" to assert their legitimacy by distinguishing themselves from a provincial, ethnic rival.[48]

But the results frustrated elite businessmen. Of at least 133 indictments issued against craft unionists between 1920 and 1929, only twelve ended in conviction or a guilty plea, and some were property crimes largely unrelated to the question of craft governance, such as robbery. Out of 39 indictments issued between 1925 and 1929, the prosecution won only four – the candy jobbers, bootblacks, bakers, and the machinery movers. State's attorneys often declined to try union officials fearing the wrath of their constituents. In eleven cases between 1921 and 1929, cleaners, teamsters, garage workers, and other tradesmen won their freedom, either because of public sympathy for unions or because of jury tampering. Those convicted often obtained pardons from Illinois Governor Len Small, allegedly after paying "large sums" to his lieutenants. The final blow was the Illinois Supreme Court's decision upholding injunctions restraining the CCLA from interfering with the United Brotherhood of Carpenters.[49]

"Police Hunt Fifty More for Bomb Terrorism," *CDN*, December 5, 1925, 1; "New Grand Jury Is In; Goes after Bombers," *CDN*, December 7, 1925, 1; *People v. Stavrakas*, 335 Ill. 570 (1929); Landesco, *Organized Crime*, 160–63.

[48] The National Association of Retail Meat Dealers did recognize the Retail Meat Dealers of Chicago, also known as the United Master Butchers' Association. "Milkmen's Club Warned As Bomb Inquiry Widens," *CDT*, December 6, 1925, 5; Landesco, *Organized Crime*, 160–61; Untitled list of criminal records of union officers, n.d., Folder 6, Gerhardt Meyne Papers, CHS.

[49] Untitled list of criminal records of union officers, n.d. in Folder 6, Gerhardt Meyne Papers, CHS; Landesco, *Organized Crime*, 127, 158–61, 164–66. Conviction rates for conspiracy were generally low. During that period, conviction rates only rose above thirty percent once, falling as low as 9 percent in 1927. See Police Department of Chicago, *Annual Reports*, 1926–1931. For

With Prohibition dominating the headlines, public interest in labor waned. Police and prosecutors spent their energy enforcing laws barring the sale and production of alcoholic beverages. Gangs had provided Chicago residents with gambling and prostitution since the nineteenth century, but the gigantic demand for illegal alcohol during the 1920s created heated competition among underworld factions, leading to a series of lurid murders. Moreover, bootleggers used their incredible wealth to buy influence among politicians and police. In this context, the citizens of Chicago unsurprisingly pushed the State's Attorney to use his resources to pursue gangsters, drawing energy away from the employers' complaints about collusive dry cleaners.[50]

This reality forced businessmen to revise their view of gang violence. Corporations initially saw bootlegging as a distraction, less serious than property crimes. But as the decade wore on, they concluded that gangsters threatened to subvert the city's politics and destroy its image. At the very least, bootlegging drew public attention away from labor violence. In 1928, Sears and Roebuck chairman Julius Rosenwald swore to withdraw financial support from the Chicago Crime Commission (CCC) unless that organization took a stronger stand against organized crime. Following Rosenwald's lead, the wealthy members of the CCC overwhelmingly elected Frank Loesch, a corporate attorney who promised to fight Al Capone, as their new president.[51]

the political pressures on prosecutors, see Hostetter, *It's a Racket!*, 10, 37, 41, 168–69; Carroll Hill Wooddy, *The Chicago Primary of 1926: A Study in Election Methods* (Chicago: University of Chicago Press, 1926), 18, 137, 176, 181–82; "Chicago Gangland Celebrates Victory," *Lightnin'* 2:8 (July, 1928): 8; Harold F. Gosnell, *Machine Politics: Chicago Model* (Chicago: University of Chicago Press, 1937), 10–1; "Judge Says Criminals Rule in Unions," *WP*, March 12, 1922, 3; *"People v. Walsh*, 322 Ill. 195 (1926); *People v. Walczak*, 310 Ill. 441 (1923); *People v. Quesse*, 310 Ill. 467 (1923); "Justice or Politics," *Employers' News*, November, 1928, 1; "Information Wanted," *Criminal Justice* 54 (September–October 1927): 8–9; Foster, *Misleaders*, 180; "Brave Leader of Strike is Dead," *Federation News*, November 26, 1938, 1, 3; "Scandals Fill Eight Years of Small Regime," *CDT*, November 5, 1932; *Carpenters' Union v. Citizens' Committee to Enforce the Landis Award*, 333 Ill. 225 (1928).

[50] Landesco, *Organized Crime*, 97–106, 169–190; Sinclair, *Prohibition: The Era of Excess*, passim; Daniel McDonough, "Chicago Press Treatment of the Gangster, 1924–1931," *Illinois Historical Journal* 82:1 (1989): 30–2; Michael Willrich, *City of Courts: Socializing Justice in Progressive Era Chicago* (New York: Cambridge University Press, 2003), 288–89.

[51] Dennis E. Hoffman, *Business vs. Organized Crime: Chicago's Private War on Al Capone, 1929–1932* (Chicago: Chicago Crime Commission, 1989), 9–11; David Johnson, "Crime Fighting Reform in Chicago: An Analysis of its Leadership, 1919–1927," Unpublished M.A. thesis, University of Chicago,

To refocus public attention on price fixing, bribery, and extortion, these businessmen conceived a new rhetoric. Since the mid-nineteenth century, the word "racket" had suggested an illicit form of business. During the early twentieth century, the term allegedly came to refer to a particular brand of political extortion. Party factions, beneficial societies, and unions required their members sell tickets to dance parties. Because of the noise they produced, these boisterous fundraisers were allegedly called "rackets." Since members sold tickets either by proclaiming a charitable purpose or by threatening buyers with harm, the word racket came to refer to an exploitative organization that masked its selfishness behind a facade of benevolence. By 1924, newspapers occasionally used the word "racketeer" to refer to a person who made his living through criminal enterprise.[52]

In 1927, Hostetter first began using the gerund "racketeering" to equate certain local unions and trade associations with criminal gangs. In a series of promotional writings, including a monthly newsletter and a popular book, titled *It's a Racket!*, Hostetter defined a racket as a "scheme by which human parasites graft themselves upon and live by the industry of others, maintaining their hold by intimidation, force and terrorism." Acknowledging that the public used the term to describe varied forms of illicit enterprise such as bootlegging, prostitution, and gambling, Hostetter purposefully added another category: organizations that set prices and wages in trades like laundry, drycleaning, barbering, construction, and trucking.[53]

The militantly antiunion EA charged racketeering in order to discredit trade agreements. Hostetter identified two categories of rackets, the first of which was the "Collusive Agreement," a compact between a local businessmen's association and a union allowing them to

1966; Andrew Wender Cohen, "The Chicago Crime Commission: Business Reform, Business Philanthropy, and Social Science in the 1920s," unpublished paper in author's possession, 1991.
[52] *Oxford English Dictionary* (Oxford: Clarendon Press, 1989), v. 13, 80–1; "Gangland Calls Truce While It Buries Caponi," *CDT*, April 6, 1924, 1; U.S. Senate, *Hearings before a Subcommittee of the Committee on Commerce United States Senate Investigation of So-Called "Rackets"* (hereafter *Racket Hearings*), v.1, Parts 1–6 (Washington, DC: U.S. Government Printing Office, 1934), 244. For other origins of the word, see Murray Gurfein, "Racketeering," *Encyclopaedia of the Social Sciences*, v. XIII (New York: Macmillan, 1934), 43–50.
[53] Hostetter, *It's a Racket!*, 4–5, 9. Thomas Quinn Beesley was a publicist who worked for the EA for only two years. In his previous career as a journalist, Beesley never wrote about crime, labor, or racketeering. Thus, I credit Hostetter with the innovations in *It's a Racket! Who's Who in Chicago*, v. 5 (Chicago: A.N. Marquis Co., 1931), 77–8.

administer rules regulating prices and wages. Hostetter's primary example was drycleaning, the so-called "'Daddy' of Them All." Here various unions and associations conspired to control competition, using threats and violence to force compliance among the plant owners and retail shopkeepers who made up the trade.[54]

But Hostetter's conception of racketeering also accommodated the emerging corporate faith in association. Hostetter's second type of racket – the "Simon Pure Racket" – was a phony union or association established by a criminal solely for the purposes of extortion. He argued that nefarious individuals masqueraded as labor leaders in order to demand cash from the public. His best example was "Big Tim" Murphy, who, he argued, saw unions as nothing more than a useful vehicle for graft. Implicit in this notion of fraud was the assumption that unions could be legitimate. Thus, while the doctrine of criminal conspiracy broadly forbade the enforcement of trade agreements, the idea of racketeering attacked existing organizations as corrupt, creating room for a supposedly pure, legitimate, and corporate form of association.[55]

By comparing union officers to mobsters, Hostetter transformed anti-union ideology. Progressive-era critics charged craftsmen with political crimes such as "conspiracy," "monopoly," and "tyranny," implying a threat to the commonwealth. Muckrakers called building trades unions "corrupt machines" or "trusts," administered by "bosses." A few newspapers compared union officials to so-called "Black Hand" extortionists. But, by using the gang as a metaphor for illegal collective action, Hostetter argued that drycleaners like Simon Gorman deserved no more sympathy from courts than did a beer runner, pimp, or gambler.[56]

Nevertheless, Hostetter did not see racketeer as a mere synonym for "gangster." That might have located the problem as external to labor, presenting unions as victims. For Hostetter, racketeers were the officials who hired "hoodlums"; they were not the gunmen themselves. He clearly made this distinction in his retelling of the story of Morris Becker, the drycleaning executive who hired Al Capone for protection against his rivals. In *It's a Racket!*, Hostetter defended Becker's alliance with "Scarface." He excoriated States' Attorney Robert Crowe for failing to protect the small businessman and praised Capone for his patriotic defense of individual liberty. As this suggests, Hostetter saw the

---

[54] Hostetter, *It's a Racket!*, 29–44.
[55] Hostetter, *It's a Racket!*, 15, 42, 129–56 "The Plain Truth," January 18, 1928, 3.
[56] "Kikulski, Labor Leader Shot by Sluggers, Dies," *CDT*, May 22, 1920, 3.

officials of the Retail Cleaners Association, not Capone, as the problem. Hostetter was trying to divert the public gaze away bootleggers
towards the potent organizations governing the local economy.[57]

By focusing a spotlight on Chicago's craft economy, the word racketeering re-cemented the close relationship between the EA and Cook
County Criminal Court. The grand jury indicted teamsters, bootblacks,
florists, candy, circular distributors, dental technicians, bakers, pop
peddlers, garage workers, glaziers, meat cutters, and waitresses between 1927 and 1929. In 1929, Harry Olson, the Chief Judge of the
Municipal Court of Chicago, founded a "racket court" with special trial
judges and prosecutors. The EA also pushed U.S. Attorney George
E. Q. Johnson to indict local associations engaged in protective forms
of collusion. For example, in 1928, district attorneys successfully used
antitrust laws to prosecute thirty-five members of the Chicago Association of Candy Jobbers for controlling the trade by assaulting retailers,
smashing windows, and throwing stink bombs. Five were sentenced to
prison including gunman John Hand and Albert Hoffman, the president of the association.[58]

Observers immediately questioned Hostetter's interpretation of
racketeering. Functionalist social scientists accepted his basic definition, but blamed antitrust law for the craftsmen's brutality. John
Landesco, the University of Chicago sociology graduate student who
authored the seminal *Organized Crime in Chicago* (1929), believed that
restraint of trade laws prevented craftsmen from enforcing their agreements in court, forcing them to turn to gunmen for help. Labor redefined racketeering, chiding the sociologist for repeating lurid tales
of collusion, violence, and corruption concocted by Hostetter and antilabor newspapers such as the *Chicago Tribune*. Pointing to the 1928
murder of John Clay, who died refusing to turn the well-funded Laundry Drivers Union treasury over to unknown gunmen, the CFL painted
their officials as the victims of racketeers who assaulted, kidnapped,
and murdered those that declined to pay tribute.[59]

[57] Hostetter, *It's a Racket!*, 37–41, 167–87 esp. 176, 257–58, 204–12, 215.
[58] *Boyle et al. v. U.S.*, 40 F.2d 49 (1930); *Boyle v. U.S.*, USCA, 7th Circuit, case #
4207 (1928) in NARA-GL; Hostetter, *It's a Racket!*, 188–203, 267–76; Willrich, *City of Courts*, 307.
[59] Landesco, *Organized Crime*, 149–52, 167; "Seeks to Expose Racketeer Bodies," *Federation News*, July 7, 1928, 2; "Robber Barons," *Federation News*, January 28, 1928, 4; "Accuse Employers' Association of Extortion," *Federation
News*, November 10, 1928, 8, 11; "Press Endorsed Racketeers Stick," *Federation News*, March 23, 1929, 3; "G. L. Hostetter Dives into Literary Art,"
Federation News, April 27, 1929, 3; "Mourn Killing of Racketeer Victim," *Federation News*, November 24, 1928, 1,3,5; "Laundry Drivers Defy Racketeers,"

Showing far more interest in gangsters than price fixing, the public casually endorsed labor's definition. The 1927 hit Broadway production, *The Racket*, told the story of an honest Chicago police captain fighting a bootlegger and his political allies. The play ran 119 performances, and, within the year, famed director Lewis Milestone turned it into an Oscar-nominated silent film. The 1929 Carole Lombard feature, *The Racketeer*, offered a similarly broad understanding of the term, depicting the love between a young woman and a New York City bootlegger.[60]

New contexts accelerated this change in meaning. In 1928, racketeering justified a close relationship between the EA and the criminal justice system, validated corporate trade associations, and marginalized craft governance. But in 1930, the crash of the stock market and the subsequent decline in production reconfigured American attitudes towards unions, associations, and competition. These conditions inspired a new political consensus and laws favoring unions, associations, and collective bargaining. In this environment, racketeering took on new meanings, justifying an altogether different role for the state in governing the economy.

Federation News, December 8, 1928, 3.; Editorial "Truth Clears Labor," *Federation News*, March 30, 1929, 4; "Organized Labor Again Proves Innocence in Gang Killing," *Federation News*, 1929, 6.

[60] Bartlett Cormack, *The Racket* (New York: Samuel French, 1928); *The Racket*, Lewis Milestone, dir. (United States: Caddo Productions, 1928), feature film; *The Racketeer*, Howard Higgin, dir. (United States: Caddo Productions, 1929), feature film.

Reverend Elmer Lynn Williams, "the Fighting Parson," inspecting his ruined home after a 1924 bombing. The director of the Better Government Association and editor of the scandalous magazine *Lightnin'*, Williams was a stalwart if idiosyncratic enemy of political corruption. In the 1930s, he turned his wrath towards the Kelly–Nash machine, State's Attorney Thomas Courtney, the International Brotherhood of Teamsters, and the New Deal. Courtesy of Chicago Historical Society (DN-0076879).

8

The New Deal Order from the Bottom Up

New Deal industrial policies originated in the construction sites and garages, storefronts, saloons, and union halls of cities like Chicago. Laws like the National Industrial Recovery Act (NIRA) expressed not corporate ideals, as scholars often assert, but rather the values of the tradesmen who had battled corporations over the definition of legitimate association. These men who built the political machine that helped elect Franklin Roosevelt president of the United States in 1932. Just as significantly, the craftsmen's agreements influenced policymakers. Roosevelt's advisors were urban intellectuals, suspicious of competition and intrigued by agreements in trades like construction, drycleaning, kosher meat, and milk delivery. When the administration began experimenting with statutes mandating unions, associations, and agreements, craft governance served as one model for economic stabilization.

For this reason, the legitimacy of the early New Deal programs pivoted on the contested meaning of the word racketeering. At the peak of the Prohibition era, Employers' Association (EA) secretary Gordon Hostetter had promoted the term to highlight the similarities between craft governance and extortion. But statutes like the NIRA dismissed Hostetter's assumptions, not only authorizing previously unlawful trade agreements, but also enforcing their provisions. The state lent its authority to men with vivid histories and long rap sheets. In pivotal cases like *Schechter Poultry* (1934), judges acknowledged this turnaround, and their understanding of racketeering profoundly affected their assessment of New Deal economic policy.

This shift suggests both the radicalism of the New Deal and the limitations of its ideology. The Democrats used the criminal justice system to protect rather than to destroy unions and associations. This was a major achievement that later proved ironic. Conspiracy, the predecessor to racketeering, was a potent historical concept charged with implications for the market, rights, and sovereignty. By contrast, "racketeer" was an epithet, referring to a generically evil individual, driven by selfishness rather than any principle. With the ascendance of racketeering, public discourse became susceptible to name-calling and fixated upon gangsters. Labor's legal status came to depend on the goodwill of criminal justice officials and thus upon its political might.

Politics and Legitimacy during the Downturn

The Great Depression transformed the context for the craftsmen's struggle, validating for many their views on competition, weakening their enemies, and allowing them to participate in a powerful political coalition. In the early years of the depression, it seemed unlikely that urban tradesmen could either provide a model for industrial governance or bolster any reform coalition. The downturn began just as unions began recovering from the defeats of the post-World War I period. Tradesmen depended upon the health of the city's transportation, manufacturing, and mercantile sectors. Unemployed railroad, factory, and warehouse workers skipped rent, making it impossible for landlords to afford repairs and banks to finance new buildings. As basics became luxuries, the market for haircuts, movies, and drycleaning evaporated. Tax revenues plummeted and public spending dropped, disproportionately affecting contractors, construction workers, and teamsters. Though craftsmen still governed these trades, deflation vigorously tested their ability to set prices, maintain wages, and retain members.

Meanwhile, the craftsmen defended their organizations against unprecedented physical attacks. A steady stream of officials met with unnatural ends: John Hand of the launderers, Tim Murphy of the gas workers, John Clay (1928), Ely Orr (1931), Timothy Lynch (1931), and Patrick Burrell (1932) of the teamsters, William Rooney of the flat janitors (1931), Dennis Ziegler of the operating engineers (1933), Louis Alterie of the theater janitors (1935), Thomas Maloy of the film projectionists (1935), and Michael Galvin of the machinery movers (1936). Some of these men were casualties of power struggles within their trades, but others died at the hands of outsiders like Murray "The Camel" Humphreys, a Capone lieutenant who sought to co-opt their organizations, steal their assets, and exploit their members.[1]

---

[1] David Witwer, "The Columnist and the Labor Racketeer," unpublished paper, Gotham Center Conference on New York City History, 2001, 18–20, 32 n. 50; Lyle, *Dry and Lawless Years*, 194–96.

Despite these pressures, the craftsmen slowly regrouped, strengthened by an outpouring of public sympathy. If economic conditions hindered them in their attempts to bargain, the downturn also prompted the utter collapse of Gilded Age individualism. For the better part of two decades, both workers and businessmen had questioned classical liberalism, promoting either private associationalism or state intervention in the market. During the 1930s, with prices falling and businesses failing, people became hostile towards "cut-throat" competition and friendly toward radical forms of collective action. Embracing the idea of organization, the public took an interest in preserving the integrity of collective bargaining.[2]

Even more than past reformers, Depression-era intellectuals saw the craftsmen's violence as justifying the reconstruction of the state's relationship to collective bargaining. Wisconsin economist John Commons and his students defended the stabilizing effects of what critics like Hostetter called "racketeering." Columbia University political scientist Raymond Moley wrote a 1930 *New York Times Magazine* essay painting racketeering as a crude expression of a natural tendency to stem "cut-throat competition." Prohibited from enforcing their agreements in court, they turned to gunmen, who provided "primitive" administration. Moley proposed that the state enforce cooperation among labor and capital, as it did with the railroads. Through "political and economic statesmanship," he argued, "the lesser forms of disorder that we call the racket may be abated."[3]

Journalists also called for a shift in criminal justice priorities. Anticipating the end of Prohibition, newspapermen wondered where bootleggers might turn when alcohol again became legal. In books with colorful titles like *Only Saps Work* (1930) and *Muscling In* (1931), reporters concluded that men like Al Capone were likely to conquer unions and associations. Meanwhile, left-wing writers often adopted the functionalism of academics like Landesco, Commons, and Moley. For instance, in his 1931 history of labor violence, *Dynamite*, Louis Adamic argued that workers turned to gangsters out

[2] Ellis Hawley, *The New Deal and the Problem of Monopoly* (New York: Fordham University Press, 1966), 10–4; Colin Gordon, *New Deals: Business, Labor, and Politics in America, 1920–1935* (New York: Cambridge University Press, 1994), 2; Himmelberg, *The Origins of the National Recovery Administration,* 88–150.

[3] John Commons, "Stabilization through Racketeering," *The New Republic* 68 (1931): 183. For Taft, see note on Letter, Hostetter to EA members, August 1933 in Box 66, Olander Papers, CHS; Raymond Moley, "Behind the Menacing Racket," *NYT Magazine*, November 23, 1930, 1–2, 19.

of desperation, seeking to compensate for the marginality of their organizations.[4]

These interpretations gained authority with the ascendance of the "Chicago Tammany," a Democratic coalition of pols and intellectuals, wage earners, and businessmen. Anton Cermak's victory in the mayoral election of 1931 signaled the debut of this juggernaut, long awaited by progressives like Hutchins Hapgood. For the sake of party unity, Cermak overcame his opposition to white-shoed Wilsonian, Franklin Roosevelt, while reformers like Harold Ickes conquered their distaste for "Pushcart Tony," an immigrant teaming contractor with close ties to the liquor dealers. Cermak appealed to ethnic populations by constructing balanced tickets, opposing Prohibition, and endorsing the national party's liberal policies. But the machine also enticed the men who commanded blocs of voters. The Democrats slowly enlisted African-American ward leaders by offering defectors like William Dawson positions of authority, while punishing stalwart Republicans, denying them patronage, and raiding their "Policy Wheels" and "Black and Tan" clubs. The party toyed with labor leaders as well, protecting those that favored the Democrats and pursuing those that backed the GOP, the Communists, or anyone else. Faced with this choice, craft workers and their employers became one the machine's core constituencies.[5]

Labor's active participation in Democratic politics allowed the craftsmen to control the Municipal Court of Chicago, the entry point for most criminal cases. In the 1920s, its chief judge was Harry Olson, a reform Republican who had strongly supported Hostetter's crusade against racketeering, founding the nation's first "racket court" in 1927 to address violent crimes related to trade, labor, or politics. But in the election of 1930, the voters rejected Olson in favor of John J. Sonsteby, a former union official tied to both progressives and Democratic machine politicians. If businessmen had demanded the new court in 1905

[4] Courtenay Terrett, *Only Saps Work: A Ballyhoo for Racketeering* (New York: The Vanguard Press 1930); Fred Pasley, *Muscling In* (New York: I. Washburn, 1931); Louis Adamic, *Dynamite: The Story of Class Violence in America* (Gloucester, MA: Peter Smith, 1963), 325–72.

[5] Gosnell, *Machine Politics*, 12–4, 93–4, 126, 146–48, 158–59; Ickes, *Autobiography*, 254–57; Gosnell, *Negro Politicians*, 79, 133–34, 189–90, 201, 232; Christopher R. Reed, "Black Chicago Political Realignment During the Depression and New Deal," *Illinois Historical Journal* 78:4 (Winter 1985): 242–56; Mark Haller, "Policy Gambling, Entertainment, and the Emergence of Black Politics: Chicago from 1900 to 1940," *Journal of Social History* 24:4 (Summer 1991): 724–29; Milton Rakove, *We Don't Want Nobody Nobody Sent* (Bloomington: Indiana University Press, 1979), 262; Cohen, *Making a New Deal,* 255–56.

to end the craftsmen's immunity to policing, new political conditions placed that body in hands sympathetic to labor.[6]

Tradesmen established a close but complicated relationship with the state's attorney. In 1932, with the help of campaign manager Harold Ickes, Democrat Thomas Courtney defeated Republican prosecutor John Swanson. Unlike Judge Sonsteby of the Municipal Court, Courtney had neither prior connection to the labor movement, nor special sympathy for workers. An ambitious politician who saw himself as presidential timber, Courtney had obtained reform backing by promising to rid the city of "racketeers and gangsters." Never letting him forget this pledge, opponents of the New Deal continuously pressured the new state's attorney to prosecute union officers. But compared to his predecessors, Crowe and Swanson, Courtney was a proponent of collective bargaining, who generally used his authority to guard unions and associations – at least those that supported him, his party, and the New Deal.[7]

Labor also struggled to transform the federal courts, bringing the debate over racketeering to a boil. In 1932, President Hoover appointed U.S. District Court Judge James Wilkerson to the Seventh Circuit U.S. Court of Appeals. Local labor federations opposed Wilkerson because of his record. As a corporate lawyer, United States attorney, and federal judge, Wilkerson had both sought and issued many injunctions, most notably the 1922 order restraining striking railway shopmen. But Wilkerson was famous for something else; the judge had sent Al Capone to Alcatraz Federal Prison for income tax evasion the year before. Frank Loesch, the president of the Chicago Crime Commission and a former council to the Pennsylvania Railroad, told judiciary committee that, "fully two thirds of the unions in Chicago are controlled by, or pay tribute directly to, Al Capone's terroristic organization." Loesch was a stalwart foe of political corruption, but, like many elites, he saw honesty as a sole possession of his class and faction. By claiming that Capone was behind worker resistance to Wilkerson, the wealthy corporate attorney asserted the fraudulence of labor's voice and the criminality of labor itself.[8]

---

[6] Willrich, *City of Courts*, 308; "John J. Sonsteby," *NYT*, April 16, 1941, 23; Harold Ickes, *The Secret Diary of Harold L. Ickes: The First 1,000 Days, 1933–1936* (New York: Simon & Schuster, 1953), 520; Staley, *History of the Illinois State Federation of Labor*, 216, 291.

[7] Ickes, *Autobiography*, 259–65; *Lightnin'* 6:6 (October 1934): 1.

[8] Authors repeatedly use Loesch's quote without fully comprehending the bias of its author. Irving Bernstein, *The Lean Years* (New York: Da Capo, 1960), 339; John Hutchinson, *The Imperfect Union* (New York: F. P. Dutton, 1972), 115–16; Harold Seidman, *Labor Czars: A History of Labor Racketeering* (New York: Liveright Publishing, 1938), 116; U.S. Congress. *Hearings Before*

Previous lawmakers had bowed to men like Loesch, but the Depression-era Senate affirmed not only labor's definition of racketeering but also the authenticity of its opposition to Wilkerson. In a letter to Senator Borah, Victor Olander of the Illinois State Federation of Labor's (ISFL) called Loesch's charge "maliciously untrue," a "smoke screen of vilification" clouding the real reason for protesting Wilkerson: his attitude towards unions. Donald Richberg, the attorney for the railway unions in 1922, charged Loesch with conflating "organized crime with organized labor." He accused the wealthy lawyer with misrepresenting "opposition from decent, self-respecting, organized labor" as an "instrument of criminal effort to punish a judge for having sentenced Al Capone." The four members of the committee, realizing the political sensitivity of Loesch's claim, dismissed the suggested connection between the federation and Capone as unproven and immaterial. The Senate delayed the appointment until after the election of Franklin Roosevelt, who withdrew Wilkerson and nominated district court judge and former Wilsonian Congressman Louis FitzHenry to the position.[9]

As the political winds shifted, Hostetter grew shrill, while labor's retorts became more confident. Having praised Capone in 1929 for protecting drycleaning executive Morris Becker, Hostetter now protested the bootlegger's omnipotence. In the past, Hostetter recalled, "organizations of businessmen and organized labor were principally responsible, with the criminal acting merely as a tool or agent." But now, he suggested, "the criminal" had gained "the ascendancy." In 1933, Hostetter abandoned this dichotomy altogether, warning EA members that: "racketeers and underworld alcohol criminals are indistinguishable." The ISFL responded with an open letter excoriating "the more fortunately situated elements of the community," for continuing to deny the worker's right to organize. Acknowledging the employers'

---

a Subcommittee of the Committee on the Judiciary United States Senate Seventy-Second Congress, First Session on the Nomination of James H. Wilkerson to be United States Circuit Judge Seventh Circuit (Washington, DC: Government Printing Office, 1932), 294; Rayman L. Solomon, *History of the Seventh Circuit, 1891–1941* (Bicentennial Committee of the Judicial Conference of the United States, 1991), 113–14; Kobler, *Capone*, 131, 305, 312–25.

9 Letter, Victor Olander to William Borah, March 28, 1932, 1–8 in Olander Papers, Box 51, CHS; "Mr. Loesch Shown Up," *Federation News* 27:14 (April 2, 1932): 1; *Hearings on the Nomination of James H. Wilkerson*, 296, 297; Dennis E. Hoffman, *Business vs. Organized Crime: Chicago's Private War on Al Capone, 1929–1932* (Chicago: Chicago Crime Commission, 1989); Peter H. Irons, *The New Deal Lawyers* (Princeton: Princeton University Press, 1982), 28–9; Solomon, *History of the Seventh Circuit*, 114–16.

right to defend their notion of fair wages and work conditions, the ISFL attacked "leaders who are so antagonistic towards the organizations of working people that they seem willing to ignore professional gangster activities of a known criminal nature, when such activities are directed against trade unions." The tradesmen were winning the battle to reshape criminal justice.[10]

The New Deal and the Problem of Racketeering

Because craftsmen provided the Roosevelt administration with votes, money, and some intellectual inspiration, the racketeering issue moved to the center of debates over the New Deal. Skilled workers, shopkeepers, and contractors helped urban political machines win elections, and they expected the state to repay them with laws promoting employment and higher prices. Conveniently, the tradesmen's resilient governing schemes intrigued federal administrators. In the early 1920s, the president himself had led the reformist American Construction Council. Secretary of the Interior Harold Ickes, National Recovery Administration general counsel Donald Richberg, Agricultural Adjustment Administration general counsel Jerome Frank, and National Labor Relations Board member Harry Millis all had extensive experience with craftsmen in Chicago. Most significantly, Raymond Moley – the Columbia professor who proposed the legitimization of the violent price agreements in 1931 – authored the NIRA, the Roosevelt administration's most expansive piece of legislation, in 1933.[11]

[10] Gordon Hostetter, "The Growing Menace of the Racketeer," *NYT Magazine*, October 30, 1932, 3; Letter, Hostetter to EA members, August 1933 in Box 66, Olander Papers, CHS; Letter, Illinois State Federation of Labor to Trade Unionists and All Other Interested Citizens in Illinois, September 1933 in Box 62, 2, Olander Papers, CHS.

[11] The role of contractors in the New Deal coalition is too complex to encapsulate here. Nevertheless, their prevalence in urban Democratic machines is indisputable. Jason Scott Smith, *Building New Deal Liberalism: The Political Economy of Public Works, 1933–1956* (Cambridge University Press, forthcoming); Caro, *The Power Broker*, 703–54; "Construction Men Form Council which Aims to Put Industry on Higher Plane," *Chicago Commerce* 18:14 (July 1, 1922): 28; Bernstein, *The Lean Years*, 116–17; Irons, *The New Deal Lawyers*, 28, 60, 120–21; "Roosevelt Sets Up a New Labor Board," *NYT*, July 1, 1934, 20; Moley, "Behind the Menacing Racket," 19. Other major New Deal officials from Chicago were Clarence Darrow, attorney for the Chicago drycleaners, teamsters, and others, Charles Merriam, a political scientist, alderman, and mayoral candidate, and Frederick Delano, the president's uncle, a railroad executive, and a founding member of the EA. Irving Stone, *Clarence Darrow for the Defense* (Garden City, NY: Doubleday, Doran & Co.,

For these reasons, the two main recovery acts of the first New Deal – the NIRA and the Agricultural Adjustment Act (AAA) – ratified schemes existing in the craft economy. Both laws established administrative frameworks allowing the state to promote, supervise, and enforce contracts between private groups of workers and businessmen. Under the observation of government attorneys, producers gathered together to form "industrial codes" (in the case of NIRA) or "marketing agreements" (in the case of AAA), which set wage scales, working hours, as well as the terms for business competition. The statutes suspended antitrust laws, making it possible for these agreements to go much farther in limiting competition than permitted before 1933. And Section 7A of NIRA specifically granted workers a right to join labor unions and participate in the code making process. Though the laws bore the imprint of many influences, the statutes clearly embodied the "economic statesmanship" envisioned by Moley in his 1930 article on racketeering.[12]

Finding validation for their organizations in the New Deal, urban tradesmen were conspicuous in the constitutional history of this period. As Peter Irons notes, two-thirds of the challenges to the NIRA involved trades like drycleaning, lumber, and kosher foods, while the earliest tests of the AAA occurred in Chicago's milk delivery business. According to most scholars, these cases show the dissatisfaction of small business with "corporatist" statutes that allegedly served the interests of national firms and, to a lesser extent, industrial workers. In fact, they show the reverse – that New Deal laws affirmed once-suspect patterns of craft governance and criminalized the city's nonunion laborers, open shop entrepreneurs, and anti-union corporations. The passage of the recovery acts implicated the federal government in the craftsmen's schemes and thereby brought the open shoppers' longstanding grievances to a new venue: the United States Supreme Court.[13]

1941), 507–14; Hawley, *The New Deal and the Problem of Monopoly*, 24; Mark G. Schmeller, "Charles E. Merriam," *American National Biography Online* (Oxford University Press, 2000); "Frederic A. Delano is Dead in Capital," *NYT*, March 29, 1953, 54; *Employers' News*, April 1928, 6.

[12] Hawley, *The New Deal and the Problem of Monopoly*, 19–20, 33–6, 191–92; Gordon, *New Deals*, 171–73; Irons, *The New Deal Lawyers*, 115–16.

[13] Irons, *The New Deal Lawyers*, 55. With the exception of Christopher Tomlins, Donald Brand, and Sidney Fine, historians agree that corporations and industrial unions – not craftsmen – were the authors and beneficiaries of New Deal recovery statutes. Himmelberg, *The Origins of the National Recovery Administration*, 181–218; Colin Gordon, *New Deal*, 166–67; Steve Fraser, "Dress Rehearsal for the New Deal: Shop Floor Insurgents, Political

Writing their arrangements into NIRA codes, the craftsmen entwined the New Deal with the ongoing debate about the criminal law. The recovery acts turned corporate price-cutters into outlaws and craftsmen into defenders of the public good. Attorneys on both sides of the constitutionality question exploited this reversal. In the *Schechter* case, the Roosevelt administration prosecuted kosher butchers because the Supreme Court had ruled that trade subject to federal interference in criminal prosecutions of the previous decade, establishing a precedent for national action. Opponents of the New Deal favored appeals that connected the Democrats to sketchy business practices and notorious public figures. Thus, by mutual consent, the legitimacy of the New Deal depended upon the acceptance of the new definition of racketeering.

Early experiments with private regulation provided the first tests of the New Deal's reversal of criminal law. In 1931, Benjamin Squires, an arbitrator and University of Chicago economics lecturer, created a plan to legally stabilize competition in Chicago's drycleaning industry. Like Landesco, Moley, and Commons, Squires believed that laws promoting competition caused tradesmen to ally themselves with gunmen, who used violence to uphold trade rules. Squires argued that carefully crafted agreements could offer drycleaners the benefits of combination without subjecting them to the exploitation of gangsters and the risk of criminal prosecution. Accepting a dual responsibility, Squires arbitrated labor disputes and chaired a new trade association: the Cleaners and Dyers Institute (CDI). Squires signed contracts with every member giving him the power to set their prices. Consulting with Morris Kaplan, an attorney specializing in trade law, Squires concluded that such agreements were lawful, since Illinois' antitrust law covered commodities, not services.

The plan proved only modestly effective at either ending gang violence or controlling competition. Surviving bombings, chain stores hardly feared the bespectacled professor's strikes and lawsuits. Seeing an opportunity, Al Capone and his lieutenant, Murray Humphreys,

Elites, and Industrial Democracy in the Amalgamated Clothing Workers," *Working-Class America: Essays on Labor, Community, and American Society*, Frisch and Walkowitz, eds. (Urbana: University of Illinois Press, 1983), 212–55; Christopher Tomlins, *The State and the Unions: Labor Relations, Law, and the Organized Labor Movement in America, 1880–1960* (New York: Cambridge University Press, 1985), 99–129; Donald Brand, *Corporatism and the Rule of Law: A Study of the National Recovery Administration* (Ithaca, NY: Cornell University Press, 1988); Sidney Fine, *Without Blare of Trumpets*, 257–73.

offered to enforce industry agreements for a fee in March 1931. When Squires refused the offers and appealed to government officials for protection, the plant owners went behind his back, paying off Humphreys for his assistance. When the United States Supreme Court held the Sherman Antitrust Act applicable to drycleaners in May 1932, members began to quit the CDI.[14]

As the high court's ruling suggested, Squires' efforts were well intentioned but still quite illegal. On July 27, 1933, State's Attorney Thomas Courtney announced the indictment of eighteen men, including Squires, Al Capone, Murray Humphreys, Republican alderman Oscar Nelson, well-known lawyer Aaron Sapiro, and a range of union officers and businessmen. The prosecutor accused these men of fixing prices in the laundry, drycleaning, carbonated beverage, and linen supply trades through strikes, boycotts, and coercion. The grand jury's action left Squires "astounded." He replied, "My dealings with manufacturers and labor have always been open and aboveboard. I attempted to go in and clean up the cleaning and dyeing industry in Chicago, and when I found I could not do it, I resigned."[15]

Courtney prosecuted the drycleaners under pressure from the Employers' Association of Chicago, which saw the "racket trial" as an extension of its campaign against collusive trade agreements. Having spent the previous five years decrying the rough governance of the drycleaning industry, Hostetter had watched Squires' experiment with some anxiety, and he asked the state's attorney to make an example of the professor. The EA financed the prosecution, paying staff attorney Edwin Raber to try the cleaners. Its values permeated the case. When Raber determined he could not try Capone and Humphreys – the former was already incarcerated in Atlanta Federal Penitentiary and the latter remained a fugitive – he commented: "We don't need the presence of Capone and Humphries [*sic*] to prove that a conspiracy to control prices, to exact tribute from business men and working men existed here." Though Hostetter now preached the indistinguishability

---

[14] Morrison Handsaker details the history of the institute in meticulous detail using his personal experience with Squires, see Handsaker, 214–80 esp. timeline 215–19; *Atlantic Cleaners & Dyers Inc. v. United States*, 286 U.S. 427 (1932).

[15] "Sapiro is Indicted in Chicago Rackets," *NYT*, July 28, 1933, 1; "Dr. Squires is Astounded," *NYT*, July 28, 1933, 2. Though Squires unquestionably opposed the use of violence, thus justifying his shock at being indicted, he actually refused to resign from the CDI even after it became moribund, leading to confusion regarding his role in the 1932 strikes. John Fitzpatrick Papers, Box 18, Folder 131, CHS.

of racketeers and gangsters, he still viewed union officials and allied businessmen as the primary problem.[16]

The trial pitted Hostetter's ideology against the values of the New Deal. On June 12, 1933, over one month before the indictment, President Roosevelt had signed the NIRA, which mandated that businessmen establish trade agreements similar to those tried by the Chicago cleaners. Benjamin Squires learned of his indictment while serving as a federal conciliator at a hosiery strike in Reading, Pennsylvania appointed by Secretary of Labor Frances Perkins. Written in late 1933, the code for the drycleaning industry ratified the private agreements it replaced, setting prices, favoring small firms against the chains, and formalizing relations between the master cleaners and the three unions. As the trial unfolded in 1934, Roosevelt expressed support for the defendants by appointing Squires the code administrator for the Chicago drycleaning industry.[17]

Because of the stakes, the trial attracted intense public scrutiny, remaining on the front page of the Chicago newspapers for months despite competition from the economic downturn and strike waves. The defendants hired a powerful set of attorneys to plead their case, including former chief justice of the Illinois Supreme Court, Floyd Thompson, former congressman Frank Reid, former judge of the Municipal Court William Fetzer, and prominent Socialists William Rodriguez and William Cunnea. The prosecution and its backers responded by investing $250,000 in trying the case. They presented piles of evidence, a parade of witnesses and more than 300 documents. As a result, the trial lasted over four months, longer than any trial in Cook County history.[18]

The defendants' two main arguments played on changing attitudes towards competition, governance, and racketeering. First, they

[16] "Labor Blasts Courtney," *Federation News*, May 12, 1934, 7; "Labor Rallies to Alderman Nelson," *Federation News*, 34:6 (February 10, 1934): 1, 8; "Edwin J. Raber," *NYT*, April 2, 1947, 27; "Now Ready to Try Chicago Racket Case," *NYT*, September 18, 1933, 38; Letter, Hostetter to EA members, August 1933 in Box 66, Olander Papers, CHS.

[17] Hawley, *The New Deal and the Problem of Monopoly*, 57–8, 96, 98, 115; "Miss Perkins to Study Charges," *NYT*, July 28, 1933, 2; "Dr. B. M. Squires as 'Conspirator,'" *Federation News* 34:5 (February 3, 1934): 1, 3; "Union Objections Delay Dyers Pact," *NYT*, November 12, 1934, 6; "New Plan is Adopted to End Silk Strike; 36-Hour Week at Higher Pay Agreed On," *NYT*, November 10, 1934, 3.

[18] *Who's Who in Chicago, 1936*, 235, 314, 1005; *Who's Who in Chicago, 1941*, 689; *Who's Who in Chicago, 1950*, 499.

exploited the differential between the grounds for the indictment – antitrust laws banning price fixing – and the public's understanding of racketeering as gang control over business and labor. The tradesmen asked the jury to ignore the law, telling the court that they had established the CDI to keep Capone out of the industry. Second, the cleaners reminded the jurors that the New Deal had subsequently legitimized their governing scheme. According to one union official, the case hinged on whether their actions were "a conspiracy against the peace and dignity of the people" or "an attempt to do the identical thing which the government of the United States is now attempting to do under the National Recovery Act." The defendants argued that they suffered merely for being prescient, writing an industrial code before the president asked them to do so.[19]

The jury acquitted everyone, thus affirming the New Deal. Observing the similarity between the CDI agreement and the NRA code for drycleaning, the jury concluded that Squires, the labor leaders, and the drycleaners were pillars of the anticipated recovery, not racketeers. State's Attorney Courtney defended his decision to prosecute the case: "Since it started there has been no bombing, acid throwing, window smashing or slugging." But the defendants unsurprisingly saw the verdict differently. James Gorman, the president of the retailers' union proudly commented the verdict "vindicated" not only the drycleaners, but also "the policy of the President of the United States."[20]

If the passage of the recovery act allowed Squires and the drycleaners to defend themselves against charges of racketeering, the history of the kosher food trade shows how the legitimacy of the NIRA itself came to hinge upon changing understandings of criminal law. As in many similar crafts, unions and associations governed the intense competition of the kosher foods business. A large number of tradesmen

---

[19] "Gang Threat Death Charged in Trial," *NYT*, January 25, 1934, 2; "Fog Clears as to Conspirators," *Federation News* 34:7 (February 17, 1934): 1, 4, 5; Everything but Conspiracy Seen," *Federation News* 34:8 (February 24, 1934): 7; "Raber's Threats Aired in Court," *Federation News* 34:11 (March 17, 1934): 1, 3; "Kaplan's Story Some Knockout," *Federation News* 34:16 (April 21, 1934): 1, 6; "Raber Raves as Trial Nears End," *Federation News* 34:17 (April 28, 1934): 2; "Gang Threat Death Charged in Trial," *NYT*, January 25, 1934, 2; "Is Dr. Squires Big Bad Wolf," *Federation News* 34:15 (April 14, 1934): 1, 3; "Case May Last Three Weeks," *Federation News* 34:12 (March 31, 1934): 10–1.

[20] Handsaker, 227–42; "Labor Blasts Courtney," *Federation News*, May 12, 1934, 7; "Verdict Brings Widespread Joy," *Federation News* 34:20 (May 19, 1934): 6; "Sapiro and 16 Win 'Racket' Acquittal," *NYT*, May 6, 1934, 8; Newell, *Chicago and the Labor Movement*, 39–40.

supplied the demand for ritually prepared meat in cities with large immigrant Jewish populations, such as Chicago and New York. In 1933,
the New York metropolitan area contained from 400 to more than
500 kosher slaughterhouses earning a combined $50 to $90 million
annually. Overseeing this market were three allied organizations: the
Greater New York Live Poultry Chamber of Commerce (LPCC), the
Official Orthodox Slaughterers of America (OOS), and the Teamsters
Local #167. As in Chicago, these groups used strikes, boycotts, fines,
and violence to set prices, enforce wage standards, and limit entry.[21]

The officers of the New York organizations struggled to rein in the
smallest and largest competitors in their jurisdiction. Small tradesmen
often failed to pay dues, skirted associational rules, and rejected standard prices. But the greater challenge came from the most ambitious
firms. The ultimate example is A. L. A. Schechter Poultry Co., the
Brooklyn chicken dealer whose opposition to NIRA eventually led to
the legislation's demise. Historians paint the four Schechter brothers
as struggling entrepreneurs, and indeed, they were recent immigrants,
three of whom lived modestly with their father, a rabbi. But by 1934,
they were not small businessmen. The *New York Times* described their
wholesale house, chicken market, and retail stores as the "largest concerns in Brooklyn, which, in turn, is the centre for a $60,000,000
annual business in the New York metropolitan area." The Schechters
earned revenues totaling over $1 million per year, as much as eight
times the average firm. They accomplished this in part by bucking the
associations that ran the trade. For instance, the brothers allegedly
refused to pay the standard rate for renting chicken coops, leading
their peers to pour emery powder into the crankcase of one of their
trucks.[22]

[21] Irons, *The New Deal Lawyers*, 86–7; "Fifty-five in Court in Poultry War," *NYT*,
August 28, 1928, 12; "66 Found Guilty in Poultry Trust," *NYT*, November 22,
1929, 28. For more on violence and criminal trials in the kosher food trade,
see Jenna Joselit, *Our Gang: Jewish Crime and the New York Jewish Community,
1900–1940* (Bloomington: Indiana University Press, 1983).

[22] "Witnesses Testify of Poultry Bills," *NYT*, October 24, 1929, 20; "Schechter
Takes Decision Gloomily," *NYT*, May 28, 1935, 13; "Government Asks NIRA
Test at Once in Poultry Case," *NYT*, April 15, 1935, 1,18; Frank Freidel,
"The Sick Chicken Case," in *Quarrels that Have Shaped the Constitution*, John
Garrity, ed. (New York: Harper & Row, 1964), 192; Irons, *The New Deal
Lawyers*, 55–7, 86–8; Idem, *A People's History of the Supreme Court* (New York:
Viking), 301–2; Brand, *Corporatism and the Rule of Law*, 290; David Schechter
household, 1930 U.S. census, Kings County, New York, population schedule,
city of Brooklyn, enumeration district 671, supervisor's district 30, sheet 2B,
dwelling 19, family 37, National Archives micropublication T626, roll 1527.

Between 1928 and 1933, the federal government repeatedly defended businesses like Schechter, charging organized kosher chicken dealers, butchers, and drivers with conspiracy to violate antitrust law. In 1929, a federal jury convicted sixty-six men, including LPCC supervisor Benjamin Simon, teamsters' union official Arthur "Toots" Herbert, and slaughterer's union delegate Charles Herbert, for conspiring to raise the price of chicken 10 to 15 cents per pound, to the tune of $500,000 per year. The judge sentenced the ringleaders to as much as three months in jail, and in April 1931, the Second Circuit Court of Appeals affirmed the butchers' conviction. But this judgment did not end the assault. In 1932, Assistant U.S. Attorney Walter L. Rice obtained an injunction from the district court restraining the poultry men. And in 1933, Rice not only obtained contempt citations against the poultry dealers, but also began new investigations into alleged "rackets," price fixing, and gang violence in the Bronx's chicken trade.[23]

By the time the Supreme Court affirmed the district court's 1932 injunction in *Local #167 v. U.S.* (1934), New Deal statutes had not only legalized the agreements in question, but also given them the force of law. The National Recovery Administration (NRA) built the kosher poultry code upon existing arrangements, endorsing the right of the merchants, butchers, and teamsters to bargain collectively and assuming responsibility for enforcing the resulting terms. Enjoying protection from competition, fearing the effects of the depression, and perhaps welcoming federally administered fines as a replacement for gunplay, the butchers overwhelmingly supported the recovery act.[24]

---

[23] "Fifty-five in Court in Poultry War," *NYT*, August 25, 1928, 12; "Ninety in Poultry Case on Trial Tomorrow," October 6, 1929, 25; "Eighty-four in Poultry Trust Tried in 'Bleachers'," *NYT*, October 8, 1929, 1; "Says Poultry Ring Exacted Big Toll," *NYT*, October 17, 1929, 22; "Witnesses Testify of Poultry Bills," October 24, 1929, 20; "Poultry Defense Closes," *NYT*, November 19, 1929, 12; "Sixty-six Found Guilty in Poultry Trust," *NYT*, November 22, 1929, 28; "Sentencing is Ended in Poultry Trust," *NYT*, December 19, 1929, 22; "Ask Writ to Block New Poultry Trust," *NYT*, February 8, 1930, 32; "Poultry Men Lose in Conviction Fight," *NYT*, April 21, 1931, 25; "Says Poultry Trust Exacts Huge Tribute," *NYT*, November 17, 1931, 3; "Bolan Offers Aid to Racket Victims," *NYT*, April 26, 1933, 7; "Poultry 'Racket' Faces New Inquiry," *NYT*, May 4, 1933, 13; "Eleven Are Accused in Poultry Racket," *NYT*, August 1, 1933, 2; "Injunction Upheld in Poultry Racket," *NYT*, February 6, 1934, 14.

[24] *Local #167, International Brotherhood of Teamsters, v. U.S.*, 291 U.S. 293 (1934); Irons, *The New Deal Lawyers*, 88–9, 103; "Schechter Takes Decision Gloomily," *NYT*, May 28, 1935, 13.

As before the New Deal, A. L. A. Schechter & Co. was the exceptional firm. A corporation among a mass of proprietors, Schechter kept their edge by defying the poultry code. The firm demanded its workers labor seventy-three hours per week for 30 cents an hour, violating union agreements setting the workweek at forty-eight hours and wages at 50 cents. Perhaps even more troubling, they sold uninspected poultry, including birds carrying tuberculosis. Caught by the code authority, the Schechter brothers became the first businessmen convicted under the felony provisions of the NIRA. Judge Campbell sentenced the brothers to as much as three months in the federal penitentiary and fines totaling $7,425.[25]

The NIRA thus inverted the logic of the criminal law. As late as August 1933, upon the testimony of the Schechters, federal prosecutor Walter L. Rice had prosecuted the men who governed the poultry trade as racketeers. One year later, the federal government had empowered men like "Toots" Herbert, and Rice was trying the Schechters as conspirators. When asked years later why he rebelled against the recovery act, Joseph Schechter replied, "I honestly think the NRA could have been a good thing if there had been safeguards against racketeering. That was what wrecked us." Schechter was not saying that gangsters forced him to pay his employees forty percent less than the code prescribed. Rather, he was lamenting that the NIRA embraced Herbert, legitimizing men considered racketeers before the New Deal. Schechter proved this after the demise of the recovery act by endorsing the Roosevelt administration, voting Democrat in the 1936 presidential election.[26]

By reversing the Schechter brothers' conviction, the Supreme Court not only invalidated the NIRA, but also rendered judgment on the new criminal law. Solicitor General Stanley Reed argued that the court's 1934 decision affirming the district court injunction against Local #167, occurring just one year earlier in the exact same industry and location, was an obvious precedent for federal authority over the chicken trade. But Justice Charles Evans Hughes denied this argument by making a tenuous distinction between direct and indirect effect on commerce, a line so fine as to suggest that the old-school reformer was eager to end the "Blue Eagle" experiment. Hughes' desperation flowed from the facts of the case, which showed that NIRA not only overthrew antitrust – a major achievement of his

[25] "Government Asks NIRA Test at Once in Poultry Case," *NYT*, April 5, 1935, 1,18; Irons, *The New Deal Lawyers*, 87–8.
[26] Freidel, "The Sick Chicken Case," 209; Irons, *A People's History*, 301; "Arch Foes of NRA Vote for New Deal," *NYT*, November 4, 1936, 6.

generation – but also set no clear "primary standard" to determine who received state power. The law contained no provision to keep notorious characters from controlling the apparatus for enforcing the kosher poultry code.[27]

Similar concerns explain Justice Brandeis' opposition to NIRA. The famed liberal voted with the majority in *Schechter* not only because he opposed centralization of federal power and the delegation of legislative authority to the executive branch, but also because NIRA validated patterns of collective action Brandeis had long attacked. In 1910, Brandeis opposed railroad regulations that Moley and Richberg saw as one model for New Deal governance. An advocate for consumers and the inventor of the term "scientific management," Brandeis condemned limits on productivity. His early writings insisted that the legality of labor be premised on its liability to civil suits, a provision not spelled out by the section giving unions the right to exist. Brandeis might have endorsed an NIRA that truly required codes to emulate the "Protocol of Peace" arbitration agreement he had negotiated in 1910 between progressive clothing manufacturers and well-administered unions, linking wage and hours to productivity. But the kosher poultry code embraced disreputable associations, long criticized by the respectable elements of the Jewish community to which Brandeis himself belonged. He could hardly accept any law that empowered organizations without regard to character and enforced agreements without regard to content.[28]

[27] *Schechter Poultry v. U.S.*, 295 U.S. 495 (1935) and *Schechter Poultry v. U.S.*, 295 U.S. 723 (1935). *Landmark Briefs and Arguments of the Supreme Court of the United States: Constitutional Law*, v. 28, ed., Philip B. Kurland and Gerhard Casper (Arlington, VA: University Publishers of America, 1975), 667–69; Irons, *The New Deal Lawyers*, 101–3; Idem, *A People's History*, 302; Betty Glad, "Charles Evans Hughes," *American National Biography Online* (Oxford University Press, 2000). This response was common to other Republican reformers. See Willrich, *City of Courts*, 315–18.

[28] Gerald Berk, "Historical Alternatives to Regulated Monopoly: Brandeis, Scientific Management, and the Railroads," in *Constructing Corporate America: History, Politics, Culture*, Kenneth Lipartito and David B. Sicilia, eds. (New York: Oxford University Press, 2003); Idem, "Neither Markets nor Administration: Brandeis and the Antitrust Reforms of 1914," *Studies in American Political Development* 8 (Spring 1994): 24–59; K. Austin Kerr, "Decision for Federal Control: Wilson, McAdoo, and the Railroads," *Journal of American History* 54:3 (Dec. 1967): 553; Hofstadter, *The Age of Reform*, 172; Louis Brandeis, "The Incorporation of Trade Unions," *Green Bag* 15 (1903): 11; Steve Fraser, *Labor Will Rule: Sidney Hillman and the Rise of American Labor* (New York: The Free Press, 1991), 62, 68, 82–3; Irons, *The New Deal Lawyers*,

The legitimacy of the Agricultural Adjustment Act, like the NIRA, also depended upon the shifting meaning of racketeering and the legal status of craft governance. Early tests of the AAA's constitutionality began in Chicago's milk trade, an industry, like drycleaning and kosher foods, long regulated by unions and associations. Contracts between the Chicago Milk Dealers Association (MDA), the Pure Milk Association (PMA), and the Milk Drivers' Union, Local #753 (MDU) set the terms for competition in the business. Before 1916, these agreements protected the middling local dealers, farms, and dairies against newcomers, usually the smallest and largest competitors from outside the Chicago area. But by the 1930s, courts and consumers had prodded the dairymen's association to absorb a New Jersey corporation, Borden Farm Products, into its system. Though this move stripped away the milkmen's anticorporate panache, their agreements remained a bulwark against two potent economic pressures. First, they reduced the amount of abundant Wisconsin milk available in the Chicago market. And second, the contract maintained door-to-door milk delivery against those who favored its direct sale to consumers in groceries.[29]

The depression heightened the tensions surrounding these agreements. Between 1930 and 1933, the price of milk fell by half, leaving Wisconsin farmers all the more determined to crack the big city market and the Chicago area dairy interests desperate to maintain their monopoly. In the first half of 1932, Wisconsin farmers circumvented the local agreements by selling 1,200 tons of milk through a new Chicago firm, the Meadowmoor Dairy. The milk interests responded, using every weapon in their arsenal. The retailers and drivers not only refused to sell Meadowmoor milk, they also convinced Chicago Health Commissioner, Herman Bundesen, to order his inspectors to bar its sale. The Milk Dealers' Bottle Exchange broke Meadowmoor containers, and then declined to replace them. Finally, the PMA, MDA, and MDU blocked trucks, robbed trains, and attacked retailers trafficking in Meadowmoor products.[30]

Critics had long charged Bundesen and the Chicago diary organizations with racketeering. In *It's a Racket!* (1929), Gordon Hostetter briefly sketched the milk delivery agreements as an example of collusive agreements, enforced by violence. That same year, Elmer

104; "Head of Butchers Held in Two Bombings," *CDT*, September 4, 1932; "Julian Mack Dies; 40 Years on Bench," *NYT*, September 6, 1943, 17.
[29] Irons, *The New Deal Lawyers*, 136–38.
[30] Declaration, 1932, *Meadowmoor v. Chicago Milk Dealers Assn.*, USDC, case #41533 (1932) in NARA-GL.

Lynn Williams, a Methodist minister dedicated to exposing political corruption in Chicago, noted that milk prices in the city were 28 percent higher than in Milwaukee. Williams, the so-called "Fighting Parson," commented, "sometimes on early summer mornings we are convinced that the milk delivery business is a 'racket.' Maybe it will get that way all year around." As the milk drivers became a cog in the Democratic machine, Williams – a reform Republican, who hated Bundesen and the New Deal – grew increasingly angry. In 1933, he accused the health inspector of accepting bribes and called the milk agreement a "business racket" and an "illegal boycott."[31]

For this reason, it was remarkable when, in 1933, the Agricultural Adjustment Act essentially ratified the milkmen's private arrangements. AAA attorneys established a milk marketing agreement for the City of Chicago that favored the PMA, CMDA, and Teamsters Local #753. For instance, the code set a single retail price for milk, regardless of whether it was sold in a store or delivered door-to-door, greatly favoring the dealers using milk drivers. Meanwhile, the law gave the associations state power, eliminating the need for physical violence. Under the AAA licensing system, the Secretary of Agriculture could deny a firm selling milk at a cut-rate price its right to operate. Because the agreement also prohibited selling unsanitary milk, the AAA also effectively bestowed federal authority upon the city official responsible for inspecting Chicago's milk, health commissioner Dr. Herman Bundesen.

Chains and independents successfully skirted the law, and the marketing agreement broke down at the end of 1933. But the Chicago milk interests acted swiftly to restore their brand of order to the trade. On January 6, 1934, 18,000 farmers affiliated with the PMA withheld milk from the Chicago market, beginning a four-day milk strike. As they had in 1932, the farmers, dealers, teamsters destroyed loads of milk headed for the city, even stopping mail trains and destroying their contents. On January 10, hemmed in by a federal court injunction and under pressure from municipal and federal authorities, the various sides reached a new settlement, which retained the price setting components of the 1933 marketing agreement,

[31] "The 'Milk War,'" *Lightnin'* 3:3 (March 1929): 5; "'Milk Shake' for Bundesen," *Lightnin'* 5:7 (April 1933): 9; "Doc Bundesen's Milk Racket Turns Sour," *Lightnin'* 7:3 (October 1936): 8–9; Hostetter, *It's a Racket!*, 137–38; Elmer Lynn Williams, "The Truth About Racketeering and the Press," *Federation News*, July 26, 1930, 14; Idem, "Newspapers Make Gunmen Factor in Chicago Affairs," *Federation News*, February 1930, 14, 16.

but at a 10–20 percent lower rate, more favorable to the direct retailers.[32]

This renegotiated agreement led to the very first suits challenging the validity of the AAA. Though the legal issues in these cases were constitutional, testing the power of the federal government to regulate retail prices, the cases were a manifestation of conflicts that had raged in the city for three decades. The plaintiffs fell into three main types: cash-and-carry retailers, dairies like Meadowmoor selling milk produced by unlicensed out-of-state farms, and Wisconsin farm cooperatives. Companies like Meadowmoor had petitioned for injunctions restraining the Chicago milkmen before the Congress ever enacted AAA. Indeed, the Borden Condensed Milk Co. had raised the same issues in 1916 before it made peace with the system. Time reshaped the conflict, but the dispute continued to revolve around the legitimacy of craft governance as a response to changing consumer habits and the developing national market.[33]

The Chicago milkmen publicly defended themselves by arguing that administered competition was the only alternative to violence. If the federal government declined control the price-cutters, then the craftsmen would do it themselves, as they did in the "milk strike" of January 1934. Milk Drivers' Union official Steve Sumner commented, "you take a bunch of young, red blooded huskies like we've got, and they're not going to stand by idly while their wages and homes disappear. That is what men go to war for; they'd be cowards if they didn't." Likewise, the farmers asserted that "ruinous prices" had brought them to the brink of the "poorhouse." Defending Roosevelt, the AAA, and Health Inspector Bundesen, they charged that "bootleg milk" distributors had

[32] Irons, *The New Deal Lawyers*, 135–37; Bill of Complaint, January 29, 1934, *Meadowmoor v. Borden*, USDC, case #13697 (1934), 22, 28–30 in NARA-GL; "Milk Strike Stops Flow into Chicago," *NYT*, January 7, 1934, 21; "Striking Farmers Halt Mail Train," *NYT*, January 10, 1934, 29; "Truce at Chicago Ends Milk Strike," *NYT*, January 11, 1934, 16; "Chicago Milk Strike Settled," *Federation News* 34:2 (January 13, 1934): 1, 3.

[33] "Chicago Milk Code Injunction Sought," *WSJ*, August 2, 1933, 12; "Sue on Price Fixing," *WSJ*, August 12, 1933, 8; "Acts under Milk Act," *WSJ*, September 1, 1933, 2; *United States v. Shissler*, 7 F. Supp. 123 (1934); *Edgewater Dairy Co. v. Wallace*, 7 F. Supp. 121 (1934); *Columbus Milk Producers Co-op. v. Wallace*, 8 F. Supp. 1014 (1934); *Meadowmoor v. Borden*, USDC, case #13697 (1934) in NARA-GL; *Meadowmoor v. Chicago Milk Dealers Assn.*, USDC, case #41533 (1932) in NARA-GL; Irons, *The New Deal Lawyers*, 136–38, 145–46, 149–150; *Borden's Condensed Milk v. Milk Producers' Association*, USDC, Equity case #636 (1916) in NARA-GL.

undercut "legitimate dealers," a rhetorical twist first made in the 1920s. Positioning themselves as victims of vicious competition, as the only alternative to "chaos," and as patriotic defenders of the New Deal spirit, the milkmen's organizations justified not only denying the city milk for four days, but also reestablishing market regulation.[34]

The milkmen employed new definitions of racketeering to defend themselves and the AAA. The farmers' reference to "bootleg milk," once merely a metaphor, was now a reference to the role of gangsters in the industry. The Chicago milk interests contended that Murray Humphreys had targeted their trade in 1931, showing special interest in Local #753's vast treasury. To obtain this money, Humphreys offered his "protection" to Secretary-Treasurer Steve Sumner and President Robert G. Fitchie. Sumner and Fitchie resisted. Aged eighty-five and sixty-five years respectively, they were hardened veterans of industrial warfare, not without resources. When Humphreys riddled their headquarters at 220 S. Ashland Street with bullets, Sumner turned his office into a fortress, complete with machine gun turrets, and purchased an armored car from bankrupt utilities executive Samuel Insull. Humphreys responded by kidnapping Fitchie, freeing him only when the union paid the gunman a $50,000 ransom. Humphreys allegedly used this money to found Meadowmoor Dairies, obtaining transportation from Michael Galvin of the Chicago Teamsters' Union, a group of independent locals that had defected from the International Brotherhood after the bloody strike of 1905.[35]

Arguing that exclusive agreements, backed by the AAA, were the only way to prevent Humphreys from controlling the milk trade, the retailers, drivers, farmers, and dairies inverted Gordon Hostetter's understanding of racketeering. They not only used the New Deal to legitimize their organizations and agreements, they briefly convinced the government that their rivals were criminals. In part, they managed to reverse the criminal law because the facts of Humphreys' role of in the trade suited their interpretation. But this shift also very much

---

[34] Bill of Complaint, January 29, 1934, *Meadowmoor v. Borden*, USDC, case #13697 (1934), 28–30 in NARA-GL; "Complaints of Bad Milk Stir City to Action," *CDT*, January 11, 1924, 12.

[35] Joint Answers of Robert G. Fitchie, et al., March 13, 1934, case # 13697. *Meadowmoor v. Borden*, USDC, ND of IL, case #13697 (1934) in NARA-GL; Touhy, *The Stolen Years*, 84, 88; Lyle, *Dry and Lawless Years*, 194–96; *Racket Hearings*, 416–17; "Robert G. Fitchie, 82, Chicago Labor Man," *NYT*, June 11, 1946, 23; Harold Seidman, "Labor Racketeering," *The Nation* 137:3554 (August 16, 1933): 180.

reflected a broader shift in public attitudes towards competition and government that accompanied Roosevelt's recovery program.

This transformation was temporary, for as in *Schechter*, the courts rejected the state's new role in the market. A few judges initially supported the AAA experiment in milk regulation as a necessary response to a national emergency, but in mid-1934, courts began striking down the price fixing provisions of the Chicago milk agreement as unconstitutional overextensions of federal authority. Again, as in *Schechter*, judges forbade the federal government from punishing price cutters as criminals, but they attacked neither the legitimacy of collective action itself, nor the milkmen's redefinition of racketeering. Thereafter, the word referred to the infiltration of presumably legitimate associations, unions, and industries by gangsters like "The Camel."[36]

The New Criminal Law

A new federal antiracketeering law, enacted in 1933, ratified labor's definition of that term and accommodated New Deal recovery laws. Between 1932 and 1940, the United States government expanded its role not only in the regulation of the peacetime economy, but in criminal justice as well. Beginning in August 1933, a United States Senate subcommittee held hearings pursuant to Senate Resolution #74, "authorizing an investigation of the matter of so-called 'rackets' with a view to their suppression." But if racketeering was the topic of the hearings, the testimony tended to focus on criminal justice generally, emphasizing ways in which the federal government could aid local police in catching those who broke the law.[37]

The few experts that discussed commerce endorsed adjustments to the criminal justice system rather than restrictions on labor unions. Nearly all of the academic witnesses were sociologists and child psychologists concerned with the causes of crime. The administration's official representative to the subcommittee, Raymond Moley, barely participated in the hearing. While Michigan law professor John Waite mentioned the problem of extortion, his solutions were greater court

[36] Irons, *The New Deal Lawyers*, 149–55.
[37] U.S. Senate, *Hearings before a Subcommittee of the Committee on Commerce United States Senate Investigation of So-Called "Rackets,"* v.1, Parts 1–6 (Washington, DC: U.S. Government Printing Office, 1934). Hereafter referred to as *Racket Hearings*.

efficiency, improved sentencing, and sharper media representations of the criminal (he asked the press to discourage children from criminal careers by giving gangsters less flattering names, such as "White Livered" Kelly). Sociologist Clayton J. Ettinger described how gangsters demanded money from tradesmen in exchange for limiting competition, but he blamed the disorganization of business and the absence of legal collective bargaining for this phenomenon. Ettinger then proposed a national police force, limitations on firearms, improved methods of fingerprinting, and civil service reform.[38]

The majority of witnesses were prosecutors, police officers, and judges concerned with catching and convicting offenders rather than broader issues of political economy. With few exceptions, these witnesses viewed racketeering as a synonym for gangster, and they focused on ways of improving the effectiveness of the criminal justice system. But even those concerned about economic coercion avoided criticizing labor unions, trade associations, and collective bargaining. For example, former U.S. Attorney George E. Q. Johnson was strong supporter of Hostetter's crusade, who worked at Chicago's original "racket court," contributed an appendix to *It's a Racket!*, and prosecuted the candy jobbers for violating the Sherman Antitrust Act. Yet in 1934 he testified almost exclusively about jury reform and federal jurisdiction. Similarly, Chicago criminal court judge and mayoral candidate John Lyle told the Senators endless stories about gang violence in the city. But he not only condemned gunmen like Edward "Spike" O'Donnell for robbing union treasuries, he also defended the "honest labor unions" that were working with the state's attorney and the EA to purge their ranks of gangsters.[39]

Though few workers spoke at the hearings, the committee overtly appealed to organized labor. A few angry former unionists testified about violence, corruption, collusion, and arbitrary authority, but the committee either ignored them, invited rebuttal witnesses, or directly halted their testimony. For example, when Patrick McNicholas alleged that corrupt gunmen, including Joseph V. Moreschi of Chicago, expelled him from the presidency of the International Hod Carriers Union in 1922, the committee chair asked him to focus on the ways that the federal government could assist local officials in controlling crime. When McNicholas disregarded this request, calling AFL members "traitors," the chairman stopped him entirely, initiating a

---

[38] *Racket Hearings*, 161–62, 310–24, 457–63, 618–29, 633–36, 665–69, 698–702, 730–31, 736–45, esp. 45–6, 244–53. "Rackets and Recovery," *Business Week* 207 (1933): 17.

[39] *Racket Hearings*, 296–305, 389–91.

monologue on the defects in the jury system and the need for an American version of Scotland Yard.[40]

The subcommittee rebuffed requests that they consider problems within the labor movement, focusing on the threat posed by outsiders like Capone. A labor lawyer for the AFL building-trades unions, Adolph Dzik noted systemic patterns of corruption in the industry and recommended a labor board to deal with issues of legitimacy. The Senators replied that Dzik's proposal was outside their jurisdiction, which was criminal justice, but suggested he might mention it to Senator Wagner's committee. Senators expressed greater enthusiasm for Steve Sumner, the eighty-six-year-old president of the Chicago Milk Drivers Union. Charming them by detailing how he defied Murray Humphreys, Sumner identifying the racketeering problem as external to labor. At the end of January 1934, the committee heard extensive testimony about collusion, corruption, and violence in New York City's music trade. But by this time, the hearings were basically over, and this evidence ended up in a separate published volume.[41]

Even businessmen called for more, not less, economic regulation. Some seconded Sumner, perceiving racketeering as an outcome of, rather than a justification for the recently enacted recovery law. William Fallowes Morgan, an owner of a cold storage company working in the highly collusive fish industry in New York, proposed that the NRA require antiracketeering clauses in its codes. Morgan accepted the legitimacy of the unions, but suggested the need for greater supervision of their leaders. When poultry shippers shocked the Senators with tales of organized inefficiency at New York City's rail terminal, the legislators proposed not to prosecute the perperators, but rather to extend the Secretary of Agriculture's authority over the unloading of beef to poultry as well. John A. Carroll, a Chicago banking executive, dairy farmer, and president of the Holstein–Friesian Association denounced the complex web of corporations, associations, and rules that governed the city's milk trade, only to bewilder the senators by then demanding the Congress protect banks from robbers.[42]

[40] *Racket Hearings*, 74–7, 78–81, 159–61, 416–19. McNicholas' grievances were longstanding. "Hod Carriers Charge New Union is Racket," *NYT*, January 4, 1931, 7; "Building Racket Charged," *NYT*, November 13, 1930, 29.
[41] *Racket Hearings*, 798–825, esp. 814–15, 416–19.
[42] *Racket Hearings*, 142–43, 357–375, 826–35; Cornelius W. Wickersham, "The NIRA from the Employers Viewpoint," *Harvard Law Review* 48 (1935): 954–77. Carroll presented himself as a poor farmer, but the census shows him as a comfortable banker, which explains his detour. John A. Carroll household, 1930 U.S. census, Cook County, Illinois, population schedule, city

Once the law left committee, Congressional debates emphasized criminal justice priorities, severing the word racketeering from its original connection to conspiracy. U.S. Attorney General Homer Cummings noted that prosecutors had found the Sherman Antitrust Act of limited utility against racketeers. Created to stop corporations from restraining trade, Cummings concluded that the "act is not well suited for prosecution of persons who commit acts of violence, intimidation, and extortion." Still worse, Cummings argued, antitrust law required evidence of "conspiracy, combination or monopoly," something he found "difficult to prove." Finally, violating the Sherman Act was a misdemeanor, insufficient to deter "extortion violence, coercion, or intimidation." Seeking to create conditions favorable to conviction, Cummings pushed for a law that condemned *individuals* rather than combinations, gangsters rather than unions.

Though Congress wrote a bill that embodied labor's definition of racketeering, unions remained resistant to any law that empowered the federal government to expand its own criminal jurisdiction. The 14th Amendment barred Congress from outlawing a specific type of person, such as a "gangster," requiring instead general laws prohibiting specific actions. Remembering how judges used antitrust laws against labor unions, men like United Mine Workers' counsel Harry Warrum strongly objected to restrictions on broad categories of coercion. They feared that future courts would use an act barring extortion not to prosecute men like Murray Humphreys but rather to punish union officers who threatened strikes.

Labor held up the bill for months, but the president wanted it passed, pitting the nation's most powerful interest group against a politically dominant chief executive. After consulting with AFL president Green, the House passed a new bill containing three passages explicitly liberating any "bona fide employee" to strike to obtain higher wages from a "bona fide employer" and cautioning the courts not to use the act "to impair, diminish, or in any manner affect the rights of bonafide labor organizations in lawfully carrying out the legitimate objects thereof." Within the month, the Senate and president approved of the amended bill.[43]

of Chicago, enumeration district 166, supervisor's district 29, sheet 2B, dwelling 2, family 73, National Archives micropublication T626, roll 421.

[43] *Congressional Record*, Senate, March 23, 1934, 5735; *Congressional Record*, 78, Part 10, 73rd Congress, 2nd Session, March 1934, 11403; Letter, Harry Warrum to William Green, April 21, 1934 in Box 10, Folder 7, Philip Taft Papers, Kheel Center, Cornell University; W. C. Roberts, "Memorandum," November 12, 1934 in Box 10, Folder 7, Philip Taft Papers, Kheel Center, Cornell University.

The Anti-Racketeering Act of 1934 ratified the definition of racketeering set out by union officials and social scientists, offering specific protections for labor protest and collective bargaining. Racketeering was a form of corruption that plagued unionism but was not intrinsic to it, a crime perpetrated *upon* unions and associations by evil individuals, rather than a crime committed *by* craft organizations. This was a victory for labor, as it freed unions from the semi-outlaw status that had left them vulnerable to prosecution throughout the nineteenth century. But even before the passage of the act, the pitfalls of this new legitimacy were apparent. It empowered the state to punish union officers but placed few limits on how that power might be used.

Politicized Legitimacy and the New Deal Order

For the rest of the decade, unions, businessmen, politicians, and commentators wielded the word racketeering in struggles to determine who could participate in New Deal order. By the time of the Senate hearings, racketeering had become an epithet synonymous with organized crime and almost unconnected to any particular set of practices. Separated from its original relationship to conspiracy and antitrust, people used racketeering as a code word to condemn labor leaders without issuing any precise charge against them. It became a smear, a counterpoint to the term "Red," designating the types of unions and businesses to be barred from a place at the table.[44]

Craft unions used the increasingly vague term to deny their rivals access to labor's new legitimacy. For example, sometime around 1930, William Stratton, the Republican Illinois Secretary of State granted ISFL secretary Victor Olander the right to approve all applications for charters submitted by worker organizations. When Democrat Edward Hughes replaced Stratton, this agreement became void. In 1933, three middle-class men – a bond salesman, an attorney, and a doctor – requested a corporate charter for a new association of garage mechanics. Uncertain how to proceed, Hughes asked Cook County State's Attorney Courtney whether the new union was legitimate. Courtney encouraged Hughes to issue the charter. When J. J. Uhlmann, the

---

[44] In 1945, Harry Millis and Royal Montgomery noted this vagueness: "The expression 'racket' is used so loosely as to include a great variety of things one does not like." *Organized Labor* (New York: McGraw-Hill, 1945), 670. For examples of the racket-red pairing, see Budd Schulberg, *What Makes Sammy Run?* (New York: Bantam, 1968), 117; Joseph A. Wise, "Midwest To Be Again Racketed," *Federation News*, December 18, 1937, 1; Howard Kimmeldorf, *Reds or Rackets: The Making of Radical and Conservative Unions on the Waterfront* (Berkeley: University of California Press, 1988).

secretary of the Chicago Metal Trades Council, discovered that Hughes
had allowed the new organization, he wrote outraged letters to Courtney, Hughes, Olander, Illinois Director of Labor Martin Durkin, and
Governor Henry Horner.[45]

Uhlmann, like many members of the AFL, saw the federation as the
source of legitimacy. Never stating any specific crimes, he called the
garage workers' association a "racketeer union" charging it with being
"antagonistic to the recognized bona fide organization," and he asked
the politicians to revoke its charter. Uhlmann asked Courtney for an
investigation, and threatened to expose the prosecutor's betrayal. In
protesting Hughes' decision to grant the charter, Uhlmann reminded
the secretary that, "the American Federation of Labor and the affiliated
International Unions are recognized by everybody as the spokesmen
for the workers."[46]

The AFL eventually reestablished its authority, forging an agreement
with Hughes and convincing judges and the legislature to bar the Secretary of State from issuing corporate charters to unaffiliated worker
organizations. But such incidents led craft unions to seek stronger relationships with the Cook County State's Attorney, whose power had
grown with public concern about racketeering. For decades, prosecutors had policed union tactics, challenged certain labor leaders, and
attacked trade agreements. In the 1930s, prosecutors used racketeering issue to justify their intervention into disputes between unions and,
more broadly, to determine which groups had authority over which
trade. But the vagueness of racketeering gave prosecutors the ability
to punish or exonerate unions and associations for purely political and
even personal reasons.[47]

Thomas J. Courtney was among the first prosecutors in the nation to use the racketeering issue to build a political career. Fighting high-profile criminals like Humphreys sold papers, and Courtney
hoped to ride the resulting notoriety to higher office. But fighting
racketeering also allowed Courtney to play the defender of New Deal

---

[45] Letter J. J. Uhlmann to Victor Olander, October 12, 1933 in Victor
Olander Papers, Box 72; Letter J. J. Uhlmann, to Martin Durkin, Octo-
ber 12, 1933 in Olander Papers, Box 72; Letter J. J. Uhlmann, Henry
Horner, October 12, 1933 in Olander Papers, Box 72; Letter J. J. Uhlmann to
Hughes, October 12, 1933 in Olander Papers, Box 72; Letter J. J. Uhlmann,
Thomas Courtney, October 12, 1933 in Olander Papers, Box 72.

[46] Letter J. J. Uhlmann to Hughes, October 12, 1933 in Olander Papers, Box
72; Letter J. J. Uhlmann, Thomas Courtney, October 12, 1933 in Olander
Papers, Box 72.

[47] "Unions Cannot Be Incorporated," *Federation News*, January 29, 1938, 6;
People ex rel. Padula v. Hughes, 296 Ill. App. 587 (1938).

collective bargaining. In this strategy, Courtney was not alone. Within a few years, New York City prosecutor Thomas Dewey followed a similar path to the governor's mansion and beyond. But while Dewey was a Republican who used racketeering to challenge labor without offending his state's working-class constituency, Courtney was a Democrat who used his growing authority to marshal specific unions behind him.[48]

Courtney intervened in rivalries like the conflict between the International Brotherhood of Teamsters (IBT) and the Chicago Teamsters Union (CTU). The CTU was a local district council, composed of unions from the North side of the city that had defected from the IBT and the AFL after the giant strike of 1905. For over two decades, 13,000 coal, ice, and machinery teamsters retained their independence by establishing ties to the city's Republican political machine. In 1933, the state's attorney began investigating the CTU, citing a letter from the Department of Justice urging him to prevent men engaged in "illegal liquor traffic," from being "admitted into membership in legitimate labor unions." In May 1933, Mayor Edward Kelly, CFL president John Fitzpatrick, and IBT president Daniel Tobin met with Courtney and agreed to push the independents to join the federation. For his support, the prosecutor demanded for the right to veto the admission of certain individuals to the newly organized locals.[49]

Five years of violence followed this meeting. Throughout the conflict, Courtney allied himself with the IBT and AFL, using charges of racketeering to justify his role in the dispute. Courtney alleged that the CTU had become a prize in a gang war between Roger Touhy, the beer baron from the northern suburbs, and members of the Capone organization, including Murray Humphreys and George "Red" Barker. Courtney assigned Chicago Police Captain Daniel Gilbert to be his chief investigator. Gilbert's men forced CTU members to join parallel IBT locals and restored union officials like James "Lefty" Lynch to power. Lynch had administered the CTU Coal Teamsters Local

---

48 Touhy, *The Stolen Years*, 89–90; Mary M. Stolberg, *Fighting Organized Crime: Politics, Justice, and the Legacy of Thomas Dewey* (Boston: Northeastern University Press, 1995), 162–92; Richard Norton Smith, *Thomas E. Dewey and His Times* (New York: Simon and Schuster, 1982).

49 The CTU president, Michael Galvin, was a Republican 27th ward committeeman. "Politics Seen in Chicago Murder," *NYT*, November 29, 1936, E6; *International Teamster* 30 (December 1933): 7, quoted in Barbara Warne Newall, *Chicago and the Labor Movement* (Urbana: University of Illinois Press, 1961), 95–6; Sterling Rigg, "The Chicago Teamsters Unions," *Journal of Political Economy* 34 (1926): 12–36 esp. 12–6; Sterling Rigg, "The Chicago Teamsters Unions," M.A. thesis, Northwestern University, 1925, 24–9.

#704 until 1928, when George Barker sent two associates to Wisconsin, where Lynch and his family were on vacation. The gunmen shot "Lefty" in the legs, warning him to stay away from Local #704. Lynch survived the attack, but stayed away until 1932, when Barker's murder (allegedly the work of the Touhys,) Gilbert's ascension, and his affiliation with the IBT enabled him to regain his union.

The independent teamsters and their allies responded by calling Courtney, Gilbert, and Lynch racketeers. In a brief submitted to Judge Denis Sullivan, Joseph Harrington, the attorney for the CTU and later for Touhy, condemned Courtney's actions as conspiratorial, claimed the IBT was the criminal organization, and requested a special grand jury investigation of the state's attorney. Muckrakers like Elmer Lynn Williams noted that James Lynch was a convicted felon, printing Lynch's mug shots from a previous larceny conviction. Williams called Captain Gilbert a "former labor racketeer," reporting the investigator's past as a CTU official once charged, but not tried, for murder. And many years later, Roger Touhy claimed that Courtney and Gilbert had conspired with the Capone gang to dominate the city's labor movement.[50]

On one level, the two sides simply disagreed about definitions. Like Gordon Hostetter, Elmer Williams focused on Lynch's career as an outlaw labor leader. In 1914, a federal jury had convicted "Lefty" on charges of conspiracy to violate the Sherman Act, when he refused to allow teamsters to cart coal belonging to a blacklisted corporation. Williams highlighted Lynch's larceny conviction. By contrast, Courtney saw Lynch as the rightful leader of the Coal Teamsters, expelled from his position by Barker, a bootlegger with no labor ties. Reflecting the new attitudes of the 1930s, Courtney painted "Red" as the racketeer and "Lefty" as the victim.[51]

[50] Newell, *Chicago and the Labor Movement,* 97–107; Joseph T. Harrington, *Petition . . . to Appoint Some Competent Attorney to Prosecute the Conspiracy Alleged to Have Been Committed by Thomas J. Courtney, States Attorney for Cook County and Edward J. Kelly Mayor of the City of Chicago as Set Forth Within. Presented on March 2, 1935 to Honorable Denis E. Sullivan* (Chicago, 1935); "Chicago Prepares to Attack Gangs," *NYT,* March 26, 1935, 3; "A Comedy of Errors," *Lightnin'* 6:6 (October 1934), 1–15; "Captain Dan Gilbert," *Lightnin'* 6:8 (March 1935): 16; Elmer Lynn Williams, *The Fix-It Boys: The Inside Story of the New Deal and the Kelly–Nash Machine* (Chicago, 1940), 74–7; Idem, *The Curious Career of Tom Courtney Unveiled: A Documented Report of that Little Known Political History of a Payroll Patriot* (Chicago, 1944), 39–40; Touhy, *The Stolen Years,* 89–92.
[51] Newell, *Chicago and the Labor Movement,* 98–9; "A Comedy of Errors," *Lightnin'* 6:6 (October 1934), 1–15; "Capt. Dan Gilbert: Now Under Two Indictments," *Lightnin'* 8:6 (January 1939): 14; Landesco, *Organized Crime in*

But the disagreement attests to the politicization of the word. With definitions of racketeering increasingly vague, both sides judged union officials by their affiliations, not by their actions. Courtney and Williams differed about Michael Galvin, the often-indicted CTU president who happened to be a Republican ward committeeman. They also argued over Marcus "Studdy" Looney, the head of the Chicago Excavators, Pavers, and Asphalt Teamsters' Union and a man convicted of labor slugging as early as 1905. Looney was a Republican, so Elmer Williams lionized him as a "white haired representative" who did "not care for money." But Looney allegedly worked for Capone, leading Roger Touhy to call him a "pimp who had graduated into labor muscling." For once, Courtney agreed with Touhy. The state's attorney expelled "Studdy" from the excavating trade, giving his jurisdiction to the IBT.[52]

Courtney and Gilbert had the authority to interpret the new law, and they used their power to destroy the CTU. In 1934, a jury convicted Roger Touhy of kidnapping, sending him to prison for the next twenty-five years. CTU president Michael Galvin was murdered in 1936. And by 1938, all but one of the CTU locals had affiliated with the IBT. Meanwhile, the state's attorney and his captain thrived. Though Courtney never became mayor or governor, he did manage to win a seat on the Cook County Circuit Court. Gilbert remained a police captain, earning the title, "world's richest cop," in 1950 when he revealed to Estes Kefauver's Senate Hearings on Organized Crime that he owned property worth $360,000 despite a salary of less than $10,000 per year.[53]

Chicago, 247; Motion for new trial on behalf of James Lynch, indicted as John Lynch, December 19, 1918, *U.S. v. Norris et al.*, USDC, case #5554 (1914); *U.S. v. Norris et al.*, 255 F. 423 (1918).

[52] "Politics Seen in Chicago Murder," *NYT*, November 29, 1936, E6; Indictment, January 8, 1915, *United States v. Artery*, case #5545, (1915); Bill for Injunction, March 18, 1929, *Hartigan Brothers v. Chicago Teamsters*, Circ.C.C. case #177949; The Joint and Several Answers of Robert G. Fitchie et al., March 13, 1934, *Meadowmoor Dairy v. Borden*, case #13697 (1934), 51; Records and Briefs, *Scavenger Service v. Courtney*, USCA, 7th Circ., case #5768 (1936), 220, 303, 335, 499; Touhy, *The Stolen Years*, 84; "Marcus 'Studdy' Looney," *Lightnin'* 6:9 (June 1935): 5; *Shields v. People*, 132 Ill. App. 109 (1907); True Bill, May 23, 1905, *People v. Miller*, case #77028, Crim. C.C., IR 134, 213–14.

[53] "Chicago Investigator Testifies," *NYT*, October 18, 1950, 40; Ovid Demaris, *Captive City* (New York: Lyle Stewart, 1969), 133–34, 245. Touhy received a ninety-nine-year sentence, but gained release in 1959. He was murdered within a month of his return. "Touhy and Two Aides Get 99 Years Each," *NYT*, February 23, 1934, 1; "Touhy Goes Free Today," *NYT*, November 24, 1959, 22; "Touhy Slaying Laid to Gang-Era Foes," *NYT*, December 18,

As AFL officials gained the political power to define legitimate unionism, they found themselves forced to sort through allegations of racketeering. For example, in 1938, two unions vied for control over the city's drycleaning workers. The newly established International Dry Cleaning Workers Union had revoked the charter of Local #17742 and granted the jurisdiction to a new union, Local #3. For years before the New Deal, critics had called the drycleaning industry a racket; now both factions drew upon this well-known history, but without any reference to closed shop anticompetitive agreements, coercion, or bribery. The leaders of Local #17742 charged that gangsters ran Local #3 and contacted State's Attorney Courtney. The president of the AFL, William Green, supported Local #3, responding, "The word 'racketeer' has been used quite freely by both sides" of the dispute. With no real basis for choosing between the two unions, he merely endorsed Local #3 and the status quo.[54]

Meanwhile, for American labor radicals, racketeering represented the tar with which to blacken craft unions. During the 1930s, labor's left flank waged a paper war with the AFL. When the AFL labeled socialists, communists, and industrial unionists "Reds," these leftists found in racketeering a viable response. But, however righteous their cause and accurate their accusations, the left did not shy away from using the crimes of a few to incriminate the entire federation. In 1930, David Saposs wrote an expose for the socialist journal, *Labor Age*, in which he defined graft, election fraud, labor directories, entry fees, and craft jurisdictions all as forms of racketeering. Labor leaders as progressive as John L. Lewis did not escape his broad net.

The left's attacks on craft unions often placed it in common cause with open shop employers. In 1933, Louis Budenz, writing in the Communist journal, *Common Sense*, explained how bootleggers like George Barker had risen to control Chicago's craft labor unions.

1959, 1; "Politics Seen in Chicago Murder," *NYT*, November 29, 1936, E6; Touhy, *The Stolen Years*, 246–73; Newell, *Chicago and the Labor Movement*, 106–7; "Lynch the Thief Repeats," *Lightnin'* 6:9 (June 1935): 8; Master's Report, December 2, 1937, *Truck Drivers v. International Brotherhood of Teamsters*, case #15634, USDC, ND, E. IL (1937).

54 Local #17742 was a "Federal" union, a local directly affiliated with the AFL. When the AFL gave the new International to a group from Cleveland, Local #17742 refused to recognize it, leading the Clevelanders to form Local #3. Letter, John Fitzpatrick to William Green, July 1, 1937, 3 in Box 22, Folder 152, John Fitzpatrick Papers, CHS; Letter, William Green to John Fitzpatrick, May 10, 1937, 2 in Box 22, Folder 150, John Fitzpatrick Papers, CHS; Memo, Ivor Fitzgerald to members of cleaning and dyeing locals, March 27, 1937 in Box 21, Folder 147, John Fitzpatrick Papers, CHS.

Budenz quoted Gordon Hostetter, his logical enemy, arguing that racketeering had emerged from the business community to infect labor's ranks. It was the continuing engagement of the AFL with capital, Budenz argued, that led to the corruption of the labor movement. Nor was Budenz the only radical who cited men like Hostetter. In the future, Socialists and Communists drew heavily from conservative sources, such as *It's a Racket!*, Chicago Crime Commission president Frank Loesch, and the *Chicago Tribune*.[55]

Craftsmen won major victories during the Great Depression, but they could not entirely escape such accusations. After years of conflict, labor's right to organize was guaranteed and racketeering had become a blight afflicting, but not intrinsic to, businesses and unions. But by replacing the deeply ideological doctrine of conspiracy with the shallow notion of racketeering, craftsmen gave their critics the opportunity to brand them as criminals without being forced to define their principles. Racketeer was a slur, not a concrete set of practices. As the law grew vague, legitimacy became a matter of political might, rather than a question of political economy.[56]

---

[55] David J. Saposs, "Cut the Racket," *Labor Age* 19:8 (August 1930): 9–12; Louis Francis Budenz, "Racketeers of Organized Labor," *Common Sense* 1:4 (February 1933): 27–9; Gordon Hostetter, "Human Liberty and How to Lose It," *Vital Speeches* 15:51 (November 15, 1948): 83–7; Harold Seidman, *Labor Czars*, 116, 282–303.

[56] One index of the craftsmen's success is the size of the AFL, which nearly doubled its membership between 1933 and 1940. Christopher Tomlins, "AFL Unions in the 1930s: Their Performance in Historical Perspective," *Journal of American History* 65:4 (March 1979): 1021–42.

Epilogue: Policing the Postwar Consensus

The economic order that emerged from the Great Depression synthesized the ambitions of corporate executives, the ideas of reformers, and the defiance of urban tradesmen. During the prior decades, craftsmen organized to protect their livelihoods, eventually inspiring New Deal laws that rearranged the relationship between the state, civil society, and the underworld. This outcome was a triumph for millions of Americans, but one fraught with ambiguity, for the combatants who made it were often coercive, bigoted, and selfish. This history provides few lessons, neither heroes nor villains, no halcyon past that we might today restore. Even if desirable, such a restoration is unnecessary, for unions and associations still dominate trades like construction in older cities such as Boston, New York, and Philadelphia, a living reminder of the problems and prospects of craft governance. By granting the tradesmen's resistance legal protection, the New Deal also cemented the conditions in these industries for decades to come.

In the years after World War II, urban tradesmen moved to the center of American political life, and their "clout," once defiantly local, became increasingly national in ambition and scope. Freed from the need to obtain employer recognition, unions enrolled millions of workers, and this electoral strength gave them immense influence. Indeed, if ethnic, religious, and racial loyalties were the basis for Progressive-era urban politics, unions fueled the machines of the postwar period. The growth of cities themselves gave the tradesmen who controlled voters, party structures, and municipal government unprecedented sway in national affairs. In this context, both Democrats and Republicans courted union officials like Chicago steamfitter and later U.S. Secretary of Labor, Martin Durkin, giving them considerable authority over candidates and platforms.

The "New Men of Power" who ruled the interest-group politics of the Cold War period were petite bourgeois survivors rather than educated technocrats. Richard J. Daley, the child of a union sheet metal mechanic, obtained the mayoralty with the strong support of men like Service Employees International Union (formerly the Chicago Flat Janitors' Union) president William McFetridge. But with the craftsmen's rising standing, Daley gained pull within the nation's dominant political party previously reserved for governors, senators, and media barons. Henry Crown, a Chicago gravel broker, built the nation's largest defense contractor, General Dynamics, upon the strength of his connections to the Cook County Democratic Party. American domestic and foreign policy bore the stamp of New York plumber and AFL–CIO president George Meany. Even President John F. Kennedy, a wealthy banker's son, depended upon a political coalition that included boss politicians, contractors, craft unionists, and gangsters.[1]

The prominence of these former craftsmen drew the attention of prosecutors, judges, and legislators. During the radical 1930s, racketeering served to promote alternative visions of labor's role in governing America's economy. Union officials actually wanted New York District Attorney Thomas Dewey to protect them from alleged murderers like Louis "Lepke" Buchalter. Similarly, in 1940, Deputy Attorney General Thurman Arnold's antitrust suits against the United Brotherhood of Carpenters fulfilled a progressive notion of "responsible" collective bargaining. Like his hero Louis Brandeis, Arnold mocked Gilded Age individualism while asserting labor's duty to protect members without reducing productivity, inflating prices, or committing acts of violence. For Arnold, who had lived in Chicago between 1914 and 1917, when federal courts repeatedly indicted building tradesmen for exceeding the latitude given them by the new Clayton Antitrust Act,

[1] C. Wright Mills, *The New Men of Power: America's Labor Leaders* (New York: Harcourt Brace, 1948); "Martin Durkin," *Biographical Dictionary of American Labor Leaders*, ed., Gary Fink (Westport, CT: Greenwood University Press, 1974), 89; *Alex Gottfried, Boss Cermak of Chicago: A Study in Political Leadership* (Seattle: University of Washington Press, 1962), 212. Milton Rakove, *We Don't Want Nobody Nobody Sent* (Bloomington: Indiana University Press, 1979), 27, 262, 284–85; Len O'Connor, *Clout: Mayor Daley and His City* (Chicago: Regnery, 1976), 107–12, 115, 145–62; Adam Cohen and Elizabeth Taylor, *American Pharaoh: Mayor Richad J. Daley, His Battle for Chicago and the Nation* (New York: Little Brown, 2001), 127–8, 249–79, 459–85; John Jentz, "Labor, the Law, and Economics: The Organization of the Chicago Flat Janitors' Union, 1902–1917," *Labor History* 38:4 (Fall 1997): 413; Ovid Demaris, *Captive City* (New York: Lyle Stuart, 1969), 213–32; Robert Zeiger, "George Meany: Labor's Organization Man," in M. Dubofsky and W. Van Tine, eds., *Labor Leaders in America* (Chicago: University of Illinois Press, 1987), 324–49, esp. 344; Seymour Hersh, *The Dark Side of Camelot* (New York: Little Brown, 1997), 131–37, 143–46.

New Deal statutes legitimizing unions undermined the functional reason for monopolistic agreements. Though his view did not control at the time, it gained force in the following decade.[2]

Over the years, the disappearance of the Democrats' ironclad majority emboldened less thoughtful critics, who pummeled organized labor with assertions of graft, collusion, and subversion, exploiting the vagueness of the term racketeering to create significant doubts about unions. In 1940, columnist Westbrook Pegler wrote a series of articles savaging union officials like William Bioff of the theater workers and George Scalise of the janitors for their connections to professional criminals. Focusing on their personal qualities to the exclusion of work conditions, Pegler created broad distrust for the labor movement without promoting any corresponding sympathy for exploited workers. Unions could not deflect Pegler's charges, not only because the allegations were often true, but also because they focused on individual officers rather than any larger political issue. Honest unions bore some responsibility for this dilemma, for, in the 1930s, they had promoted the personalization of the racketeering problem as a way of securing the legality of collective action.

In the 1950s, American lawmakers of both parties began crusading against racketeers, holding hearings investigating both organized crime and unions like the Teamsters. The Kefauver (1950), Kennedy (1957), and McClellan hearings (1963) all exposed how selfish leaders, gunmen, gamblers, and pimps corrupted unions, an exploitation that was all too real, if less common than witnesses implied. But unlike the Anti-Racketeering Act of 1934, which followed a pro-labor recovery statute, postwar criminal laws – the Hobbs Act (1946), the Landrum–Griffin Act (1959), and the Racketeer Influenced and Corrupt Organization Act (1970) – were uncoupled from any expansion of worker rights. Quite the opposite, allegations of extortion actually built support for the Taft-Hartley Act of 1948, a law severely curtailing union activism. Accusers aimed less at protecting American institutions than

---

[2] "Minutes of Executive Committee, October 6, 1935" in Box 10, Folder 7, Philip Taft Papers, Kheel Center, Cornell University; Steve Fraser, *Labor Will Rule: Sidney Hillman and the Rise of American Labor* (New York: The Free Press, 1991), 245–55, esp. 254; Alan Brinkley, "The Antimonopoly Ideal and the Liberal State," *Journal of American History* 80:2 (September 1993): 557–79; Idem, *The End of Reform: New Deal Liberalism in Recession and War* (New York: Knopf, 1995) 119–20; *United States v. Hutchinson*, 312 U.S. 219 (1941); Thurman Arnold, *The Folklore of Capitalism* (New Haven: Yale University Press, 1937). For another case where Arnold's antitrust division successfully stipulated the limits of urban craft governance under the New Deal, see *Milk Drivers' Union v. Lake Valley Co.*, 311 U.S. 91 (1940).

discrediting the New Deal or – in the case of Democrats like Kefauver and Kennedy – demonstrating to a middle class public their virtuous independence from their own core supporters.[3]

Almost as much as the Cold War, the crusade against racketeering bounded the so-called "liberal consensus." That so many presidential candidates established their visibility by addressing the issue suggests its overwhelming appeal. And like charges of Communist subversion, racketeering prosecutions served to dampen the ferocity of the labor movement without openly attacking the New Deal order. Critics used racketeering less to promote a more honest labor movement than to warn labor leaders that assertiveness invited investigation. It is no defense of Teamsters' president Jimmy Hoffa to say that his incarceration flowed both from his aggressiveness as a union official and from his exploitative, brutal, and sometimes reactionary stewardship.

Moreover, dissatisfaction with the craftsmen helped prompt the breakdown of New Deal liberalism. In his comments upon leaving the presidency in 1961, Dwight Eisenhower warned America about the "military industrial complex," implicitly rebuking defense contractors like Henry Crown who applied the rough-and-tumble rules of construction in Chicago to weapons procurement. The assassination of John F. Kennedy – a signal event in the fragmentation of the Democratic majority – is often blamed on Teamsters' officials and Chicago gunmen, angry at investigations of their activities. Though the New Left of the 1960s found common cause with some elements of the labor movement, they bitterly attacked craft unionists like George Meany as dinosaurs, implicated in racial segregation and an anticommunist foreign policy. If some of these charges were unfair, they nevertheless indicated the uneasiness with which many on the left viewed a coalition with urban tradesmen.[4]

[3] David Witwer, "The Columnist and the Labor Racketeer," unpublished paper, Gotham Conference on New York City History, October 6, 2001; William Moore, *The Kefauver Committee and the Politics of Crime, 1950–1952* (Columbia, MO: University of Missouri Press, 1974); Estes Kefauver, *Crime in America*, ed., Sidney Shalett (Garden City, NY: Doubleday, 1951); John McClellan, *Crime Without Punishment* (New York: Duell, Sloane, & Pearce, 1961).

[4] Arthur Sloane, *Hoffa* (Cambridge, MA: MIT Press, 1991); Dwight D. Eisenhower, "Farewell Radio and Television Address to the American People," *Public Papers of the Presidents of the United States, Dwight D. Eisenhower, 1960–1961* (Washington, DC: Government Printing Office, 1961), 1035–40; Robert Griffith, "Dwight D. Eisenhower and the Corporate Commonwealth," *American Historical Review* 87:1 (February 1982): 120; Pamela Colloff and Michael Hall, "Conspiracy Theories," *Texas Monthly*, November 1998; Hersh, *The Dark Side*, 295–96, 317–21, 450–51; Joshua

Such dissatisfaction and outright criticism chipped away at the consensus favoring New Deal industrial policies, partly explaining their waning influence during the last decades of the twentieth century. Criticized by the left, right, and center, in newspapers, novels, and popular films, craft unions developed a reputation – sometimes deserved – as corrupt and mob dominated. Being a pillar of the establishment, craft unions lost the air of sympathy that caused men like Hutchins Hapgood to rationalize their misbehavior earlier in the century. After 1960, people began viewing tradesmen as another special interest, and a dangerous one at that.

Time also transformed the economic context for the settlement of 1933. Laws modeled upon urban craft governance failed to function when applied to new conditions. Farm workers' unions never succeeded in organizing the bulk of the nation's agricultural labor, partly because conditions on the farms contrasted so sharply with those in industries like construction. National and international forces hampered manufacturing unions, allowing employers to escape collective bargaining by exporting jobs to states and countries unfriendly to unions and by hiring workers not yet acculturated to union values. The rise of new mills in new places has likewise undermined the traditional strength of potent unions like the steelworkers.

But while manufacturing unions shrank, the urban craft economy remained a bastion of Wagner Act collective bargaining. Many scholars attribute the post-1970 decline of the labor movement to the rise of a service economy, never noting the successful organization of these trades in cities during the first half of the century. Unions remain strong in construction and local transport – trades that inherited craft governance directly, while other unions succeed because they share traits with the early twentieth-century craft economy. Strong public sector unions rely upon the immobility of their jobs, political connections, and special legislation in their collective bargaining. Growing organizations like the Service Employees' International Union organize a foreign born and semiskilled workforce using a similar combination of geographic advantage and political savvy. Though hardly a workable model for all unions, its success shows the potential of a legal regime modeled on Chicago's craft economy.[5]

Freeman, *Working-Class New York: Life and Labor Since World War II* (New York: New Press, 2001), 187–92, 237–46; Hunter S. Thompson, *Fear and Loathing: On the Campaign Trail '72* (New York: Warner Books, 1992), 134–35.

5 J. Craig Jenkins, *The Politics of Insurgency: The Farm Worker Movement in the 1960s* (New York: Columbia University Press, 1985); Barry Bluestone and Bennett Harrison, *The Deindustrialization of America: Plant Closings, Community*

The difficulty for the labor movement rests less with service jobs themselves and with the workers who do them than with their location. Corporations made headway when demographic shifts allowed them to fundamentally alter the geography of work. During the 1960s and 1970s, city populations began declining. People moved to new suburbs, not only creating budgetary crises in cities placing pressure on mayors to cut costs, but also moving work to areas where neither Democratic politics nor unions thrived. Outside of central cities, even the most potent building trades unions have found it difficult to govern skilled construction work. For example, the Levitts of Levittown fame built some of the first inexpensive suburban homes under open shop conditions only miles from New York City at the peak of the AFL's power. Similarly, by shifting work from public streets to private spaces such as malls, employers severely hampered labor's ability to picket businesses.[6]

For historians, the declining relevance of state-sponsored collective bargaining illustrates again the hazards of portraying industrialization and political responses to it as inevitable. Legal revolutions depend on the coalitions that create them. In the dwindling years of the Reconstruction period, the Republican Party built a seemingly unstoppable alliance by favoring the Gold Standard, high tariffs, African-American patronage, Union Army pensions, and imperial foreign policy. By 1930, this partnership was in pieces, its constituencies dejected, defected, or defunct. In the subsequent four decades, the statutes of the New Deal, the Fair Deal, the New Frontier, and the Great Society, came to seem the natural results of "political development" and "industrial maturity." Only later did it become plain that liberal economic policy of the 1930s was no more eternal than the Gold Standard. Progressive movements, worker protest, and even craft governance remain. But the legal triumphs of the past are castles resting on shifting sands, buffeted by the struggles of the present.

Abandonment, and the Dismantling of Basic Industries (New York: Basic Books, 1982); "Springtime for Steel," *CDT,* June 21, 1998, C1; Richard B. Freeman and Casey Ichnowski, *When Public Sector Workers Unionize* (Chicago: University of Chicago, 1988); "Largest Union Victory in Decades is a Big Boost for Labor," *St. Louis Post-Dispatch,* February 28, 1999, E6.

[6] H. G. Bissinger, *A Prayer for the City* (New York: Random House, 1997); Freeman, *Working-Class New York,* 256–87; Barbara M. Kelly, *Expanding The American Dream: Building and Rebuilding Levittown* (Albany: State University of New York Press, 1993), 26.

Bibliography

Manuscript Collections

Chicago, IL. Chicago Historical Society. Archives and Manuscripts Department

Chicago Federation of Labor Papers.
Chicago Building Trades Council. Minutes Book, 1912–1914.
William Dever Papers.
John Fitzpatrick Papers.
Landis Award Employers' Association Papers.
Gerhardt Meyne Papers.
Victor Olander Papers.
Howard Levansellaer Willett Papers.

Chicago, IL. Cook County Circuit Court Archives

Cook County Circuit Court. Case Files, 1890–1930.
Cook County Criminal Court. Case Files, 1900, 1935–1937.
Cook County Criminal Court. Indictment Volumes, 1900–1940.
Cook County Criminal Court. Docket Books, 1900–1940.
Cook County Superior Court. Case Files, 1890–1930.

Chicago, IL. National Archives and Research Administration. Great Lakes Division

United States Court of Appeals, 7th Circuit. Record and Briefs, 1891–1959.
United States Court of Appeals, 7th Circuit. General Index, 1891–1936.
United States Court of Appeals, 7th Circuit. Docket Books, 1891–1953.
United States District Court. Case Files.

United States District Court. General Index.
United States District Court. Docket Books.

Chicago, IL. Newberry Library

Eugene Prussing Papers.
Graham Taylor Papers.

Chicago, IL. University of Chicago. Joseph Regenstein Library Special Collections

Ernest Burgess Papers.
Frank Knight Papers.
Charles Merriam Papers.
Bessie Louise Pierce Papers.
George Schilling Papers.

Ithaca, NY. Cornell University. Kheel Center for Labor Management

Philip Taft Records.

Reported Cases

Aberdeen-Franklin Coal v. City of Chicago, 315 Ill. 99 (1924).
Adams v. Brenan, 177 Ill. 194 (1898).
Allen v. the Chicago Undertakers' Association, 232 Ill. 458 (1908).
American Dental Company v. Central Dental Laboratory Company, 256 Ill. App. 279 (1930).
American Steel Foundries v. Tri-City Central Trades Council, 257 U.S. 184 (1921).
Anderson & Lind Manufacturing v. Carpenters' District Council, 308 Ill. 488 (1923).
Arms v. City of Chicago, 314 Ill. 316 (1924).
Atlantic Cleaners & Dyers Inc. v. United States, 286 U.S. 427 (1932).
Banghart v. Walsh, 339 Ill. 132 (1930).
Barnes v. Typographical Union, 232 Ill. 424 (1908).
Baxter v. Board of Trade, 83 Ill. 146 (1876).
Beaton v. Tarrant, 102 Ill. App. 124 (1902).
Bedford Cut Stone Co. v. Journeymen Stone Cutters, 274 U.S. 37 (1927).
Beesley v. Chicago Journeymen Plumbers' Protective Association, 44 Ill. App. 278 (1892).
Blais v. United Brotherhood of Carpenters & Joiners, 169 Ill. App. 596 (1912).

Board of Trade v. Nelson, 162 Ill. 431 (1896).

Boston Store of Chicago v. Retail Clerks Local 226, 216 Ill. App. 428 (1920).

Boyle v. United States,40 F.2d 49 (1930).

Brennan v. Purington Paving Brick Company, 171 Ill. 276 (1912).

Bricklayers v. Bowen, 183 N.Y.S. 855 (1920).

Bridge, Iron, and Structural Workers' Union v. Sigmund, 88 Ill. App. 344 (1900).

Brims v. United States, 6 F.2d 99 (1925).

Builders' Painting and Decorating v. Advisory Board Building Trades, 116 Ill. App. 265 (1904).

Building Trades Council v. Board of Education, 1 Ill.C.C. 378 (1898).

Cahill v. United Association of Plumbers, 238 Ill. App. 123 (1925).

Carlson v. Carpenter Contractors' Association, 305 Ill. 331 (1922).

Carpenters' Union v. Citizens' Committee to Enforce the Landis Award, 333 Ill. 225 (1928).

Chicago Branch National Stonecutters v. Journeymen Stonecutters, 2 Ill. C.C. 118 (1906).

Chicago Federation of Musicians v. American Musicians Union, 234 Ill. 504 (1908).

Chicago German Hod Carriers Union v. Security Trust, 315 Ill. 204 (1924).

Chicago, Wilmington and Vermillion Coal Co. v. People, 214 Ill. 421 (1905).

Christensen v. Kellogg Switchboard, 110 Ill. App. 61 (1903).

City of Chicago v. A. M. Forbes Cartage Company, 1 Ill. C.C. 473 (1901).

Cleaning and Dyeing Plant Owners v. Sterling Cleaners, 278 Ill. App. 70 (1934).

Clifford v. Hedrick 159 Ill. App. 63 (1910).

Columbus Milk Producers Co-op v. Wallace, 8 F. Supp. 1014 (1934).

Commonwealth v. Hunt, 45 Mass. 111 (1842).

Cook County Brick Co. v. Lebahn Brick Co., 92 Ill. App. 526 (1900).

Cook County Brick v. W. Bach & Sons, 93 Ill. App. 88 (1900).

Critchfield v. Bermudez Asphalt Paving Company, 174 Ill. 466 (1898).

Debs v. United States, 249 U.S. 211 (1919).

Doremus v. Hennessey, 176 Ill. 608 (1898).

Dr. Lietzman, Dentist, Inc. v. Radio Broadcasting Station WCFL, 282 Ill. App. 203 (1935).

Dunbar v. American Telephone and Telegraph, 224 Ill. 9 (1906).

Dunbar v. American Telephone and Telegraph, 238 Ill. 456 (1909).

Duplex Printing Press v. Deering, 254 U.S. 443 (1921).

Edgewater Dairy Co. v. Wallace, 7 F. Supp. 121 (1934).

Employers' Teaming Co. v. Teamsters Joint Council, 141 F. 679 (1905).

Engel v. Walsh, 258 Ill. 98 (1913).

Everett v. People, 216 Ill. 478 (1905).

Faxon v. Grand Lodge Brotherhood of Locomotive Firemen, 87 Ill. App. 262 (1899).
Fenske Brothers v. Upholsterers #18, 358 Ill. 239.
Fields v. United Brotherhood of Carpenters & Joiners, 60 Ill. App. 258 (1895).
Fishburn v. City of Chicago, 171 Ill. 338 (1898).
Flannery v. People, 127 Ill. App. 526 (1906).
Flannery v. People, 225 Ill. 61 (1907).
Forbes Cartage Co., R. J. Mix Transfer Co. v. City of Chicago, 1 Ill. C.C. 473 (1901).
Ford v. Chicago Milk Shippers Association, 155 Ill. 166 (1895).
Franklin Union No. 4 v. People, 121 Ill. App. 647 (1905).
Franklin Union No. 4 v. People, 220 Ill. 355 (1906).
Garrigan v. United States, 163 F. 16 (1908).
Gillespie v. People, 188 Ill. 176 (1900).
Glay v. People, 94 Ill. App. 598 (1900).
Glay v. People, 94 Ill. App. 602 (1900).
Grand Lodge Brotherhood of Locomotive Firemen v. Cramer, 60 Ill. App. 212 (1895).
Grand Lodge Brotherhood of Locomotive Firemen v. Orrell, 97 Ill. App. 246 (1901).
Green v. Board of Trade, 174 Ill. 585 (1898).
Hillenbrand v. Builders Trade Council, 14 Ohio Decisions, N.P. 628 (1904).
Hitchman Coal v. Mitchell, 245 U.S. 229 (1917).
Humphreys v. Internal Revenue, 42 B.T.A. 857 (1940).
In re Phelan, 62 F. 803 (S. D. Ohio, 1894).
International Brotherhood of Electrical Workers v. Western Union, 6 F.2d 444 (1925).
Jarrett, Admr. for Peter Kaehler v. Johnson, 216 Ill. 212 (1905).
Johnson v. People, 124 Ill. App. 213 (1906).
Kemp v. Division #241, 255 Ill. 213 (1912).
Kent Stores v. Wilentz, 14 F. Supp. 1 (1936).
Klever Shampay Karpet Kleaners v. City of Chicago, 238 Ill. App. 291 (1925).
Koebel v. the Chicago Landlords' Protective Bureau, 210 Ill. 176 (1904).
Linn v. United Brotherhood of Carpenters and Joiners, 191 Ill. App. 117 (1915).
Local #167, International Brotherhood of Teamsters, v. U.S., 291 U.S. 293 (1934).
Loewe v. Lawlor, 208 U.S. 274 (1908).
Lowenthal v. City of Chicago, 313 Ill. 190 (1924).
Marshall Field & Co. v. Becklenberg, 1 Ill. C.C. 59 (1905).
McNamara v. People, 183 Ill. 164 (1899).

Mears Slayton Lumber Co. v. District Council Carpenters, 156 Ill. App. 505 (1922).

Milk Drivers' Union v. Lake Valley Co. 311 U.S. 91 (1940).

Moody v. Farrington, 227 Ill. App. 40 (1922).

Moores v. Bricklayers Union, 23 Weekly Law Bulletin (Ohio) 48 (1890).

Nusbaum v. Retail Clerks' International Protective Association, 227 Ill. App. 206 (1922)

O'Brien v. People ex rel Kellogg Switchboard and Supply Co., 216 Ill. 354 (1905).

O'Donnell v. People, 110 Ill. App. 250 (1903).

People ex rel. Akin v. Butler Street Foundry, 201 Ill. 236 (1903).

People ex rel. Deneen v. Sullivan, 218 Ill. 419 (1905).

People ex rel. Padula v. Hughes, 296 Ill. App. 587 (1938).

People v. Bissett, 246 Ill. 516 (1910).

People v. Board of Trade, 45 Ill. 112 (1867).

People v. Board of Trade, 80 Ill. 134 (1875).

People v. Boyle, 312 Ill. 586 (1924).

People v. Brautigan, 310 Ill. 472 (1924).

People v. Cobb, 343 Ill. 78 (1931).

People v. Connors, 253 Ill 266 (1912).

People v. Connors, 253 Ill. 266 (1912).

People v. Curran, 207 Ill. App. 264 (1918).

People v. Curran, 286 Ill. 302 (1919).

People v. Davis, 3 Ill.C.C. 516 (1898).

People v. Enright, 256 Ill. 221 (1912).

People v. Graves, 304 Ill. 20 (1922).

People v. Lloyd, 304 Ill. 23 (1922).

People v. Mader 313 Ill. 277 (1924).

People v. McDonald, 314 Ill. 548 (1924).

People v. Novotny, 371 Ill. 58 (1937).

People v. Patris, 360 Ill. 596 (1935).

People v. Pouchot, 174 Ill. App. 1 (1912).

People v. Quesse, 310 Ill. 467 (1923).

People v. Richards & Kelly Manufacturing Company, 1 Ill. C.C. 171 (1900).

People v. Seefeldt, 310 Ill. 441 (1923).

People v. Stavrakas, 335 Ill. 570 (1929).

People v. Walczak, 310 Ill. 441 (1923).

People v. Walczak, 315 Ill. 49 (1924).

People v. Walsh, 322 Ill. 195 (1926).

Piano and Organ Supply Co. v. Piano and Organ Workers Union, 124 Ill. App. 353 (1906).

Platt v. National Association of Retail Druggists, 1 Ill. C.C. 1 (1905).

Preble v. Architectural Iron Workers' Union, 260 Ill. App. 435 (1931).
Prussing v. Jackson, 208 Ill. 85 (1904).
Prussing v. Jackson, 85 Ill. App. 324 (1899).
Purington v. Hinchliff, 120 Ill. App. 523 (1905).
Purington v. Hinchliff, 219 Ill. 159 (1905).
Rubin v. City of Chicago, 330 Ill. 97 (1928).
Sanford v. People, 121 Ill. App. 619 (1905).
Schechter Poultry v. U.S., 295 U.S. 495 (1935).
Schechter Poultry v. U.S., 295 U.S. 723 (1935).
Shields v. People, 132 Ill. App. 109 (1907).
Strong v. International B.L.& I. Union, 82 Ill. App. 426 (1899).
Sturges v. Board of Trade, 86 Ill. 441 (1877).
Sullivan v. People, 108 Ill. App. 328 (1903).
Taff–Vale Railway Co. v. Amalgamated Society of Railway Servants, A.C. 426 (1901).
United States v. Brims, 21 F.2d 889 (1927).
United States v. Brims, 272 U.S. 549 (1926).
United States v. Brims, 6 F.2d 98 (1925).
United States v. Norris, 255 F. 423 (1918).
United States v. Spotless Dollar Cleaners, 6 F. Supp. 725 (1934).
Union Pressed Brick Co. v. Chicago Hydraulic Pressed Brick Co., 3 Ill. C.C. 290 (1899).
United Mine Workers v. Coronado Coal, 259 U.S. 344 (1922).
U.S. v. Shissler, 7 F. Supp. 123 (1934).

Unpublished Cases in National Archives, Great Lakes Division

Babcock and Wilcox Co. v. Boilermakers et al., case #9360, USDC, ND, E. IL (1929).
Borden's Condensed Milk v. Milk Producers' Association, case #636, USDC, ND, E. IL (1916).
Boyle v. U.S., case #4207, USCA, 7th Circ. (1928).
Brims v. U.S., case #3436, USCA, 7th Circ., (1923).
Chicago Poultry Merchants v. Chicago Poultry Handlers, case #4176, USDC, ND, E. IL (1924).
Coyne Brothers et al. v. Teamsters, case #4183, USDC, ND, E. IL (1924).
Dahlstrom Metallic Door Co. v. Iron Workers, case #5724, USDC, ND, E. IL (1926).
Lamson v. Reliable Transit Co., case #8060, USDC, ND, E. IL (1928).
Meadowmoor Dairy v. Borden Farm Products, case #13697, USDC, ND, E. IL (1934).
Meadowmoor Dairy v. Chicago Milk Dealers, case #41533, USDC, ND, E. IL (1932).

Peterson v. Teamsters, case #8428, USDC, ND, E. IL (1928).

Scavenger Service v. Courtney, case #5768, USCA, 7th Circ., (1936).

Truck Drivers v. Teamsters, case #15634, USDC, ND, E. IL (1937).

U.S. v. American Terra Cotta and Ceramic Co. et al., case #9333, USDC, ND, E. IL (1922).

U.S. v. Andrews Lumber, et al., case #7518, USDC, ND, E. IL (1918).

U.S. v. Andrews Lumber, et al., case #8302, USDC, ND, E. IL (1921).

U.S. v. Artery, case #5545, USDC, ND, E. IL (1915).

U.S. v. Artery, case #5546, USDC, ND, E. IL (1915).

U.S. v. Artery, case #5547, USDC, ND, E. IL (1915).

U.S. v. Boyle, case #5648, USDC, ND, E. IL (1915).

U.S. v. Brims, case #3436, USCA, 7th Circuit (1923).

U.S. v. Chicago Association of Candy Jobbers, case #7906, USDC, ND, E. IL (1928).

U.S. v. Chicago Master Steam Fitters' Association, case #7902, USDC, ND, E. IL (1921).

U.S. v. Chicago Mosaic Tiling Co. et al., case #6068, USDC, ND, E. IL (1917).

U.S. v. Dohney, case #5649, USDC, ND, E. IL (1915).

U.S. v. Dohney, case #5650, USDC, ND, E. IL (1915).

U.S. v. Dohney, case #5651, USDC, ND, E. IL (1915).

U.S. v. Feeney, case #5652, USDC, ND, E. IL (1915).

U.S. v. IBEW Local #9, case #14, USDC, ND, E. IL (1913).

U.S. v. James Clow & Sons et al., case #7788, USDC, ND, E. IL (1921).

U.S. v. Lehigh Portland Cement Co. et al., case #9312, USDC, ND, E. IL (1922).

U.S. v. Louis Biegler Co. et al., case #7901, USDC, ND, E. IL (1921).

U.S. v. Murphy, case #8330, USDC, ND, E. IL (1921).

U.S. v. Norris, case #5554, USDC, ND, E. IL (1914).

U.S. v. Poster Advertising Association, case #7648, USDC, ND, E. IL (1921).

U.S. v. Stretch, case #5653, USDC, ND, E. IL (1915).

U.S. v. Painters District Council #14, case #8556, USDC, ND, E. IL (1928).

Weller v. Chicago Hebrew Butchers, case #1447, USDC, ND, E. IL (1920).

Western Union v. IBEW #134 et al., case #4047, USDC, ND, E. IL (1924).

Williams v. Teamsters, case #4183, USDC, ND, E. IL (1924).

Unpublished Cases in Cook County Circuit Court Archives

Abrams v. Master Bakers Association, case #294250, Sup.C.C. (1912).

Advisory Board Building Trades v. Builders' Painting, case #227537, Sup.C.C. (1903).

Allen v. Chicago Federation of Musicians, case #234926, Sup.C.C. (1904).

American Ideal Cleaning v. Master Cleaners & Dyers, case #369807, Sup.C.C. (1921).

American Musicians Union v. Chicago Federation of Musicians, case #271650, Circ.C.C. (1906).

Anderson v. Lake Seamen's Union, case #241609, Sup.C.C. (1905).

Bent v. Piano and Organ Workers Union, case #204497, Sup.C.C. (1900).

Bindley v. Chicago Federation of Musicians Local #10, A.F.M., case #255626, Circ.C.C. (1904).

Builders' Painting v. Advisory Board Building Trades, case #227537, Sup.C.C. (1903).

Building Trades Council of Chicago v. State Bank of Chicago, case #217048, Sup.C.C. (1901).

Burgher v. Painters, Decorators and Paper Hangers of America, case #234118, Sup.C.C. (1903).

Butchers and Grocery Clerks v. U.S. Fidelity & Guaranty, case #205590, Sup.C.C. (1900).

Chicago Cigar Manufacturers v. Cigar Makers Union, case #238016, Sup.C.C. (1904).

Childs & Co. v. Franklin Union #4, case #234227, Sup.C.C. (1903).

Chimera v. Chicago Federation of Musicians, case #256082, Sup.C.C. (1906).

Chmelik v. Teamsters, case #163790, Circ.C.C. (1928).

Cohen v. Bakers and Confectioners, case #105070, Circ.C.C. (1923).

Doehne v. Chicago Federation of Musicians, case #255329, Circ.C.C. (1904).

Donahue v. Book Binders, case #229852, Sup.C.C. (1903).

Donnelley v. Book Binders, case #229851, Sup.C.C. (1903).

Donnelley v. Franklin Union #4, case #234015, Sup.C.C. (1903).

Eagle Cleaning & Dying v. Master Cleaners & Dyers, case #370500, Sup.C.C. (1921).

Ellery v. American Federation of Musicians, case #286182, Circ.C.C. (1908).

Fendl v. Gubbins, case #207473, Circ.C.C. (1900).

First Trust and Savings Bank v. Brotherhood of Painters, case #278195, Sup.C.C. (1910).

Gavin v. Bricklayers and Masons International Union, case #227562, Sup.C.C. (1903).

Gavin v. Bricklayers and Masons International Union, case #218594, Circ.C.C. (1901).

Gavin v. Bricklayers and Masons International Union, case #243717, Sup.C.C. (1905).

Gavin v. Bricklayers and Masons International Union, case #266991, Sup.C.C. (1908).

Gray v. United Order American Bricklayers, case #212310, Sup.C.C. (1901).

Gustav F. Ouclay v. Franklin Union #4, case #232812, Sup.C.C. (1903).

Guthrie v. Chicago Federation of Musicians, case #220809, Sup.C.C. (1902).

Hartigan Brothers v. Teamsters, case #177949, Circ.C.C. (1929).

Henneberry Co. v. Book Binders, case #229849, Sup.C.C. (1903).

Heusner Baking Co. v. Bakers and Confectioners Union #2, case #272931, Circ.C.C. (1906).

Holland Construction v. Amalgamated Sheet Metal Workers, case #229657, Sup.C.C. (1903).

Huecker v. Cigar Makers International Union, case #211775, Sup.C.C. (1901).

International Freight Handlers v. International Freight Handlers, case #254260, Sup.C.C. (1906).

Kellogg Switchboard and Supply v. Brass Workers, case #230199, Sup.C.C. (1903).

Kretchmar v. Brotherhood of Painters, case #315610, Sup.C.C. (1915).

Kretchmar v. Brotherhood of Painters, case #333282, Sup.C.C. (1917).

Kryl v. Chicago Federation of Musicians, case #256083, Sup.C.C. (1906).

Lyon & Healy v. Piano and Organ Workers Union, case #236230, Supp.C.C. (1904).

Martin v. Chicago Flat Janitors' Union, case #143895, Circ.C.C. (1927).

Montgomery Ward & Co. v. Teamsters, case #243939, Sup.C.C. (1905).

People ex rel Emerich v. Chicago Masons and Builders Assn., case #219410, Circ.C.C. (1901).

People v. Bausk, case #74791, Crim.C.C. (1904).

People v. Carney, case #76979, Crim.C.C. (1905).

People v. Carney, case #78365, Crim.C.C. (1905).

People v. Cleary, case #s 7793–7819, Crim.C.C. (1915).

People v. Conn,case # 71812, Crim.C.C. (1903).

People v. Dold, case #59120, Crim.C.C. (1900).

People v. Egger, case #69701, Crim.C.C. (1903).

People v. Eisenlord, case #s 80445–80447, Crim.C.C. (1906).

People v. Foster, case #71884, Crim.C.C. (1904).

People v. Gilhooley case #77030 Crim.C.C. (1905).

People v. Gubbins, case #58583, Crim.C.C. (1900).

People v. Haley, case #91483, Crim.C.C. (1909).

People v. Illinois Brick Co., case #s 79340–79341, Crim.C.C. (1905).

People v. Johnson, case #66201, Crim.C.C. (1902).

People v. Johnson, case #71762, Crim.C.C. (1903).

People v. Johnson, case #71818, Crim.C.C. (1903).

People v. Kearney, case #24995, Crim.C.C. (1921).

People v. Kearney, case #25124, Crim.C.C. (1921).

People v. Kearney, case #26588, Crim.C.C. (1921).

People v. Kearney, case #27077, Crim.C.C. (1921).

People v. Kearney, case #27446, Crim.C.C. (1921).

People v. Lindemann, case #s 72078–72079, Crim.C.C. (1904).

People v. Madden, case #s 90527–90530, 90577, 90579, 91317, Crim.C.C. (1909).

People v. McCaffery, case #25125, Crim.C.C. (1921).

People v. Miller, case #28640, Crim.C.C. (1921).

People v. Miller, case #70799, Crim.C.C. (1903).

People v. Miller, case #77028, Crim.C.C. (1905).

People v. Mix, case #86389, Crim.C.C. (1907).

People v. O'Donnell, case #24996, Crim.C.C. (1921).

People v. Obermeyer, case #72033, Crim.C.C. (1904).

People v. Olson, case #75529, Crim.C.C. (1904).

People v. Olson, case #75530, Crim.C.C. (1904).

People v. Pelkus, case #71594, Crim.C.C. (1903).

People v. Prussing, case #s 77368–77372, Crim.C.C. (1905).

People v. Ruth, case #91386, Crim.C.C. (1909).

People v. Sanitary Specialty Manufacturing Company, case #71392, Crim.C.C. (1903)

People v. Seefeldt, case #26946, Crim.C.C. (1924).

People v. Shea, case #76994, Crim.C.C. (1905).

People v. Spiess, case #75430, Crim.C.C. (1904).

People v. Tatman, case # 78213, Crim.C.C. (1905).

People v. Veltman, case #26751, Crim.C.C. (1921).

People v. Walczak, case #18895, Crim.C.C. (1921).

People v. Wilson, case #71395, Crim.C.C. (1903).

People v. Woerner, case #71762, Crim.C.C. (1903).

People v. Wright, case #26752, Crim.C.C. (1921).

Piano and Organ Supply Company v. Piano and Organ Workers, case #232465, Sup.C.C. (1903).

Platt v. Barry, case #244201, Sup.C.C. (1905).

Prucha v. United Order of American Bricklayers at Chicago, case #207992, Circ.C.C. (1900).

Rand McNally v. Franklin Union #4, case #232947, Sup.C.C. (1903).

Rand McNally v. Franklin Union #4, case #233046, Sup.C.C. (1903).

Rili v. United Order of American Bricklayers, case #246928, Circ.C.C. (1903).

Schmidt v. United Order of American Bricklayers, case #276661, Circ.C.C. (1906).

Sherman v. Chicago Federation of Musicians, case #206264, Sup.C.C. (1900).

Stamos v. Chicago Bakers' Joint Council, case #191865, Circ.C.C. (1929).

Stiles v. Brotherhood of Painters, case #232122, Sup.C.C. (1903).

Stiles v. Brotherhood of Painters, case #231675, Sup.C.C. (1903).

Sykes Steel Roofing Co. v. Amalgamated Sheet Metal Workers, case #228903, Sup.C.C. (1903).

Tischler v. Cigar Makers International Union, case #265964, Circ.C.C. (1905).

Typothetae v. Franklin Union #4, case #232708, Sup.C.C. (1903).

Union Pressed Brick Co. v. Chicago Hydraulic Pressed Brick, case #216762, Circ.C.C. (1901).

Union Pressed Brick Co. v. Chicago Hydraulic Pressed Brick, case #216762, Circ.C.C. (1901).

Union Pressed Brick Co. v. Hydraulic Pressed Brick Co., case #196935, Circ.C.C. (1899).

Vessella v. Chicago Federation of Musicians, case #254135, Sup.C.C. (1906).

Weldon v. Chicago Federation of Musicians, case #263907, Circ.C.C. (1905).

Winslow Brothers v. Building Trades Council, case #198400, Sup.C.C. (1899).

Index

Fake, Frederick, 178
Falkenau, Victor, 125–126, 129
Farwell, Jr., John V., 31
Feather, William, 51
Feeley, Edward, 94, 96
Feeney, William J., 211
Fetzer, William C., 275
Field, Marshall, 30, 31, 53, 102, 104
Fieldstack, Charles, 107
Film Exhibitors' Association of Chicago, 204
Firefighters' unions
  Fireman's Association, 149
First National Bank of Chicago, 30
Fitchie, Robert G., 284
FitzHenry, Louis, 270
Fitzpatrick, John, 118, 245, 291
Flannery, William, 91
Fleet, John A., 63
Floerch, John, 147
Food riots, 200–201
Ford, Henry, 206–207
Ford, Percy, 94
Forgan, James B., 30
Foster, William Z., 226, 245
Frank, Jerome, 271
Franklin Union #4 decision (1906), 161
Freight Handlers' Unions
  International Freight Handlers Union, Local #4, 69
Fridley, Albert, 94
Friedman, Clara, 201
Fuller Construction Co., 104, 208
Fuller, George A., 44–45, 139
Fultonham Brick Company of Ohio, 101

Gallagher, John, 95, 193
Galvin, Michael, 266, 284, 293
Ganton & Co. (1908), 99, 134, 235
Garland, Mahlon, 154
Garment workers' unions, 54, 178
  International Ladies Garment Workers Union, 75
  Seamstresses' union, 108
  United Garment Workers District Council, 73
Garrick Theater, 74
Garrigan, Daniel, 116, 178
Garrison, Wendell Philips, 136
Gary, Joseph, 182, 183
Gas Workers' Union, 232

Gavin, James
  charges conspiracy, 164
  expelled from bricklayers, 75, 104
  injunction against bricklayers, 176, 193
  labeled a "scab", 66
  lawsuit against bricklayers, 163, 183
Geeting, John, 165
General Dynamic, 298
General Electric, 27, 211, 214
Gentleman, William "Dutch", 56, 222
Gentleman, Mrs., 222
Georgson, Nicholas, 229
German Americans, 17, 19, 27, 30, 149
Gilbert, Daniel, 291–293
Gilbreth, Frank B., 45
Gilhooley, Charles, 90, 94, 96
Glaziers' Union, 224
Goldberg (plastering contractor), 238
Goldstein, Philip, 224
Gompers, Samuel, 6, 67, 152, 154, 245
Gorman, James, 276
Gorman, Simon, 227, 229, 261
Grand Jury
  investigations, 116
  selection system, 172–174
Grand Pacific Railway, 32
Grant, Luke, 137
  hired to write corruption law, 189
  support for unions, 140
  view of African Americans, 141
  view of masculinity and violence, 92–93, 143, 148
Grant, Ulysses, 169
Great Depression (1929–1941), 266
Great Northern Hotel, 79
Great Northern Theater, 74
Greater New York Live Poultry Chamber of Commerce, 277, 278
Greek Americans, 19
Green, William, 288, 294
Greenbaum, Jacob, 92
Gubbins, George P., 52–53, 66, 87–89, 110

Hagen, Marinius, 96
Haley, Margaret, 73
Hand, John, 227, 231, 262, 266
Hanson, D.C., 74
Hapgood, Hutchins, 93, 155, 268, 301
Harding, George Sr., 101

Protocol of Peace garment industry
agreement, 280
Prussing, Ernst, 149
Prussing, Eugene E., 150
Prussing, George C., 149–151
Puck, 120, 139
Pullman Company, 23, 25, 32
Pullman Strike of 1894, 165
Pullman, George, 30
Pure Milk Association, 281–284
Purington Brick Co., 89
Purington, Dillwyn V., 53, 82, 83

Quackenbush, Frank, 213
Quesse, William, 226
Quinn, Charles, 74
Quinn, Timothy P., 175
Quirk, John, 213

Raber, Edwin, 256
Race Riot of 1919, 92, 217–218
Racket court, 262, 268, 286
Racket hearings of 1933, 285
Racket, The (1927), 263
Racketeer Influenced Corrupt
Organization Act of 1970, 299
Racketeer, The (1929), 263
Racketeering, 1, 9–10
changing definitions during 1930s,
265–268, 284
defined as "collusive agreements",
260–261
defined as extortion, 261
growing imprecision of term, 289–295
origins of term, 233–234, 254–255,
260–262
relation to gangsters, 261
relation to New Deal, 271–273
Ragen family, 91–92
Frank Ragen, 92, 217
James M. Ragen, 92, 217
Ragen's Colts, 92, 217–218
Railroads, 22, 32
Ramier, John, 92
Rand McNally, 185
Ravinia Park, 76
Ream, Norman B., 32
Reed, Stanley, 279
Reformers, professional, 122
belief in rule of law, 136, 145
class identity of, 137

critique of craft governance, 120, 122,
123, 135, 143
industrial peace as priority, 129
notion of "responsible unionism", 142
view of African Americans, 141–142
Reger, Frank P., 224
Reid, Frank, 275
Reimer, Louis, 82
Reliable Transit Co, 214
Replacement workers, 76, 99, 113–116
Republic Steel, 22
Republican Party
Chicago, Deneen reform faction, 268
Chicago, Madden-Thompson-Crowe-
Small machine, 217, 218, 291
Illinois, 150
United States, 211
Restaurant Keepers' Association of
Chicago, 80
Retail Coal Dealers Association of Illinois
and Wisconsin, 80
Reynolds, George M., 31
Rice, Walter L., 278, 279
Richberg, Donald, 270, 271, 280
Richman Brothers Cigars, 94
Roach, Joseph, 95
Robb, J.S., 124, 128
Robb, Mrs. J.S., 124–126, 128
Robins, Raymond, 91, 148
Robinson, F.B., 41
Rock Island Depot, 90
Rockefeller family, 45, 104, 139, 208
Rodriguez, William, 275
Rooney, William, 266
Roosevelt, Franklin D., 265, 271, 275,
283
Julian Mack and, 177
American Construction Council, 236
urban political machines, 268
Wilkerson appointment, 270
Roosevelt, Theodore, 169, 171
Rosenwald, Julius, 30, 31, 37, 208, 248,
259
Rubin, Samuel, 230, 231
Russian Americans. See Jewish Americans
Ryan, Frank, 71
Rysdon, Eli A., 90–91, 104, 139, 159, 163,
165

Sanborn, Arthur Loomis, 244
Sanitary Cleaning Shops, Inc., 230